R. S. Thoma

# R. S. Thomas
## *Serial Obsessive*

M. WYNN THOMAS

University of Wales Press
Cardiff
2013

*www.uwp.co.uk*

British Library Cataloguing-in-Publication Data.
A catalogue record for this book is available from the British Library.

ISBN  978-0-7083-2570-4 (hardback)
ISBN  978-0-7083-2613-8 (paperback)
e-ISBN  978-0-7083-2661-9

Typeset in Wales by Eira Fenn Gaunt, Cardiff
Printed by CPI Antony Rowe, Chippenham

*I fy annwyl wraig*

*Ac er cof am ein hen gyfaill ni'n dau,*
*Hywel Teifi Edwards (1934–2010)*

# CONTENTS

Acknowledgements        ix

Illustrations        xi

Abbreviations        xii

Introduction        1

1    War Poet        13

2    For Wales, See Landscape        37

3    The Disappearing Clergyman        67

4    Son of Saunders        93

5    Family Matters        117

6    The Leper of Abercuawg        147

7    Irony in the Soul: R. S.(ocrates) Thomas        171

8    'Time's Changeling'        193

9    'The fantastic side of God'        219

Contents

10     Transatlantic Relations     241

11     'The fast dipping brush'     263

12     'The brush's piety'     293


Index     321

# ACKNOWLEDGEMENTS

Permission has very kindly been granted by Gwydion and Rhodri Thomas to publish extracts from R. S. Thomas's published works, and the R. S. Thomas Centre at Bangor University has generously allowed publication of some unpublished materials.

Several parts of this book have appeared in present or previous form elsewhere. I am grateful to those associated with the following for permission to mine those sources: *The New Welsh Review*; *Wales at War, Critical Essays on Literature and Art*; *Welsh Writing in English, A Yearbook of Critical Essays*; *Internal Difference, Literature in Twentieth-Century Wales*; *Miraculous Simplicity, Essays on R. S. Thomas*; *Cawr i'w Genedl, Cyfrol i gyfarch Hywel Teifi Edwards*; *Agenda*; *Echoes to the Amen, Essays after R. S. Thomas*; *Renascence, New Perspectives in Scholarship and Criticism*; *Poems of Earth, Poems and Essays in Honour of Jeremy Hooker*.

Permissions to include entirely or in part from the following works have been kindly granted: *The Collected Poems 1945–1990* by R. S. Thomas, by permission of The Orion Publishing Group, London; 'A Flickering Mind', 'Joy', 'Mysterious Disappearance of May's Past Perfect' and 'Thinking About Paul Celan' by Denise Levertov, from *New Selected Poems* (Bloodaxe Books, 2003); 'Infant Sorrow' by William Blake, from *William Blake: Selected Poetry and Prose*, edited by David Punter (Routledge, 1988); 'Michael' by William Wordsworth, from *William Wordsworth: Selected Poetry and Prose*, edited by Philip Hobsbaum (Routledge, 1989); 'No Second Troy' by W. B. Yeats, by permission of A. P. Watt Ltd on behalf of Gráinne Yeats; 'On the Shore' by R. S. Thomas, from *The Bread of Truth* (1968), by permission of Kunjana Thomas; 'Psalm Fragments (Schnittke String Trio)' by Denise Levertov, from *The Stream and the Sapphire*, © 1997 by Denise Levertov, reprinted by permission of New

Directions Publishing Corp.; 'Reaping' by Joseph P. Clancy, *Twentieth-Century Welsh Poems* (Gomer Press, 1982) from the original Welsh poem 'Medi' by Dic Jones, *Cerddi Dic yr Hendre* (Gomer Press, 2010); 'Reluctance', from *The Poetry of Robert Frost*, edited by Edward Connery Latham, published by Jonathan Cape, reprinted by permission of The Random House Group Limited; 'Some Notes on Organic Form' by Denise Levertov, from *New and Selected Essays*, © 1973 by Denise Levertov, reprinted by permission of New Directions Publishing Corp.

Over a quarter of a century, I have published more than a dozen books with the University of Wales Press, and am more appreciative than ever of the exceptional services they have rendered me. My sincerest thanks go to Sarah Lewis, Dafydd Jones, Siân Chapman, Charlotte Austin, Steven Goundrey, Eira Fenn Gaunt, Janet Davies and all the other members of a team that, despite the outrageous challenges and difficulties of recent times, have remained devoted to the highest standards of professional performance.

The dedication of this book to my wife and recently departed friend Hywel Teifi Edwards is an inadequate return for all their love, affection and support. And included equally in the embrace of my very warmest thanks are those others dearest to me, Elin, Bob, and of course little Joseph. Mae'r llyfr hwn, gyda chariad mawr, yn gyflwynedig ichi i gyd.

# LIST OF ILLUSTRATIONS

Between pages 146 and 147

1.  Richard Hilder, *Cottages at Litlington* (n.d.). Donated by the Pilgrim Trust. © Victoria and Albert Museum, London.
2.  Mildred Eldridge, *Addoldy-y-Bedyddwyr* (n.d.). © Victoria and Albert Museum, London.
3.  Mildred Eldridge, *Maes yr Onnen*, reproduced in R. S. Thomas, *Selected Prose* (1982). © Kunjana Thomas 2001.
4.  Mildred Eldridge, *Soar-y-Mynydd*, reproduced in R. S. Thomas, *Selected Prose* (1982). © Kunjana Thomas 2001.
5.  Mildred Eldridge, *Peat Cutting, Cefn Coch* (n.d.). © Victoria and Albert Museum, London.
6.  Kenneth Rowntree, *Conway Castle and Coracle* (n.d.). © Victoria and Albert Museum, London.
7.  Mildred Eldridge, drawing of R. S. Thomas (n.d.). Private collection.
8.  Mildred Eldridge, drawing of R. S. Thomas (n.d.). Private collection.
9.  Edgar Degas, *Portrait of a Young Woman*, 1867. Musée d'Orsay, Paris; Giraudon; The Bridgman Art Library.
10. Edgar Degas, *Mademoiselle Marie Dihau at the piano*, oil on canvas, c.1869–72. Musée d'Orsay, Paris; Giraudon; The Bridgman Art Library.
11. Edgar Degas, *The Opera Orchestra*, oil on canvas, c.1870. Musée d'Orsay, Paris; Giraudon; The Bridgman Art Library.
12. Ben Shahn, *Father and Child*, painting (n.d.).
13. Toyen, *Hlas Lesa I*, painting (n.d.).
14. Iwan Bala, *Land*, painting (n.d.).
15. Wil Rowlands, *At the End*, painting (n.d.).
16. Christine Kinsey, *Yr Adwy 1*, pencil and charcoal on paper (n.d.).

# ABBREVIATIONS

CP    *Collected Poems, 1945–1990* (Guernsey: Phoenix/Orion, 2000)

CLP  *Collected Later Poems, 1988–2000* (Tarset: Bloodaxe, 2004)

But this one, had he ever been anything but solitary?

R. S. Thomas, *The Echoes Return Slow*

# Introduction

There are deaths that have affected the very weather of the Welsh mind, and for two days after R. S. Thomas's passing in September 2000, the country was swept by storms. What mattered to many, towards the end of his long life, was that he was still there, magnificently cussed, wilfully bloody-minded, incorrigibly anachronistic. In a world glib with yes-men, his was a voice ever ready to say No! in thunder. And, as a connoisseur of irony, he would have relished the moment at his funeral when, during the still moment of prayer, the jets he had so often cursed screeched unheeding overhead, inscribing their own hostile obituary in the skies of Llŷn. As for the cremation that followed, it was perfectly suited to one who, contrary to public perception, was never a grave man. 'Poor old Arnold,' one of the Victorian sage's friends is reported to have commented on hearing of the great man's passing: 'he won't like God.' It's easy to understand why the Almighty put off calling R. S. Thomas home for as long as possible: He knew He would face cross-examination to all eternity. Nor did the ageing Thomas lose his notorious capacity to shock. When I interviewed him a couple of years before his death, he startled his respectable audience by saying that, were he persuaded that drugs would improve his performance as a poet, he would not scruple to take them.

That remark underlined how very seriously he took his vocation – not only as a priest, but as a poet. But how good a poet was he? A century after his birth, but a mere dozen years after his death, it is far, far too early to tell. Quiet consensus – eloquent in its neglect of him – currently murmurs 'not very': a marginal figure at best, minor in his achievements, limited in vision, briefly interesting in his early Iago Prytherch years. I belong to the dissenting minority, but have to concede a special, and probably distorting, interest. I deeply sympathise with both his political and his religious convictions, while by no means fully subscribing to either. For me he remains the 'Solzhenitsyn of Wales', a necessary extremist, an irritating troubler of conscience, a fully signed up member of the awkward squad. He is a true 'Son of Saunders', as explained in one of the chapters that follow. I also particularly value those 'laboratories of the spirit', his late, religious poems, each attenuated text isolated on its page like some gaunt Giacometti figure imaging the modern condition. And however haunting the poetically substantial figure of Iago Prytherch, I feel it is high time for some critics fixated on the early poetry to break free of their arrested development: IP, RIP. When in 1992 I asked Thomas if he would very kindly contribute an unpublished poem for inclusion in a book I was editing about his work, he sent me 'The One', which captures the essence of his religious poems at their incomparable best. Referring to 'the word' of ultimate truth, he notes that

> It is buried under the page's
> drift, and not all our tears,
> not all our air-conditioning
> can bring on the thaw. Our sentences
> are but as footprints, arrested
> indefinitely on its threshold.[1]

That he was uneven is self-evident – what poet, including the undeniably important, is not? Such volumes as *Experimenting with an Amen*, *Counterpoint* and *Mass for Hard Times* might not be greatly missed were they somehow to become completely unavailable, but any narrative of terminal decline in his later years would have to contend with the impressive final achievement of *No Truce With the Furies*, probably as good a volume as ever he published, despite his ironic prepublication aside to me that the title was the best thing about it.

To the very end he scorned an increase of popularity through compromise with the modish or the fashionable, either in poetry or in life. Among my most treasured possessions are two of the red ties, one identical with the other, that he invariably wore. 'He who marries the spirit of the age,' he mordantly reflected, 'will find himself a widower tomorrow.' Of that there was never any danger. With all the perverse stubbornness (or admirable consistency?) evident in his taste for red ties, Thomas persisted in writing a species of poetry sufficiently experimental, in its own way, to exasperate many well-established critics, to whom it seemed limp and formless. Derwent May put it pithily: '[In too many of his later religious poems] the lines are more like furrows than lines of verse – the eye goes backwards and forwards along them as monotonously as Prytherch's plough in the stony fields.'[2] High-risk such poetry certainly is. During the time of the frontier wars, Native Americans were reputed to fear only one thing – damp weather that caused bow-strings to lose their tautness. The danger for the later Thomas was the slackening of his deliberately bald, verbally minimalist sentences as he dared eke them out, phrase by phrase, over several broken lines. That said, I have considerable sympathy with his testy comment on the critics of his later poetry: 'I see some people are still nit-picking about my so-called lack of form. I wish they'd catch up.'[3]

In Ysbaddaden Bencawr, the Welsh-language writer Gwyn Thomas found a perfect avatar for him, capturing the ambivalence of his looming presence as man and poet.[4] Culhwch's task in the *Mabinogion* is to confront and outwit this fierce, unkempt, one-eyed giant custodian of a beautiful daughter. The monstrousness of which Thomas knew himself to be capable is sadly confirmed not only by any number of his casual acquaintances but also by his son, whose account of his early upbringing makes for sobering and distressing reading.[5] Thomas's own poignant confession in an interview one year before his death with the *Daily Telegraph* journalist Graham Turner tells us all we need to know:

> I don't think I'm a very loving person . . . I wasn't brought up in a loving home – my mother was afraid of emotion – and you tend to carry on in the same way, don't you? I suppose my son Gwydion . . . could say he was the victim of the same lovelessness . . . I'm always ready to confess the

3

things that are lacking in me . . . and particularly this lack of love for human beings. If you said that this is a dimension of my work which disqualifies me from being a poet of great significance, I'd agree with you. There is a kind of narrowness in my work which a good critic would condemn.[6]

No wonder he heard 'the voice / of God in the darkness cursing himself / fiercely for his lack of love' (*CP*, p. 319). Whether or not one judges Thomas here to be his own best critic, it would be difficult to deny that he was his own best enemy.

In his defence, one might note an observation he made over lunch when entertaining my wife and myself at his home. Commenting on his chronic impression of self-alienation, of standing at a distance even from himself, he mused that, while certainly not schizophrenic, he might nevertheless be that way inclined, because of his chronic inability to experience himself as a solid, fully integrated personality. Intensely inner-directed at core, as evidenced in his obsessively repetitive creativity, he could certainly be awkward and even wounding in his relationships with others. Yet he was decidedly capable of kindness and of sympathy, if not of sustained affection. When his second wife's only daughter, Alice, died at the age of 40 in 1997, Thomas wrote to his friend Raymond Garlick: 'We knew she could not live, but it didn't make it easier to lose such a vivid and brave person.'[7] And people of my acquaintance sadly experiencing the loss of a loved one to Alzheimer's Disease have found themselves inexpressibly moved by 'Geriatric', the opening poem of Thomas's final collection, *No Truce With the Furies*, with its impassioned, darkly enigmatic conclusion:

> I come away
> comforting myself, as I can,
>     that there is another
> garden, all dew and fragrance,
>     and that these are the brambles
> about it we are caught in,
>     a sacrifice prepared
> by a torn god to a love fiercer
>     than we can understand. (*CLP*, p. 213)

4

And then there are those lovely, gentle poems in remembrance of his first wife, Elsi. They rival those of Hardy to Emma after her death and are, perhaps, rooted in the same tragically belated feelings of guilt and self-bafflement.

> Impalpable,
> invisible, she comes
> to me still, as she would
> do, and I at my reading.
> There is a tremor
> of light, as of a bird crossing
> the sun's path (*CLP*, p. 237).

Boorish Thomas could certainly be, but his reputation for it was also lavishly embroidered by others, in particular by 'mainstream' journalists, commentators and critics piqued by the brutalities of Thomas's dismissal of fools and the short shrift he invariably gave to anti-Welsh arrogance, pretension and condescension. He was good at England-baiting, managing to provoke comments such as the following on his poems about Wales: 'his poems reveal the mediocre origins of most modern nationalism, in many countries besides his own'.[8] What, one wonders, are the supposedly contrasting origins of the earlier, non-modern, nationalisms presumably exemplified by the English?

Not the least complex of the tangle of contradictions at the core of his being was the contrast between his hostility to most things English and a snobbishness consistent with his rather plummy, consciously cultivated Episcopal accent. This fierce champion of Welsh-language culture chose to provide his son with a thoroughly anglicising education at a leading English public school. Yet, in discussion with me, he caustically remarked that any Welsh-language poets who contemplated publishing a bilingual volume should be warned that in including English they would just be making up to a cannibal. And if on occasions in later life he seemed to have fallen victim, then it was to a legend at least partly of his own conscious making and deliberate manipulation.

After all, he had begun by reinventing himself. Christened Ronald, he added the name 'Stuart', later accounting for it in several different ways.

(Two of the three great poets of the twentieth century – the third being Wallace Stevens – were, he noted, distinguished by a brace of initials: T. S. Eliot and W. B. Yeats. He preferred to leave unspoken an aspiration to emulate them.) His rationalisations are perfectly credible, but it also seems pretty clear that adopting 'Stuart' had been a critically important means of denying any substantial indebtedness to his natural parents with whom he nevertheless remained locked in psychic conflict until the very end of his life. It was also the first step in a career of formidable self-fashioning strikingly at odds with his reputation for full-frontal directness and searing honesty. From the Yeats he so greatly admired he had learnt much about the wearing of masks.

He overshadowed other poets, Welsh and otherwise, like a great Upas tree, legendary for dropping only poisoned fruit: rarely was he generous in his acknowledgement even of younger writers. Objectionable, offensive, silly, provocative, outrageous, R. S. Thomas could undoubtedly be – but at times he could also border on the sublime in his moral and cultural defiance, as in some of his singular poems. And he could be captivating as a man, as I can vouch from personal experience. During the last decade of his life I met him some two dozen times in all, at occasions private and intimate, public and formal. The numerous interviews I conducted with him included some destined for radio and television as well as several public events that invariably attracted a capacity audience – an interview at the Hay Literature Festival in the summer of 1997 was first scheduled for some peripheral venue, then moved to a substantial tent, and ended up packing the main marquee with some 750 people (as R.S. – always more alert than he liked to admit to the attention he was receiving – proudly informed me the following day).

In all my conversations with him, never did I feel more shaken, or more inadequate, than when, staring into the fire, he remarked, with quiet finality, that although he still wrote compulsively, true poetry would no longer come. 'What is it makes a good poem?', he humbly asked, as if, for a terrible moment, he genuinely trusted me to supply the answer. I, of course, was speechless. There was such sadness in his question: writing poetry had, after all, been his very *raison d'être*, and the fading of talent signified, for him, no less than the slow extinction of personal existence itself. The silence was broken only by his wistfully recalling the one late poem he still cherished as his own:

> The archer with time
> as his arrow – has he broken
> his strings that the rainbow
> is so quiet over our village?
>
> Let us stand, then, in the interval
> of our wounding, till the silence
> turn golden and love is
> a moment eternally overflowing. (*CLP*, p. 223)

Such intensity was not, however, a trademark of his presence. Expecting to meet an ogre, visitors instead met with courtesy, kindness and consideration: women, in particular, were prone to sense that R.S.'s monkish ascetism was, in fact, the self-restraint of a sensuous nature. Teasing and being teased seemed to come naturally to him, and his dryness of wit was always accompanied by a twinkle of the eye. A *Daily Telegraph* journalist sent to brave the Welsh Cyclops reported that Thomas had arrived late, apologising for having been detained at a hospital where he'd been receiving treatment for a heart condition. Sympathising, the reporter solicitously expressed the hope that his ticker would hereafter prove more reliable. 'Yes,' came the grave reply, 'I'm very aware at my age that I'm living only on tick.' Over lunch, he might pass on the gravy, explaining that he was known to be a dry man; and he would decline pudding, since to eat it would be more than his des[s]erts. Puns and wordplay were second nature to him, and they abound in his poetry, yet only in one (brilliant) essay has this been adequately recognised by his critics and persuasively related not only to his philosophy of language but to his vision of existence.[9] After all, his intimate colloquies with Iago Prytherch and with God were conducted in the related key of irony, and he could be withering about the eminent critics who were blind to the logopeia in his poetry.

He never lost his genius for delighting strangers by speaking and acting in character. When I took my American friend William Virgil

Davis, a poet and R. S. Thomas scholar, to meet him in Maentwrog some twenty years ago, R.S. suggested we rendezvous at the Oakley Arms. Bill and I found the place vibrant with young people playing the pin-ball machines to raucous musical accompaniment. Then R. S. materialised and brusquely pre-empted introduction by harrumphing 'This place is hopeless'. He also delighted in mischievously wrong-footing his friends. Scheduled to conduct a public interview with him, in front of a packed house at the Royal Hotel in Cardiff, I met him as he began to climb the stairs to the meeting room. He had no sooner reached me than he suddenly turned on his heel, saying 'I am just going outside and may be some time.' Recalling his notorious reputation for unexpected rudeness on certain public occasions, I quailed at the prospect of having to explain his absence to the restless awaiting audience. Then the penny dropped. The meeting was being held in the Captain Scott room, its walls adorned with pictures of the ill-fated Antarctic expedition of 1912 that had embarked at Cardiff. R.S. was teasingly quoting the famous last words of Captain Oates. His honesty could also be disconcerting. Interviewed on the BBC Radio Cymru programme *Beti a'i Phobl*, he confessed to a physical cowardice the implications of which for his poetry will be explored in one of the chapters that follow. When it was pointed out he'd been robust enough to play rugby, he retorted that he'd only ever played safely out on the wing, 'a position most useful for nursing cold feet'.

Boorish and humourless as a man, narrow as a poet: these are the distorting clichés that continue to dog R. S. Thomas. Narrow, no: obsessive, yes, or so this study will argue. The *OED* brings out several meanings of the verb 'obsess' relevant to his case. Deriving from *ob* + *sidere* (to sit), it originally meant 'to sit down before a fortress . . . to besiege, invest (1647)': what could better capture Thomas's life-long preoccupation with a distant divinity? 'Of an evil spirit; to beset (a person); to haunt (1540)'; how apt for a poet who, well into his eighties, declared there could be 'no truce with [his] furies'. 'In mod. use . . . to haunt and trouble as a "fixed idea", which persistently assails or vexes (1680)': Iago Prytherch, Wales, the self, his mother, and of course God – what were these but the *idées fixes* of his serially troubled poetic imagination? And paintings, too,

8

or so this study will conclude by suggesting, became a little-recognised 'obsession' of his later years, allowing him to bring several of his deepest concerns into arrestingly sharp focus.

The stigmatising of Thomas as 'narrow' has, it seems to me, consistently bedevilled the reading of his work. Both as man and as poet, his complexity has tended in retrospect to be reduced to convenient simplifications. This has been the unintentional consequence even of many of the excellent critical and biographical studies that have appeared since his death. Concentrating illuminatingly and intensively as they have done on his religious poetry, his poetics, his theology, his politico-cultural ideology and the like, they have made him seem monocular.[10] One rare exception is Tony Brown's outstanding brief study of the complete gamut of his work set in the total context of his life.[11] Other exceptions include the valuable multi-author collections of essays on his career and achievement and special issues of journals dedicated to his work.[12] Designed to advertise the multiplicity of contexts within which Thomas's poetry operates, the study that follows is written and composed very much in the catholic spirit of these latter publications. While not claiming to be comprehensive, it does seek to study Thomas's poetry in a number of very different locations, contexts and connections, all a little more unexpected in character, perhaps, than those encountered in most other studies. Thus his emergence as a poet under wartime conditions is given prominence, as are his frequently strange dealings, through the medium of poetry, with key members of his family. An international dimension to the work of a poet so frequently stigmatised for being narrow and provincial in his allegiances is recognised through consideration of its relations to the work of Borges and of Denise Levertov. The reach and complexity of his commitments to the culture of Wales are explored by tracing his deep indebtedness to the thought and example of Saunders Lewis, while the fact that some of his English texts have a kind of troubled and troubling Welsh cultural subconscious is established through an examination of the ways in which a deep fascination with Abercuawg functions in his poetry. That his religious poems are not only modern but post-modern in theological stance and radical poetics is suggested, and a case is made for considering his exercises in autobiography as experiments in writing the modern history of a soul. An interest in paint-ing is tentatively demonstrated to have been more central to his concerns than he was prepared to admit, and than most of his critics have been ready to recognise: and in the often fruitful creative response of painters to his poems is discerned an implicit acknowledgement of his sensitivity to their medium.

Talk of 'facets' and 'contexts' don't begin to cover the case, though. I have always been perplexed by any imposing totality of critical reading presented as a comprehensive, let alone authoritative, study of an author. That is surely a mausoleum of the imagination. This volume accordingly lays no claim to being thorough or systematic. A poem, the ageing Frost used to tell students, was just like a carrot. A critic's job was simply to point out in it the merest hint of a nose – eyes and mouth would then spontaneously suggest themselves. And firmly believing the best criti-cism to be thus light of touch and inclined to humour, I might even perhaps have profitably titled this volume *The Parson's Nose*.

Thomas himself was chronically footloose. Friends of his such as Raymond Garlick and Brynmor Thomas used to recall how, when visit-ing, he would often decline the offer of a bed for the night, preferring to pitch his tent on their lawns, Gaddafi-fashion. It was no doubt one more symptom of his acute discomfort with intimacy – and indeed with domesticity – in almost any form. It was also undoubtedly a genuine expression of his lifelong instinctive affinity for the natural world, which he was inclined to favour over the human. And to me it seems perfectly expressive of his 'default' condition as a peregrine soul, an eternally journeying spirit, chronically 'lost in his own breath' (as he memorably wrote of his Iago Prytherch), a 'waif spirit' (*CLP*, p. 295). This is the Thomas who seems to have fully discovered the natural idiom of his soul only late in his career, in his haunting religious poetry.

And if his death seemed to affect the very weather of the Welsh mind, then today, a century after his birth, it is clear that his writing has per-manently altered perception of the Welsh landscape itself. R. S. Thomas country is as unmistakeable as Hardy country, or for that matter, Faulkner country. In Malcolm Pryce's comic noir, *The Unbearable Lightness of Being in Aberystwyth*, his private eye finds himself confronting signs ominously

warning 'You are now entering Iago Prytherch country', and passing
signposts to 'The bald Welsh hills'.[13] Viewing a farmer working in the
fields during the sixties, the poet Harri Webb imagined him as a kind
of escapee from an early Thomas poem, a Iago Rhydderch who had
narrowly avoided being turned into a Iago Prytherch. This figure recalls
being approached 'by a figure gaunt and tall,' who 'carried on at tedious
length/ About my life so grim,/ It took all my idiot peasant strength/
To be polite to him.'[14] Almost forty years later, on Thomas's passing,
Peter Finch wrote in his sprightly irreverent way:

> A pioneer of dark wounds and internal tensions. In old age bird song and
> reliable grouch. Stood, was counted, still no change. To live in Wales is to
> become unassailable. 'An angel-fish' (Clarke). Expect retrospective, marvel-
> ling and statue.[15]

The short-hand style is an affectionately teasing tribute to Thomas's
familiarity: he has himself become part of the mental landscape of a
Wales his poetry has refashioned. A dozen years after his death, such a
poet needs no solemnising retrospective, no worshipful marvelling, no
marmoreal statue – and no critical study.

## Notes

1  M. Wynn Thomas (ed.), *The Page's Drift: R. S. Thomas at Seventy* (Bridgend:
   Seren, 1993).
2  Derwent May, 'Drystone verses by a bleak bard', *The Times* (Monday, 5 April
   1993).
3  Jason Walford Davies (ed.), *R. S. Thomas: Letters to Raymond Garlick, 1951–1999*
   (Llandysul: Gomer Press, 2009) (letter dated 8.iii.93), p. 146.
4  Gwyn Thomas, 'Barddoniaeth R. S. Thomas', in M. Wynn Thomas (gol.),
   *R. S. Thomas: Y Cawr Awenydd* (Llandysul: Gwasg Gomer, 1990), p. 1. Thomas
   points out that 'Ysbaddaden' derives from an old Welsh name for 'bramble',
   and that this image, like the ancient story in which it occurs, seems to suggest
   a powerful primal energy such as is embodied in R.S.'s poetic persona.
5  '"Quietly as snow": Gwydion Thomas talks to Walford Davies', *New Welsh
   Review*, 64 (Summer 2004), 15–48.

6   'God is a poet who sang creation', *Daily Telegraph* (4 December 1999).

7   Davies, *Letters to Raymond Garlick*, p. 157 (letter of 18.xii.97).

8   May, 'Drystone verses'.

9   Damian Walford Davies, '"Double-entry Poetic": R. S. Thomas – Punster', in Damian Walford Davies (ed.), *Echoes to the Amen: Essays after R. S. Thomas* (Cardiff: University of Wales Press, 2003), pp. 149–82.

10  Valuable studies include Dewi Z. Phillips, *R. S. Thomas: Poet of the Hidden God* (London: Macmillan, 1986); M. J. J. van Buuren, *Waiting: the Religious Poetry of Ronald Stuart Thomas* (Nijmegen: Katholieke Universiteit van Nijmegen, 1993); Elaine Shepherd, *R. S. Thomas: Conceding an Absence* (London: Macmillan, 1996); Grahame Davies, *Sefyll yn y Bwlch: R. S. Thomas, Saunders Lewis, T. S. Eliot, a Simone Weil* (Caerdydd: Gwasg Prifysgol Cymru, 2000); John Powell Ward, *The Poetry of R. S. Thomas* (Bridgend: Seren, 2001); Jason Walford Davies, *Gororau'r Iaith: R. S. Thomas a'r Traddodiad Llenyddol Cymraeg* (Caerdydd: Gwasg Prifysgol Cymru, 2003); Christopher Morgan, *R. S. Thomas: Identity, Environment, and Deity* (Manchester: Manchester University Press, 2003); Barry Morgan, *Strangely Orthodox: R. S. Thomas and his Poetry of Faith* (Llandysul: Gomer, 2006); William V. Davis, *R. S. Thomas: Poetry and Theology* (Waco: Baylor University Press, 2007); Daniel Westover, *R. S. Thomas: A Stylistic Biography* (Cardiff: University of Wales Press, 2011). Also two biographies: Justin Wintle, *Furious Interiors: Wales, R. S. Thomas and God* (London: HarperCollins, 1996); Byron Rogers, *The Man Who Went into the West: the Life of R. S. Thomas* (London: Aurum Press, 2006).

11  Tony Brown, *R. S. Thomas* (Cardiff: University of Wales Press, 2006).

12  *Y Cawr Awenydd*; *The Page's Drift*; *Echoes to the Amen*; Sandra Anstey (ed.), *Critical Writings on R. S. Thomas* (Bridgend: Seren, new edn 1995); William V. Davis (ed.), *Miraculous Simplicity: Essays on R. S. Thomas* (Fayetteville: University of Arkansas Press, 1993).

13  Malcolm Pryce, *The Unbearable Lightness of Being in Aberystwyth* (London: Bloomsbury, 2006), pp. 135–7.

14  Harri Webb, 'Ianto Rhydderch: Tch Tch', in Meic Stephens (ed.), *Harri Webb: Collected Poems* (Llandysul: Gomer, 1995), pp. 140–1.

15  *New Welsh Review*, 51: xiii (Winter 2000/2001), 11.

I

# War Poet

In 1942, the enterprising and arrestingly exotic M. J. Tambimuttu edited *Poetry in Wartime*, which the publishers Faber claimed to be 'unique in that it is not an anthology of war poems', but a collection (including the work of Brenda Chamberlain, Alun Lewis, Lynette Roberts, Dylan Thomas and Vernon Watkins) of the best poems written since the beginning of war – some of which are also 'war-poems'.[1] The distinction is an important one, pointing up the complexity of the relationship between literature and war, another facet of which is the inevitable inflection of any work produced during wartime by the special conditions that enter, however insensibly, or indirectly, into the very marrow of its making. When Dylan Thomas entitles his 1937 poem 'I make this in a warring absence', he is referring primarily to his wish for a 'peace' in his turbulent relationship with his wife Caitlin; 'an armistice of a moment, to come out of the images on *her* warpath'.[2] But the image is rootedly expressive of the time in which it was written, when memories of the Great War haunted a young generation uneasily eyeing the ever grimmer circumstances that, passing for 'peace' in contemporary Europe, ominously threatened to turn the two decades since 1918 into a mere 'armistice'.

Thomas's poem was included in Keidrych Rhys's groundbreaking 1944 anthology *Modern Welsh Poetry*.[3] Among its thirty-seven mostly young contributors were conscientious objectors like Pennar Davies, Glyn Jones and Roland Mathias; First World War veterans like Wyn Griffith and David Jones; home-front writers like Lynette Roberts, the Argentinian incomer suspiciously eyed as a spy at Llan-y-bri, and Brenda Chamberlain, who from her Llanberis cottage helped with mountain rescue of wrecked aircrew; and serving soldiers such as the reluctant combatant Alun Lewis and the wholly unlikely Vernon Watkins. Several of them were to produce war-related volumes that have been forgotten but would bear revisiting – Brenda Chamberlain's remarkable *The Green Heart* (1938) and Nigel Heseltine's *The Four-Walled Dream* are as undeservedly neglected as the wartime poetry of T. Harri Jones and Harri Webb.[4] And because of the range of contributors, Rhys's volume itself deserves to be better appreciated as a valuable record, such as perhaps poetry alone could offer, of the otherwise elusive sensibilities and modalities of wartime Wales. Here, for instance, a survivor of Mametz stands aghast in Wyn Griffith's 'farewell to . . . all remembering': 'If there be time enough before the slaughter/ Let us consider our heritage/ Of wisdom' (*MPW*, p. 53). A young Nigel Heseltine is devastated by the venerable T. Gwynn Jones's refusal, in August 1939, to countenance the awarding of the main prizes at that year's National Eisteddfod at Denbigh: 'An old man speaking of poetry/ Gave us no crown no chair/ No father no mother no voice/ For tomorrow// For tomorrow death' (*MWP*, p. 66). And a similar need (sometimes desperate, always urgent) for an adequate, answerable 'voice', a language to make sense of direst experience, is to be felt in most, if not all, of this poetry. It is what prompts Ken Etheridge to fulminate against indulgence in 'the lechery/ Of much used metaphors', and to plead 'Let us be clean in language' (*MWP*, p. 42). And it leads many to reconnect themselves to Wales, either by finding appropriate symbolic language in Welsh myth, or by grounding themselves, Antaeus-like, in Welsh land, in Welsh communities, and within the continuities of Welsh history. As Keidrych Rhys's case demonstrates, mobilisation could result in a newly palpable realisation that 'I'm not English', 'My roots lie in another region'; so that, in an intense, reflexive effort of cultural recovery, 'I try to remember the things;/ At home that mean Wales but typical [*sic*]/ Isn't translated across The Channel' (*MWP*, pp. 112–13).

The rural landscape and community life Rhys thus recuperates was at that time being experienced somewhat ambivalently by his wife, Lynette Roberts: 'To the village of lace and stone/ Came strangers. I was one of these', writes Roberts, implicitly associating herself, after a fashion, with evacuees (*MWP*, p. 115). She, however, was a refugee of a very different kind, in search of her ancestral roots and attempting, in the process, to recall a Welsh people alienated from their own historical origins and ignorant of their authentic cultural inheritance. Hers was therefore a wartime enterprise closely paralleling that attempted, through the *Caseg Broadsheets*, by Brenda Chamberlain and Alun Lewis, to whom Roberts addressed her 'Poem from Llanybri', inviting him to visit.[5] The poem itself seeks to reenact ancient social customs and poetic conventions, and to discover the kind of English that alone can vouch for the distinctively Welsh locality, and authoritatively speak for it. It becomes what Tony Conran would later call 'a gift poem' – a poem that is offered as a gift, as if it were a proffered piece, a real substantial token, of the landscape itself. 'I will offer you/ A fist full of rock cress fresh from the bank' (*MWP*, p. 116). But it is her own insuperable alienation from this place that comes through in 'Lamentation', a poem which, in properly insisting that the anguish of miscarriage can exceed even that caused by a local air-raid, is a rare reminder of how 'normal', quotidian life will always continue to furnish experiences as searing as those that war may bring. The poems in the collection also remind us of other continuities between pre-war life and wartime experiences. In industrial south Wales, war followed hard upon the heels of a decade and a half of economic crisis and social devastation. This is indicated in Huw Menai's case, through the juxtaposition of a poem on the terrible siege of Stalingrad with others on the mental torment of working underground: 'Where shall the eyes a darkness find/ That is a menace to the mind/ Save in the coal mine, where one's lamp/ Is smothered oft by afterdamp?' (*MWP*, p. 95).

All the important writers of the time – from Dylan Thomas to Alun Lewis, and from Emyr Humphreys to Idris Davies – are included in Rhys's *Modern Welsh Poetry*. And yet it is with a start that one comes upon R. S. Thomas in this company. Rarely has he been regarded a wartime poet, let alone as a 'war poet'. And to read two of his poems in this context is to be bewildered, disorientated, discomfited. 'Iago Prytherch his name' (*MWP*, p. 130): what on earth is Thomas's celebrated 'ordinary man of the bald Welsh hills' doing in this company? And who would have expected Thomas's chronically absconding God to make his absent presence first known here, as 'the voice that lulled/ Job's soothing mind to a still calm/ Yet tossed his heart to the racked world' (*MWP*, p. 131)? Could it somehow be, against all probability, that the early R. S. Thomas, too, was a war poet?

The answer, as we shall see, is yes; and to read a signature poem of Thomas's such as 'A Peasant' in the context of this collection is to begin to notice that his early poetry shares several of its central concerns with the poetry of his 'wartime' generation of (mostly) young Welsh poets. Writing under duress, they sought for new forms, new themes, and above all a new language adequate for expressing their situation. As their Wales became luridly back-lit by the glare of conflict, they found that everything they had previously unconsciously valued about their country – the land, the people, the communities – was rendered newly precious, sharply silhouetted by the fires that threatened to consume them. The antiquity of Wales, whether suggested by myth and legend or embodied in the ancientness of rocks and mountains, became for them the warrant of survival; even the devastations that pre-war Wales had endured – the dreadful depression years commemorated by Idris Davies and Huw Menai, the decline of Welsh rural and upland communities angrily mourned by R. S. Thomas – were now paradoxically metamorphosed into proofs of invincible endurance. And, with eyes rawly exposed to the ubiquity of violence, these poets could look differently even upon the most conveniently tranquil and reassuring scenes:

When birds and brittle leaves come down
When trees and grass freeze out their blood
And fishes die in floods of rain,
This is the time for Death.
A mouse is spiked on blades of grass
A sparrow swings from the gibbet of a twig. (*MWP*, p. 103)

It is by bearing features such as these in mind that we may best prepare ourselves for understanding important aspects of R. S. Thomas's ground-breaking first collection, *The Stones of the Field* (1946).

There we are stopped in our tracks by passages like this:

> Nor shot, nor shell, but the fused word,
> That rocks the world to its white root,
> Has wrought a chaos in the mind,
> And drained the love from the split heart;
>
> Nor shock, nor shower of the sharp blows,
> That fall alike from life and death,
> But some slow subsistence within,
> That sinks a grave for the sapped faith.[6]

Here, surely, is a poem that – with its self-conscious sonorities, declamatory rhetoric, dramatic off-rhymes and impacted images – could almost pass for one by Dylan Thomas? Or that would not be out of place in *Raiders' Dawn*, that disturbing first volume by Alun Lewis, whose language is so fraught with violence and from which several poems were extracted for Rhys's *Modern Welsh Poetry*? And yet, this is 'Propaganda' by R. S. Thomas, one of those short lyrics he effectively disowned by choosing not to reprint them in his later, mature collection *Song at the Year's Turning*. That these poems have been overlooked by critics is understandable since, by omitting them, Thomas presumably meant to indicate that they were only apprentice pieces and that the early growing points of his distinctive, authentic talent lay elsewhere – in the farmer poems (including those about Prytherch) that were also included in *The Stones of the Field*.

But those discarded early lyrics are not, I feel, entirely without interest or indeed without significance. They seem to bespeak a 'chaos in the mind', a sensibility under stress. And the affinity between 'Propaganda' and certain poems by Dylan Thomas and Alun Lewis is, in my opinion, one that is worth noting – not because of any suggestion of influence but because it dramatically highlights a shared social experience. All three writers were living through a period when, as Yeats put it, 'mere anarchy' had been loosed upon the world – and it was Yeats himself, of course, who showed younger poets in his poetry how to construct a language strong enough to convey the brutalities of breakdown.[7] R. S. Thomas, in his turn, showed he had learnt lessons from the master by writing Yeatsian poems in the early 1940s like the following, 'On a Portrait of Joseph Hone by Augustus John':

> As though the brute eyes had seen
> In the hushed meadows the weasel
> That would tear the soft down of the throat
> And suck the veins dry
> Of their glittering blood . . . (*CP*, p. 15)

It is with a poem like this very much in mind that I would like to suggest that *The Stones of the Field* might usefully be read as war poetry. Obviously I do not mean that the collection directly addresses the subject of war. What I do mean is that the poetry frequently comes from an imagination fearfully alerted by war to the ferocities of existence: 'Your love is dead, lady, your love is dead;/ Dribbles no sound/ From his stopped lips, though swift underground/ Spurts his wild hair'.[8] Indeed, there is a terrible Jacobean relish about such lines, that shows how R. S. Thomas, like Alun Lewis, understood how sexually arousing and sensually heightening the experience of violence and disaster could be.

So much has been written, not least by R. S. Thomas himself, about the move to Manafon that precipitated the Iago Prytherch poems, and a *rite de passage* it clearly was, involving the rude awakening of an innocent, sentimental, cosseted, romantic bourgeois to the harsh and sometimes cruel facts of life on the upland farms. But what the critics seem to have consistently overlooked is one of the reasons for the move, as R. S. Thomas recalled it in his autobiography *Neb*. He is remembering the period he spent from 1940 to 1942 as a curate at Hanmer, in Flintshire border country:

By now the war had started in earnest, and although there was not much risk locally, the parish was in the path of the German planes as they aimed at Merseyside. Every night, when the weather permitted, the planes came across on their way in and they soon began to get on the curate's nerves, not so much because of the fear but because of despair and hopelessness at the thought that they were on their way to drop their evil loads on help-less women and children . . . Although Merseyside was about twenty miles away as the crow flies, as he stood at the door with his wife listening to the sound of bombs in the distance and watching the flame lighting the sky, he felt an occasional puff of air going through his hair and lifting his wife's skirt. Sometimes the Germans would drop a few bombs in the area, after seeing a light somewhere perhaps, but without harming anyone, thanks to the open character of the land. One night he happened to be looking through the window when he heard a bomb screaming on its way down quite near. He waited for the explosion, but nothing happened. The follow-ing day it was discovered that the bomb had plummeted to earth a yard or two away from a zinc-roofed cottage, where an old couple was living. They were sleeping soundly at the time, not realising anything unusual was happening! The curate decided to build a defensive wall against the wall of the parsonage opposite the place under the stairs, as a place to shelter in, should more bombs start to fall. One night when he was leaving the church that was next door to the house he heard a terrible explosion quite near. He ran in and urged his wife to come to shelter under the stairs, and there they were for hours, while the enemy aircraft circled above their heads. They heard afterwards that there were Italians as well as Germans, and that they were having difficulties in trying to get near Merseyside. Several bombs were dropped in the area that night, and the hill-country was set on fire in the neighbourhood of Minera. Seeing the flames, they started to drop bombs there too, and some shepherd that was living near the moorland got the fright of his life. The curate so hated to think about the damage that was occurring almost every night, and so longed for the hills in the distance (Moel Famau could be seen clearly enough towards the north-west) that he decided to learn Welsh, in order to come back to Wales.[9]

It took more than forty years for R. S. Thomas to reflect directly on these events in a poem. It was in *The Echoes Return Slow* (1988) that he at last confronted feelings whose repressed presence had, it now seems, covertly influenced the poetry of *The Stones of the Field*. He admitted that he had known 'the instinctive fear// of the animal that finds/ the foliage about its den/ disarranged and comes to know/ it can never go there again' (*CLP*, p. 20). The implications of such experiences for Thomas's under-standing of his own character will be considered in chapter 6. But at this point it is worth noting how, in recalling that 'the wind that [had] ruffled/ [his wife's] skirt came/ from no normal direction', Thomas was registering a profound reorientation of his psychic existence (*CLP*, p. 20). The shock wave from the bomb had shaken him to the foundations of his inner being, creating a fundamental sense of mistrust and insecurity. It was this 'animal' experience of 'instinctive fear' that, in actual, historical, reality prompted him to try to make his home safe, best he could, and to construct a sanctuary for his wife and himself under the stairs. And it was also the same fear of the animal, which finds its very den has been disturbed, that perhaps led him half-admiringly to associate the Manafon upland farmers with 'The land's patience and a tree's/ Knotted endurance' (*CP*, p. 12).

In his wartime poetry he invests Prytherch and his kind with a power of survival that makes them more reassuringly trustworthy than any 'cwtsh dan stâr' ('the place under the stairs'). Moreover, baffled and pained though R. S. Thomas chronically is by Prytherch's 'uncouth ways', he is also ambiguously attracted to his unselfconsciousness. And this attraction, usually explained in terms of Thomas's reaction against his urban bourgeois background, can also be seen in a new light – the light of the Merseyside bombing, as it were – if we remember what Thomas reveals about his wartime self in *The Echoes Return Slow*. The portrait he there paints is of a lonely, isolated, figure tormented by the unceasing arguments he was having with himself. He even half-envied the men of action, who had gone to war with promptness and conviction: 'Yes, action has its compensations. What does one do when one does not believe in action, or in certain kinds of action? Are the brave lacking in imagination? Are the imaginative not brave, or do they find it more difficult to be brave? What does a man do with his silence, his aloneness, but suffer the sapping of unanswerable questions?' (*CLP*, p. 21). Full consideration of the implications of these comments must be postponed until chapter 6, but it is clear that through the 'unimaginative' figure of Prytherch he was able at once to articulate his inner doubts aloud and also to imagine a human experience proof against 'the sapping of unanswerable questions'. When reading his wartime poems we should, I feel, bear in mind the revealing picture of his wartime self that R. S. Thomas gave us for the first time in *The Echoes Return Slow*: 'Casualty of the quarrel with strong men, bandaging himself with Yeats's sentence about the quarrel within, he limped on through an absence of sympathy. His poetry was bitter' (*CLP*, p. 22).

R. S. Thomas's pre-Manafon experience of the bombing of Merseyside obviously underlies the only poem in *The Stones of the Field* that deals directly with the war. 'Homo Sapiens 1941' is a mock-epic study of man the hubristic aviator, the Icarus of modern technological warfare, and it exposes the spurious glamour of the Romantic will-to-power that was prevalent in the aesthetics as well as in the politics of the 1930s:

> Murmuration of engines in the cold caves of air,
> And, daring the starlight above the stiff sea cloud,
> Deadly as a falcon brooding over its prey,
> In a tower of spirit-dazzling and splendid light,
> Pedestrian man holds grimly on his way.
> Legions of winds, ambushed in crystal corries,
> Conspiring to destroy him, and hosts of ice,
> Thronging him close, weigh down his delicate wings;
> But loud as a drum in his ear the hot blood sings,
> And a frenzy of solitude mantles him like a god.[10]

The episode is reminiscent of Satan's sinister flight towards earth in Book II of *Paradise Lost*, when he 'heroically' withstands the buffeting of chaos. But the poem reads primarily as an ironic pastiche of the Romantic modernist style favoured by those worshippers of the Machine, the Futurist artists and writers. R. S. Thomas's imagination sweeps the sky like a flurry of searchlights as he tries to fix the image of self-intoxicated modern man, caught in all the destructiveness of his mad daring. There are moments of particular resonance. Take that opening line, 'Murmuration of engines in the cold caves of air'. Is Thomas recalling and rewriting the famous lines about the First World War in *The Waste Land*? 'What is that sound high in the air/ Murmur of maternal lamentation'.[11] It could be that this distorted echo of Eliot is Thomas's way of introducing into his poem those feelings about the women and children of Merseyside that he mentions in *Neb* – so the murmur of maternal lamentation becomes the dark accompaniment to the murmuration of masculine engines.

Concern with aerial warfare had, of course, been a commonplace of the thirties, greatly exacerbated by the infamous case of Guernica – and

'Homo Sapiens 1941' could profitably be juxtaposed with the Huw Menai poem 'In the Vale of Glamorgan' of around the same period, included in Rhys's *Modern Welsh Poetry*:

> Bird-men, the devil's alloy in their metal,
> Go soaring Southward while a throstle sings;
> Above, then below the clouds – wonder of wonders!
> The sunset's beauty flashing on their wings.
>
> And I, with humble sparrows in the cornfield,
> Know less of exultation than of pain
> For thinking that these miracles of conquest
> May not come home again! (*MWP*, p. 94)

Very different in their style though these poems are (and for once Menai's reactionary Georgian pastoral seems to serve a poignantly ironic purpose), they exhibit a shared nexus of edgy feelings – a kind of modern, tortured version of the sublime, where awe at human conquest of the air is accompanied by terror at the consequences.

Because there is no other poem like it in *The Stones of the Field*, 'Homo Sapiens 1941' has tended to be discussed in isolation.[12] I have never seen it referred to in connection with the Iago Prytherch poems, and yet it is with reference to 'Homo Sapiens 1941' that R. S. Thomas's early farmer poems acquire a pointed 'period' meaning that immediately politicises them. To put it simply, Prytherch is the elemental opposite of 'Homo Sapiens 1941' – earth-bound where the latter is air-borne, doggedly ancient where the latter is dangerously modern. The point seems to be underlined by R. S. Thomas when, in *Song at the Year's Turning*, he arranges 'Homo Sapiens 1941' opposite his familiar poem 'A Labourer'. If 'legions of winds, ambushed in crystal corries' have conspired to destroy the modern aviator, then the question with which 'A Labourer' opens is: 'Who can tell his years, for the winds have stretched/ So tight the skin on the bare racks of bone/ That his face is smooth, inscrutable as stone?' (*CP*, p. 2). If the airman is mockingly depicted as braving the fury of the skies, then the 'peasant' in Thomas's poem of that name, season after season 'Against siege of rain and the wind's attrition,/ Preserves his

stock, an impregnable fortress/ Not to be stormed even in death's confusion./ Remember him, then, for he, too, is a winner of wars' (*CP*, p. 4).
I take that admonition to be more than a casual rhetorical gesture, since
the early figure of Prytherch seems to be, in certain of his features, partly
the product of a wartime imagination.

The opening poem of *The Stones of the Field* is 'Out of the Hills', where
the upland farmer, 'Dreams clustering thick on his sallow skull,/ Dark
as curls', comes 'ambling with his cattle/ From the starved pastures' (*CP*,
p. 1). Thomas follows his progress down into the valley with distinct unease, unwilling to 'witness his swift undoing/ In the indifferent streets:
the sudden disintegration/ Of his soul's hardness, traditional discipline/
Of flint and frost thawing in ludicrous showers/ Of maudlin laughter;
the limpid runnels of speech/ Sullied and slurred, as the beer-glass chimes
the hours'. There is obviously a lot that could be said about Thomas's
distaste for the corrupting softness of life on the valley bottom, but in
the context of this period study it is worth noticing the belief that was
current when the poem was written.

It was generally accepted at the time that the dwellers in the valleys
along the Welsh borders belonged to an entirely different race of people
from the farmers who lived in the neighbouring uplands.[13] The former
were the English descendants of the foreign invaders from post-Roman
times onwards, while the latter were the Welsh remnants of the original
pre-Celtic tribes that had retreated into the hills. This belief seemed solidly
based on scholarly, 'scientific' evidence. Disputing the new anthropological approach of Franz Boas, the eminent Professor of Geography at
Aberystwyth, H. J. Fleure, had from the 1920s onwards been conducting
a systematic study of the different racial elements in the Welsh population. He was able to report in the October 1939 issue of *Wales* that 'The
work of measuring the types of Welsh people has been proceeding very
rapidly during the last five years and there are now measurements of
between 4000 and 5000 men of ascertained localised ancestries.'[14] The
reference here is to the measuring of human skulls, a practice undertaken
because it was believed that there was a precise correlation between skull
size and shape and racial antecedents. In his article, Fleure listed and
described six different racial types that could be readily distinguished

in the Welsh population. He labelled these from A to F, and then roughly explained which categories predominated in the different areas of Wales. He concluded, for instance, that 'Montgomeryshire [where Manafon, of course, was located], Brecknock, and Radnor show increasing proportions of F as one goes towards England and increasing proportions of B as one goes towards the western hills' (269). By F he meant 'tall, rather long headed fair men with sharp profiles', who were descended from 'the post-Roman invaders of Britain' (268). These, he added, were 'the famous or should we now say, thanks to the wild exaggerations of Nazi propaganda, notorious Nordic types'. As for B, these were 'the little dark Welshmen occurring everywhere, short or medium in height, with oval faces and long, rather than extremely long heads, dark eyes less deeply set than those of A, but sometimes the eye pigment has been almost lost' (267).

To call attention to Fleure's categories is not, for one moment, to suggest that Prytherch is simply a version of this type B, a 'little, dark Welshman'. But it does seem possible that the idea, which could be extrapolated from such evidence as Fleure offered, that the 'aboriginal' Welsh could still be found stubbornly surviving in the western hills above Manafon, proved attractive to an R. S. Thomas who had been so disturbed at Hanmer by modern images of violent invasion. If so, then as the pages of *Wales* during that period show, he was certainly not the only writer to be influenced directly or indirectly by anthropological thinking such as Fleure's. There are two other particularly interesting examples. In the July 1943 issue a Lieutenant J. B. Sidgwick from Leicester, stationed apparently in the Newtown area, just down the road from Manafon, published a poem called 'Welsh Station':

> The hills in this part of the world
> Are hard worked and domestic, harrowed
> And horse drawn to their summits.
> Slick smooth-pastured hill flanks
> Slip into the valleys, usurp the old wild
> Strongholds of the long-headed defenders,
> Saturnine and slight, who burnt their earth
> Before the encroaching east. Barrow
> Is buried now beneath black-suited Sabbaths
> Hard cash, alicks and social pretenders.[15]

The poem concludes on a note of lament for the defeated aboriginal inhabitants, now assimilated into the invading culture: 'Rout leaps out of planned retreat –/ And liquid vowels, gentle eyes/ Merely serve to emphasise/ Dolichocephalic defeat'. R. S. Thomas was, of course, to press beyond these domesticated hills around Newtown and to find in the harsher upland areas farmers whose faces and accents were still as yet unsubdued by modern civilization.

Sidgwick was an unknown writer, but John Cowper Powys was not. During the course of an article on 'Wales and America' in the summer 1944 issue of *Wales*, Powys cited Fleure in support of his claim that 'there exists in Wales a deep tradition of pre-historic understanding between the mountains and the people such as is rare on our migratory planet.'[16] He went on to elaborate the point, in terms that seem almost to anticipate some of R. S. Thomas's feelings about the 'native' Welsh:

> Geographically and historically – pre-historically too, no doubt! – Wales is the last stronghold of the oldest race in Europe. Here, in the mountain–plateaus and the deep valleys, with the Irish Sea to prevent further escape, migratory invaders have been forced, for some ten thousand years, to amalgamate with aboriginals who, as Professor Fleure hints, go back in long uninterrupted descent to a branch of our Homo Sapiens who succeeded the hardly human Neanderthal. And it may well have been that the difficult and delicate art of sinking into your native soul and your native soil, while wave after wave of warlike invaders pass over you, has in all these thousands of years given the Welsh their predominant characteristics.

Alerted by this, we can see signs of Fleure's influence everywhere in the piece on 'Welsh Aboriginals' that Powys published in the July 1943 issue of *Wales*. In his own inimitable fashion he there gloried, with eccentric Romantic zeal and panache, in his own 'real Aboriginal Welsh blood', which was 'true Non-Aryan Berber'.[17] He enthusiastically agreed with Dr Iorwerth Peate 'that it is the inaccessibility of certain parts of our land that has saved our "remnant" of Real Welshmen'. He further quoted Peate's opinion that the 'People of the mountains were the natives; but men of the plains were Romans. *There* you get the story of every new influence in our land':

*I'r estron, os mynu* [sic]
*Boed hawl tros y glyn;*
*I ninnau boed byw*
*Ar ymyl gwisg Duw*
*Yn y grug – yn y grug –*

(Let the stranger, if so must be
Stake his claim in the valley:
Give us to live our life
Where the Deity garments himself
In the heather – in the heather.)

This Welsh folk-rhyme is the very one quoted by R. S. Thomas in 'The Depopulation of the Welsh Hill Country' (first published in *Wales* in 1943), at the end of a passage where he argues that it is in the hill country that 'there beats the old heart of Wales'.[18] And further attention will be paid in chapter 3 to the significance of the rhyme for Thomas's later readings of Wales in his poetry of the 1960s. To set his poem 'Out of the Hills' in this extensive context is to understand why that poem ends with Thomas reassuring himself and us that at midnight the farmer will extricate himself from the clutches of the valleys folk and make his way home. 'Be then his fingerpost/ Homeward', the poem urges us: 'The earth is patient; he is not lost' (*CP*, p. 1).

As *The Echoes Return Slow* shows, Thomas's imagination had become particularly sensitised to ideas of invasion during his stay at Hanmer. He recalls listening as 'All night the freight trains thundered over the viaduct on their way south. The English coast was in danger. The tall headlines in the papers marched grimly into an uncertain future' (*CLP*, p. 20). There may be an ironic emphasis here on the way the English (as opposed to the Welsh) react to the threat of invasion. What Thomas later became aware of, at Manafon, was that the arming of England to repel invasion meant the 'invasion' of Wales by the 'modernising' required by the war effort. As he recalls in *The Echoes Return Slow*: 'The tractor invaded the age-old quietness of the land. As the war proceeded, technology directed its infiltration. The farmer changed his allegiance from Ceres to Mars, from subsistence to profit. The priest again questioned his vocation' (*CLP*, p. 25). Invasion came in a cruder form – in the form of 'barbarians'

26

from Hackney, evacuees who were quartered on the vicar and his wife during the latter stages of the war. Thomas's later testimony was that the women neglected their children scandalously, preferring to spend most of their time in the local pubs, when they were not 'flirting' with the wounded soldiers housed at Gregynog. And this, he adds with disgust, when their men-folk were 'in danger of their lives on the continent'.[19] There are traces – even sources? – here of the misogyny that sometimes seems so evident in Thomas's later poetry.

It will not do, though, to see Prytherch and his people, full though they are of the 'artistry of [their] dwelling on the bare hill', simply as the kind of figure of traditional endurance outlasting cataclysm that we famously get in Hardy's poem 'In Time of the Breaking of Nations'. Because another of the ways in which the war leaves its mark on the poetry of *The Stones of the Field* is by foregrounding for Thomas the violence that is so troublingly a part of existence itself – whether it be noticed in nature, or in man's dealings with nature. It is a violence that Thomas sometimes sees as inseparable from sexuality and fertility. Notice, for example, the question on which 'A Labourer' ends: 'Is there love there, or hope, or any thought/ For the frail form broken beneath his tread,/ And the sweet pregnancy that yields his bread?' (*CP*, p. 2). It is in the neglected lyrics, though, rather than in the much more promising and relatively accomplished farmer poems, that one feels exactly how exposed and raw were R. S. Thomas's emotions at this time. The poem he simply called 'Song' can still startle us because it is so uncharacteristic of the R. S. Thomas we know – the poet's mature self. But it is in the very immaturity (in this sense) of the sentiments that the interest of the poem lies:

> We, who are men, how shall we know
> Earth's ecstasy, who feels the plough
> Probing her womb,
> And after, the sweet gestation
> And the year's care for her condition?
> We, who have forgotten, so long ago
> It happened, our own orgasm,
> When the wind mixed with our limbs,
> And the sun had suck at our bosom;[20]

27

Regretting how we 'have affected the livery/ Of the time's prudence,' Thomas yearns to 'quicken again/ To the lust and thrust of the sun/ And the seedling rain'. This enthusiastically primitivistic account of man's intercourse with nature is not exactly convincing – R. S. Thomas is no Stravinsky, and his 'Song' is no orgiastic *Rite of Spring*. In fact, one seems to sense a desperation behind the affirmation – a will to wholeness that is itself a symptom of sickness. And the sickness, judging at least from other poems in this debut collection, is his dismayed awareness not only of a misfit between man and nature but also of the inherent mis-shapen character of nature herself; the equivocal character of her energies.

This is most simply evident from the two poems R. S. Thomas chose to pair at the precise centre of *The Stones of the Field*. On one page is 'Country Church (Manafon)'; on the other is 'Birch Tree', a short poem full of rapturous wonder at the world's power of self-transfiguration:

> When the cloud left you, you smiled and sang
> With the day's brightness, O birch tree among
> The envious moors, sullen and frowning;
> Your long veins filled with light,
> And broke in showers on the night,
> Your dark head with silver crowning. [21]

Here the released joy of the birch tree is literally radiant – that is, it radiates outwards until, in darkness, it becomes the light and fire that we know as stars. The image appears to be a spiritual one, since the Virgin Mary is traditionally represented in iconographic tradition as crowned with stars, in accordance with the famous passage from the Book of Revelation (12: i) – 'And there appeared a great wonder in heaven: a woman clothed with the sun and the moon under her feet, and upon her head a crown of twelve stars' – but fused with this Christian imagery is the older Celtic association of the birch tree with love. As Alwyn and Brinley Rees pointed out long ago in their classic study of *Celtic Heritage*, medieval Welsh love poetry (including that of Dafydd ap Gwilym) is full of 'lines associating the birch-tree with love. The lover's bower usually stood beneath a birch-tree or in a birch-bush; wreaths of birch were presented as love-tokens, and in Wales the may-pole was usually a birch-tree'.[22] So R. S. Thomas has here combined Christian with pagan elements, to produce what might be loosely called a sacramental image, finding a sacred, celebratory joy in the sensuous and even the sensual life of nature.

But before resting content with such intense lyrical affirmation, we should glance at the qualifying poem with which 'Birch Tree' is, as it were, paired in *The Stones of the Field*. 'Country Church (Manafon)' is obviously as precisely accurate an evocation of that building as the title would suggest. (Indeed, in his late autobiography *Neb*, R. S. Thomas described the church in terms strikingly similar to those he had used in his poem forty years before.)

> The church stands, built from the river stone,
> Brittle with light, as though a breath could shatter
> Its slender frame, or spill the limpid water,
> Quiet as sunlight, cupped within the bone.
>
> It stands yet. But though soft flowers break
> In delicate waves round limbs the river fashioned
> With so smooth care, no friendly God has cautioned
> The brimming tides of fescue for its sake. (*CP*, p. 11)

'No friendly God' – what a fine, minatory title that would make for a study of R. S. Thomas's religious poetry. But the phrase also warns us that in *The Stones of the Field* the natural world is not seen as benignly spiritual in character. If in 'Birch Tree' light comes to triumph over darkness, then in 'Country Church' light makes even 'built' stone 'brittle' – an inspired conjunction of terms that makes one word ('brittle') seem the virtual disarrangement of the other ('built'), so that language itself, in its unsettling pliability, seems to endorse the sense of an unstable universe. Indeed, the quiet, haunting power of this poem derives in good part from what might be called the metaphysics of its sonic patterns. Throughout, moments of confidence instilled in us by concatenations of sounds that link words of solidly like meaning ('stands . . . Stone') alternate with unnerving moments when like sounds leave us adrift among unlike meanings: 'built . . . brittle . . . spill . . . limpid'. In the last stanza an effect of magical idyll, of a suspension of time, is created by the lulling repetition of soft consonants – 'soft flowers . . . delicate waves . . . limbs . . . fashioned . . . so smooth', only for the very same sounds to lead us unawares into a very different world – of 'no friendly God' and of the 'brimming tides of fescue'. Again, R. S. Thomas highlights this aspect of his wartime experience at Manafon in *The Echoes Return Slow*, when he recalls that 'life in the remotest backwater is prompter of a hundred and one questions. As to be alive is to be vulnerable to pain, so it is to be conscious that peace is transitory' (*CLP*, p. 25).

'Peace is transitory': when we bear in mind that this comment on the general nature of life is made in the context of R. S. Thomas's recollections of wartime life in Manafon, we notice how implicit in it is a sense that war, with its pain and violence, exemplifies – in extreme and obscene form – abiding aspects of existence itself. And there are poems in *The Stones of the Field* where R. S. Thomas seems to me to be forcefully reminding himself of that – anxious to lose any lingering Romantic innocence he had about the pastoral life. Take his poem 'Winter Retreat', for example:

> Accustomed to see death like a wild boar
> Running amok, eyes red, great jaws
> Slavering horribly with their mad lust for blood;
> Accustomed to listen to the bewildering uproar
> Inseparable from its usual method,
> These last stragglers through a world of snow,
> Failing to recognize under the glib mask
> Of innocent whiteness the traditional foe,
> Abandoned themselves with a child's trust to sleep
> On its dissembling pillow.[23]

One wonders to what extent the lurid nightscape of burning Merseyside influenced those opening lines. It is difficult to disconnect Thomas's image of 'death like a wild boar' not only from the legend of the depredations of the Twrch Trwyth in the *Mabinogion*, but also from Alun Lewis's evocation in 'Post-Script: For Gweno', of 'the mad tormented valley/ Where blood and hunger rally/ And Death the wild beast is uncaught, untamed'.[24] Or the same poet's memory (modernising, of course, the

Adonais story) of the invasion of Greece: 'When the raving tusked boar /
Gored the sensual innocent.' In other words, even if Thomas was not
specifically thinking of the war in those opening lines, the Behemoth
images he used were very much part of the vocabulary of psychic stress
during the Second World War, as of course they had been during the
First World War.

In so far as it is a collection in which R. S. Thomas, partly challenged
by war, determined to face up undeviatingly to the harshness of existence,
*The Stones of the Field* is also what Whitman famously called a 'language
experiment'. The poems are the record of his search for a truthful vocabulary for experience, and he effectively says as much in the final poem in
the volume. But before we consider that, it is worth remembering what
Thomas had to say about language in the essay on Scottish writing that
appeared in *Wales* in the same year that *The Stones of the Field* was published. There he enviously praised the fierce, uninhibited style of Scots
writers such as Douglas Young: 'Scots has . . . a braw quality in keeping
with its environment which makes one wonder why in equally stern surroundings so much modern Welsh writing is jingling and sweet. There
are people living under the harsh crags of Cadair Idris and Yr Wyddfa,
or on the bare gaunt moorlands of central Wales, but their verse is tame
to the point of lifelessness.'[25] With those comments in mind we should
be better able to understand the significance of the closing poem of *The
Stones of the Field*:

> Do not say, referring to the sun,
> 'Its journey northward has begun',
> As though it were a bird, annually migrating,
> That now returns to build in the rich trees
> Its nest of golden grass. Do not belie
> Its lusty health with words such as imply
> A pallid invalid recuperating.
> The age demands the facts, therefore be brief –
> Others will sense the simile – and say:
> 'We are turning towards the sun's indifferent ray'.[26]

'The age demands the facts' is a phrase that could have served as an
epigraph to *The Stones of the Field*. But the poem is very much about the

different pictures of the world that lurk behind our 'factual' descriptions of it – because these pictures reveal the faith by which we actually live. In the examples he gives, Thomas brings several buried similes to light only in order to reject them. But he concludes by admitting that we can offer no substantial description of the world that is completely simile-free – in which there is no implied suggestion of what the world is *like*. The real work therefore is the work of finding appropriate similes and, viewed in the light of the concluding assertion, the whole collection can be seen as an exercise in figurative language. Not only are the poems in *The Stones of the Field* full of similes, they are ostentatiously full of similes, to an extent that almost invites us to see them as poems about similes. This is clear enough in a short poem like 'A Thought from Nietzsche' which is an extended conceit, based on a trope that treats the human body as if it were an acre of ground.[27] Related conceits occur throughout the collection – particularly comparisons, verging on the mythopoeic, between men and trees. And it is not only in the short lyrics that troping is so prominent as virtually to constitute the topic of the poetry.

The farmer-portraits are full of foregrounded figures of speech, as in the long narrative poem 'The Airy Tomb' (*CP*, pp. 17–20). And just as, in the final lines of the final poem, the emphasis is on the 'indifference' of nature to the human condition, so throughout the collection the similes tend to work to establish the same harsh truth about the elemental nature of the universe and man's place in it – whether Iago Prytherch is described as penning 'a few sheep in a gap of cloud', or a farmer is described (wonderfully) as 'Gaitered with mud, lost in his own breath', or a labourer is seen 'as his back comes straight/ Like an old tree lightened of the snow's weight'.[28] In other words, R. S. Thomas's wartime response to his demanding age was to render life in uncompromising similes that pictured the world not as reliably ordained or managed by a humanity-orientated God, but as provocatively neutral – glorious and harsh in equal measure, and expressing something of divinity in both its aspects. Indeed to reread *The Stones of the Field* is to discover how consistent with that view of a distant God he articulated in his poetry over the last thirty years of his life is the troubled sense of the divine one gets from this, his first collection.

And with this in mind, it is easy to understand why R. S. Thomas took the collection's title from the Book of Job. The phrase 'the stones of the field' occurs during the following passage:

> In famine he shall redeem thee from death: and in war from the power of the sword. Thou shalt be hid from the scourge of the tongue; neither shalt thou be afraid of destruction when it cometh. At destruction and famine thou shalt laugh: neither shalt thou be afraid of the beasts of the earth. For thou shalt be in league with the stones of the field; and the beasts of the field shall be at peace with thee. And thou shalt know that thy tabernacle shall be in peace; and thou shalt visit thy habitation, and shalt not sin. (Book of Job, 5: xx–xxiv)

Here, indeed, one might say, is a vision of a providential God. But placed in the context of the Book of Job as a whole, these words have a tragically hollow ring to them. They are not Job's words, but the words of Eliphar the Temanite, as he rebukes the afflicted, tormented Job for his loss of faith in the Almighty. But, by the end of the Book of Job, it is with this very same Eliphar the Temanite that God is angry: 'for ye have not spoken of me the thing that is right, as my servant Job hath' (42: i). By then, Job has been brought to realise that God is like the mighty ungovernable Leviathan, not to be measured or constrained by a human being: 'Canst thou draw out leviathan with a hook? Or his tongue with a cord which thou lettest down?' (41: i). It is this vision of God that became R. S. Thomas's mastering vision, his answer to the irreducible puzzle of existence as presented to him in general by the nature of the universe, and in particular by the cruelties of his demanding age. And it is with the Job who reaches this understanding that he identifies in *The Stones of the Field*, as is shown in that poem included by Rhys in *Modern Welsh Poetry* and aptly entitled 'The Question':

> Who is skilled to read
> The strange epitaph of the salt weed
> Scrawled on our shores? Who can make plain
> The thin, dark characters of rain,
> Or the hushed speech of wind and star
> In the deep-throated fir?

Was not this the voice that lulled
Job's seething mind to a still calm,
Yet tossed his heart to the racked world?[29]

'Then answered the Lord unto Job out of the whirlwind, and said "Gird up thy loins now like a man: I will demand of thee, and declare thou unto me. Wilt thou also disannul my judgement? Wilt thou condemn me, that thou mayst be righteous? Hast thou an arm like God? Or canst thou thunder with a voice like him?"' (Book of Job, 40: vi–ix). This was the voice that eventually spoke to R. S. Thomas out of that wind of war that lifted his wife's skirt as they stood at the door watching Merseyside burn. It was also the voice that intermittently spoke to him out of the stones of the field above Manafon. It lulled his seething mind to a still calm; but it also tossed his heart to the racked world. And the poems of *The Stones of the Field* show him to us in this double aspect.

But if these were the longer-term implications of the title *The Stones of the Field*, the short-term message was somewhat different. It was that humankind should seek to renew its ancient peaceful acquaintance with 'the stones of the field' and 'the beasts of the field', so as to be redeemed 'from death . . . and from the power of the sword'. Born of wartime, every bit as much as those poems Rhys included in *Modern Welsh Poetry*, Thomas's collection remains a singular and compelling record of Wales's complex response to the Second World War.

## Notes

[1] M. J. Tambimuttu (ed.), *Poetry in Wartime* (London: Faber and Faber, 1942), cover blurb.

[2] Walford Davies and Ralph Maud (eds), *Dylan Thomas, Collected Poems 1934–53* (London: J. M. Dent & Sons, 1988), pp. 68, 216.

[3] Keidrych Rhys (ed.), *Modern Welsh Poetry* (London: Faber and Faber, 1944). Hereafter *MWP*.

[4] Brenda Chamberlain, *The Green Heart* (London: Oxford University Press, 1958); Nigel Heseltine, *The Four-Walled Dream* (London: The Fortune Press, 1941).

[5] Brenda Chamberlain, *Alun Lewis and the Making of the Caseg Broadsheets* (London: Enitharmon, 1970).

[6] R. S. Thomas, *The Stones of the Field* (Carmarthen: The Druid Press Limited, 1946), p. 10.

[7] W. B. Yeats, 'The Second Coming', in *Collected Poems* (London: Macmillan, 1963), p. 211. *The Stones of the Field* contains a poem – to be considered in the next chapter – addressed to Yeats, 'Memories of Yeats whilst Travelling to Holyhead' (p. 22).

[8] R. S. Thomas, 'Madrigal', *Stones of the Field*, p. 35.

[9] R. S. Thomas, *Neb*, gol. Gwenno Hywyn (Caernarfon: Gwasg Gwynedd, 1985), pp. 38–9. My translation.

[10] Thomas, *The Stones of the Field*, p. 22.

[11] T. S. Eliot, *The Waste Land* (V: 'What the Thunder Said'), in *Collected Poems, 1909–1962* (London; Faber, 1965 impression), p. 77.

[12] The poem 'Homo Sapiens 1941' is well discussed in Ned Thomas, 'R. S. Thomas: the Question about Technology', in *Planet*, 92, 54–60.

[13] The belief that the mountains provide the key to the Welsh character is, of course, an old one, and it was reinforced towards the end of the nineteenth century and the beginning of the twentieth century by the work of geographers who emphasised the influence of environment on the development of national character. One writer who was interested in these theories was O. M. Edwards, as has been pointed out in E. G. Millward, 'O. M. Edwards', in Geraint Bowen (gol.), *Y Traddodiad Rhyddiaith yn yr Ugeinfed Ganrif* (Llandysul: Gwasg Gomer, 1976), pp. 37–51, especially pp. 48–9. Millward adds an appendix (pp. 52-3) of Edwards's statements, in both Welsh and English, on this subject. I am grateful to Professor Dafydd Johnston for drawing this essay to my attention. For discussion of the broader appeal of this concept to writers and artists in the 1930s and 1940s, see Linda Adams, 'Fieldwork: the Caseg Broadsheets and the Welsh Anthropologist', in Tony Brown (ed.), *Welsh Writing in English: A Yearbook of Critical Essays*, 5 (1999), 51–85.

[14] H. J. Fleure, 'The Welsh People', in *Wales*, 10 (October, 1939); reprinted in *Wales: 1–11* (London: Frank Cass and Company, 1969), 265–9 (269).

[15] J. B. Sidgwick, 'Welsh Station', in *Wales*, 1 (July 1943), 32; subsequently collected in Keidrych Rhys (ed.), *More Poems from the Forces* (London: Routledge, 1943), pp. 258–9.

[16] John Cowper Powys, 'Wales and America', in *Wales*, 4 (Summer 1944), 66–71 (69).

[17] John Cowper Powys, 'Welsh Aboriginals (or the Real Welsh)', in *Wales*, 1 (July 1943), 60–9 (61).

[18] 'The Depopulation of the Welsh Hill Country', in *Wales*; reprinted in Sandra Anstey (ed.), *R. S. Thomas: Selected Prose* (Bridgend: Poetry Wales Press, 1983), pp. 19–25 (p. 24). Anstey also cites other places where Thomas quotes these lines. For his other uses of this folk rhyme, see Jason Walford Davies, *Gororau'r Iaith: R. S. Thomas a'r Traddodiad Llenyddol Cymraeg* (Caerdydd: Gwasg Prifysgol Cymru, 2003), p. 244.

[19]  Thomas, *Neb*, p. 112.

[20]  Thomas, *The Stones of the Field*, p. 23.

[21]  Thomas, *The Stones of the Field*, pp. 24–5. For the echoes of Welsh language literature and tradition in the poem, see *Gororau'r Iaith*, p. 190.

[22]  Alwyn and Brinley Rees, *Celtic Heritage* (London: Thames and Hudson, 1961), p. 287.

[23]  Thomas, *The Stones of the Field*, p. 28.

[24]  Alun Lewis, *Raiders' Dawn* (London: Allen and Unwin, 1942: 1946 reprint), p. 45.

[25]  Anstey, *R. S. Thomas: Selected Prose*, p. 31.

[26]  Thomas, *The Stones of the Field*, p. 48.

[27]  Thomas, *The Stones of the Field*, p. 13.

[28]  Thomas, *The Stones of the Field*, pp. 14, 20, 8.

[29]  Thomas, *The Stones of the Field*, p. 15.

# 2

# For Wales, See Landscape

That Thomas first effectively emerged as a poet under wartime conditions – as indicated in the previous chapter – seems appropriate: born on the very eve of the Great War, he had in effect been a war baby. 'We were in Liverpool for most of the First World War', Thomas wrote in an autobiographical essay: 'There were ferries over the Mersey to the Wirral . . . One day on the sands at Hoylake my father pointed southward to where some blue-green hills loomed. "That's Wales", he said. Prophetic words.'[1] That silhouetting on the distant horizon of a mysterious, enticing Wales is a feature that recurs in his writings about his younger self. It emblematises what might be lightly characterised as his Liverpool complex: his lifelong sense of being internally exiled from his own country and its ancient aboriginal culture. It conveys his lifelong frustrated yearning and struggle to return 'home' from that exile. But it also instances the way his imagination repeatedly worked to fashion a *Pura Wallia*, a pure, unconquered and invincible Wales of quintessential Welshness. So, for instance, even when recounting how he grew up in Holyhead, he recollects the saying that Anglesey is only a platform for viewing distant, magnificent Snowdonia, the great fastness of authentic Welshness. Having moved to study at the University College of North Wales, Bangor, he exulted at the proximity of Snowdonia: '[I] was confronted by the whole sweep of the mountains . . . I stood on a hillock and shouted "Mae hen wlad fy nhadau," the Welsh national anthem, for no reason I knew' (p. 4). In his 1968 essay, 'The Mountains', Thomas recalls that, to the people of Anglesey,

> The hills are asleep. They lie at their ease like lions, and are of the same colour. Or they crouch above the water, as if waiting to spring . . . But to live near mountains is to be in touch with Eden, with lost childhood. These are the summer pastures of the Celtic people. On the darkest of days there is that high field, green as an emerald.[2]

And in recalling his journeys home by train from theological college in Cardiff to his old home, in Holyhead, he vividly remembers travelling the border line and wistfully admiring the seemingly impenetrable Welsh hills, sternly standing sentry to the west:

> In the west, the sky would be aflame, reminding one of ancient battles. Against that light, the hills rose dark and threatening as though full of armed men waiting for a chance to attack. There was in the west a land of romance and danger, a secret land. (*SP*, 137–8)

It was on a similar train journey that he was supposedly to meet his *alter ego*, W. B. Yeats, and it was out of those hills that his Muse was to appear.

It was this romantically remote Wales that he tentatively began to explore through his long walks in the Ceiriog Valley in 1936, during his first curacy at Chirk. His travels became more adventurous once he got to know a certain young woman with an Austin Seven. She was Mildred Eldridge, an English lady and a painter, and together they made a romantic couple, making pilgrimages to Romantic locations, such as the Highlands and Islands of Scotland – and the Ceiriog Valley – in search of surviving traces of Celtic culture akin to that of aboriginal Wales. Interestingly enough, though, little attention has yet been paid to his creative partnership with Eldridge, whom he called 'Elsi'. That is somewhat remarkable, given Thomas's own important statement in his autobiographical essay:

> The girl he had started to court was a recognized artist with experience of art school in London and also of Italy. Looking at her paintings, he identified

with the artistic life. She had already exhibited her work in galleries in London, and he too yearned to prove himself in [the artistic] field.[3]

From the beginning, therefore, his poetry existed in a complex symbiotic relationship with her painting, and her distinguished work as an artist was to help Thomas develop his own, distinctive interest in visual art (to be further considered in later chapters).

\* \* \*

The year 1946 saw the publication of R. S. Thomas's first collection of poems, *The Stones of the Field*. By that time, Mildred Eldridge was busy contributing to a major 'national' project to 'Record the Changing Face of Britain'. Sharply aware that the war threatened to obliterate much that was historic and distinctive in the British landscape and cityscape, the Ministry of Labour and National Service, prompted by Sir Kenneth Clarke, set up a high-powered Committee on the Employment of Artists in Wartime, on the Roosevelt model, early in the war, and one of its programmes was the visual recording of precious landmarks. Teams of artists were recruited to image key sites for posterity, and at war's end these portraits – constituting a kind of map of a vanishing country – were published in several substantial volumes entitled *Recording Britain*. The format of each was the same. The General Editor provided a textual intro-duction to the collection of images of a specific region. The images then followed, each accompanied by a page of interpretative text. As has re-cently been noted, 'The result was less a record of change than a tribute to continuity, a celebration of "Englishness" (Scotland was not covered and Wales was represented by only seventy-six pictures, substantially fewer than London)'.[4] Indeed, while the immediate urgent occasion for the exercise was the threat to England's national heritage presented by war, the project in fact typified the kind of work of conservation and protection that had been under way since the nineteenth century and that had intensified during the inter-war period as organisations were formed and mobilised in opposition to ever-more powerful agencies of 'modernisation', not infrequently supported by the British government.

A leading role was taken by societies such as the National Trust, the Commons and Footpaths Protection Society, the Society for the Protection of Ancient Buildings, and the Council for the Preservation of Rural England, one of whose most doughty campaigners and most influential writers was Clough Williams-Ellis. Perhaps the best known of the latter's books was *Britain and the Beast*, a collection of essays by prominent figures (including J. M. Keynes, C. E. M. Joad and G. M. Trevelyan) published in 1937. Typical of works of this kind, it hymned the glories of an old England threatened by the ugliness of urban sprawl, road-widening schemes and jerry building, and it comfortably included Wales (and indeed Scotland) within the purview of its nostalgically constructed 'England'. Edmund Vale's contribution to the volume, 'Wales: Its Character and its Dangers', reeks of the old colonial condescension and peddles the usual Arnoldean Celtic stereotypes: Welsh sloth is attractive to the busy Englishman but leaves Wales undefended against 'hustlers' and 'spoilers'; the Welsh are artists but Nonconformity has atrophied their sensitivity to the visual; an imaginative people, they enrich their scenery with 'romance [that is] indigenous'.[5] Similarly, in another of his influential works, *On Trust for the Nation*, Williams-Ellis himself, cheerfully generalising about 'our characteristically illogical English way', notes that whereas in England National Trust properties are of great historical and aesthetic value in their own right, in Wales they are little more than '"Amenity Hedgehogs" commanding view-points from which one can survey wide landscapes of which they themselves are an integral part', and so 'that landscape itself should perhaps be given more attention than the actual properties'.[6] For Wales, then, see landscape – it is the classic English Romantic colonial representation of the country as barren of indigenous cultural interest but as precious for its scenery. Whereas Williams-Ellis proudly trumpets the properties of English notables in the National Trust care – the birthplaces of Wordsworth, Newton, Coleridge, Kipling and Lawrence of Arabia – there is no hint that Wales could possibly claim figures of comparable 'national' significance.

The *Recording Britain* volumes, then, offer in some ways a definitive visual expression of this conservative cult of 'Englishness', a 'home front' culture whose appeal became very greatly magnified by war conditions (fig. 1). It was a cult closely connected with efforts to preserve traditional 'English' craft skills and traditions – including the great English tradition of watercolour sketches deriving from John Sell Cotman and J. M. W. Turner. It was in the name of this native topographic tradition that the managers of the *Recording Britain* project decided to have key sites visually captured not as photographs but in the form of sketches and wash-drawings. And indeed, many of the artists associated with the scheme (including Mildred Eldridge) were Fellows of the Royal Watercolour Society, a body dedicated to the conservation of an important English craft. As such, their work defined itself not only against the many styles of international Modernism (to the consternation of many Modernist artists among those newly-arrived in England from Nazi Europe, who were fearful that English art might become xenophobically nationalist) but also against Neo-Romanticism, the English expressionist movement that was galvanising the British art scene during the war period, and several of whose most prominent painters gravitated to Wales. But the broadly conservative practice of the *Recording Britain* artists itself en-compassed an interesting variety of individual styles, including the theatricality of John Piper's tempestuous images and the much more quietly visionary work of the Quaker, Kenneth Rowntree.

By temperament, upbringing and artistic training Mildred Eldridge was perfectly suited to a cultural milieu in which traditional crafts were revered, the social function of the artist was respected, delicate genres such as pencil sketches, wash drawings and watercolours were highly valued, and intense importance was attached to the preservation of the national environment. As she reveals in her enchanting, beautifully illus-trated memoir, her father, a jeweller who had early schooled himself in his trade through repeated visits to the British Museum and the Victoria and Albert museum, had a workshop at home with a lathe 'on which he turned the most delicate of ivory boxes and other treasures'.[7] An indiffer-ent pupil at school, Eldridge cared only for art, and 'with great detail and brilliant manuscript colours [she] was able to make Duc de Berry manu-script paintings of the drawings' she found in her copy of the Prologue to Chaucer's *Canterbury Tales*. At home, she loved 'making intricate things for the Doll's House' and produced dozens of paper figures dressed in clothes from many of the folk cultures of the world, 'all painted with great detail'. She came into her own only when she later attended first Wimbledon School of Art and then the Royal Academy of Art. With the removal of her family to Leatherhead in Surrey when she was sixteen, she revelled in exploring the fields and woods that surrounded what was still then largely a village community. Despite her subsequent rapturous exposure to Italian art and culture (Bernard Berenson even introduced her to the great collection he had amassed at I Tatti) she was to remain in many ways a quintessentially English artist of her period. Among the effects she left at her death were volumes (on the work of Nash, Hodgkins and Moore) from the important wartime Penguin Modern Painters series; original drawings for the C.P.R.W. annual report of 1967–8; a manuscript of the lost Mills in the County of Merioneth; a book by John Maddison on the land of the crofters; and photographs of corn ornaments from the National Museum of Wales. Given this touching late evidence of her long devotion to both cultural and environmental conservation, it is no surprise to discover the kind and quality of work she produced for the *Recording Britain* project during the early years of her marriage to R. S. Thomas.

* * *

The cultural nationalist link between the *Recording Britain* project and the watercolour movement was reinforced by the appointment of Arnold Palmer, a latter-day Georgian and a 'partisan of the Royal Watercolour Society', as secretary of the scheme.[8] He also served as general editor of the great post-war volumes that were the public record of the work done, and his introduction to these publications proves most interesting, reveal- ing as it does the thinking behind the selection of Welsh sites to record. Equally importantly, by virtue of its tone as much as its actual content, it tells us much about English perceptions of Wales at this time. While the bulk of the Welsh images actually produced by the artists did indeed, the editor informs us, record life in modern industrialised Wales, the few that were selected for inclusion in the second of the published volumes reflected his own preference for 'wild scenery . . . musical streams . . .

and stone cottages'. He cherishes all that is 'evocative of the ancient and separate life of the Principality . . . Farm wagons and sleigh wagons, river boats, costume, chapels, peat-digging, slate fences and slate tomb-stones as well as the quarries themselves, summer dairy houses high on the mountain slopes, open-air baptism by immersion, an eisteddfod'. And, he adds, 'many of them could hardly have been procured from a foreigner; they are due to the knowledge, skill, and enthusiasms of a resident artist, Mildred Eldridge' (*RB* 3, p. 91). It is worth noting, then, that it is in these specific terms that he singles her out from the team of thirteen artists who had contributed to the visual recording of Wales.

At several points Palmer is at great pains to point out that the images compiled for *Recording Britain* counter several of the prejudiced, hostile or condescending images that the English have of the Welsh. So, for instance, whereas the English make fun of monotonously repetitive Welsh surnames, and of unpronounceable Welsh place names, 'there is nothing comical in a national life that in [*sic*] such evidences of persistence, resist-ance; and nothing surprising in the bearers of those names speaking a language of their own'. 'Not enough', he adds assertively, 'not nearly enough, attention has been paid to the Welsh character' (*RB*, p. 92). His comments are striking proof that a combination of factors had sensitised some English writers, at last, to the situation of a Welsh Wales threatened by extinction through the irresistible advance of Anglophone culture. Vul-nerability to air attack was, of course, the most immediate and dramatic of the threats England faced, but there was also the much older, and in some ways less controllable, threat represented by the modernising process, particularly when sponsored by instruments of state. Moreover, the increasing power of the United States of America was threatening to reduce England to subordinate economic, political and even cultural status. The *Recording Britain* project itself had been carefully selected in part to please the US market by conforming to American images of English cultural quaintness.

This general editor's text is revealingly complex in its ideological as-sumptions. Much of what has so far been quoted could be said to mirror the standpoint of the young R. S. Thomas: the true Wales is not the Wales of coalmines and of slate quarries, but the ancient Wales of the rural and upland areas; the Welsh are a proud people, persisting by resisting; and the key to their resistance is the Welsh language, the true repository of authentic Welsh 'character'. Indeed, so close a match would there seem to be between these sentiments and those of Thomas that one begins to wonder whether some of Thomas's views might not have been communicated to the editor via Mildred Eldridge, and whether Thomas might not even have had an invisible hand in the selecting of the sites she chose to image.

But Palmer's text is also susceptible to being understood a little differently. 'Man's ingenuity and constant pressure are much more easily forgotten in Wales than in England', writes the editor in his opening sentence (p. 91). This sense of Wales as a pastoral refuge, as sanctuary of ancient British values, and therefore as essentially consisting of its mysteriously expressive landscape, exerted powerful appeal on a large number of English painters during the Second World War. Barred from travel to the Continent – that traditional resort of painters in search of a subject – they turned instead to that which, while nearer home, still promised a hint of the primitive and the exotic; the dark interior, so to speak, of Britain and continuing source of ancient Britishness. This was a cultural reading of Wales that particularly appealed to artists of the Neo-Romantic movement, some of whose leading figures settled for a period in the country.[9] Like that of the *Recording Britain* artists, their vision was in some ways a late manifestation of a view of Wales that had originated with the proto-Romantic travellers of the late eighteenth century in search of the picturesque and the sublime, a view that had reached maturity in the work of several of the great writers and artists of the English Romantic movement, including Wordsworth, Shelley and Turner. Interestingly enough, it is with one of these writers of the Romantic period – Thomas Love Peacock – that Palmer specifically identifies during the course of his introductory essay, as he also identifies with that definitive Victorian inventor of 'Wild Wales', George Borrow. 'Something of [these] two authors' qualities – simplicity and sophistication, tenacity and independence, eagerness for knowledge and argumentativeness – marks the Welsh nation', writes the editor (*RB*, pp. 92–3), and at this point it seems that in primitivising the Welsh he is continuing the Matthew Arnold tradition of representing them, like Edmund Vale, as 'Celtic' – as too temperamental and imaginative by ethnic nature to be suited to the practicalities of commercial and political power. There, of course, Palmer parts company with R. S. Thomas and seems to reveal a 'colonial' dimension to his thinking.

His essay then modulates into a somewhat different key, with a passage that is worth quoting in full:

> The English are handicapped by certain notions which, however hot the pace of world citizenship, they are loath to discard, and high among these comes suspicion of the linguist. The Welsh are bilingual, worse, they share the island of Shakespeare and Herrick, Keats and Wordsworth, Cowper and Crabbe, whose works they are free to enjoy, while keeping themselves a treasure of lyric and nature poems locked away for ever in their native tongue.
>
> The defenders of native cultures are everywhere, and more than ever, up in arms; yet their opponents are numerous, undeclared and, what is worse, usually unintentional. The border counties, once the guardians of Welsh life, are now the open-door to Anglo-Saxon views and amenities. Even in the heart of the country, people who used to make their own music, may now have to travel forty miles to hear harp-playing of a standard that would have satisfied Owain Glyndwr. Welsh wild-fowl, hunted from lake to lake, find their way most easily to the London market than to the bird sanctuaries. Welsh farms are apt to pass into the hands of 'enterprising' men from other parts of the island. The natives will need all their persistence, all their imagination and acumen if they are to maintain their character and their way of life and, at the same time, their progress and their place. (*RB*, p. 93)

Palmer is here echoing, almost word for word, the kind of sentiments one comes across repeatedly in R. S. Thomas's prose writings in the 1940s. The resemblance is uncanny, almost as if he were ventriloquising Thomas's views: and perhaps indeed he was, if one bears in mind that something of Thomas's view of Wales could well have been communicated to the editor by Mildred Eldridge. But it is also equally possible that what we have here is not a ventriloquising but a revealing coincidence of viewpoints – revealing because it shows us how much the thinking of the early R. S. Thomas of Chirk, Hanmer and Manafon about Wales derived from what one might loosely term 'English' Romantic, Victorian and Neo-Romantic constructions of the country as, by the 1940s, they were evolving into a more sophisticated semi-comprehension by English cultural conservationists of threatened Welsh cultural singularity. The early Thomas's Wales was also Borrow's wild Wales. It is worth recalling what Palmer had noted about the images produced by Mildred Eldridge: 'many of them could hardly have been procured from a foreigner; they are due to the knowledge, skill, and enthusiasms of a resident artist'. Here the antithesis of 'foreigner' is not 'native' but 'resident', a term here used, as it will be throughout this essay, to suggest an outsider who takes up more or less permanent residence in another country. Eldridge was after all English, but sympathetically resident in Wales. And she was also married to one who felt himself, in fundamental respects, to be 'resident' in the Wales of which, by birth and upbringing, he was 'native'. That reflects an important strand in Thomas's own feelings about himself and helps explain how, though a Welsh native, he could, at one level, hold views virtually identical with those expressed by Palmer and reflected in *Recording Britain*.

\* \* \*

But, of course, R. S. Thomas's case is much more complex than that. It would not be difficult, certainly, to deconstruct his early prose, and even his poetry, by showing how they are built out of 'foreign' materials – that is, out of images of Wales characteristic of a 'resident' rather than of a native.[10] This is certainly one aspect of his 'Liverpool complex', his sense of himself as an internal exile. But to deconstruct his writings in this reductive way would be to overlook the power that is in the poetry – the power that *is* that poetry – and that is a power of distinctive anguished engagement with the defining paradox of his identity, as neither resident nor native but as resident native, or native intellectual, to borrow a phrase from Frantz Fanon. To appreciate this, one needs to set examples from his own set of textual images of Wales, as recorded in his 1946 collection *The Stones of the Field*, alongside a sample of Mildred Eldridge's corresponding collection of visual images.

One of the buildings featured by Eldridge is the Baptist chapel, 'Addoldy-y-Bedyddwyr, Glyndyfrdwy' (fig. 2). The accompanying text by Palmer attempts to offer a judicious assessment of Nonconformity, beginning by noting the awesome ugliness of Welsh chapels, erected by people intent on escaping the 'mysterious shadows' of Anglican churches, but 'often without the knowledge, taste and money to devise a dignified substitute' (*RB*, p. 100). Recognising that these institutions provided 'good education in self-government', it notes that the chapels remained important community centres. As for Eldridge's drawing, its treatment of the subject is altogether more romantic than Palmer's text. The chapel is viewed beyond a cemetery overrun by grass, with sheep grazing in the foreground – a composite image suggestive of the rough pastoral long associated with wild Wales. In some ways, this interest in Nonconformist chapels is typical of the English cultural movement with which Eldridge was associated. John Piper was, in 1948, to produce a series of celebrated prints of Welsh chapels; Kenneth Rowntree was to feature several of them in *A Prospect of Wales* (a text to which we will return); and important essays on Nonconformist architecture by John Betjeman and others appeared in *The Architectural Review*, a house journal of the English conservationist movement. By 1955 Betjeman had, of course, become one of the high priests of the English cultural conservation movement, and it was partly in that capacity that, in his brief preface to *Song at the Year's Turning*, he bestowed his blessing on R. S. Thomas and 'introduced' him to an English readership as 'essentially a local priest' and as twentieth-century heir of the distinctively English tradition of 'local descriptive poets'.[11]

There are close parallels between R. S. Thomas's early work and the sentiments textually expressed and visually inscribed in Eldridge's sketch of 'Addoldy-y-Bedyddwyr'. But an essay of his from 1948, 'Dau Gapel', shows how infinitely more tangled than hers was his emotional and intellectual response to Welsh Nonconformity. There, in a text adorned by Mildred Eldridge's drawing, Thomas contrasts the ancient, mysterious, otherworldly spirituality of Maes-yr-Onnen (fig. 3) with the neatness of Soar-y-Mynydd (fig. 4) which, for all the little chapel's remoteness, shows that it continues to be cherished by the upland farmers as a place of meeting and of worship. In both localities, he experiences a dream-vision – a point worth noting for future reference. But attracted though Thomas is to the vision of the spiritual oneness of Creation that he received at Maes-yr-Onnen, it is the vision he received at Soar-y-Mynydd that finally claimed him:

> In Maes-yr-Onnen I had a glimpse of the spirit of man; here [at Soar-y-Mynydd], I saw the soul of a special type of man, the Cymro or Welshman. For the very source of Welsh life as it is today is here in the middle of these remote moorlands of Ceredigion. And it is in places of this sort that the world of the true Welshman is formed. (*SP*, p. 46)

How much of that vision is conveyed by Mildred Eldridge's drawing? Not very much, it must be admitted. The very style of her draughtsmanship precludes it. Although her English interest in Nonconformist architecture is clearly inflected by her appreciation, probably thanks to her husband, of Welsh Nonconformity's distinctive cultural significance – she does not seek merely to highlight the purely architectural qualities of a chapel façade, in the manner of Piper and Rowntree's full-frontal representations – her image is nevertheless essentially a record made by a Romantically-inclined cultural outsider who is a sympathetic resident. R. S. Thomas's text, by contrast, is invested with the turmoil of unfocused feeling of a resident native.

Another of Eldridge's images is that of 'Peat Cutting, Cefn Coch, Montgomeryshire' (fig. 5). This time Palmer's accompanying text informs us that 'Peat is cut and used for fuel in all the hill districts of Wales from north to south'. Moreover, 'In an old manuscript in the Cardiff Free Library [MS50] the artist found a reference to the use of peat in fulling-mills and kilns in the time of Queen Elizabeth' (*RB*, p. 114). Underpinned by conscientious antiquarian research, Eldridge's image thus possesses its own delicate fidelity not only to visible scene but to historical record. It is impeccably authenticated by history, so to speak. And yet it lacks the entirely different authenticity of Thomas's own signature, indeed savagely idiosyncratic, reaction to the kinds of human figures that he found in the uplands of Montgomeryshire, and which are so lightly rendered by Mildred Eldridge's feathery pencil as to seem wispy outgrowths of the landscape itself. While broadly adopting his wife's approach, Thomas reverses her practice, and views his Welsh landscape through the looming

figure of Iago Prytherch. This is more than an alternative aesthetic strategy; it is intended to reveal and to counteract the politics of cultural
subordination inscribed in the whole English topographical tradition –
from the eighteenth-century cult of the Picturesque to *Recording Britain*
– of rendering Wales merely as landscape, or (later) as the peripheral site
of residual social and cultural values. 'What is Wales to England after
all', Thomas writes caustically in his important 1946 essay 'Some Contemporary Scottish Writing', 'but a kind of western county that is not
worth bothering about apart from its scenery and its natural resources?
Wild Wales! Yes, but it all resides in the landscape' (*SP*, p. 37). In this
comment on the kind of images of Wales favoured by *Recording Britain*
may surely be heard the spirit of colonial rebellion, deriving from an
entirely different 'eye' for Wales, and inscribed in what can only therefore
be called an anti-colonial, or post-colonial text, that manifests itself in,
and as, the opening poem of *The Stones of the Field*.

   The volume is full of materials drawn from the English repertoire of
images of Wales – the repertoire on which Eldridge herself draws, in
more than one sense.[12] But *The Stones of the Field* plays variations on those
materials in a style that may best be understood by viewing this, Thomas's
first volume of poetry, in the light of post-colonial theory. The collection
opens with 'Out of the Hills':

> Dreams clustering thick on his sallow skull,
> Dark as curls, he comes, ambling with his cattle
> From the starved pastures. He has shaken from off his shoulders
> The weight of the sky, and the lash of the wind's sharpness
> Is healing already under the medicinal sun.
> Clouds of cattle breath, making the air heady,
> Remember the summer's sweetness, the wet road runs
> Blue as a river before him; the legendary town
> Dreams of his coming; under the half-closed lids
> Of the indolent shops sleep dawdles, emptying the last
> Tankards of darkness, before the officious light
> Bundles it up the chimney out of sight. (*CP*, p. 1)

It is appropriate that the first word in the very first poem in Thomas's
very first collection is 'Dreams', because we are, in truth, entering – or

rather being engulfed by – Thomas's own dream vision. The figure is not so much consciously summoned, as felt to loom, mysterious and unbidden, into view. And it is only by arising from the remote, inaccessible recesses of Thomas's own imagination that this peasant figure is able to come primordially 'out of the hills'. The invasive entry of this figure that seems more like an atavistic memory of the old wild drovers than a mid-twentieth-century hill farmer has about it all the mythopoeic quality of the lone Clint Eastwood figure riding into a spaghetti western. The writing is unmistakably trance-like, obsessional, as it was to remain throughout the decade and a half that Thomas continued to write about his upland 'peasants'. Indeed, Thomas here deliberately includes a mention of the route that might have led to a more complete, balanced, psychologically rounded, realistic portrait, only to reject it. 'No, wait for him here', he insists, refusing the artistic invitation to follow his peasant down into the town, where a very different side of his character will be revealed. In other words, the poem shows us how R. S. Thomas, at the very outset, sets limits on where his imagination shall go, because he knows that his psycho-mythopoeic vision can be maintained and focused only within those narrow, deliberately excluding, limits.

Thomas here uses words in a way that strongly, and perhaps pointedly, contrasts with the way in which Mildred Eldridge uses the pencil. Hers is the lightest of touches, the mark, so to speak, of an artistic intelligence intent on accurate draughtsmanship to convey a romantic fragility of presence, leaving only a fleeting impression. In an admiring and discriminating essay published in *Art Quarterly*, Mark Bourne commends Eldridge's commitment to 'beauty':

> And beauty is what she achieves. Beauty cut down to perfect facets. Her paintings disturb. For all that is familiar in them, they quiver with an unexplained force. What fragment of the mortality is it that she catches in a flower or a reed? . . . Beauty is seen in these paintings ('ethereal' they have been called) for what she is – a ghost. A shudder of wonder, a shiver of fear, a thrill of meeting, a reluctance at parting – that is our encounter with beauty. Yes, a ghost, and, so often, a stranger.[13]

Eldridge's elusive 'beauty' finds no counterpart, however, in Thomas's 'Out of the Hills'. On the contrary: his figure is sculpted out of words laid on so thick that they seem almost tactile to the reading eye, just as one cannot look at a picture by Cézanne without becoming aware that it is an image fashioned out of paint. Indeed, the thickness of his verbal pigment, his linguistic impasto, seems in itself to be an implicit comment on the English watercolour tradition favoured by the *Recording Britain* artists who imagined Wales: it is perhaps no accident that, a few years later, Thomas should memorably dismiss 'the watercolour's appeal/ To the mass' as being wholly unequal to 'the poem's/ Harsher conditions' (*CP*, p. 194). Already in his early poetry the medium is itself the message, in the sense that 'Out of the Hills' is a poem *about* language. Just as it is a poem *about* seeing – about compulsive, as opposed to romantically select-ive, vision.

Attention has already been drawn to Thomas's review essay, 'Some Contemporary Scottish Writing', published in 1946, the same year as *The Stones of the Field*. In it he expresses his admiration for Scottish writers who, following the lead of Hugh MacDiarmid, were producing a poetry quite distinct from that of England in character, fashioned out of a lexicon as rough and chunky as Highland rocks. This is an essay crucial for understanding the early poetry of R. S. Thomas. It was written at a time when he remained convinced that the responsibility for rendering Wales in poetry, and thus ensuring its continuity, was being passed from Welsh-language writers to the English-language writers of Wales. It was therefore vital that these writers, prominently including himself, should ensure that they wrote an English poetry consonant in language, as much as in theme, with the 'stern surroundings' of the typical Welsh environment. 'Out of the Hills' is thus an experiment in such a language. In its lexical thickness, the poem is meant to emerge out of its bald physical environment, just as the figure himself emerges as a mysterious emissary 'Out of the Hills' instead of merging with a lightly sketched landscape as the retiring figures of the peat cutters do in Mildred Eldridge's fine drawing. It will be remembered that, in another poem from *The Stones of the Field*, Thomas notes how Manafon church stands, 'built from the river stone' (*CP*, p. 11). Similarly, in 'Out of the Hills', both the figure and the language that constitutes it are meant to bespeak their origin in a distinctively Welsh landscape, and in a distinctively Welsh

51

culture. And they are able to speak, and thus to reveal themselves, in these terms only through the medium of the poet's consciousness. It was a consciousness deeply inward with their character, a character Thomas felt to be all the more authentic because for him it remained 'foreign' to a significant degree.

\* \* \*

In *Les Damnés de la Terre* (1961), a famous pioneering study of post-colonial culture, the French Algerian psychoanalyst and sociologist Frantz Fanon drew upon his lived experience of the African anti-colonial struggle to construct a composite picture of the native intellectual. His mind, as well as his country, having been colonised, he is at first anxiously concerned to demonstrate his own sophisticated command of the colonising culture's values and style. But then he gradually awakens to his self-alienated condition: his condition as a resident native, so to speak. And the earliest sign of this dawning consciousness is the new, violent twist he semi-consciously gives to the colonial cultural styles he has self-woundingly internalised and that remain the sole medium of expression available to him. The result is a 'harsh style, full of images, for the image is the drawbridge that allows unconscious energies to be scattered on the surrounding meadows. It is a vigorous style. . .'.[14] That would seem to be a perfect description of the style of 'Out of the Hills'. The figure who comes from the upland country himself crosses that psychic drawbridge, and brings with him the images that allow unconscious energies to be scattered on the surrounding meadows of the lowlands of valley bottom and plain. This signature poem, signifying the arrival of Thomas's Muse, reveals, in Fanon's words, 'the need that man has to liberate himself from a part of his being which already contains the seeds of decay' (p. 177):

> At the very moment when the native intellectual is anxiously trying to create a cultural work he fails to realize that he is utilizing the techniques and language [such as those on display in *Recording Britain*] which are borrowed from the stranger in his country. He contents himself with stamping these instruments with a hallmark which he wishes to be national, but which is strangely reminiscent of exoticism. (p. 180)

Such is exactly the impression left by R. S. Thomas's early poetry. On the one hand it is arrestingly aboriginal in its power; on the other it is 'exotic' in that it is a variant on the colonisers' exoticising images of wild Wales; the images that featured both in the work of Welsh-based Neo-Romantic artists of the war period and (in an altogether more sober and sympathetic key) in the work of Mildred Eldridge and other artists of the *Recording Britain* project.

The subversive rhetorical strategies of the 'native intellectual', as characterised by Frantz Fanon and as employed by R. S. Thomas in *The Stones of the Field*, are also very interestingly exemplified in the work of Gwyn Jones, another important Welsh Anglophone writer of the immediate post-war period. In 1948, just two years after the publication of Thomas's volume and of the first volume in the *Recording Britain* series, Jones provided an introductory essay for *A Prospect of Wales*, an enchanting little King Penguin featuring visual images by Kenneth Rowntree, one of the most talented of the team of artists who had worked on *Recording Britain* (fig. 6). The essay is Jones at his inimitable and irresistible best. A flamboyant, and in places florid, example of mannered eloquence, it is also a fascinating instance of Welsh post-colonial rewriting of English topographical tours of Wales.

Gwyn Jones's prose in *A Prospect of Britain* may be read as offering a striking instance of a native intellectual in his transitional state. He is in part working within a display culture – a member of the subaltern group displaying his mastery of the dominant culture's most sophisticated verbal and rhetorical forms. (The same deep impulse to 'pass' as English was evident in R. S. Thomas throughout his long life. His frequently bitter renunciation of English culture and all its works was accompanied by a litany of examples of his craving for it – from his refined accent, to his dispatch of his unfortunate son to English boarding-schools, to abundant evidence of his social and cultural snobbishness.[15]) However, Gwyn Jones seems also to venture (however consciously) into mimic mode, slightly exaggerating his command of the discourse of English topographical writing. Hence, or so one might suggest, the glittering histrionics of his prose, the ever-so-slightly overblown character of the writing, the knowing seductiveness with which he acts the part of tourist guide.

He begins by appearing to conform to English colonial textual practice, as he draws a picture of the glorious rural and upland Wales of the west and north-west as seen from the vantage point of his hillside cottage, between Aberystwyth and neighbouring Clarach. With characteristic elan, Jones delineates the great curve of Cardigan Bay, from the 'long peninsula of Lleyn', past 'the spike of Cnicht', to the 'exquisite cone of Snowdon' and 'across seventy miles of heaped-up water' to the 'claw-tip at St David's Head, with the magic mountains of Prescelly hanging in-land like a haze'.[16] He captures the way the scene metamorphoses with the constant shifts in the weather, recalling a sublime vision he had one evening in July 1943, when, looking towards Snowdonia, '[b]etween the mountains that were islands the sea poured pale smoky streams, and one saw the sea *behind* them, fluorescent as a fresh-caught mackerel' (*PW*, p. 7). Then from the distant prospect he switches attention to a fore-ground that includes the Prytherch-like form of a 'farmer in broken-nosed cloth cap and flapping army greatcoat [leading] a horse and cart to where he is dunging next year's pasture' (*PW*, p. 8).

These passing details of the present next give way to reflections on the geological ancientness of the Welsh land and of the corresponding ancientness of Welsh-language culture. Having recently completed (with Thomas Jones) a great English translation of *The Mabinogion*, Gwyn Jones was naturally alive to 'the sense of history, of other worlds around one' everywhere in the Welsh heartland, sheltering as it did behind 'the mountains of defeat. A lair and sanctuary from the pursuit of a victorious foe' (*PW*, p. 14). Drawing on a geo-political model of Wales favoured, as mentioned in the previous chapter, by such Welsh anthro-pologists of the time as Iorwerth Peate – a model that deeply influenced Welsh-language intellectuals and came to be passionately adopted by R. S. Thomas – Jones notes how, as wave upon wave of invaders swept into the country, 'the Welsh kept the mountains still and licked their unhealing wounds' (*PW*, p. 14). This is the quiet beginning of his departure from English topographical convention, and his adoption of a 'native' perspective. This subversive strategy is further developed through his assertion, counter to the long-standing English topo-graphical practice of reducing Wales to picturesque landscape, that 'there is more than beauty here, for this is sacred soil, rich with history and legend' (*PW*, p. 15).

But, after giving due weight to this dimension of Welsh scenery, Jones marks his most decisive break with the colonial traditions of visual representation of the country by turning from the famed areas of Welsh landscape 'to that crumpled blanket of the South Wales industrial valleys in which I was born' (*PW*, p. 18). Passionately resisting the impulse 'to call them ugly', he celebrates the history of this region whose history is so recent that it 'may be read without a book, in the valley bottoms themselves, in the glow of molten metal and the dark magnificence of pitheads, in the hands of men and the faces of their women' (*PW*, p. 18). And now ready to make crystal clear his break with colonial traditions of pictorial representation, he exclaims:

> What do they know of Wales who only Snowdon know? It has always roughed my heel, and I trust it ever shall, to find seekers after the 'truly picturesque' by-pass the industrial region of south Wales with an assurance that 'We shall find nothing to detain us here!' May their tyres ever burst, and their walking boots sprout nails! It would seem as reasonable to discuss the scenery of Wales without reference to this idiosyncratic region, as to discuss Welsh cheeses without reference to Caerphilly. (*PW*, pp. 19–20)

For *A Prospect of Wales*, Gwyn Jones had been teamed with a gifted member of the *Recording Britain* team, Kenneth Rowntree, and, with respect to its representational practices, the Jones-Rowntree combination is a fascinating mixture of cultural convergence and cultural divergence. A particularly sensitive and talented illustrator, Rowntree was in some respects naturally inclined to be sympathetic to the Welsh scene. A Quaker, he was fascinated by the silent eloquence of letters, and so was able to produce a powerful image of the Creed and the Lord's Prayer in Welsh as depicted on wall panels in the parish church at Yspytty Cynfyn (Cardiganshire). A colonial counterbalance to that, however, was supplied in the form of a picture of a wine shop in Brecon, above it a sign, 'The Siddons Wine and Spirit Vaults', clearly signifying that this was the birthplace of England's onetime stage darling, Sarah Siddons. Taking his cue from Jones, Rowntree includes, alongside marvellously atmospheric representations of a variety of Welsh landscapes, a couple of strong images of industrial townscapes. They are peculiarly striking, however, in that they are totally devoid of people; a totally deserted 'Street in Neath' therefore seems as mysterious, not to say sinister, an image as any found in de Chirico's paintings. Such uncanny representations are all the more strange, since Gwyn Jones, in his essay, had particularly emphasised the 'warm gregariousness' that characterised the Welsh industrial valleys, and had celebrated the human resilience of communities in 'a district which has kept its grin through all that spoliation, depression and neglect could do to it' (*PW*, p. 19).

Rowntree's empty streets are unconsciously powerful testimony to the failure of the English topographical tradition to operate outside the limits of a colonial vision, so as to comprehend not just the scenery of Wales but its society and its culture as manifest both in its ancient rural land-scapes and in its modern industrial townscapes. With the best will in the world, therefore, his images testify against themselves, unconsciously bearing witness to the accuracy of the subversive, post-colonial thrust of Gwyn Jones's introductory text. A like relationship may be discerned between Mildred Eldridge's images of Wales for *Recording Britain* and R. S. Thomas's verbal images of Wales in *The Stones of the Field*.

\* \* \*

What we have in the poem 'Out of the Hills', is a moment of encounter which sees the birth of authentic self-recognition. In encountering the anonymous figure out of the hills, R. S. Thomas is meeting with an aspect of himself, and this becomes a means of accessing a dimension of his own identity that is otherwise inaccessible to him. It is a special kind of recognition, the knowing of the self that Thomas didn't know he knew. This moment is a meeting between the resident Thomas, who is the speak-ing observer, and the native in Thomas, who is disclosed in and by this figure 'out of the hills'. And the gap between Thomas and his figured other self can be crossed only in, and as, obsessive dream vision. Otherwise, in normal waking life, the gap remains. To the end of his life, Thomas remained haunted by the inability to close it fully, to integrate himself, doomed as he therefore was to exist as a resident native; as native intellectual.

And yet, as he also came to understand, it was this very psychologically divided existence, repeatedly seeking final resolution in dream, that made Thomas not only a poet but a national poet. 'It is a formidable task this winnowing and purifying of the people', writes Thomas in 'Some Contemporary Scottish Writing':

> because it so nearly forms a vicious circle. There can be no national art without a people, and there can be no people without artists to create them and give form to their dreams and aspirations. This seems to bring us to the crux of the matter. The poet's chief problem is, how by virtue of his mind and vision he can best save his country – directly through political action, or indirectly through his creative work. (*SP*, p. 38)

Thomas here formulates the dilemma in exactly the same way as does Saunders Lewis, whose influence on Thomas's development into a national poet is considered in chapter 4. But in conceiving of the poet as saviour of his country, he is also indebted to English Romantic poetry, to the American example of Walt Whitman,[17] and, most immediately at the time of writing *The Stones of the Field*, to the poetry of W. B. Yeats and Hugh MacDiarmid.

Not only is this belief in poetry as originating in dream fundamental to one's understanding of his debut collection, it is actually addressed in one of the poems from *The Stones of the Field* that has been consistently misread as a reporting of fact on the few occasions it hasn't been completely overlooked. In 'Memories of Yeats Whilst Travelling to Holyhead', Thomas writes of sharing a compartment with the great Irish poet on one of his journeys home along the coastal line to see his parents in Anglesey. When, more than fifty years after the poem was published, he was asked whether any such incident had ever occurred he said no, adding that the whole episode was pure invention. Or, one might suggest, a dream vision, which would be appropriate since the poem, full of echoes as it deliberately is of Yeats's own poetry, is actually about the poet as dreamer. The poem pivots around a contrast. First, Thomas notes how beautiful is the scenery – sea on one side, mountains on the other –

through which the train passes; and he imagines passengers drawing the attention of the famous poet to this seeming wealth of picturesque and poetic material. But that is not how poetry comes. Yeats is therefore scornfully, and revealingly, impervious to such conventionally romantic scenery:

> But who would have sensed the disdain of his slow reply
> Of polite acquiescence in their talk of the beautiful?
> Who could have guessed the futility even of praising
> Mountain and marsh and the delicate, flickering tree
> To one long impervious and cold to the outward scene,
> Heedless of nature's baubles, lost in the amazing
> And labyrinth paths of his own impenetrable mind? (*CP*, p. 10)

Thomas found himself as a poet when, in the poems of *The Stones of the Field*, he turned his back on the outward scene as conventionally perceived and romantically described in colonial topographical texts, and 'lost himself in the amazing/ And labyrinth paths of his own impenetrable mind'. That is precisely what we see happening at the very outset of 'Out of the Hills'. The emergence of that figure paradoxically marks Thomas's entry into the labyrinth. The as yet unnamed figure comes out of the dream time of Thomas's mind. And the poem tacitly confesses this by displacing Thomas's dream experience onto the town: 'the legendary town/ Dreams of his coming' (*CP*, p. 1). This trope is then elaborated into a conceit, as Thomas notices how 'under the half-closed lids/ Of the indolent shops sleep dawdles'. The town is obviously a border town which, like Shrewsbury, retaining memories of the uncouth marauding Welsh, has taken steps to disarm and tame them by seducing them with the soft luxuries of civilisation. In its geographical and historical dimensions the actual border town in which this poem is set is the appropriate site for what is, in psychological terms, a border or liminal or threshold experience – Thomas's crossing of the border within him between resident and native.

So Thomas's poem about meeting Yeats on the Holyhead train (which was, for Thomas, literally the train home) is the occasion for what may be termed his own summary of the growth of a national poet's mind. He therefore concludes his poem in this fashion:

> But something in the hair's fine silver, the breadth of brow,
> Had kept me dumb, too shy of his scornful anger
> To presume to pierce the dark, inscrutable glasses,
> His first defence against a material world.
> Yet alone with him in the indifferent compartment, hurled
> Between the waves' white audience, the earth's dim screen,
> In mutual silence closer than lover knit
> I had known reality dwindle, the dream begin. (*CP*, p. 10)

Given the complex nexus of meanings that the term 'dream' carries in Yeats's poetic lexicon, that last line reverberates with possibilities. It calls to mind, for example, the lines from an old play that served as epigraph to Yeats's great, pivotal collection *Responsibilities*: 'in dreams begin responsibility'. Implicit in Thomas's line is the belief that established reality has to dwindle for the dream to begin from which new, mature responsibilities are born. For Thomas, established reality was the reality of the colonial condition of Wales. And out of dream vision would be born the responsibility to create a new, post-colonial Wales. Illuminating attention has recently been paid to the influence of Patrick Kavanagh's magnificent anti-Yeatsian poem, *The Great Hunger*, on the early Thomas.[18] But counterbalancing attention also needs to be paid to Thomas's prior, and in some ways deeper, commitment to Yeats himself. 'Out of the Hills' is, in a way, a poem corresponding to that signature poem of Yeats's cultural identity, 'A Fisherman': 'A man who does not exist,/ A man who is but a dream'.[19]

What the poem about meeting Yeats shows is that Thomas had learned he could become a Welsh poet only when his resident's material images of Wales, so evident still in the prose of the early period, and his resident's 'external' relationship with the country, were metamorphosed into a politically and culturally empowering 'insider knowledge'. Not, as noted already, that he was ever to succeed in becoming fully 'native', at least not in the sense he understood and wished to be; but he did become a 'resident native' who compulsively refashioned a resident's images of Wales, artistic images deriving in good part from English colonial practice with regard to the country, into a tormented dream of native belonging. Much the same, of course, could be said for Yeats himself, the Anglo-Irishman who paradoxically became a national Irish poet by dreaming his perverse dreams of belonging. That train on which R.S. 'met' Yeats was therefore the appropriate trope for representing both their conditions – figures permanently in transit, personalities actually constituted of psychic passage, poets all of whose poems were transitional, and individuals who were restlessly travelling towards that endlessly deferred 'home' which, in the poem, is represented by Holyhead.

Recording the changing face of Britain was the government artists' wartime project. *The Stones of the Field* could be read as Thomas's alternative version of such a record, making ambiguously visible the process on which he was embarking: the process of turning colonial images of Wales long familiar from English pictorial, and picturesque, tradition, into images marking Wales as a separate distinctive country, and recording that about it which was genuinely most distinctive and most at risk of being obliterated.

As has been noted, he and Mildred Eldridge gravitated towards the same kinds of subjects, the same kinds of landscapes, but they treated them very differently. For her, they functioned as points of reference; for him they were points of entry. Where the lightness of her sketches and the fluidity of her paintings suggest that her eye has briefly alighted here to trace the flowing energy lines of the cosmos, the physicality of his writing powerfully conveys the sensation of being bogged down, caught by a compulsive and obsessive vision of a single and singular locale. Whereas this difference is partly that of sensibility – and also, or so Thomas was always to suggest in his poems to his wife, a gender difference – it also records a fundamental difference of relationship to that which is being depicted. This is expressed in the celebrated poem in which we are first introduced to Iago Prytherch.

'A Peasant' is the memorable poem in which that figure out of the hills is first named: 'Iago Prytherch his name, though, be it allowed,/ Just an ordinary man of the bald Welsh hills,/ Who pens a few sheep in a gap of cloud' (*CP*, p. 4). It is a strange poem throughout, and one that begins and ends with an enigma. Why write 'Iago Prytherch his name, *though*, be it allowed,/ Just an ordinary man of the bald Welsh hills"? Why that *though*? What is the force of it? Why shouldn't a Welsh peasant farmer be called 'Iago Prytherch'? Many answers are possible. For instance,

'Iago Prytherch' is a mouthful of a name, and could sound comically pretentious to an English ear. But, in the present connection, a different possibility may be suggested, one that relates to the double vision characteristic of an obsessive state. This is most familiar to us through love: with our rational understanding we are perfectly capable of seeing that the man or woman with whom we are besotted is, to the disinterested eye, perfectly ordinary; but, with the eye of love, we cannot fail to see him or her very differently, as charismatically exceptional. So it is with R. S. Thomas in relation to Iago Prytherch, who is introduced to us as simultaneously wholly typical and wholly unique. In this initial moment of recognition, Thomas registers the dawning of an inexplicable obsession – and the dawning of an understanding that obsession is by definition inexplicable – an obsession that was even to long outlast the decade in which it found its most repeated expression. In naming him into being as 'Iago' at this point Thomas is, therefore, acknowledging the peculiar intimacy of their relationship.

There is a parallel, and related, enigma in the poem's last line: 'he, too, is a winner of wars,/ Enduring like a tree under the curious stars'. Much ink has been spilled over the meanings of that adjective 'curious' so unexpectedly applied to the stars. It has, for instance, been pointed out that 'curious' can mean intricately fashioned. So it can, and therein may lie part of the word's point.[20] But it is worth staying with its more immediate, common and obvious meaning. The stars are indeed curious about Iago, because he is as much an enigma to the natural cosmos as he is to the human world. After all, he is at once 'like' a tree yet not a tree, defying the categories not only of understanding but of the very cosmos by inhabiting a border between man and nature. And it is precisely this ability to escape categorisation, and therefore to escape definitive conceptualisation, that guarantees his endurance – his power not just to survive the attrition of the elements, season after season, but also to survive the infinitely more dangerous process of appropriation by the colonising gaze of human observers, as will be further established in chapter 4. As such, Iago at this point embodies R. S. Thomas's dream of locating, in a safe place of refuge, what, in 'Some Contemporary Scottish Writing', he was to call 'that dignity, that personality, that soul [which] is so different, even alien in the Celtic peoples that it has aroused the unfailing antagonism of generation after generation of English official classes and their quisling admirers' (*SP*, p. 38). But 'curious' also exactly expresses Thomas's own intuition that while he will forever be baffled in his every attempt to know Iago (see chapter 3), such a futile attempt will, for that very reason, be his lifelong obsession. To be empowered to name Iago is not in fact to know him. The last line of 'A Peasant' therefore echoes the first line of the poem only in order to cancel it. And in that image of Iago's supra-natural rootedness is encapsulated, of course, Thomas's own yearning for the total aboriginal belonging of ur-nativeness. Between them, therefore, the opening and concluding lines of 'A Peasant' convey, through their several meanings, Thomas's privilege, plight and pain as 'resident native', as burgeoning native intellectual. In 'Affinity', another poem from *The Stones of the Field*, Thomas invites us to consider a 'man in the field beneath,/ Gaitered with mud, lost in his own breath' (*CP*, p. 8). 'Lost in his own breath': I have long found that to be a haunting, breathtaking line. It seems a poignant portrait of Thomas himself – as someone who never knew who he himself really was.

\* \* \*

In R. S. Thomas's later years, English press photographers loved to capture what came to seem definitive images of his stubborn, indomitable, defiant and cantankerous nature, his xenophobic Welshness. But his wife saw a different, deeper truth about his character (fig. 7; fig. 8). It is impossible to know what the half-century relationship between R. S. Thomas and Mildred, Elsi Eldridge was actually like, nor would one in any case want to intrude even posthumously on their privacy. It can, however, be reasonably inferred, from the poems Thomas left on record, that the relationship was subtle and complex, as will further be recognised in a later chapter.[21] That, too, is the impression given by a sketch Eldridge herself made in her later years (in private ownership), consisting only of two free-standing, or perhaps free-floating, heads. It suggests a tenderness in a relationship that was, however, predicated on distance, on respecting clearly separate living spaces. Her down-turned head is indistinctly drawn, her half-formed Sybilline features inscrutable. By contrast, his head, tilted upward in her direction, is more firmly rendered, the wisps of fine hair floating free making him seem like a wild, ageing, Celtic bard, dreams clustering thick on his skull. In that respect, this image is the culmination of Mildred Eldridge's Romantic approach to things Welsh; the apotheosis of a Welsh 'resident's' view of R. S. Thomas as Romantic Welshman. His upturned eye gives him a passing resemblance to the ecstatic visionary St John on the Island of Patmos, in a celebrated painting by Velázquez. Yet the total effect of his image is that of a lost waif and stray, who looks towards his wife across a yawning gap, in futile yearning. Although the more lightly sketched of the two figures, she somehow nevertheless seems much the more firmly grounded, the more self-possessed. He, by contrast, seems to be firmly caught in a gesture conveying his incompleteness, his neediness, his fundamental insecurity. And in that respect, this delicate and immensely touching late drawing seems to convey the unhoused and peregrine condition of the resident native, a native intellectual at home nowhere, least of all in his 'own' country; the condition out of which, or so this chapter has endeavoured to suggest, his poetry had, from the very beginning, come: 'lost, as he was, in the amazing/ And labyrinth paths of his own impenetrable mind'.

## Notes

1   William V. Davis (ed.), *Miraculous Simplicity: Essays on R. S. Thomas* (Fayetteville: University of Arkansas Press, 1993), p. 1.
2   Sandra Anstey (ed.), *R. S. Thomas: Selected Prose* (Bridgend: Poetry Wales Press, 1983), pp. 104–5. Hereafter *SP*.
3   R. S. Thomas, *Autobiographies*, trans. Jason Walford Davies (London: Dent, 1997), p. 45. Hereafter *A*.
4   Gill Saunders, 'Introduction', *Recording Britain: A Pictorial Domesday of Pre-War Britain*, David Mellor, Gill Saunders, Patrick Wright (eds) (Newton Abbot & London: David & Charles, in association with the Victoria and Albert Museum, 1990), p. 7.
5   Edmund Vale, 'Wales: Its Character and its Dangers', in Clough Williams-Ellis (ed.), *Britain and the Beast* (London: Dent, 1937), pp. 256–65. The elision of Wales is apparent from the very beginning of the book: in the commendatory

messages, the Rt. Hon. Kingsley Wood, Minister of Health, trumpets that 'Mr Clough Williams-Ellis is a doughty champion of the Beauty of Rural England' right after the Rt. Hon. David Lloyd George has declared that 'A task of supreme importance for our times is the awakening of the nation to the treasures of our neglected countryside' (p. v).

6  Clough Williams-Ellis, *On Trust for the Nation* (London: Elek, 1947), p. 47.

7  *www.meeldridge.blogspot.com*. Eldridge's work is passingly placed in a wider cultural perspective in Pyrs Gruffudd, 'Prospects of Wales: Contested Geographical imagination', in Ralph Fevre and Andrew Thompson (eds), *Nation, Identity and Social Theory: Perspectives from Wales* (Cardiff: University of Wales Press, 1999), pp. 149–67. I should like to thank Robert Meyrick, Aberystwyth University, for his assistance in locating materials by and relating to Mildred Eldridge, particularly relating to her large masterpiece, the multipart mural *The Dance of Life*, painted over three years at Eglwys-Fach for the nurses' dining room of the Orthopaedic hospital at Gobowen. It is a 120-foot long visionary allegory, consisting of six panels. Enthusiastic responses to it included a remarkable letter to Eldridge by Stanley Spencer (14 November 1958). He praises the painting ecstatically, mentioning 'this extraordinary degree of unity you can ramify into all places near and far', and stating that 'I feel when I look at the scheme that you hold much the same beliefs that I hope I have in painting; namely that imagination is found in the bearest [*sic*] reality and that is what I think is exciting'. A central theme of the murals is 'the story of civilized man's alienation from nature, and his attempts to reclaim a lost natural wisdom' (*The Advertizer*, 7 September 1988), and urban life is represented as the site of such alienation. This is, of course, a theme Eldridge shared with R. S. Thomas.

8  *Recording Britain* (Oxford: Oxford University Press, in association with the Pilgrim Trust), p. 10. Hereafter *RB*. See also *www.thepilgrimtrust.org.uk*.

9  See Clare Morgan, 'Exile and the Kingdom: Margiad Evans and the Mythic Landscape of Wales', *Welsh Writing in English: A Yearbook of Critical Essays 6* (2000), pp. 89–118.

10  At the same time, he was also beginning to draw upon materials from the Welsh-language literary tradition, which he was slowly mastering. See Jason Walford Davies, *Gororau'r Iaith: R. S. Thomas a'r Traddodiad Llenyddol Cymraeg* (Caerdydd: Gwasg Prifysgol Cymru, 2003). Some of the material covered in this seminal study is anticipated in the same author's '"Thick Ambush of Shadows": Allusions to Welsh Literature in the work of R. S. Thomas', *Welsh Writing in English*, 1 (1995), pp. 75–127.

11  John Betjeman, 'Introduction', in R. S. Thomas, *Song at the Year's Turning* (London: Rupert Hart-Davis, 1955: 1965), pp. 11–14.

12  At the same time, *The Stones of the Field* includes some early, and striking, examples of Thomas's rapidly-deepening acquaintance with Welsh-language literary culture. See Davies, *Gororau'r Iaith*.

[13] Mark Bourne, 'Mildred Eldridge', *Art Quarterly* 3/4 (1960), 136. Elsewhere in the article, though, Bourne claims that 'As meticulous care combined with ascetic vision has enabled her husband R. S. Thomas to achieve his poetry, so by selection and economy, Mildred Eldridge has created the stark splendour of her work. And the universe is both stark and splendid' (137).

[14] Frantz Fanon, 'On National Culture', in *The Wretched of the Earth*, trans. Constance Farrington (Harmondsworth: Penguin, 1990), p. 177.

[15] See, for example, the comments of his son, Gwydion, in a recent interview: 'one of the things that emerged in the mid 1990s during the years leading up to his second marriage, to Betty Vernon, was that in moving to be near her in Titley, Herefordshire, he was able to indulge his hankering to be an English country gentleman. He used to appear regularly in tweed jackets and cavalry twills like a retired Colonel'. '[W]hen Rhodri, at Westminster School, wisely chose to read Law at Bristol rather than at Oxford, R.S.'s comment was "Well, Westminster can't be that much of a school if it can't secure him a place at Oxford!"' '"Quietly as Snow"; Gwydion Thomas interviewed by Walford Davies', *New Welsh Review*, 64 (Summer, 2004), 30, 29.

[16] Kenneth Rowntree and Gwyn Jones, *A Prospect of Wales* (London: Penguin, 1948), p. 7. Hereafter *PW*.

[17] See the unpublished BBC radio talk (April, 1957), 'A Time for Carving', in the R. S. Thomas Study Centre, Bangor University, drawn to my attention by Tony Brown. For Whitman and Wales, see chapter 9 of M. Wynn Thomas, *Transatlantic Connections: Whitman US-Whitman UK* (Iowa City: University of Iowa Press, 2005).

[18] Patrick Crotty, '*The Great Hunger* and R. S. Thomas's *The Minister*', in Andrew Hiscock and Katie Gramich (eds), *Dangerous Diversity: the Changing Faces of Wales* (Cardiff; University of Wales Press, 1998), pp. 131–49. See also Sam Perry, 'Passionate and simple: R. S. Thomas and Irish Writing', *Almanac*, 13 (2008–9), 126–61.

[19] W. B. Yeats, *The Collected Poems of W. B. Yeats* (London: Macmillan, 1963), p. 167. See '"Yeats said that": R. S. Thomas and W. B. Yeats', *Almanac*, 13 (2008–9), 1–26.

[20] For an interesting discussion of 'A Peasant', see J. P. Ward, *The Poetry of R. S. Thomas* (Bridgend; Poetry Wales Press, 1987), pp. 15ff.

[21] In 'Parallel Lives? The Art of M. E. Eldridge', *Planet*, 129 (June–July, 1998), 17–26, Peter Lord concludes that 'Saunders Lewis was right to sense some relationship between the art of M. E. Eldridge and R. S. Thomas, though its nature is unusually elusive. It may have more of the quality of parallel lives, sometimes closing together to touch, at other times moving starkly apart, than of lives inextricably entwined.'

# 3

# The Disappearing Clergyman

One image in particular seems conveniently to offer itself as a paradigm of aspects of R. S. Thomas's situation, both during the 1960s and indeed onward into the 1970s. It appears in the form of an episode, or more strictly speaking a brace of episodes, from his childhood, as recalled in *Y Llwybrau Gynt*:

> Another time, going to one of the parks [in Liverpool]: it is the middle of winter and the lake there is frozen over. A crowd of people are sliding on it. Near to the bank, there is a patch which has not frozen. A clergyman comes into view, sailing along like a ship with the wind behind it. Suddenly, to my astonishment, he disappears into the pool. Others come straight away to pull him out, dripping wet. He goes off, crestfallen. Life carries on. It is nice in the park in the summer as well. The breeze is full of the scent of roses. I bend over to sniff one of the flowers – but something nasty is waiting for me there! Quick as a flash it's up my nose, and I start to scream. My mother rushes over to me, scared out of her wits. After I have blown my nose like a dragon into her handkerchief, the enemy is revealed: a harmless little black fly! But I remember the experience to this day, and I still take great care when smelling a flower.[1]

Here we see how life first got up R. S. Thomas's nose – as it did so notably and so frequently thereafter. In its comically, but calculatedly ingenuous way, the passage is a reflection on the black treachery of life – or rather the black fly treachery of life – and how to guard against it. There are, of course, other elements in the story, such as R. S. Thomas's familiar impatience with his younger self, whom he seems often to want to represent as a cosseted mummy's boy. And in its teasingly modest way, the episode summarises the tragi-comedy of the encounter of human dreams with reality. But above all, it embryonically suggests the twin fears that seem to me to be the two most important concerns of R. S. Thomas's poetry during the 1960s: fears that correspond to the double threat of collapse from within and invasion from without. And bearing in mind those memories from childhood as related above, we could conveniently think of these threats as (a) the disappearing clergyman syndrome, and (b) the black fly syndrome.

Emily Dickinson once spoke of acquiring, in her poetry, 'that precarious Gait/ Some call Experience'. R. S. Thomas, watching an old man, sees him 'trying/ Time's treacherous ice with a slow foot'.[2] That 'slow foot' seems sometimes to be the careful measure of his own song. 'Time's treacherous ice' is, in this case, not a metaphysical nicety. It refers to the social, economic and political processes which are putting the skids under everything that makes his Wales culturally distinctive. The question, then, is how to keep one's footing, or how and where to stand one's ground.

In his comprehensive study of the Welsh-language poetry of the 1960s, Alan Llwyd refers to the decade as the period when the whole tempo of life seemed to change.[3] He then proceeds to show how a host of poets made this acceleration the subject of their poetry, with many deploring its consequences while a few revelled excitedly in the new opportunities – both experiential and linguistic – that the rapidly developing social and cultural situation offered. R. S. Thomas was certainly not among the latter. But neither can he be simply aligned with the former since, although he shared their cultural conservatism, he was not as ready as they to express it through the unqualified eulogy of the 'peasant' and pastoral life of a rural Wales whose time was clearly passing. A poem by perhaps the greatest modern exponent of *cynghanedd*, Dic Jones, who was himself a working farmer, can serve as an example of this genre, although due allowance must be made for the high toll the English language takes on such an irreducibly foreign form of writing:

Yellow ears' rustle of praise
Weaves through the valley meadows;
Grain dances in summer haze;
They bow to the wind's power
From ridge to ridge, the patterns
Of rust and gold interlaced . . .

Once horns would invite our strong
Elders to the same battle,
Early scything's fearless men,
Forefathers of his fathers,
Old fellowship, unselfish,
Cheerful reaping's peerless troop.
Oppression had made it strong,
Hardship had made it wealthy.

Mother and children turned out,
And sweetheart, to the cornfield,
In autumn perseverance,
To tie its top-heavy gold,
And an unmatched battalion
Of craft-bound ricks clothed a ridge.

They have not, today's farmers,
One-third of the old crew's craft;
His field will hold tomorrow
Of its long gold drooping ears
Merely the battle's stubble,
And a lustreless clipped mane.[4]

R. S. Thomas himself seemed set to settle in, and to settle for, the country at the beginning of the 1960s. Initially, in *Tares*, it seemed that he would stay where, as a poet, he already was; namely in Manafon. As is well known, though, his Manafon, the Manafon of the early poetry, was the product of an educative disillusionment. In the John Ormond film about his life and work, R. S. Thomas spoke of the shock of coming up against 'the harsh realities of rural life', and characterised himself, with characteristic self-deprecation, as coming 'out of a kind of bourgeois environment which, especially in modern times, is protected: it's cushioned from some of the harsher realities'.[5] What he didn't mention there, of course, was the contribution made by Welsh-language literature to the dream of rural beauty he'd brought with him to the Montgomeryshire uplands. 'To him', he wrote in *Neb*, referring to himself in the third person, 'the locality and the neighbouring country was beautiful. He wished to continue to write poems of praise to the whole area. But how was he to reconcile this with the farmers' own attitude and way of life?'[6] For more than a century, Welsh culture had celebrated the stock figure of cultured shepherd and farmer, who epitomised all that was best in the unique Welsh *gwerin* (volk). And that image was not simply replaced by Iago Prytherch. It survived, in drastically modified form, as one of the several contradictory elements of which the poetic character of Iago is compounded. Furthermore, as late as 1968, the original dream could surface, with its naivety virtually intact, in a passage from the prose-work 'The Mountains'. Ruined buildings remind R. S. Thomas of the men who 'spent long days . . . swapping *englynion* over the peat cutting. They have gone now; the cuttings are deserted, yr *hafotai* in ruins' (*SP*, p. 105). An irony worth our notice is the fact that the lonely figure of the farmer in his poetry is the product of the depopulation of the hill country that had been a feature of the preceding half-century. Yet Thomas frequently treats the figure as an emblem of the eternal condition of rural life, unchanged and unchanging. His farmer is seemingly imbued 'with a tree's patience,/ Rooted in the dark soil' (*CP*, p. 88). This is a view of the country very different from that offered in *Neb*, when he records 'that more than thirty thousand people had left Montgomeryshire between the two world wars . . . The rector [R. S. Thomas himself] began to sing with longing of the life that had been, and of the life of loneliness and of poverty endured by those who had stayed' (p. 51).

Still, there is no doubt that Manafon flies did get up R. S. Thomas's nose. Their blue, uncertain, stumbling buzz can be heard throughout his many perplexed dialogues with the gaunt, remote figure of Iago Prytherch. Yet his poetry evades much more than it admits of the realities of the region. Considered as an approximation to, let alone as an accurate report of, life in an upland rural community, the Prytherch poems are non-starters. As R. S. Thomas himself points out, the Manafon district was 'a sociologist's nightmare' – its social structure was so complicated. He himself gives an interesting analysis of that structure, and of the resultant social psychology of the area in *Neb*:

> The rector's name was expected to head any list of gifts, and they would then adjust their contributions according to the size of the farm: a farmer of two hundred acres would give two pounds, say, a farmer of one hundred acres one pound, and so on – as simple as that. (*Neb*, p. 57)

But one thing is certain. There were no 'peasants' there, in spite of this Welsh bard and his English reviewers. Indeed, when one reads the social comments passed by Anglo-American critics on these poems, one feels like referring them to Raymond Williams's wise words about the terms appropriate for a mature discussion of Hardy:

> First, we had better drop 'peasant' altogether. Where Hardy lived and worked, as in most other parts of England, there were virtually no peasants, although 'peasantry' as a generic word for country people was still used by writers. The actual country people were landowners, tenant farmers, dealers, craftsmen, and labourers.[7]

There are, in fact, occasions when R. S. Thomas implicitly makes related points and distinctions in his poetry. For instance, he speaks very deliberately of a hired landless labourer in the poem called 'Hireling', and of the wealthy farmer with large capital in 'Rhodri'. In other words, he sometimes allows us to glimpse a rural world that does not so much contrast with as reproduce in its own terms the capitalist structure of commercial town and industrial centres. Prosperity, greed and materialism are not then treated as foreign imports; they are seen as endemic to the rural economy, to rural society, as they are to its urban and suburban counterparts. And this, I take it, is precisely why R. S. Thomas will not, cannot, allow us or himself to contemplate the social structure of the real Manafon for too long in his poetry. If he did, the ground would be cut from under his feet, as surely as the ice disappeared under his Liverpool clergyman's skates. R. S. Thomas's Manafon, as embodied in Iago Prytherch, exists in and for the sake of a contrast with the commercial and industrial capitalism that R. S. Thomas regards as the threat of anglicisation:

> He will go on; that much is certain.
> Beneath him tenancies of the fields
> Will change; machinery turn
> All to noise. (*CP*, p. 178)

Iago Prytherch is also his great and deliberate exercise in mystification. He is the counterpart, in the earlier poetry, of the *Deus Absconditus* who is the dominant dramatis persona of the later poetry. As critics have frequently noted, and as even the poet himself more or less agreed, the descriptions of Iago's personality border on (if they do not actually cross over into) the self-contradictory. Is he an avid, devoted reader of 'the slow book/ Of the farm'? Or is he as mindless as the soil he tills? And if he is so mindless, is he blissfully, enviably so; or brutishly so? Moreover, to pursue Iago Prytherch is, as Roland Mathias admirably demonstrated forty years ago, to become entangled in R. S. Thomas's confusions about the status and character of the natural world itself.[8]

No way seems yet to have been found by commentators to dissolve these contradictions, except perhaps by seeing them as variants of the primitivism that is commonly the bourgeois townie's view of country life. After all, both the pastoral and the anti-pastoral have been popular bourgeois genres. Naturally, though, interpreters are content to talk about the Iago Prytherch poems as consisting of R. S. Thomas's arguments with himself, without enquiring too deeply into the social content, or context, of this arguing. Their explanation tends to gravitate towards those familiar opening lines of 'Servant':

> You served me well, Prytherch.
> From all my questionings and doubts;
> From brief acceptance of the times'
> Deities: from ache of the mind
> Or body's tyranny, I turned,
> Often after a whole year,
> Often twice in the same day,
> To where you read in the slow book
> Of the farm, turning the fields' pages
> So patiently, never tired
> Of the land's story; not just believing,

> But proving in your bone and your blood
> Its accuracy; willing to stand
> Always aside from the main road,
> Where life's flashier illustrations
> Were marginal. (*CP*, p. 146)

I also find these lines revealing – revealing of the need or the needs that Prytherch is brought into existence to serve. To identify these needs is also to begin to understand why Iago's serviceableness consists of his being an enigma; of his being 'inscrutable'; of his being eminently visible and yet permanently beyond the reach of sight. In chapter 2, Prytherch's origins in Thomas's own impacted psychic struggles were emphasised. In this chapter, attention needs to be paid to the way in which Prytherch's loomingly mysterious figure offers Thomas a temporary expedient for dealing with the centuries-old Welsh problem of how to resist the invading, appropriating, eyes of the English.

As was suggested in chapter 2, behind not only the original con-struction but also the subsequent eccentric maintenance of the character lies the whole complex matter of the history and the sociology of the picturesque: 'a pose/ For strangers, a watercolour's appeal/ To the mass, instead of the poem's/ Harsher conditions' (*CP*, p. 194). In an uncollected 1958 essay for *The Listener*, Thomas had a fair bit to say about Wales in these terms: 'Because it is a small country', he explains, 'one is always arriving.'[9] For the inhabitant, this rules out the possibility of using physical distance as a trope for the mystery and depth of one's own culture – a favourite ploy, of course, of American writers. It also rules out the possibility of using physical distance or vastness as either an actual or metaphorical barrier against invasion, of the kind spectacularly instanced by the history of Russia. All of Wales is exposed as Border Country – a point R. S. Thomas was, however unconsciously, making when he chose to make his stand at Manafon, a mere stone's throw from Offa's Dyke. The 1958 essay continues like this: 'Certainly in Wales, the country and the people have, like Mr Eliot's roses, the look of things that are looked at. How tired one is of the South Stack [lighthouse near Thomas's boyhood home in Holyhead], anchored for ever in its mono-chrome calm.'

It has been fairly widely remarked that Iago Prytherch was brought into being partly by a counter-cultural, anti-picturesque, post-colonial impulse, but it remains to suggest that it was the same impulse, properly understood as being of national and not merely of local or aesthetic origin, that kept Iago in a state of perpetually perplexing existence. It was of the essence, if he was to avoid being appropriated by the very attention the poetry invited. Therefore, the more he seemed to abide R. S. Thomas's questioning, the more he remained free. One arrives at Iago very quickly in the early collections, and yet each arrival is only the point of a new departure. One could paraphrase a splendid remark once made by Hugh MacDiarmid and assert that 'the prodigiousness of Iago's character itself becomes a safeguarding excellence.' What it safeguards is the mystery of a way of life that is a synecdoche for Wales.

A useful point may be made here in passing. To the customary talk about R. S. Thomas's indebtedness to the Romantics should perhaps be added a mention of his significant adaptation of at least one import-ant pre-Romantic genre. A half century ago, Geoffrey Hartman wrote a fascinating essay on what seemed to him to be virtually the missing link between eighteenth-century poetry and Romantic poetry.[10] This link was *inscription verse* – verses written as if intended to be carved on a seat, say, or an elm-tree. Verses, too – and this is where R. S. Thomas's poetry comes in – written as if an object, or a feature of the landscape (such as a waterfall), were itself addressing the reader, inviting him to stand and ponder the hitherto unnoticed significance of the scene in front of him. It was, as Hartman pointed out, a genre well suited to the task of con-veying the mysterious hidden life of the natural world. 'Invasion on the Farm' can usefully be regarded as just such an inscription poem – verses inscribed on Iago Prytherch, as it were. It is no more an authentic dramatic monologue than lines 'addressed' to the reader by a waterfall are actually, credibly, spoken by it:

> I am Prytherch. Forgive me. I don't know
> What you are talking about; your thoughts flow
> Too swiftly for me; I cannot dawdle
> Along their banks and fish in their quick stream
> With crude fingers. I am alone, exposed

> In my own fields with no place to run
> From your sharp eyes. I, who a moment back
> Paddled in the bright grass, the old farm
> Warm as a sack about me, feel the cold
> Winds of the world blowing. The patched gate
> You left open will never be shut again. (*CP*, p. 60)

Even as he speaks, Iago's essential existence is left safely wrapped in the impenetrability of muteness. This irreducible distance between him and the inner life of his characters is something that R. S. Thomas seems to value and regret equally, and almost simultaneously, as can be seen in the poem 'The Watcher':

> He was looking down on a field;
> Not briefly, but for a long time.
> A gate opened, it had done so before,
> A sluice through which in a flood came
> Cattle and sheep, occasionally men,
> To fan out in a slow tide,
> The stock to graze, the men busy
> In ways never to be divulged
> To the still watcher beyond the glass
> Of their thin breath, the ear's membrane
> Stretched in vain, for no words issued
> To curse or bless through those teeth clenched
> In a long grip on life's dry bone. (*Tares*, p. 41)

The ambivalence of this poem is palpable, as Thomas on the one hand wants to participate in the life he is observing and on the other respects the stubborn, impenetrable self-absorption of the workers in their inscrutable tasks. That one long sentence, beginning in the third line and concluding with the poem itself, starts with the promise to the eye of admission to the secret existence of the scene, but ends with the frustration of the ear's attempt to eavesdrop on the meaning of what is going on. The whole passage is rather like a reversal of the famous opening to Wordsworth's 'Michael', where at first the landscape presents a forbidding aspect to the outsider, only to relent once the traveller persists in his willingness to leave the public way, and its public ways, and to learn the customs of this country. Then, says Wordsworth, he may be admitted, or initiated into the discovery that 'the mountains have all opened out themselves,/ And made a hidden valley of their own.'[11]

'The Watcher' is a poem from the collection *Tares* (1962), and that is the last of R. S. Thomas's collections to be devoted to the Manafon experience. Indeed one might venture to suggest that it is the last of his volumes to be imbued with a sense of a particular place – a specific human and natural locality. After that, it could be argued, Thomas becomes a displaced person. One finds him struggling to realise his dreams, not through a particular place and time, as he was doing, however imperfectly, ambiguously and uncertainly in the earlier Manafon poems, but *against* the temptation to trust to any human place or time. In retrospect, it can be clearly seen that the poetry after *Tares* was being written somewhere along the road leading from Manafon to Abercuawg, that place which is no place that is extant, but 'somewhere evermore about to be'. It could well be that the social and political events in Wales during the 1960s were partly responsible for this change. It is worth noting his bitter comments in 'Movement': 'Move with the times?/ I've done that all right:/ In a few years/ Buried a nation/. . . None of those farms/ In the high hills/ Have bred children./ My poems were of old men' (*CP*, p. 141).

Another key poem of this period is 'The Untamed', included in what seems to me to be the key volume of the 1960s, *The Bread of Truth* (1963), which is full of the disappearing clergyman syndrome and the black fly syndrome – in other words, fears of inward collapse and invasion:

> My garden is the wild
>   Sea of the grass. Her garden
> Shelters between walls.
>   The tide could break in;
>   I should be sorry for this.
>
> There is peace there of a kind,
>   Though not the deep peace
> Of wild places. Her care
>   For green life has enabled
>   The weak things to grow.

Despite my first love,
   I take sometimes her hand,
Following strait paths
    Between flowers, the nostril
    Clogged with their thick scent.

The old softness of lawns
    Persuading the slow foot
Leads to defection; the silence
    Holds with its gloved hand
    The wild hawk of the mind.

But not for long, windows,
    Opening in the trees
Call the mind back
    To its true eyrie; I stoop
    Here only in play. (*CP*, p. 140)

This poem seems to be constructed out of the tension Thomas feels between his old passion for that realm of independence and freedom that nature had represented for him ever since he was a boy in Holyhead, and a reluctant, wary, yet genuinely affectionate attachment to domestic life. Starting from here, one can see how much of Iago Prytherch there is in R. S. Thomas. And while his bleak confession of a failure to love has already been noted in my introduction to this book, a different aspect of that condition appears here: his avoidance of emotional closeness, or intimacy, because he fears it will render him vulnerable.

The poem ends on a note of heroic, strenuous individualism reminiscent of the writings of Kierkegaard. When Thomas himself mentioned the Dane during the 1970s he made reference, interestingly enough, to *The Present Age*, which is primarily a work of social rather than spiritual analysis. In *The Present Age*, Kierkegaard attacks the various devices – of protracted dispassionate reflection – by means of which his age safeguarded its sophisticated inertia, and avoided being brought to the raw moment of decisive, irreversible choice. Yet only in that extremity of personal choosing, that moment of self-exposure, does the individual come authentically into being, according to Kierkegaard. Only then does his life acquire the depth – or what Kierkegaard calls the inwardness –

that constitutes true character. With that in mind, it is interesting to read
the following:

> And he dared them;
> Dared them to grow old and bitter
> As he. He kept his pen clean
> By burying it in their fat
> Flesh . . .[12]

Here Thomas depicts Saunders Lewis, no less, as a Kierkegaardian hero,
a man whose daring commitment to an idea and an ideal was in itself
an indictment of tepid, unresisting modern conformism, and in particular
a devastating indictment of the morally and politically supine character
of the Welsh people (to be discussed further in chapter 4). What also
strikes me, though, is the totally unexpected similarity that lurks within
the apparent dissimilarities between the figure of Iago Prytherch and
Saunders Lewis, as seen by R. S. Thomas. The words of another poet can
help us here, the words of Robert Frost in a poem called 'Reluctance':

> Ah, when to the heart of man
>     Was it ever less than a treason
> To go with the drift of things,
>     To yield with a grace to reason,
> And bow and accept the end
>     Of a love or a season.[13]

What both Iago and Saunders Lewis unexpectedly prove to possess is
this distaste for the 'treason' of yielding to 'the drift of things'; of following
the flow. It is their blessed unreasonableness in this respect that commands
R. S. Thomas's respect. They have an ungracious unyieldingness in common. Yet, of course, the heroic unreasonableness of the one is fundamentally different in kind from that of the other. This difference is the difference
between two periods of R. S. Thomas's writing, and between two reactions
by him to the Welsh situation.

Iago Prytherch is invented to represent a communal way of life which
possesses the sort of brute integrity that goes with force of habit. He is,
to the best of R. S. Thomas's ability, invested with permanence. If he is

presented as occupying a non-verbal fastness, then by writing poems about him Thomas constructs a kind of verbal fastness for his own hopes of some principle of endurance in Welsh cultural affairs. 'Not choice for you', as R. S. Thomas puts it in one version, at least, of this myth of permanence, 'But seed sown upon the thin/ Soil of a heart, not rich, nor fertile,/ Yet capable of the one crop,/ Which is the bread of truth that I break' (*CP*, p. 146). Saunders Lewis, on the other hand, is the contrary individual who chooses quite consciously to devote his accusatory life to the preservation of values that have been jettisoned by the community in its unseemly haste to catch up with what it considers to be progress. The great enemy of such an authentic, committed individual, according to Kierkegaard, is 'the public' – a phenomenon he equates with modern mass society:

> A nation, a generation, a people, an assembly of the people, a meeting or a man, are responsible for what they are and can be made ashamed if they are inconstant and unfaithful, but a public remains a public . . . no single person who belongs to the public makes a real commitment . . . made up of individuals at the moments when they are nothing, a public is a kind of gigantic something, an abstract and deserted void which is everything and nothing.[14]

And then one remembers that Thomas, too, has used that word 'public' and invested it with the same charge of contempt:

> I am invited to enter these gardens
> As one of the public, and to conduct myself
> In accordance with the regulations;
> To keep off the grass and sample flowers
> Without touching them; to admire birds
> That have been seduced from wildness by
> Bread they are pelted with.
>                                   I am not one
> Of the public; I have come a long way
> To realise this. (*CP*, p. 165)

It may very well be no more than coincidence that the key Kierkegaardian term turns up so prominently in 'A Welshman at St James' Park'. After all, the obvious source for the term is the formal public language of the familiar public notices, the disciplinary courtesies of which the poem begins by mockingly imitating. Nevertheless, the uncompromisingly simple, absolute contrasts – between British 'public' and Welsh man; between seductively trim gardens and wild hills – upon which the poem turns are the very materials of a Kierkegaardian choice, which brings a genuine individual into existence out of the crowd.

No wonder R. S. Thomas explained, in 'A Grave Unvisited', that he had deliberately passed by the opportunity to visit Kierkegaard's grave. He was revolted by the thought that the Danes were now anxious to profit from the posthumous fame of a figure who had, throughout his short life, been despised and rejected by his fellow-countrymen:

> What is it drives a people
> To the rejection of a great
> Spirit, and after to think it returns
> Reconciled to the shroud
> Prepared for it? (*CP*, p. 183)

For 'people' here read 'the Welsh public'; and for Kierkegaard read Saunders Lewis – or R. S. Thomas himself.

'A Welshman at St James' Park' is a poem about the proper use by the speaker of that little word 'I', which begins with his ungraciously flat refusal of the official terms of self-description proffered him by the sign. It is very much a 1960s poem, in that it analyses the semiotics of official-dom, showing how inimical to Welshness is the concealed ideology in-scribed in the ostensibly neutral language of public discourse in Britain. This was broadly the perception that underlay the campaigns of Cym-deithas yr Iaith Gymraeg, the Welsh language society, during this period against English-only road signs and the like. Yet, while young Welsh speakers, trained by Saunders Lewis and others to read the signs of the times, found dramatic methods of exposing and dismantling the 'homely' instruments of the Anglo-British state in Wales, it commonly remained the case that the English monoglots of Wales had their eyes opened to the incurable Englishness of a supposedly British state only when they were exiled in England. In this respect, too, the poem is therefore very much of its time – and can indeed usefully be described as the classic exile's poem of the mid-twentieth century, just as Ceiriog's 'Nant y Mynydd' ('Mountain stream') is undoubtedly the classic nineteenth-century Welsh exile's poem.[15]

Familiar lines from each of these two poems help bring into focus the difference between two forms of Welsh experience of exile, separated by a hundred years. Ceiriog presents himself as an innocent child of the mountains: 'Mab y mynydd ydwyf innau/ Oddi cartref yn gwneud cân./ Ond mae 'nghalon yn y mynydd/ Efo'r grug a'r adar mân' ('I too am a son of the hills,/ Singing far away from home./ But my heart is in the mountains,/ with the heather and the small birds').[16] And R. S. Thomas turns to similar images:

> I think of a Welsh hill
> That is without fencing, and the men,
> Bosworth blind, who left the heather
> And the high pastures of the heart.

Set in the context of the complete poem, Ceiriog's imaginary mountain seems to be the location, however idealised, however romanticised, of an actual way of life. He speaks in the agrarian person of the 'gwerinwr', or 'amaethwr', who has been uprooted and transplanted to barren urban soil. In other words, there is the myth of a particular kind of society behind 'Nant y Mynydd', whereas with R. S. Thomas one is constantly aware of the bareness of that Welsh hill of which he thinks – a hill bare even, one might say, of Iago Prytherch and his resilient upland life. And that initial impression is confirmed by the phrase that soon follows: 'the high pasture of the heart'. Such a genitive construction is extremely familiar to any reader of Thomas's poetry. And here it seems to function as a means of creating a deliberate ambiguity of meaning. The phrase could refer either to actual high pastures that were dear to the heart, or to high pastures that were a figure of speech for the feelings of the heart – in other words, for a person's emotional and perhaps spiritual condition. Either way, the dream is rather a lonely one, centred not on a society but on an image of lofty self-sufficiency, and a quality of individual integrity, which is proof against all anticipated attempts to seduce it or to overcome it.

In the early poetry, such a dream had been embodied in R. S. Thomas's highly distinctive vision of the people of an actual, particular upland community. But during the 1960s, judging at least by the evidence of the poetry, Thomas began to internalise the dream for even safer keeping – becoming, in a way, his own Iago Prytherch; substituting for the upland farms around Manafon his own, internal 'high pastures of the heart'. At the end of 'A Welshman at St James's Park', therefore, he heads implicitly back not to a particular Welsh community, but to the 'high pastures of the heart'. That is to say, he simply exchanges a state of external, geo-graphical exile for a state of internal exile. He puts distance between himself and London only in order to come back and keep his distance from his fellow-Welshmen, most of whom seem 'Bosworth blind' (the reference is to the Welsh who, having assisted Henry Tudor to become Henry VII, subsequently became besotted with London).

This self-preserving attempt to keep his distance from his supposed kind is what seems to happen repeatedly in Thomas's later 1960s poetry. A poem like 'Afforestation', for example, is surely a coded expression of his distaste for Welsh consumer society, while 'Blondes' is a ferociously patronising poem on much the same subject. But above all, it's worth recalling his experiences 'On the Shore':

> No nearer than this;
> So that I can see their shapes,
> And know them human
> But not who they are;
> So that I can hear them speak,
> The familiar accent,
> But not what they say.
>
> To be nearer than this;
> To look into their eyes
> And know the colour of their thought;
> To paddle in their thin talk –
> What is the beach for?
> I watch them through the wind's pane,
> Nameless and dear.[17]

What language are these unfortunates speaking, one wonders? It's doubtful whether they're speaking a Brummy English, although there are connections between this piece and a poem like 'Eviction', where, incautiously approaching someone in the Welsh heartlands, Thomas finds that 'as in a dream/ A dear face coming up close/ Spits at us, the reply falls/ In that cold language that is the frost/ On all our nation' (*Bread of Truth*, p. 13). There the black fly syndrome can be clearly seen. The people on the shore could, though, be speaking either English or Welsh. It seems to make no difference. R. S. Thomas is equally estranged from the speakers of both languages. He is thus far advanced on the road leading from Manafon to Abercuawg.

It is in his essay *Abercuawg* (originally a lecture given in Welsh at the 1976 National Eisteddfod) that we find him saying things like this:

> [W]hatever Abercuawg might be, it is a place of trees and fields and flowers and bright unpolluted streams, where the cuckoos continue to sing. For such a place I am ready to make sacrifices, maybe even to die. But what of a place which is overcrowded with people, that has endless streets of modern, characterless houses, each with its garage and television aerial, a place from where the trees and the birds and the flowers have fled before the yearly extension of concrete and tar-macadam; where the people do the same kind of soul-less, monotonous work to provide for still more and more of their kind?
>
> And even if Welsh should be the language of these people; even if they should coin a Welsh word for every gadget and tool of the technical and plastic age they live in, will this be a place worth bringing into existence, worth making sacrifices for? Is it for the sake of such a future that some of our young people have to go to prison and ruin such promising careers? I have very often put such questions to myself, and I am still without a definite answer. (*SP*, p. 158)

Welsh-speaking Wales is there seen as being itself implicated in the process of 'afforestation' – to use an image from his own poem, which Gwenallt had made famous before him. In these paragraphs from *Abercuawg*, Welsh-speaking Wales assumes something of the threatening shape of St James's Park in Thomas's imagination, driving him to take refuge in a name from the Welsh literature of the Middle Ages, which evokes 'a place of trees and fields and flowers and bright unpolluted streams, where the cuckoos continue to sing'. It is surely the lowland equivalent of 'the high pastures of he heart'. In fact, Abercuawg sounds very like the Afallon (Avalon) to which T. Gwynn Jones's dying Arthur yearns to go: 'i ynys Afallon i wella fy nghlwy' ('To the island of Avalon to heal me of my wounds').[18] Yet it is actually presented as an image of dream, which is the opposite of Romantic escapism, and is intended to be the prelude to serious engagement with present unsatisfactory realities in the name of Abercuawg – that is, in the name of other, fuller ways of living, memories and hints of which are preserved in the 'obsolete' terms that haunt the margins of current, debased speech. Such a potentially constructive argument is indeed advanced in *Abercuawg*, and seems to be an attractive one. 'In dreams', as Yeats used to like to quote, 'begin responsibility'.

Nevertheless, having registered the argument, one is still left in a situation similar to that described by Thomas himself in his lecture 'Words and the Poet': 'My own position is usually to allow this as a legitimate theory, but to ask in practice, "Where are the poems?"' (*SP*, p. 85). The answer seems to be that there are no poems, that this positive interpretation of the dream of Abercuawg has failed to produce an answering body of work. Instead it is an altogether different and more disturbing side of the Abercuawg vision of things that seems, from the 1960s onwards, to have issued in poetry. This is the side apparent in the famous, or notorious, anecdote about Branwen included in the lecture:

> Who has not had the experience of seeing his dreams shattered? Branwen was the Helen of Wales, wasn't she? Many of us, I'm sure, hold an image of her in our hearts, not as she is in her rectangular grave on the banks of the river Alaw in Anglesey, but as she was in her lifetime – the fairest maiden alive. There are still a few Branwens in Wales. Did I not hear the name once and turn, thinking she might steal my heart away? Who did I see but a stupid, mocking slut, her dull eyes made blue by daubings of mascara – a girl for whom Wales was no more than a name, and a name fast becoming *obsolete*? (*SP*, pp. 158–9)

This is a powerful example of the black fly of modern Welsh life getting up R. S. Thomas's nose. This Branwen may well have been a Welsh speaker – Thomas does not stop to find out. It would make no difference. She would be certain to speak only plastic Welsh, in any case. He has no wish to 'paddle in [her] talk'. He wishes, no doubt, that he were 'on the shore': 'what is the beach for?' Well, it is clearly for the avoidance of such disenchantment as comes from close encounters of several kinds with his fellow-countrymen and women.

When he writes like this, R. S. Thomas shows an affinity with those conservative intellectuals who were an influential and impressive force in Welsh-language culture during the 1960s. Alan Llwyd has summarised their outlook, through extensive quotation, in *Barddoniaeth y Chwedegau*, with particular reference to the observations of Saunders Lewis and Iorwerth Peate. Peate argued that the coming of bilingualism inescapably meant the serious dilution of Welsh-language culture, with the result that no great literature could ever again be produced in Welsh. Lewis likewise concluded that the end of a 'predominantly monoglot community' was 'unmitigated loss, disability, even calamity' for writers: 'English idiom enters unconsciously into Welsh speech today', he sadly noted. 'It is all about us, even in the remotest countryside, in radio set and television screen and daily newspaper. Inevitably there's a landslide of deterioration.' R. S. Thomas, himself a Welsh-learner, took his cultural bearings from prophets like these, as will be emphasised in the next chapter.[19]

His Abercuawg vision of Welsh-language society – a view that grows parallel to his increasingly jaundiced view of English-language society in Wales – can be seen developing in the poetry of the 1960s. The point can most easily be made by a simple, and no doubt simplifying, contrast between two images R. S. Thomas uses for language. One dates from the 1950s, the other from the 1960s. Writing in *The Listener* (1958), he explained to the English that the Welsh lived not so much on two levels as in two rooms: the kitchen and the front parlour. The former was for family and friends, the latter for visitors. The Welsh, he explained, 'are a homely people, they live in their kitchen. They have their front parlour, of course, and without the language the traveller will never get beyond it.'[20]

This is one of R. S. Thomas's recurrent images of an inviolable inner sanctum. But what one notices is that the inner sanctuary here is not only the Welsh language, but the spoken and the lived language. It is identified with an existent, ongoing, securely hidden kind of social life. It is a view of the Welsh-speaking society that parallels, after an instructive fashion, his view of the Manafon farmers.

Contrast this with the way the language is imaged in the poem 'Welcome', in *The Bread of Truth* (1964):

> You can come in.
> You can come a long way;
> We can't stop you.
> You can come up the roads
> Or by railway;
> You can land from the air.
> You can walk this country
> From end to end;
> But you won't be inside;
> You must stop at the bar,
> The old bar of speech.
>
> We have learnt your own
> Language, but don't
> Let it take you in;
> It's not what you mean,
> It's what you pay with
> Everywhere you go,
> Pleased at the price
> In shop windows.
> There is no way there;
> Past town and factory
> You must travel back
> To the cold bud of water
> In the hard rock. (*CP*, p. 134)

When *The Bread of Truth* was reviewed in *The Listener*, the English reviewer singled out this poem for unfavourable comment, complaining because R. S. Thomas had put such unpleasant sentiments in the mouth of one of his peasant characters. The following week the poet replied, in a letter, that he was speaking for himself in a poem about 'the English infiltration of Wales'.[21] But, as any Welshman will realise, the poem is for home consumption, as much as for foreign or English consumption. It is indirectly

86

addressed – addressed, that is, via the English – to the Welsh people whose national anthem, it sometimes seems, is the old radio favourite, 'We'll keep a welcome in the hillsides'. There is in any case an element of bravado that lends pathos to the poetry. English is imagined as being spoken only as a Welsh guerrilla tactic, used only to fleece the tourists. As if it were possible to use the language without in any way being used, or changed, by it.

There is a great deal to be said about this change of image, from kitchen to 'cold bud of water/ In the hard rock.' And there is something to be said *for* it, as well. The difference between the two images is perhaps in part a measure of the difference between the social experiences of two decades. The 'cold bud of water' is a deeply sympathetic image produced in eloquent defiance of the fact and vile image of Tryweryn – the reservoir that supplied Liverpool with water, and which was created in October, 1965, by drowning the hamlet of Capel Celyn. This remote village had been thoroughly Welsh-speaking, and virtually the whole of Wales had been unanimous in its opposition to the English reservoir scheme that necessitated the disappearance of a whole valley and the dispersal of its Welsh-speaking community.[22]

As a result of such disastrous experiences, by the 1960s the Welsh language had been partly driven and had partly issued aggressively of its own accord out of the 'kitchen'. The realisation that the future of the language was inseparable from social, economic and political affairs revolutionised, as we know, the whole language struggle at this time. And although Thomas speaks pointedly and concentratedly of the cold bud of water in the rock, his metaphor could, at least by extension, be understood as signifying the subtly diffused and therefore infinitely ungraspable nature of a linguistic community.

Yet what strikes me most of all, I must say, is the way that a social phenomenon – language, culture – has here been essentially displaced onto, or into, landscape. Maybe in literature, as Geoffrey Hartman has wittily put it, topography is always tropography; a figure of speech. In 'Welcome' we certainly have landscape used as a trope for the Welsh language; and we have it, I would suggest, because R. S. Thomas finds it increasingly difficult to identify with any existing linguistic community.

Place replaces people, before itself being displaced later by a purely imaginary place – Abercuawg – 'a place of trees and fields and flowers and brightly unpolluted streams, where the cuckoos continue to sing'. Language is de-socialised, de-culturised, de-humanised even, by being elementalised into 'the cold bud of water/ In the hard rock'. It is an image clearly produced under conditions of great social stress, and it creates a picture of pristine linguistic source, forever preserved from corruption by Welsh speakers, as well as from invasion by English speakers. Like Edward Thomas, R. S. Thomas is searching for 'a language not to be betrayed'. His refrigerating use of the adjective 'cold' is incidentally very reminiscent of Yeats: 'the cold/ Companionable streams'; 'cast a cold eye/ On life, on death'; 'cold and passionate as the dawn'. 'Imagination must dance', as Yeats said, 'must be carried beyond feeling into aboriginal ice.'[23] And he, like R. S. Thomas, used the adjective 'cold' to describe a state of being that would not decay or rot in time. We are, then, back where we began; back with the fears of slippage, of erosion and invasion, and all the other treacheries of Time that were suggested by R. S. Thomas's childhood memories of the disappearing clergyman and the black fly.

The pathos of this linguistic crisis is very evident in *Pietà* (1966). The collection opens like this: 'Rhodri Theophilus Owen,/ Nothing Welsh but the name' (*CP*, p. 152). This is a stark example of language completely losing its meaning, because there is no correspondence between the name given an object and the real nature of that object. Under such circumstances, what is the poet to do? Should he abandon this traditional form of nomenclature, since it is now no longer appropriate? Or should he strive to reconnect modern life in Wales with the ancient native language that alone can relate it to its own past? Just two pages later in *Pietà*, Thomas contrasts the Welshman's alienated relationship to language with the comfortable linguistic situation of the English. He describes a house named 'Rose Cottage, because it had/ Roses. If all things were as/ Simple!' (*CP*, p. 155). Perhaps there is, here, in the caustic use of the word 'simple', just a hint that the Englishman's home is altogether too secure a castle, since the English language is so strong as to seem virtually a reality principle in itself. Nevertheless, Thomas's constantly embattled Welshness makes him feel a little envious of the very different cultural condition of the English:

> You chose it out
> For its roses, and were not wrong.
> It was registered in the heart
> Of a nation, and so, sure
> Of its being. All summer
> It generated the warmth
> Of its blooms, red lamps
> To guide you. And if you came
> Too late in the bleak cold
> Of winter, there were the faces
> At the window, English faces
> With red cheeks, countering the thorns. (*CP*, p. 155)

Thomas's own experience had been very different. What he saw in the faces of his fellow-countrymen and women was not a warm welcome but a grim threat. He therefore preferred to keep his distance; to withdraw and keep company with 'the cold bud of water/ In the hard rock' – and, in his final years, with the birds.

Of all the interviews R. S. Thomas gave, one of the most revealing was that shown on the Welsh television arts programme *Arolwg* in the mid 1980s. Thanks both to the interviewer and to the fact that the interview was conducted in Welsh, the poet seemed somewhat less embattled and less combative than usual. One remark he made during the course of that conversation throws interesting light on the relationship between his poetry of the 1960s and the new direction his work seemed to take with the appearance of *H'm* (1972). He explained that during his seventy and more years he had seen extensive and profound changes in Welsh life – changes that had repeatedly undermined his hopes and eroded his ideals. It was, he added, this experience of senseless or outrightly destructive change that had prompted him to wonder what view of what kind of God could be compatible with the seemingly pointless events of human history. In other words, he was explaining that the remarkable and frequently anguished religious poetry he had produced from the beginning of the 1970s onwards had arisen, in significant part, from the sorts of difficulties in negotiating Time's treacherous ice which, on the evidence of the poetry, had become more acute for him during the 1960s.

From the early 1960s onwards, therefore, any sense of attachment, however imperfect, grudging and bewildered, that Thomas had previously felt to a particular locality, seems to have been gradually replaced by feelings of dislocation and displacement. Even as he was finding in Aberdaron and on the Llŷn peninsula the strong, if threatened, remnant of a thriving Welsh-language community and becoming active in organisations and campaigns to protect it, his sense of Wales at large – which he could view at a distance across the waters of Cardigan Bay – seems to have become ever more disillusioned, for the kinds of reasons that surfaced in the poetry of the 1960s. Useful negative evidence of this may be found in the reaction to this poetry by Dafydd Elis Thomas, shortly to become Plaid Cymru MP for the Meirionnydd Westminster constituency (subsequently Meirionnydd Nant Conwy) , in an essay printed in *Poetry Wales* in 1972. It was consciously written from the point of view of a sympathiser with the young members of Cymdeithas yr Iaith Gymraeg, many of whom were being imprisoned at that time for defacing English-only road signs in an attempt to gain a place for Welsh in the public domain. And it was also an expression of the views of the rising generation of nationalist leaders: enthused by the revolutionary 1966 electoral success of Gwynfor Evans (the first Plaid Cymru MP) they confidently (and, as it turned out, accurately) predicted further 'mainstream' success for the party. Dafydd Elis Thomas's pithy accusation was that the poet was indulging in a reactionary poetry of despair, at the very time when a young generation of writers and activists was discovering, and indeed creating, in contemporary Welsh life the grounds for evolutionary hope.[24]

Now, half a century later, we can perhaps indulge the luxury of regarding the work of both these Thomases as graphic historical evidence of the crisis psychology of the period. And what is striking is how they reproduce between them the ambivalent tone of the apocalyptic work with which, in 1962, the Welsh experience of the 1960s could be said to have really, if rather belatedly, begun: namely Saunders Lewis's famous radio broadcast *Tynged yr Iaith* (The Fate of the Language), to which further attention will be paid in chapter 4. That lecture contains the following characteristic passage:

> The political tradition of the centuries, the whole economic tendency of the present age, are against the survival of the Welsh language. Nothing can change that except determination, will, struggle, sacrifice, effort.[25]

The first sentence verges on hopelessness. The second confronts it, out-faces it, and so wins through to a well-tempered, steely determination.

Although it was Saunders Lewis's example that inspired the efforts of the young activists throughout the 1960s, there is a hint of easy, rhetorical optimism in Dafydd Elis Thomas's version of the ensuing struggle. On the other hand, the accusations he levelled against the poetry were fair enough, within limits. R. S. Thomas had not really supported in his poetry (as opposed to his public remarks and actions) the courageous efforts being made at that time to protect and advance the Welsh language. He clearly could not find it in himself as a poet to muster a coherent, convinced counter-attack against the social, political and economic forces that threatened his Wales. But instead, he made his own lonely way down, through his poetry of the 1960s, to the profound and at times tragic misgivings that lie very close to the root of Saunders Lewis's unyielding determination. The result was uncomfortable and discomfiting poetry that still speaks with particular power and poignancy in the monitory and admonitory voice of its period to the would-be bilingual and bicultural Wales of our time.

## Notes

1. The English translation comes from 'The Paths Gone By,' in Sandra Anstey (ed.), *R. S. Thomas, Selected Prose* (Bridgend: Poetry Wales Press, 1983), pp. 131–45. Hereafter *SP*.
2. R. S. Thomas, 'An Old Man', *Tares* (London: Hart-Davis, 1961), p. 27.
3. Alan Llwyd, *Barddoniaeth y Chwedegau: astudiaeth lenyddol-hanesyddol* (Caernarfon: Cyhoeddiadau Barddas, 1986); especially chapter 1, 'Mae'r Tempo wedi Newid'.

[4] Translation by Joseph P. Clancy, in *Twentieth-Century Welsh Poems* (Llandysul: Gomer Press, 1982), pp. 216–17.

[5] John Ormond, 'R. S. Thomas: Priest and Poet', *Poetry Wales: R. S. Thomas Special Number* (Spring, 1972), 50.

[6] R. S. Thomas, *Neb*, Cyfres y Cewri 6 (Caernarfon: Gwasg Gwynedd, 1985), p. 42. My translation.

[7] Raymond Williams, *The English Novel from Dickens to Lawrence* (St Albans: Paladin, 1974), p. 82.

[8] Roland Mathias, 'Philosophy and Religion in the Poetry of R. S. Thomas', *Poetry Wales* (Spring, 1972), 27–45. Reprinted in Roland Mathias, *A Ride Through the Wood* (Bridgend: Poetry Wales Press, 1985), pp. 186–205.

[9] R. S. Thomas, 'The Welsh Parlour', *The Listener*, 15 January 1958, 119.

[10] Geoffrey Hartman, 'Wordsworth, Inscription, and Romantic Nature Poetry', in F. W. Hilles and Harold Bloom (eds), *From Sensibility to Romanticism* (New York: Oxford University Press, 1969), pp. 389–413.

[11] William Wordsworth, 'Michael', in Philip Hobsbaum (ed.), *William Wordsworth: Selected Poems and Prose* (London: Routledge, 1989), p. 31.

[12] R. S. Thomas, *Welsh Airs* (Bridgend: Poetry Wales Press, 1987), p. 44.

[13] Robert Frost, *Selected Poems* (Harmondsworth: Penguin, 1963), p. 32.

[14] Søren Kierkegaard, *The Present Age*, trans. Alexander Dru (London: Collins, 1962), p. 69.

[15] John Ceiriog Hughes (1832–87) enjoyed an immense popular reputation during the Victorian period as Wales's supreme lyric poet.

[16] T. Gwynn Jones (gol.), *Ceiriog; Detholiad o'i Weithiau* (Wrecsam: Hughes a'i Fab, 1932), t. 116. My translation.

[17] R. S. Thomas, *The Bread of Truth* (London: Hart-Davies, 1968), p. 29.

[18] T. Gwynn Jones, *Ymadawiad Arthur a Chaniadau Eraill* (Caernarfon: Cwmni y Cyhoeddwyr Cymreig, 1910), p. 20.

[19] Llwyd, *Barddoniaeth y Chwedegau*, pp. 84–5.

[20] R. S. Thomas, *The Listener*, 15 January (1958), 119.

[21] R. S. Thomas, *The Listener*, 14 November (1963), 797.

[22] In 2005, the city of Liverpool issued a formal apology to the Welsh people for the drowning of Capel Celyn, acknowledging the insensitivity and mistake of its action in 1965.

[23] W. B. Yeats, 'A General Introduction to My Work', *Essays and Introductions* (London: Macmillan, 1971), p. 523.

[24] Dafydd Elis Thomas, 'The Image of Wales in R. S. Thomas's Poetry', *Poetry Wales* (1972), 59–66.

[25] Saunders Lewis, *Tynged yr Iaith* (Cyfansoddiadau BBC, 1962), p. 26.

# 4

# Son of Saunders

In a lecture he delivered on 10 December 1938, Saunders Lewis enquired whether Wales had indeed recently managed to produce a distinctive national literature in the English language.[1] At that time Lewis was easily the most dominant figure on the Welsh cultural scene. A founder member of Plaid Cymru (the Party of Wales), he had recently been given a hero's welcome by a crowd of thousands upon his release from prison. He had served a term in Wormwood Scrubs for setting fire, with two companions, to the caretaker's hut on the grounds of a bombing school established by the British government, in the teeth of Wales-wide opposition, on a site of historic and cultural importance. Lewis was also a giant creative talent – poet, dramatist, novelist, political polemicist, cultural ideologue, and literary critic – and his role in Welsh-language culture has frequently been likened, in terms both of its scale and its radically innovatively conservative character, to that of T. S. Eliot in Anglo-American culture or (given the very different political orientation) of Hugh MacDiarmid in the Scottish context.[2]

A mere decade earlier, and the question 'Is there an Anglo-Welsh Literature?' would scarcely have been worth asking. In the interim, however, a conspicuously talented generation of Anglophone writers from Wales had appeared – the best known of whom, virtually from the out-set, was of course Dylan Thomas.[3] These writers came mostly from the concentration of population in the English-speaking south and south-east of Wales, an area that included the depressed coal-mining valleys with their associated iron, steel and tinplate industries, and the great industrial ports of Cardiff and of Swansea. In all its aspects – its threateningly 'foreign' language, hybrid culture, proletarian character, militant socialist politics etc. – this region, the product of the late-nineteenth-century boom that had turned south Wales into one of the great cosmopolitan industrial centres of the world, was a nightmarish dystopia to Saunders Lewis, as it was to the cultural constituency he represented.[4]

Born and raised in a prosperous middle-class Welsh family in Wallasey, Liverpool, Lewis (1893–1985) was the most brilliant member of one of the first generations of Welsh-speaking writers and scholars, mostly from a humble rural or semi-industrial background in the north and west of Wales, to have been made proudly aware at university of the grandeur and antiquity of a unique Welsh literary tradition extending back some fifteen hundred years. This tradition was perceived as being the very backbone of Welsh national identity, but it was clearly under serious threat – from within, in the curiously mixed populist and bourgeois form of the religious Nonconformity which was the drab legacy of the nineteenth century, and (much more catastrophically) from without, in the shape of the alien anglophone culture that industrialisation had brought to the south. It was perhaps this crisis mentality that energised and sponsored the twentieth-century renaissance of Welsh-language writing, a remarkable cultural phenomenon (broadly comparable, say, to the Southern Renaissance in the USA), which was at its height in 1938 when Saunders Lewis delivered his lecture.

Given his cultural allegiance, it's not surprising that Lewis draws the lecture to a close by saying, 'I conclude then that there is not a separate literature that is Anglo-Welsh' (p. 13). His carefully chosen point of comparison is Anglo-Irish literature, the autonomy and national authenticity of which is based, he argues, on four features absent from the Anglo-Welsh case: first, a 'separate world from the industrial civilization of England' (p. 7); second, a form of English that is idiomatically and rhythmically distinct from that of England; third, writers like Yeats who consciously 'write for [their] own race'; and, fourth, writers who (again in

Yeats's phrase) were 'doing something for nationalism'. By contrast, 'the growth of Anglo-Welsh writing in recent years is the inevitable reflection of the undirected drifting of Welsh national life. It will go on, becoming less and less incompletely English, unless there is a revival of the moral qualities of the Welsh people' (p. 14). As for the most famous of Anglo-Welsh writers, his case is dismissed with a benignity that is more apparent than real: 'Mr Dylan Thomas is obviously an equipped writer, but there is nothing hyphenated [i.e. Anglo-Welsh] about him. He belongs to the English' (p. 5).

R. S. Thomas (born in 1913) was an almost exact contemporary of Dylan Thomas (born in 1914), but he began publishing almost a decade later than the younger man. At more or less the same time (i.e. immediately following the Second World War) R. S. Thomas went, spurred by a sudden impulse, on a pilgrimage to meet Saunders Lewis, a man whom he did not know and had never even met. R.S., no callow impressionable youth but a man of thirty-two, had already embarked on a cultural rite of passage. Having been brought up by English-speaking (and indeed in some respects anti-Welsh) parents in the busy ferry port of Holyhead, on the overwhelmingly Welsh-speaking island of Anglesey, he had, toward the end of the war, begun to learn Welsh shortly before moving to serve as vicar of Manafon, a rural upland parish in mid-Wales close to the English border. It was from there that he travelled to Saunders Lewis's home near Aberystwyth. From Lewis, R. S. Thomas seems to have received a kind of benediction both on his cultural 'conversion' and on his work. In his turn, Thomas was, after a fashion, both paying very personal tribute to Saunders Lewis's intellectual pre-eminence and, in more general terms, acknowledging the primacy of Welsh-language culture over the Anglo-Welsh. These cross-cultural ties mark him off from the pre-war generation of Dylan Thomas – who, as a young writer, made a pilgrimage to Aberystwyth in like spirit to pay homage not to Saunders Lewis but to the brilliantly bilious Caradoc Evans, the bête noir of Welsh speakers ever since the publication in 1915 of his scarifying fictional portrait of rural Nonconformist Wales, *My People*. The ties re-established also show that R. S. Thomas belonged to the group of Welsh writers in the English language – prominent among them being the novelist Emyr Humphreys

– who, coming first to prominence in the post-war years, set out to form a common front with Welsh-language writers. And although both R. S. Thomas and Emyr Humphreys continued to write primarily in English, they can both be regarded as the literary sons of Saunders Lewis, just as Dylan Thomas and most of his inter-war generation can be labelled the sons of Caradoc.[5] Humphreys's late acknowledgement of this came in the form of his poem 'S.L. i R.S. (An Imagined Greeting)'. It is keyed from the outset to Thomas's remark, in his own notable poetic tribute to Lewis, that 'poets/ Are dangerous: they undermine/ The state', and it includes a memorable image (modelled on Humphreys's own recollections of his earliest meeting with Thomas) of Saunders Lewis's first encounter with the aspiring young poet in the early 1950s, when

> You arrived at an unexpected
> Hour, emerged
> From that Austin Seven
> Like an ostrich stretching
> His legs as he abandons
> The mechanised egg
> Eyes washed in primal light
> Unused to blinking.[6]

Recognising R.S.'s own well-advertised anguish over his inability to write poetry in Welsh (for him an acquired language rather than a mother tongue),[7] Humphreys concludes his poem by switching to that language as he celebrates Thomas's prominent public support for the young law-breakers of Cymdeithas yr Iaith Gymraeg, conclusive proof, Humphreys suggests, that 'Yn dy galon y Gymraeg a orfu' (in your heart, it was the Welsh language that won the day).

To write in English while remaining a disciple of Saunders Lewis was, of course, to be impaled on a painfully obvious contradiction, since Lewis regarded English as the language of self-alienation and the tongue that threatened the Welsh language (and hence the Welsh nation) with extinction. In some of the early essays of R. S. Thomas, however, there are unexpected moments of hope: 'There are signs now that the mantle of writers like T. Gwynn Jones, W. J. Gruffydd [two of the major figures of the modern Welsh literary renaissance] is falling not upon the younger Welsh writers, but upon those of us who express ourselves in the English tongue. We must not grow heady with this distinction and forget that we also are Welshmen. Ireland has contrived to remain Irish despite her use of English, and there is no overwhelming reason why we should not succeed also, provided we can get rid of that foolish epithet Anglo-Welsh' (*SP*, pp. 29–40). Strictly speaking, this is an heretical view that Thomas quickly abjured, but it could be argued that it continued, throughout his career, to be operative on the level of his actual writing even though he notoriously repudiated it in all his statements, insisting with ever increasing fervour that it was impossible to remain a Welsh writer while writing in English. One of the interesting paradoxes of his case is that while in his later pronouncements, over the decades, he consistently dismissed the possibility of a Welsh literature in English, his poetry not infrequently fulfilled three of the four conditions that Saunders Lewis had concluded (from the Anglo-Irish example) were necessary for the construction of a non-English literature in that language. First, Thomas confined himself to the non-industrial (and therefore supposedly non-English) regions of Wales; second, he clearly produced a significant body of his poetry for, and sometimes deliberately addressed it to, the Welsh people; and thirdly, his was a nationalist writing in the very spirit of Lewis's own brand of cultural and political nationalism at the core of which lay the belief that Welsh alone was the authentic language of Wales.[8]

There is undoubtedly a sense in which the influence on Thomas's poetry, if not of Saunders Lewis himself, then of the cultural ideology with which he was so eminently associated, was very widely pervasive. A simple example is provided by the poetry of the late 1940s through the 1950s. This is the period when, as we have seen in chapter 3, Thomas first came to prominence largely through the eye-catching poems he addressed to the endlessly enigmatic Iago Prytherch as a composite figure of the Welsh uplands farmer. The flatly contradictory elements that help make the unpredictable portrait so compelling – rustic, boor, child of nature, stoical laborer, elemental man, degenerate brute etc. – are, as by now is common knowledge, partly the mirror image of the confused expectations Thomas had brought with him to Manafon. And these, in turn, had to some extent been subsequently intensified by the concept, assiduously promoted by Welsh-language literary culture for almost a century, of a cultivated rural *gwerin*. This was believed to form the bedrock of national life, and was regarded as being the antithesis in quality of those deracinés, the hybrid and degenerate industrial Anglophone proletariat. When Thomas sees Iago 'fixed in his chair/ Motionless, except when he leans to gob in the fire', and concludes that 'There is something frightening in the vacancy of his mind' (*CP*, p. 4), he does so against the background of his earlier (1945) belief that 'the health and wealth of a country depends upon its possession of a sturdy, flourishing peasantry'. 'Here and there among the upland people', he had then been convinced, 'are poets, musicians, penillion singers, and men possessed of a rare personality' (*SP*, p. 23).

Once one is alerted to the poetry's internal connections – infinitely subtle, complex, even elusive though they sometimes are – with this whole socio-cultural context, then it seems that they constitute the very warp and woof not only of Thomas's treatment of Iago and his kind, but of all his poetry. Even the politically induced hatred he developed of the English language itself paradoxically nurtured the tortured passion of his creative appreciation, as a poet, of the incomparable range and power English possessed as a literary medium. The contempt he shared with Saunders Lewis for the moral spinelessness and genial fudging of his complaisant fellow-countrymen was translated into the terrible clarity of syllabically weighted utterance in his late, great, religious poetry:

> I had looked forward
> to old age as a time
> of quietness, a time to draw
> my horizons about me,
> to watch memories ripening
> in the sunlight of a walled garden.
> But there is the void
> over my head and the distance
> within that the tireless signals
> come from. (*CP*, p. 388)

Underlying this spare syntax of unsparing honesty is also, perhaps, a memory of the qualities of the Welsh-language poetry of the great medieval period, as identified by Saunders Lewis and others. These qualities were not the supposedly 'bardic' ones of visionary rapture, torrential eloquence and rhapsody, but rather those that Lewis liked to characterise as 'classical' and 'aristocratic', namely the epigrammatic terseness of authoritatively considered, masterful expression.

\* \* \*

Although Thomas was extensively and deeply influenced by his learned experience of Welsh-language culture whose chief conscience and custodian was, for him, Saunders Lewis, this is not the place to embark on a comprehensive study of this endlessly branching subject.[9] Instead, I propose to confine myself to some of the poems Thomas openly and directly addressed to a Wales that he viewed very much through the lens of Lewis's writing. There are enough of these to constitute a significant subdivision, or genre, of his poetry, randomly scattered though they originally were throughout the several volumes he published over a period of twenty years or so. This kind of writing was first discernible in the 1950s, and it reached its controversial conclusion in 1974, when Thomas published a group of twelve blistering pieces. The sardonic title he gave to this chapbook, *What is a Welshman?*, was clearly meant to imply that a Welshman was a pretty bizarre phenomenon, resembling more an inanimate thing than a real person.

This stiletto-slim collection is worth briefly considering, not least because it tends to be studiously ignored by the many readers who find it too bludgeoningly offensive to mention. It opens with an attack on the south Wales industrial society, and coalfield culture, which has for more than a century been at the sacred heart of the (often sentimental) self-perception of anglophone Wales. Like the sleeper in some medieval dream poem, Thomas lies 'on the black hills/ black with the dust of coal/ not yet mined' and enters the realm of visionary nightmare, experiencing, in surrealistic images, the horror of a bastardised world.[10] His language of repugnance recalls Saunders Lewis's notorious poem 'Y

Dilyw, 1939' (The Deluge, 1939), where the south Wales of the depression years was imaged as a place where 'All flesh has festered its way on the face of the earth'. 'Here once was Wales', remarked Lewis with obvious distaste, surveying a proletariat supine in its 'culture of grease'.[11] The social plight of this disorientated people was for him, as it was for Thomas, a symptom of the moral decay that accompanied the loss of the Welsh language. Thomas draws his own poem to a close by imagining the barbed welcome extended by valleys people to one like himself, who comes to them 'with a language/ filched from the dictionary/ of the tribes'. They protest that they await his sermon:

> and a pulpit grew up under my feet
> and I climbed into it and
> it was the cage
> of the mine-shaft down down down
> to preach to the lost souls
> of the coal-face reminding
> how green is the childhood
> of a glib people taunting
> them with the abandonment
> of the national for the class struggle.

This passage culminates with R. S. Thomas's hostile response to the anti-nationalist and pro-British socialism that dominated south Wales for over a century. But it begins with a wry, self-mocking allusion to the legendary occasion when, as St David (the patron saint of Wales) was attempting to address a huge congregation at Llanddewi-brefi in the open air, the ground rose up under his feet to provide him with a natural pulpit. By contrast, R. S. Thomas's elevation proves to be a literal letdown, and the self-mockery that infuses both this opening phrase and the whole of the quoted passage makes for a much more complex political statement than is usually realised. While not for an instant questioning the truth of his message, Thomas has an eye here for the futility and absurdity of his own prim sermonising, and seems to see the helpless distance at which history has placed him from his listeners.

The controlled pathos of this passage is, then, a measure of the tensile strength of its political vision, but in other poems in this collection the pathos that is unconsciously elicited is simply a sign of weakness. Thomas's dream (in 'He is sometimes contrary') of ancient battles and mythological birds is full of the wistfulness of felt impotence; the piece 'He agrees with Henry Ford' ends with a wildly grotesque image, as if his imagination had suddenly become dyslexic, in which 'Cilgwri's ousel/ on my ramshackle aerial/ keeps the past's goal/ against the balls of tomorrow'(CP, p. 261). Elsewhere in the volume his anger, too, breeds only a weak sarcasm of weaker cliché ('clerks undress/ the secretaries with/ their lean eyes' (CP, p. 255)), although there are occasional moments of reverberative power: 'Anything to/ sell? cries the tourist/ to the native rummaging among/ the remnants of his self-respect' (CP, p. 255).

In the last poem in the volume, however, the unevenness of tone, and of quality, in the writing seems functional and expressive – as if the ferocity of feeling that possesses the speaker makes him careless of taste and heedless of decorum. Accompanying this is a contemptuous sense of the banality of the means by which cultural catastrophe has actually been effected. The subject is the Welsh language and the way it has been 'sold' for social advancement. 'The decree went forth/ to destroy the language' – to describe the clauses relating to the Welsh language in the 1536 Act of Union in these terms is also, of course, to introduce Herod and the Massacre of the Innocents and, when this is realised, the concluding lines of the poem are reinforced by another dark surge of meaning:

> The
> industrialists came, burrowing
> in the corpse of a nation
> for its congealed blood. I was
> born into the squalor of
> their feeding and sucked their speech
> in with my mother's
> infected milk, so that whatever
> I throw up now is still theirs. (CP, p. 262)

That use of the vulgar colloquialism for vomiting is all the more powerful since the linguistically fastidious Thomas so rarely uses slang, and all his resentment at his early helpless and humiliating dependence upon his domineering mother (feelings evident elsewhere in his writings, as we shall see in later chapters) are here channelled into, and focused in, his attitude towards his 'foreign' mother-tongue. It should also be remembered that Thomas's actual place of birth was Cardiff, the city that was very largely the creation, in the late nineteenth century, of the mine owners who opened up the south Wales coalfield. As for the title of the poem, 'It hurts him to think' means exactly what, with almost brutal plainness, it says. Referring to himself in the third person as he frequently did – in this case conveying in the process a stark sense of self-alienation – Thomas makes it clear that it isn't only the thought of how 'the decree went forth' that hurts, but the very process of thinking itself, inseparable as it is in his tormented case from the hated English language.

The poem is all the more noteworthy because in it a Juvenalian R. S. Thomas succeeds in making poetic capital out of the very coarseness of feeling that vitiates several of the other pieces in the collection, and it could be that this coarseness has its origins in the cultural and political disappointments that had ushered in the seventies. After all, the 1960s had for the most part been, for Thomas, a relatively hopeful period of political turbulence, during which the bulk of his poetry about the 'matter of Wales' was written. Indeed, in order to understand that poetry properly one needs to know something about the important events that created the political climate of the decade.[12]

In October 1965, many years of nationwide protest in Wales came to a climax when, as noted already, Liverpool Corporation insisted on flooding the Tryweryn valley in mid-Wales, which had been home to the Welsh-speaking community of Capel Celyn, in order to create the reservoir of Llyn Celyn that would service the city's industrial expansion. Embittered reaction to this development included the blowing up of pipelines in the vicinity of the dam, but the large-scale protests were mostly confined to non-violent demonstrations led by the Welsh-speaking intelligentsia. These events helped politicise a whole generation of young Welsh men and women, regardless of language, and contributed to the formation in the late 1960s of a new nationalist consciousness that manifested itself in both the political and cultural sectors. In particular, a new group of English-language writers came to prominence who, like the

R. S. Thomas of the late 1940s, began to look to Welsh-language culture for inspiration and for political orientation.

Welsh-language poets have traditionally played a politically active part in protecting their culture, and so they did at the time of Tryweryn, being prominently involved in the campaigning while also using their poetry either to advertise or to explore the issues that were at stake. R. S. Thomas's poem 'Reservoirs' is itself an English contribution to that significant body of literature, but it takes the form not so much of protest as of a bitter elegy for the suicide of a culture. The line breaks form precipices where Thomas's mind pauses to look down with horror into new depths of moral despair: 'Reservoirs that are the subconscious/ Of a people, troubled far down/ With gravestones, chapels, villages even;/ The serenity of their expression/ Revolts me' (*CP*, p. 194). Tryweryn becomes his synecdoche for the whole Welsh geopolitical landscape, as Thomas sees mirrored in it the widespread signs of the self-mutilation of a people: 'the smashed faces/ Of the farms with the stone trickle/ Of their tears down the hills' side'. And central to Thomas's dark meditations is his sense of being an internal exile, as noted in chapter 2 – of being a man, in the words of J. R. Jones, the most important Welsh cultural philosopher of the period, whose country has left *him*, rather than he it: 'Where can I go, then, from the smell/ Of decay, from the putrefying of a dead/ Nation?'

The darkness of tone of the poem matches the undertone of pessimism in the historic radio lecture the elderly Saunders Lewis had given in February 1962.[13] He argued that the possibly terminal decline of the Welsh language was not an historical accident, but the rapidly accelerating result of deliberate English government policy. This policy had first been adopted in the 1536 Act of Union and had thereafter been consistently implemented by means that included the mental colonisation by England of the Welsh people. Central still to this ongoing process was the refusal to grant official recognition to Welsh as a language of law and of public administration. Lewis warned that by the beginning of the twenty-first century, Welsh would cease as a living language if this situation was not immediately challenged and changed. The combination in this apocalyptic lecture of cool argument, searing prophecy and astute political analysis

had a galvanising effect on his younger Welsh listeners. He had simultaneously provided them with an urgent cause, a powerful motive and
a pragmatically precise yet revolutionary programme for action. By the
end of the year a group of young university students and Plaid Cymru
activists had formed Cymdeithas yr Iaith Gymraeg, advocate of direct
non-violent action in pursuing its aims. By the end of the decade, Cymdeithas yr Iaith (by then led by prison-tested heroes and heroines) could
look back on a remarkable programme of non-violent activities that had
involved extensive, well-supported campaigns of law breaking designed
to gain official state recognition (and status) for the Welsh language.

'The political tradition of the centuries, the whole economic tendency
of the present age, are against the survival of the Welsh language', Lewis
had sadly conceded in his radio broadcast. 'Nothing can change that
except determination, will, struggle, sacrifice, effort'.[14] Warmly though
R. S. Thomas admired and supported the Cymdeithas yr Iaith campaigners, his poetry tended to concentrate broodingly, almost obsessively, on the unpromising facts of the contemporary Welsh situation.
He saw the hopes for Wales he shared with Lewis being everyday doubly
confounded – by the ever-deepening inroads made by the English, and
by the ever-weakening moral resolve of the Welsh people in general to
withstand the process of anglicisation. As noted in chapter 3, his nationalist poetry of the 1960s – and earlier – is haunted by images of invasion
and of internal collapse: 'We've nothing to offer you', he says, speaking
as 'A Welshman to Any Tourist', 'no deserts/ Except the waste of thought/
Forming from mind's erosion' (CP, p. 65). The tone of the observation is
typical. Harshly sarcastic, it speaks of a deep hidden hurt, of loathing
laced with self-loathing, of a mood of settled political depression, of a
feeling of humiliating impotence. It is this particular kind of raw sarcasm
– not a controlled explosion of savagery, but rather the by-product of an
implosion of dark feelings – that recurs in Thomas's poetry on the subject
of Wales. Much rarer are the instances of irony – those occasions when
he is able to maintain an inner detachment that comes across at the linguistic level as a poise which enables him to indulge in a kind of cultural
double entendre: 'You can come in', he airily concedes in 'Welcome',
'You can come a long way;/ We can't stop you./ . . . But you won't be

inside;/ You must stop at the bar,/ The old bar of speech' (*CP*, p. 134). This is plain enough, but prepares the way for the nice equivocation that follows: 'We have learnt your own/ Language, but don't/ Let it take you in'. The sentence turns on its polite axis to warn the outsider that to insist on admittance is also to invite deception.

A year before Saunders Lewis's lecture, Thomas published a poem that included his most fiercely Yeatsian dismissal of his fellow countrymen: 'I find/ This hate's for my own kind,/ For men of the Welsh race/ Who brood with dark face/ Over their thin navel/ To learn what to sell'. The prevalence of these and related sentiments in his subsequent poetry came to irritate not only the English-speaking Welsh but also those Welsh speakers who were heartened by the achievement of Cymdeithas yr Iaith and the brief spectacular successes of Plaid Cymru, inaugurated in 1966. In 1972, the young Dafydd Elis Thomas, himself soon to become a Plaid Cymru MP, voiced severe criticism in 'The Image of Wales in R. S. Thomas's poetry', an essay referenced in chapter 3.[15] Thomas was accused of 'contrasting mythical past with realistic present' (p. 62); of a 'middle-class contempt for the ordinary working-class people of the industrial south-east' (p. 63); of an 'elitism' involving 'the elevation of a small group who have a historical sense' (p. 64); and finally of reducing Wales to an 'image of death' (p. 64). Dafydd Elis Thomas illustrated his argument with pointed quotations from the poetry, and ended by tartly observing that, 'for my generation's poets, being Welsh is not a cause for depression' (p. 66).

There are grounds for supposing that the publication of *What is a Welshman?* in 1974 was not unconnected with Dafydd Elis Thomas's attack two years previously. The sour venom with which the poet repeated some of his bleak images of Wales in this collection may, therefore, have been in part a response to what he probably saw as his cocky young critic's callow optimism. However, as the poem 'To pay for his keep' (*CP*, p. 257) shows, R. S. Thomas also had the Investiture of 1969 at the back of his troubled mind. This was the grandiloquent ceremony, held at Caernarfon Castle, at which Charles, as eldest son of the English monarch, was declared Prince of Wales. People of Thomas's persuasion believed, not without very good reason, that the whole event had been

cynically arranged and brilliantly stage-managed by the Labour government of the day (in which virulently anti-nationalist Welshmen held key
positions) to strengthen and mobilise the British sentiments of the majority of the Welsh people. And, whether this had been intended or not, it
certainly did happen. Moreover, the Welsh-speaking community was
itself deeply divided in its reactions to the event, split between fierce
opposition (leading in particular cases to acts of violence) and qualified
support (on the hopeful supposition that Charles – who had learnt a little
Welsh – might yet turn committed advocate for Wales and its language).
Tension grew as the Investiture approached, and the authorities were
then to take advantage of the threat and the reality of violence to instigate
anti-terrorist measures that included some highly dubious but very effective police action.

Thomas found confirmation in all this both of his pessimistic assessment of the popular Welsh character and of his suspicion that the British
state would use means foul and fair, crude and subtle, to retain control
of the country. From the obvious pun in its title onward, 'To pay for his
keep' sets out to delineate the scene at Caernarfon in crudely distinct
terms that make the poem the verbal equivalent of one of the political
cartoons of the day. Thomas enters the mind of the young prince (mocked
by the popular Welsh activist and folk singer Dafydd Iwan as 'Carlo')
in order to show the Machiavellianism of the ruling mentality. Through
Charles's eyes, he sees the absurd collection of 'respectables' ('rigid with
imagined/ loyalty'), the mean Caernarfon streets 'filthy with/ dog shit',
and the expensive charade held in the huge castle, that ostentatious
symbol of occupying power constructed by Edward I, hammer of the
Welsh as much as of the Scots, which the politically subtle Charles de-
plores as unnecessary. 'A few medals/ would do now', the prince muses,
underlining R. S. Thomas's view that England's little butty had always
put an obligingly low price on its obedience and loyalty to the English
throne. The prince fills the foreground of the poem, but in the distance
and beneath his notice is 'that far hill/ in the sun with the long line/ of
its trees climbing/ it like a procession/ of young people, young as himself'. This is a shift of moral and political perspective effected by a shift
of physical perspective – a device deftly suited to the occasion, since the

Investiture had been deliberately conceived of as an inspiring ocular spectacle and actually became a great seductive television spectacular, the modern equivalent of a triumphal royal procession. And in that mention of trees on the far hill beyond the 'city' walls of Caernarfon there may also be, of course, just a hint of Calvary to suggest the sacrifices made for the language by the young people of Cymdeithas yr Iaith and others.

*What Is a Welshman?* was, then, a postscript to Thomas's nationalist writing of the previous decade, and it placed a question mark over the optimism generated by the political culture of the period. Thereafter, Thomas wrote very few poems directly on the nationalist question. When asked about this, he sometimes became mischievously flippant, remarking dismissively that he had wrung that particular dishcloth dry. Left to his own devices, on the other hand, he volunteered a much more complex and likely answer. In 1966, Thomas became vicar of Aberdaron, a tiny seaside village on the very tip of the 'remote' Llŷn peninsula, which was part of the rapidly eroding heartland of Welsh-language culture. For him, it was the culmination of a lifelong quest for the 'true' Wales he had first glimpsed, as an English-speaking boy in Holyhead, when he gazed across Anglesey and the Menai Straits at the magnificent profile of the mountains of Eryri, Snowdonia, in distant Gwynedd. And although Thomas soon found that in Llŷn he was in the very front line of the battle against the anglicisation of Welsh culture and the commercial despoliation of the Welsh landscape, he also found that his daily involvement in the life of the Welsh language made him less anxious to make its fate the subject of his poetry – although he was no less determined to fight for its survival. After his retirement, in 1978, to live a few miles from Aberdaron, he continued to be very actively involved in campaigning for various causes – CND, Cymdeithas yr Iaith, environmental protection – but his poetry became almost exclusively one of spiritual search, inspired in part by the great age of the geological formations of the Llŷn peninsula.

\* \* \*

That, then would seem to be the end of the story, except that in 1987 R. S. Thomas published a collection called *Welsh Airs*, in which for the first time he gathered most of the poems he'd written about Wales into a single volume. Appearing eight years after the Welsh electorate had rejected a proposal to establish a national assembly, the volume was produced partly to educate a new, young generation, ignorant even of immediate past history, in the politics of the Welsh situation. To read these poems now is to realise how much things have changed over the forty years and more since most of them were written, the most dramatic development, of course, being the establishing of a National Assembly for Wales following the reversal in 1997 of the 1979 anti-devolution vote. Indeed, Thomas's politico-cultural map of Wales seems almost to have been reversed by recent historical developments. Rural Wales is well on its way to being lost to Welsh-language culture, thanks to a massive in-migration of English speakers, mostly from England, whose degree of identification with Wales remains a troublingly unknown quantity. Indus-trial Wales is no more, but in the remnants of its culture can be found English speakers who have fashioned an authentically Welsh identity out of the industrial history of the valleys. In and around Cardiff – where 'a girl relieved herself/ of me' and where there is 'a stone/ doorstep I played/ on a while in a brief/ ignorance of where I belonged'[16] – there has been an extraordinary increase in the number of Welsh-medium schools. By the 1990s, Margaret Thatcher, a rampant English nationalist, had managed to accomplish what the Welsh nationalists had failed to achieve – a feeling among the majority of Welsh people, deeply alienated by her unpopular policies, in favour of a separate Assembly. And, since it has been established, it has steadily increased its limited powers.

This quick socio-political portrait of Wales is not prelude to an attack, à la Dafydd Elis Thomas, on R. S. Thomas's supposedly grotesque mis-representation of the contemporary scene. Rather, it is intended to high-light what Thomas himself wants us to see – the challenging conserva-tivism of the poems defiantly reprinted in *Welsh Airs*, poems that advertise the poet's loyalty to the cultural philosophy he learned in the 1940s under the tutelage of Saunders Lewis. Here, for the first time between two covers, can be found all those controversial elements in his nationalist poetry listed by Tony Bianchi: 'a cherishing [of] all those positions definitive . . . of the ethnic resurgence of the Welsh-speaking middle class; an hostility towards science and urban life as un-Welsh; an equivalent elevation of rural values; an essentialist or ahistorical concept of nationhood, based on a selective view of the past and notions of an organic tradition; a belief in the importance of an elite in defending this ideal, of which the Welsh language is an embodiment; a view of the English-speaking Welsh as alienated and needing to align themselves with these values to overcome this alienation; and above all, the elevation of culture, literature and even "taste" as surrogate religion which informs these convictions'.[17]

When brought together in a single collection, however, the poems on these themes trace out new and interesting patterns of interconnection. Here, certainly, are those passages and poems in which Thomas jeeringly parodies the crudely pally vernacular of the Anglo-Welsh, but along with them is included 'Welsh', the piece in which he adopts that very same vernacular in order to pillory himself: 'Why must I write so?/ I'm Welsh, see:/ A real Cymro,/. . .Only the one loss,/ I can't speak my own/ Language – Iesu,/ All those good words;/ And I outside them' (CP, p. 129). Behind this, and perhaps at the very root of his conversion to cultural nationalism, is a hatred of his snobbishly anti-Welsh mother, and an obsessive desire to 'accuse the womb/ That bore me'. His nationalist poems are that accusation, and to see that intimately personal animus in them is also to notice anew when, as in 'Border Blues', Thomas singles a woman out to represent the degeneracy of Wales: 'Olwen teasing a smile/ Of bright flowers out of the grass,/ Olwen in nylons'; 'the ladies from the council houses:/ Blue eyes and Birmingham yellow/ Hair and the ritual murder of vowels' (CP, p. 69).

To personalise Thomas's nationalist poems in this and in other ways is to recover important dimensions of their meaning. 'I must,' he tells those council house ladies in 'Border Blues', 'go the way of my fathers/ Despite the loneli – you might say rudeness' (CP, p. 69). The sudden, self-protective adjustment of meaning, mid-word, is significant. His nationalist poems are palimpsests in which the underlying loneliness intermittently shows through the overwritten rudeness. That is not, however, to say that he yearns to be reconciled with his people. These poems are full of a sense that isolation is, in the contemporary socio-political climate, the necessary precondition for integrity. This is very evident in 'A Welshman at St James' Park' where, as noted in the previous chapter, he refuses the invitation, inscribed in the public notices, to become 'one of the public', and refuses 'to admire birds/ That have been seduced from wildness by/ Bread they are pelted with' (*CP*, p. 165). But it is equally a feature of the portrait he paints, under the title 'A Lecturer', of the great Welsh-language poet Gwenallt, who is described as an insignificant-looking 'little man,/ Sallow,/ Keeping close to the wall/ Of life'. This exterior conceals and defends, however, an inner sanctum of genius reinforced by moral courage: 'Watch him,/ As with short steps he goes./ Not dangerous?/ He has been in gaol' (*CP*, p. 138). Here the syntax itself involves the reader in a double-take, as the imperative changes its meaning from an invitation simply to look at this slightly ludicrous figure to a mocking warning to keep a wary eye on him.

The syntax of several of these poems is, in fact, a reliable guide to the deep structure of Thomas's relationship to Wales. The eight uses of the connective 'but' in the first two passages of the sequence 'Border Blues' shows up the binary pattern of his thinking, his dependence on the dynamics of contrast – particularly between the Welsh present and the Welsh past. There is, indeed, a great deal of the Romantic ironist in Thomas, but he is at his best when he avoids the temptation – which is obviously strong in him – to play a sentimentally simple ideal off against a debased reality: 'A Line from St David's', for instance, is interesting because it dramatises, very effectively, the way Thomas has been surprised into uncharacteristically garrulous affirmations by the fresh, untainted beauty of the ancient Pembrokeshire landscape, so that he can believe, for once, 'That the old currents are in the grass,/ Though rust has becalmed the plough' (*CP*, p. 123). As for those many poems in which he fiercely attacks contemporary Wales, the problem with them as poetry is not, as some of his critics have claimed, that they are somehow politically unfair, but rather that their rhetoric of anger does tend to grow monotonous. There is also the unevenness of quality that in Thomas's case seems endemic to this emotionally heightened form of writing. Within the space of a very few lines, such as the following four from 'Afforestation', a poem can disconcert the reader by changing from crude invective to an image in which anger and anguish are strikingly fused: 'Thin houses for dupes,/ Pages of pale trash./ A world that has gone sour/ With spruce' (*CP*, p.130). The whole of 'Toast' divides cleanly along this fault line, with the overblown and overworked conceit of national decay in the first ten and a half lines eventually giving way to a wearily flat question that sets up, and sets off, the epigrammatic conclusion: 'What shall I say/ to a people to whom provincialism/ is a reasonable asking-price/ for survival? I salute your/ astuteness and drink to your future/ from a wine-glass brimming with acid rain' (*WA*, p. 37).

In *Welsh Airs*, R. S. Thomas repeatedly returns to the version of pastoral he particularly favours, namely the harsh political anti-pastoral. Implicit in this is a bitter satire of the pastoral of rural idyll, as is clear in 'Looking at Sheep':

> Yes, I know. They are like primroses;
> Their ears are the colour of the stems
> Of primroses; and their eyes –
> Two halves of a nut.
> > But images
> Like this are for sheer fancy
> To play with. Seeing how Wales fares
> Now, I will attend rather
> To things as they are: to green grass
> That is not ours; to visitors
> Buying us up. (*CP*, p. 151)

As was pointed out in chapter 2, English Romantic literature (think of Wordsworth climbing Snowdon or visiting Tintern) played its part in developing the Welsh tourist trade by conveniently overlooking the country's society and culture in order to reduce 'Wales' to a gloriously inviting empty landscape. It is therefore appropriate that Thomas should use his own poetry to reclaim, repopulate and repoliticise the countryside – in short, to *see* 'how Wales fares now'. He also renames it, using the indigenous names that recall the country's history – Traeth Maelgwn, Hafod Lom, Hyddgen and Llanrhaeadr-ym-Mochnant, this last being

the name of the little hamlet where in 1588 Bishop William Morgan produced the magnificent Welsh Bible, which for centuries has been the bible
(in the secular sense) of Welsh writers: 'The smooth words/ Over which
his mind flowed/ Have become an heirloom' (*WA*, p. 32).

'Welsh airs' can also, clearly, be read as 'Welsh heirs', and the whole
volume then becomes a study in sharply contrasting applications of that
term, with 'The Patriot' placed near 'The Provincial', and versions of the
past ironically shadowing a present that sees a people 'quarrelling for
crumbs/ Under the table, or gnawing the bones/ Of a dead culture' (*CP*,
p. 36). But even as it actually stands, the title of the volume is politically
pointed. 'Welsh Airs' is a phrase that brings to mind genteel Victorian
collections of melodies from 'the land of song' – the sentimental epithet
by which an anxiously ingratiating Wales made (and perhaps still makes)
itself respectable in the eyes of the English world. During the course of
*his* collection, Thomas plays several variations on this politico-musical
theme. At one point, for instance, he recalls a familiar Welsh hymn's
affirmation that in heaven the golden harp's song will continue forever,
only to sharply change key by observing that 'the strings are broken,
and time sets/ The barbed wire in their place' (*CP*, p. 72). Elsewhere,
Welsh people sing hymns that are 'not music/ so much as the sound of
a nation/ rending itself, fierce with all the promise/ of a beauty that
might have been theirs' (*CP*, p. 465).

Another musical term appears in 'Fugue for Ann Griffiths', the title
of his splendid, long, concluding poem about one of the greatest of Welsh
hymn writers. Ann has traditionally been regarded as the heroine of
Welsh Nonconformity (although the Methodists had not yet split from
the Anglican Church in her time), and indeed Thomas himself appreciates
the way her hymns blow the dust off the Welsh language '"week by week
in chapel after chapel"' (*CP*, p. 471). Yet the terms in which he celebrates
her tend to remove her from the tender care of those decaying chapels
that he elsewhere so mistrusts, those grim killjoy institutions whose
'varnish/ Wears well and will go/ With most coffins'. He depicts her as
a spirit in rapture and a pilgrim soul, 'her face, figure-head of a ship/
outward bound' (*CP*, p. 471). It is an unorthodox view of Ann, slightly
reminiscent of the one offered by Saunders Lewis in a famous public

lecture when he, too, intrigued Nonconformists by removing her from their charge and placing her in the more exalted spiritual company of the great European mystics. His lecture was an inspirational event, and it could well be of such occasions that R. S. Thomas was thinking when he wrote in 'The Patriot': 'Those, who saw/ For the first time that small figure/ With the Welsh words leaving his lips/ As quietly as doves on an errand/ Of peace-making, could not imagine/ The fierceness of their huge entry/ At the ear's porch' (*CP*, p. 150).

Unidentified though he is in 'A Patriot', Saunders Lewis is the openly avowed subject of another poem in *Welsh Airs*, a piece that is important enough to need quotation in full:

> And he dared them;
> Dared them to grow old and bitter
> As he. He kept his pen clean
> By burying it in their fat
> Flesh. He was ascetic and Wales
> His diet. He lived off the harsh fare
> Of her troubles, worn yet heady
> At moments with the poets' wine.
>
> A recluse, then; himself
> His hermitage? Unhabited
> He moved among us; would have led
> To rebellion. Small as he was
> He towered, the trigger of his mind
> Cocked, ready to let fly with his scorn. (*CP*, p. 466)

'Unhabited' seems to bring with it its sonic shadow 'Uninhabited', an accurate description of a man who, born in Wallasey, never fully felt at home in the Wales whose cultural identity he championed with such fierce passion. And such a doubling reinforces one's sense that the Saunders Lewis of this penetrating portrait can be seen as the alter ego of Thomas himself in old age (as will be further confirmed in chapter 6 of this study). Apart from physical size, the details fit both characters in almost equal respect. Of course, the likeness here to Thomas is entirely unintentional, yet it is by no means fortuitous. He had, after all, for almost half a century, instinctively developed his relationship to Wales along the demanding, unyielding lines laid down in both the life and the work of the extra-ordinary man he first met at the end of the Second World War. This particular poem, therefore, amply confirms the impression left by *Welsh Airs* as a whole when it shows us that R. S. Thomas was, indeed, in many important respects, Lewis's [Anglo-]Welsh heir: a true Son of Saunders.

## Notes

¹ 'Is there an Anglo-Welsh Literature?' (Cardiff: Cardiff section of the Guild of Graduates of the University of Wales, 1939).

² See Alun R. Jones and Gwyn Thomas (eds), *Presenting Saunders Lewis* (Cardiff: University of Wales Press, 1973); Bruce Griffiths, *Saunders Lewis* (Cardiff: University of Wales Press, Writers of Wales series, 1979).

³ For the history of the English-language literature of Wales, see M. Wynn Thomas (ed.), *Welsh Writing in English* (Cardiff: University of Wales Press, 2003); the most attractive introduction to the writers of Dylan Thomas's generation is Glyn Jones, *The Dragon Has Two Tongues* (London: Dent, 1968; revised edition (ed. Tony Brown), Cardiff: University of Wales Press, 2001).

⁴ The history of Wales during this period is covered in Kenneth O. Morgan, *Rebirth of a Nation: Wales, 1880–1980* (Oxford: Clarendon Press, 1981).

⁵ For Emyr Humphreys's vivid tribute to Lewis, see 'Outline of a Necessary Figure', in M. Wynn Thomas (ed.), *Emyr Humphreys: Conversations and Reflections* (Cardiff: University of Wales Press, 2002), pp. 84–91.

⁶ Emyr Humphreys, *Collected Poems* (Cardiff: University of Wales Press, 1999), p. 180.

⁷ See, for instance, 'The Creative Writer's Suicide', in Sandra Anstey (ed.), *R. S. Thomas: Selected Prose* (Bridgend: Poetry Wales Press, 1983), pp. 167–74. Hereafter *SP*.

⁸ In his excellent study *Sefyll yn y Bwlch: R. S. Thomas, Saunders Lewis, T. S. Eliot, a Simone Weil* (Caerdydd: Gwasg Prifysgol Cymru, 1999), Grahame Davies argues that both Lewis and Thomas, relatively ignorant of the actual existent Wales, created a country of the mind ideally suited to their conservative, anti-modernist nostalgia. For a brief English summary of the argument, see the same author's 'Resident Aliens: R. S. Thomas and the Anti-Modern Movement', *Welsh Writing in English: A Yearbook of Critical Essays*, 7 (2001–2), 50–77.

⁹ For a definitive address of the subject, see Jason Walford Davies, *Gororau'r Iaith: R. S. Thomas a'r Traddodiad Llenyddol Cymraeg* (Caerdydd: Gwasg Prifysgol Cymru, 2003). A summation in English of some of the author's findings may be read in '"Thick Ambush of Shadows": Allusions to Welsh Literature in the Work of R. S. Thomas', *Welsh Writing in English: A Yearbook of Critical Essays 1* (1995), 75–127.

[10] R. S. Thomas, *What is a Welshman?* (Swansea: Christopher Davies, n.d.), p. 1. Hereafter *WW*.

[11] Saunders Lewis, 'The Deluge, 1939', trans. Joseph P. Clancy, *Twentieth-Century Welsh Poems* (Llandysul: Gomer Press, 1982), pp. 75–7.

[12] An excellent introduction to this whole background can be found in Ned Thomas, *The Welsh Extremist* (Talybont: Gwasg y Lolfa, 1973; reprinted 1978).

[13] Saunders Lewis, *Tynged yr Iaith* (Cyfansoddiadau BBC, 1962). For a translation, see G. Aled Williams, 'The Fate of the Language', in *Presenting Saunders Lewis*, pp. 127–41.

[14] Saunders Lewis, *Tynged yr Iaith* (Cyfansoddiadau BBC, 1962), p. 26.

[15] Dafydd Elis Thomas, 'The Image of Wales in R. S. Thomas's Poetry', *Poetry Wales*, 7:2 (Spring, 1972), 59–66.

[16] R. S. Thomas, *Welsh Airs* (Bridgend: Poetry Wales Press, 1987), p. 36. Hereafter *WA*.

[17] Tony Bianchi, 'R. S. Thomas and His Readers', in Tony Curtis (ed.), *Wales, the Imagined Nation* (Bridgend: Poetry Wales Press, 1985), pp. 69–95.

5

# Family Matters

To judge from his poetry, R. S. Thomas remained chronically skeptical throughout his life about being able to measure the ultimate worth, or indeed to understand the real nature, of his personal being. His poems of unsparing self-assessment seem always to leave a wide margin for eventual correction, even as they insist on facing up to the morally inadequate self-image that 'lies in ambush' for him, regardless of how secretly or obliquely he approaches the mirror: 'And the heart knows/ this is not the portrait/ it posed for.'[1] Similarly, as will become evident in chapter 8, his essays in autobiography – *Neb* and *The Echoes Return Slow* – are constructed to give the impression of a man who does not feel in full possession of his own life: 'A Narcissus tortured/ by the whisperers behind/ the mirror'(*CP*, p. 516). He writes sometimes like a baffled spectator of his own representatively strange existence – 'ce néant indestructible, qui est moi', as the line from Claudel puts it, which Thomas chose as epigraph for *Neb*. But there are also those others close to him who are the partners in his sorrow's mystery: 'There are four verses to put down/ For the four people in my life,/ Father, mother, wife// And the one child' (*CP*, p. 83). These four have been a significant presence in his writing – indeed an obsessive presence in the case of his mother – yet very little attention has been paid to those poems in which they appear.

In *The Echoes Return Slow*, R. S. Thomas's search for origins took him farther back than ever before, although even then it is doubtful whether he himself believed he had got to the very bottom of what he elsewhere described as 'time's reasons/ too far back to be known' (*CP*, p. 516). He did, though, go back as far as the womb, in an astonishing passage invoking pre-natal experience:

> Pain's climate. The weather unstable. Blood rather than rain fell. The woman was opened and sewed up, relieved of the trash that had accumulated nine months in the man's absence. Time would have its work cut out in smoothing the birthmarks in the flesh. The marks in the spirit would not heal. The dream would recur, groping his way up to the light, coming to the crack too narrow to squeeze through. (*CLP*, p. 12)

It would be a crass and impudent piece of reductiveness to insist on explaining the character of Thomas's writing either exclusively or even primarily in terms of what is revealed here. 'Character is built up/' as he has himself reminded us, 'by the application of uncountable/ brush strokes' (*CLP*, p. 58). Nevertheless, any reader of his poetry is likely to be struck by the consonances between this memory of birth and R. S. Thomas's reported experiences of living. To put it guardedly thus is to avoid the unanswerable question: is he actually remembering a climate of pain in which his whole being had its genesis? Or is he projecting the pains and frustrations of a lifetime back into the imagined trauma of birth? There is also another possible confusion to which we need to be alert. Even if we hold that a real trauma experienced at birth did (as he himself here seems to suggest) have very far-reaching effects on R. S. Thomas's growth and development, it does not follow that his outlook on life is therefore simply the consequence of that primal trauma; merely the ugly scar of an unfortunate early psychic wound. It would be wiser to speculate that by some such means as those he chooses to mention figuratively at the beginning of *The Echoes Return Slow* he was exposed, and thus sensitised, exceptionally early to those uncomfortable aspects of life his unaccommodating mature poetry has repeatedly explored.

But at this point, it is enough to note that R. S. Thomas's was a difficult birth, and that when he was in his mid-seventies this fact (recalled as an actual experience) was deliberately chosen by him to serve as an image of the origins of his sensibility. Examined in this light, and read with the corpus of Thomas's mature work in mind, the passage quoted yields several suggestive meanings. Indeed it would seem to lay bare the deep structure of the poetry's psychology, its fundamental disposition towards life. Here can be seen, for instance, that fear of confinement that is a recurring feature of the poems. Sometimes it is expressed as a passion for freedom (associated with nature); on other occasions it emerges as a nervousness about emotional intimacies, entanglements, commitments, or as a physical distaste for any kind of close encounter with others. Most interestingly of all, it manifests itself in Thomas's identification with a God who is tired of being besieged by men's prayers, or pestered by sentimental petitions, or threatened by the encroachments of the human on his living space: 'My privacy/ Was invaded; then the flaw/ Took over' (CP, p. 230). In 'The Gap' it is the pressure of human words that God feels: 'God woke, but the nightmare/ did not recede. Word by word/ the tower of speech grew./ . . . One word more and/ it would be on a level/ with him; vocabulary/ would have triumphed' (CP, p. 324). This kind of perception culminates in that superb exercise in the theology of claustrophobia, 'The White Tiger'. The creature possesses 'a body too huge/ and majestic for the cage in which/ it had been put', and its calm, cold beauty commands awe:

> It
> was the colour of the moonlight
> on snow and as quiet
> as moonlight, but breathing
>
> as you can imagine that
> God breathes within the confines
> of our definition of him, agonizing
> over immensities that will not return. (CP, p. 358)

Arrange the meanings in that prose passage about his birth into a different pattern, and other preoccupations of his poetry seem to emerge. For instance there is a faint intimation of the impenetrable barrier between the divine and the human in that thwarted foetal sensation of 'groping his way up to the light, coming to the crack too narrow to squeeze through'. As for the brusque and rather brutal description of the actual birth, it is disturbingly peculiar. In being referred to as 'the woman', the mother is denied her motherhood: similarly the baby is denied the natural process of birth, and exists in the description only as an inference from the clinically cold fact that 'the woman was opened and sewed up'. Parenthood is the inconvenient production of 'trash', which has then to be disposed of. These aspects of the passage are, perhaps, best left uninvestigated until later, when we consider the ambivalent way in which Thomas has presented his relationship with his parents in his poetry. It is, however, worth noting the undercurrent of savagery in the writing, as if there were in the writer a feeling of resentment at having been 'from his mother's womb untimely ripp'd'. And when R. S. Thomas does use the image of Caesarean birth in his poems, it is as a symbol of the monstrously unnatural – an act of violence done to nature. 'The scientists breach/ themselves with their Caesarian/ births, and we blame them for it', he writes in 'It': 'What shall we do/ with the knowledge growing/ into a tree that to shelter/ under is to be lightning struck?'[2] Again, in 'The Other', he uses the same image to describe the birth of the fearsome Machine:

> They did it to me.
> I preferred dead, lying
> in the mind's mortuary.
> Come out, they shouted;
> with a screech of steel
> I jumped into the world
> smiling my cogged smile,
> breaking with iron hand
> the hands they extended. (*CP*, p. 410)

Hovering somewhere in the background here are surely Blake's fierce lines from 'Infant Sorrow':

> My mother groan'd! My father wept.
> Into the dangerous world I leapt:
> Helpless, naked, piping loud:
> Like a fiend hid in a cloud.

> Struggling in my father's hands,
> Striving against my swaddling bands,
> Bound and weary I thought best
> To sulk upon my mother's breast.[3]

Here baby talk is fighting talk. The infant is precociously aware of being an actor in a tense, emotionally violent family drama: it has to learn early to assume the wiles of disguise, and thus its impulses are, as it were, corrupted at source. Interestingly, there are also shades of the companion piece to 'Infant Sorrow', namely 'Infant Joy', about the poem that partners the prose description of birth in *The Echoes Return Slow*. It will be remembered that Blake's poem begins 'I have no name./ I am but two days old.' This is how Thomas's poem begins:

> I have no name:
> time's changeling.
> Put your hand
> in my side and disbelieve
>
> in my godhead. (*CLP*, p. 12)

The spiritual implications of this self-naming will be considered in chapter 8. Meanwhile, it's worth noting that, through the secondary meaning of 'changeling' – 'a child surreptitiously put in exchange for another' (OED) – he here declines to consider himself as being, in his essential identity, the child of his parents. Even the surname he inherits from them is given a sardonic twist that turns it from a genealogical fact into a human parable. He is a Thomas who *promotes* doubt – doubt about the divine innocence of infancy. Indeed, the last few lines of his poem read like an ironic commentary on Blake's 'Infant Joy'. Blake's baby is named 'Joy' by its mother in a great surge (or gush) of sentiment, which can be read either as mothering or as smothering. In Thomas's poem the baby speaks for itself:

> Her face rises
> over me and sets;
> I am shone on

through tears. Charity
spares what should be
lopped off, before
it is too late. (*CLP*, p. 12)

The power in these lines is in their delicate psychological equivocation. On the one hand, he wants the mother to be kind by being cruel and so grant him an early end to a miserably unworthy existence (with the additional half-suggestion that early castration might have spared the humiliations of specifically masculine being). On the other hand, he is deeply moved by a tenacious love that seems to involve a redeeming acceptance of him as himself ('I am shone on through tears'). This latter strain of feeling in the poem seems to connect it with the very last prose passage in the collection, where R. S. Thomas brings together, in a single act of religious meditation, his deep passion for the sea and his abiding love for his wife:

> Both female. Both luring us on, staring crystal-eyed over their unstable fathoms. After a lifetime's apprenticeships in navigating their surface, nothing to hope for but that for the love of both of them he would be forgiven. (*CLP*, p. 72)

In that last phrase, clarity of meaning (with its related determination to hope) is deliberately made to struggle free of a heavy weight of repeated monosyllables and of confusingly repeated prepositions.

The description of difficult, or unusual, birth, whether it be remembered or imagined, seems then to attract to itself, and to concentrate in itself, a mixture of feelings that is characteristic of R. S. Thomas. There are, for instance, the self-loathing, the dark mistrust of human intimacy, the general sense of alienation and dissociation that permeate his writing. At the same time there is a strong sense of the inviolable integrity of his own separate, independent being. And there is also a shy, almost grudging, doubt-full and dubious tribute to a strength and persistence of love that makes 'a thing endurable which else/ Would break the heart.'[4] These feelings consort together most touchingly, I find, in Thomas's poems about relations within the family. But perhaps because these poems are so few and so far between, secreted away on the odd page of his collections, and only barely existing, it sometimes seems, in the shadow of his towering work on Iago Prytherch and the *Deus Absconditus*, they have so far received very little attention.

R. S. Thomas may have been too painfully close to his mother for him to feel able to write much about her, although he admitted in *Neb* that 'Strange, and perhaps crucial, is the relationship between a mother and her son'.[5] 'Because my father was often at sea and because my mother was of a domineering nature I was ruled mainly by her', he told Ned Thomas.[6] In his interviews and in *Neb*, he repeatedly described her as possessive, neurotic and infuriatingly false-genteel: 'My mother gave me the breast's milk/ Generously, but grew mean after,/ Envying me my detached laughter' (*CP*, p. 83). Yet he has also consciously tried to balance the picture with other qualities, as in the following disquieting passage:

> But it became time for him to leave Holyhead and head for Bangor as a student at the college. And his mother came with him! On the pretext that she was eager to see that he had good lodgings and so on, she came also to share his first day away from home. But mercifully, because he was totally unknown, the other students did not stand in ranks to make fun of the little baby arriving with its nurse. Those were his feelings at the time. It was later that he would remember how he had returned to the house the previous night and heard the sound of crying upstairs, and the voice of his father trying to silence his wife. Then in bed, after going to sleep, he awoke and felt someone kissing him over and over. This is how a mother came to realize that she was about to lose the child of whom she had been too possessive. (*A*, p. 36)

In all his work there is, as far as I know, only one poem devoted entirely and exclusively to his mother, although one suspects his poetry has, in many intangible and incalculable ways, been 'ruled mainly by her'. Only in *The Echoes Return Slow* did he make her approaching end the subject of a poem. Seven years after his father's death it was, he tells us, his mother's turn to go: 'The woman, who all her life had complained, came face to face with a precise ill' (*CLP*, p. 50). In the opening lines there seems to be a sad, blurred echo of the poem of birth, when the baby had been condemned, by its mother's 'Charity', to live:

> She came to us with her appeal
> to die, and we made her live
> on, not out of our affection
> for her, but from a dislike
> of death. (*CLP*, p. 50)

The double edge of feeling is most sharply sensed in the studied choice of the word 'dislike', where fastidious outward courtesy is drily used to distance inner fear in a manner passingly reminiscent of Emily Dickinson. Moreover, the slightly fearful gentility that R. S. Thomas elsewhere associates with his mother now appears, ironically, as an acknowledged feature of his own reserved make-up. Powerful cross-currents of feeling can, then, be sensed under the still surface of the language, and these become even stronger towards the end, as the measured words seem increasingly to act as multipliers of meaning:

> The ambulance came
> to rescue us from the issues
> of her body; she was delivered
> from the incompetence of
> our conscience into the hospital's
> cleanlier care. Yet I took her hand
> there and made a tight-rope
> of our fingers for the mis-shapen
> feelings to keep their balance upon.

Built into the first phrase is a reproachful reminder of the opening line of the poem – 'She came to us . . . The ambulance came/ to rescue us'. Then follows the extraordinary mention of 'the issues of her body', a phrase into which black meanings are so densely compressed that no relieving gleam of comfort is at this point able to escape. Obviously the reference is partly to physical incontinence and to other kinds of bodily effluent. But beyond that is the sense of the mother as having become an insuperable problem, a dilemma, the big issue; and behind that again lies Thomas's inescapable awareness of his own binding situation as her son, himself literally one of 'the issues of her body' – indeed the phrase echoes the one he used about his birth. This last dark shade of meaning in the phrase then colours one's reading of the next sentence so that 'she was delivered/ from the incompetence of/ our conscience' is a kind of grim parody of the process of giving birth, and contains a poignant allusion to the Lord's Prayer as well as, of course, depending on the modern, humdrum meaning of the word 'deliver'. By the time one has reached the end of the piece, the picture of the son taking his mother's hand and making a tight-rope 'of our fingers for the mis-shapen/ feelings to keep their balance upon' seems applicable to the poem itself. The poet has produced, through words, a precarious miracle of emotional equilibrium, without ever pretending to have straightened out the twisted feelings of a lifetime between his mother and himself.

'Oh, could I lose all father now', wrote Ben Jonson in his great, eloquently restrained elegy 'On my son'. R. S. Thomas's related wish that he could 'lose all son', in his relationship with his mother, is just as restrained and, yes, just as eloquent too, I would argue. Indeed he is perhaps usefully thought of as sometimes being, like Jonson, a superb writer of modern epigrams, in the classical and Elizabethan sense. As a theological student he was given a grounding in Greek and Latin, and later acquired a knowledge of the great, pungently concise, *cynghanedd* writing of the golden age of Welsh poetry. Particularly interesting is his mention, in *Neb*, of the debt he owed one of his early teachers:

> ... the boy would hardly have succeeded in his A-level examination, were it not for the headmaster, Derry Evans, a man who possessed an innate gift for teaching Latin. The latter gave him an excellent foundation that enabled him not only to succeed academically, but also to develop into a poet, because of the emphasis on language. Through having to search for the right word to translate the Latin, he learned the need to do so in poetry as well. (*A*, p. 35)

But although in his mature poetry Thomas remained always in search of the precise, as he grew older he became more able to reconcile clarity and complexity, whereas in some of his earlier work there was a tendency to be inflexibly definite and decided. Take, for instance, a poem like the following, entitled 'Sorry':

Dear parents,
I forgive you my life,
Begotten in a drab town,
The intention was good;
Passing the street now,
I see still the remains of sunlight.

It was not the bone buckled;
You gave me enough food
To renew myself.
It was the mind's weight
Kept me bent, as I grew tall.

It was not your fault.
What should have gone on,
Arrow aimed from a tried bow
At a tried target, has turned back,
Wounding itself
With questions you had not asked. (*CP*, p. 127)

The immediate impact of these lines is, surely, powerful, but the piece as a whole does not wear particularly well, perhaps because the images are too insistently definite. The poem is rather like a fine metal bridge that has been built without expansion joints: there is no give in it to allow for changes of temperature in his feelings towards his parents and their relationship to himself. The possible exception to this overall impression is the one sentence that does have an echoing plangency about it: 'Passing the street now,/ I see still the remains of sunlight'. Otherwise the statements border on the dogmatic.

'Sorry', which was first collected in *The Bread of Truth* (1963), seems all the more rigid (as if with suppressed anger) when compared with the opening section of 'Album', a poem included in *Frequencies* (1978):

My father is dead.
I who am look at him
who is not, as once he
went looking for me
in the woman who was. (*CP*, p. 350)

The blank simplicity of the opening statement breaks down into the brooding Faulknerian complexity of the sentence that follows. And as is the case with Faulkner's style, the effect of this spool of syntax is to substitute for the conventional working idea of temporal chronology a sense of time's bewildering circularities: 'What does it mean/ life? I am here I am/ there'. As understood in the opening lines, the relationship between father and son becomes one that reveals a mysterious correspondence between past and present. The parallelism of syntax makes their roles seem interchangeable. Thomas realises he is now the bringer to life of his dead father, as once his father brought him to life. A particular poignancy seems to attach to that phrase: 'as once he/ went looking for me/ in the woman who was'. Underlying and underpinning these lines there appears to be a pun on the unspoken word 'conceive'. Instead of being merely the by-product of sexual intercourse, the begetting of the child is seen as a great hungering movement of the mind, in the spirit of some deep human need. What the phrase deliberately leaves unclear, however, is whether the 'me' that was actually produced did indeed satisfy that need. In other words it is uncertain whether R. S. Thomas is seeing himself as indeed his father's chosen one, or as the disappointing result of his father's search. And since the syntax makes Thomas's 'search' for his father in the photograph the double of his father's 'search' for him in the act of intercourse, the emotional ambivalence associated with the latter also becomes transferred to the former. Thomas's father is now at his mercy: he exists only in his son's 'conception' of him. And as he acts on the great need to give his father being, the son, by implication, feels both love and resentment.

Judging by the evidence freely offered by R. S. Thomas himself in *Neb*, his impulse to 'go searching' for his dead father came partly from his feeling that he had been impeded – not least by his father's early deafness – from communicating intimately with him when he was alive: 'He was a man who had seen the world and its ways, and he would perhaps have shared his experiences had he been able to have a normal relationship with his son' (*A*, p. 82). R. S. Thomas's painful sense of frustration at being unable to enjoy 'a normal relationship' with his father comes out most poignantly in two sentences he wrote about his death in *The*

*Echoes Return Slow.* 'In the order of things children bid farewell to their parents. Unable to hear his father bid him farewell in his stentorian voice' (*CLP*, p. 50). Thomas was, then, prevented from communicating with his dying parent, and had to suffer instead his father's lonely, bellowed goodbye. One wonders how much this affected the later Thomas's pre-occupation with the silence of God. As for the implications for his self-perception of his lifelong sense of masculine inadequacy, compared with his sometime masterful father – a ship's master, before being mastered, and in Thomas's view emasculated, by his wife – they will be considered in the next chapter.

The development of 'Album' is governed by a whole blend of feelings. Having begun by thinking of himself as specifically desired and searched for by his father, Thomas goes on to see himself as the addition to the family that unbalanced the whole picture:

> . . . Look! Suddenly
> the young tool in their hands
> for hurting one another.
>
> And the camera says:
> Smile: there is no wound
> time gives that is not bandaged
> by time. And so they do the
> three of them at me who weep. (*CP*, p. 350)

The hint of banality, the suggestion of conventional wisdom, in the words the camera utters, is a sign of the emptiness of the comfort it has to offer. After all, from the very beginning of the poem, Time is seen as repeating itself, not as improving on itself. As for the last sentence, it is, I feel, particularly disarming and deeply affecting because there is scarcely another one like it in the whole of Thomas's work – hardly another moment in his poems where he allows himself such an open display of 'weakness'; of helplessly naked emotion of the kind found in the work of poets so unlike him in temperament, such as Lawrence's 'Piano', or Whitman's 'Out of the Cradle'.

A rather different account of the reason for his conception is given in 'The Boy's Tale', a poem where the tension in the speaker (presumably

R. S. Thomas himself) betrays itself in the nervously clipped style of expression, a kind of psychological telegramese, where the aim seems to be to expend as little emotion as possible in words: 'Skipper wouldn't pay him off,/ Never married her' (*CP*, p. 142). As the poem proceeds, the abruptness of manner becomes a style of reporting appropriate to the dry description of a fateful *fait accompli*: 'Caught him in her thin hair,/ Couldn't hold him'. This sense of the wife-husband relationship as one, in his parents' case, where the woman trapped and tamed the man, recurs in R. S. Thomas's writing: 'My father was a passionate man,/ Wrecked after leaving the sea/ In her love's shallows. He grieves in me' (*CP*, p. 83). In 'The Boy's Tale', Thomas sees the child as his mother's chosen instrument for controlling and dominating her sailor spouse:

> She went fishing in him;
> I was the bait
> That became cargo,
> Shortening his trips,
> Waiting on the bone's wharf.
> Her tongue ruled the tides.

In fact, Thomas's portraits of his father, including the repeated suggestion of marital defeat, with a resulting impression of masculine weakness and inadequacy, are very reminiscent of Robert Lowell's pictures of 'Commander' Lowell, his easy-going sea-going father. But the comparison between the two writers, once it occurs to one to make it, is somewhat to R. S. Thomas's disadvantage in at least one respect. Lowell is able to relax in his writing without thereby losing control over it and lapsing into slackness. His consequent achievement, in *Life Studies* particularly, is to invest apparently casual and inconsequential observations with a deeper purpose. His lazily undulating lines work like slow-release tablets, and have to be tucked under the tongue of the mind for a long time in order to allow them gradually to secrete their meanings:

> 'Anchors aweigh,' Daddy boomed in his bathtub.
> 'Anchors aweigh,'
> when Lever Brothers offered to pay
> him double what the Navy paid.
> I nagged for his dress sword with gold braid,

and cringed because Mother, new
caps on all her teeth, was born anew
at forty. With seamanlike celerity,
Father left the Navy,
and deeded Mother his property. [7]

Placed next to a passage like that, Thomas's writing can seem cramped, inhibited, even grandiose and portentous. This is partly due to a passion for authoritative, clinching images, the general absence of which in the mature Lowell may help explain why Thomas has a relatively low opinion of the American's work. He once told John Barnie in an interview that Lowell 'enjoyed an inflated reputation and Heaney came under his influence. It would have been better had he not' ('Probings', 47). Elsewhere, during the same conversation, he admits his strong preference for the work of Geoffrey Hill, which is, after all, high tension like his own, although Hill's tends also to be magnificently dense and turgidly pretentious by turns. The irresistible attraction, for Thomas, of the strong image makes it next to impossible for him to write a really successful poem longer than a page or so. For one thing, the series of determinedly arresting images produces a stop/go kind of tempo, and prevents a larger overall structure from forming; for another, the images tend not to collaborate but to clash and compete with each other, rather like a whole chorus made up of prima donnas. A case in point is his extended elegy for his father, 'Salt', where he seems intent on exhausting the whole repertoire of nautical tropes in one virtuoso display.[8] Taken in small doses, however, the poetry can have considerable effect, as can be seen in the following passage:

The voice of my father
in the night with the hunger
of the sea in it and the emptiness
of the sea. While the house founders
in time, I must listen to him
complaining, a ship's captain
with no crew, a navigator
without a port; rejected
by the barrenness of his wife's
coasts, by the wind's bitterness

off her heart. I take his failure
for ensign, flying it
at my bedpost, where my own
children cry to be born. (*CP*, p. 396)

His clear signal here that he identifies in some ways, and to some extent, with his father is worth bearing in mind when he goes on to pity the ageing man's painful ineffectuality, and in particular the world-wide traveller's lack of anything substantial to show for his life's journey: 'What was a sailor/ good for who had sailed/ all seas and learned wisdom/ from none, fetched up there/ in the shallows with his mind's valueless cargo?' How far, one then wonders, was Thomas's invincible determination to be a lifelong mental traveller – a determination so frequently expressed in terms of nautical images, of crossing fathomless depths – shaped by his reaction against that image of his father as left, in old age, bereft of the becoming dignity of 'wisdom'? Certainly his father's example served as salutary warning to R. S. Thomas in several ways, hardening, in particular, his resolve to protect his separate selfhood from being compromised or invaded. Running through his poetry is the constant fear of and contempt for 'weakness', whether it be moral or emotional. He is hardest on himself when he detects such weakness in his own make-up: 'A will of iron, perforated/ by indecision. A charity/ that, beginning at home,/ ended in domestication./ An uxorious valour/ so fond of discretion as/ to defer to it/ as his better half' (*CLP*, p. 41). Regardless of whether one takes the reference to marriage here as fact or as metaphor, the relationship of husband to wife is unmistakably seen, once more, as fraught with danger for the former.

Alongside R. S. Thomas's painful sense of his father's weakness lies his envy of the power he had possessed, when a young sailor, to escape to sea from the nauseating mess human beings had made of modern life. Thomas seems sometimes scarcely able to forgive his father for having finally come ashore – which is tantamount, in Thomas's thinking, to running aground. He imagines his father's corpse as stranded, for ever, on 'this mean shoal of plastic/ and trash'. In 'Sailors' Hospital', the town of Holyhead is seen as 'time's waste/ Growing at the edge/ Of the clean sea'. That poem ends, though, in great tenderness, as Thomas finds it impossible to let go of a man whom, on a different level of feeling, he wishes to see released:

> With clenched thoughts,
> That not even the sky's
> Daffodil could persuade
> To open, I turned back
> To the nurses in their tugging
> At him, as he drifted
> Away on the current
> Of his breath, further and further,
> Out of hail of our love. (*CP*, p. 193)

These are lines that, rather unusually for R. S. Thomas, enact rhythmically the actual feel of what is being experienced.

As could probably have been anticipated, many of the feelings that Thomas has about his parents recur, but in significantly modified form, in the half-dozen or so poems he wrote about his son, Gwydion, beginning with the emphasis that 'It was your mother wanted you;/ you were already half-formed/ when I entered' (*CP*, p. 274). These, the opening lines of 'The Son', may well remind us of the claim in 'The Boy's Tale', that he had been his mother's idea, but there the resemblance between the two poems rather pointedly ends, because the remainder of 'The Son' is given over to the speaker's progressive admission of his own shyly entranced part in the making and the nurturing of the baby. Even in the act of conception he can now see 'the hunger, the loneliness bringing me in/ from myself'. But what particularly disarms him is that the tiny baby is 'too small to be called/ human'. This is an important discovery for a poet who is otherwise almost indecently quick to detect the smell of mortality in every phase and feature of human life.

Indeed almost all the rest of R. S. Thomas's poems about Gwydion insist on explicitly recognising, in some way or other, the fact that his son participates in the general human condition, and partakes of the general human frailty. 'Song for Gwydion', a lovely early lyric, approaches this theme via an evocation of the child's 'innocent' natural beauty, to

132

which the father pays enraptured tribute by bringing him a 'trout from the green river'. Its song has been stilled, and its rainbow colours faded by death, but the child selfishly exults in the gift: 'the first sweet sacrifice I tasted,/ A young god, ignorant of the blood's stain' (*CP*, p. 23). Ignorant, maybe, but no longer innocent. Father and son are united in a moment of sad communion, partners in sin. Thomas is always ready to see signs of the criminal cupidity of mankind in the gross appetitiveness of young children, even to the extent of describing his begetting of Gwydion, in 'Anniversary', as 'Opening the womb/ Softly to let enter/ The one child/ With his huge hunger' (*CP*, p. 103). This seems connected to his attack in *Neb* on man's exploitation and selfish spoliation of the environment: 'the classical word for this was "cupido", the insatiable greed in man that gave birth to machines and aeroplanes and missiles and all the technology of the contemporary world' (*A*, p. 108).

'Is there a leakage/ from his mind into the minds/ of our inventors?' he enquires in a poem from *The Echoes Return Slow* (*CLP*, p. 30). This piece, along with its accompanying prose passage, seems to be an interesting rewriting of Coleridge's great poem 'Frost at Midnight'. There, it will be remembered, Coleridge is gradually reconciled, through listening to his child breathing in the cot at his side, to the natural world that had originally seemed to him so coldly indifferent, or inimical, to human existence. The poem ends with a marvellous verse paragraph celebrating a benign, blessed, organically integrated cosmos, in which Coleridge's son will feel completely at home at all times, and in all seasons: 'Therefore, all seasons shall be sweet to thee . . .'.[9] In the prose passage that precedes Thomas's poem, he creates a scene similar to that in 'Frost at Midnight', but very different to it in tone: 'Despite the atmosphere of the nursery, that half-light before the fire, cradling the child, telling it stories, wishing it God's blessing in its small cot, dark thoughts come to the priest in the church porch at night, with the owl calling, or later at his bedside' (*CLP*, p. 30). The process here can be seen to be the reverse of that in 'Frost at Midnight', since Thomas begins with a sense of security, and ends in a state of alienation.

Coleridge was also, of course, disturbed at the beginning of his poem by 'the owlet's cry' that came 'hard and hard again', as if conveying to the human listener all the inhuman hostility of the cosmos. But eventually his disturbed and disordered thoughts are imperceptibly knit together into a new harmony by the rhythm of his son's breathing. In Thomas's case, however, his child's breathing sets the tempo for increasingly disturbed reflections about the unseen presence that haunts the universe:

> What listener
> is this, who is always awake
> and says nothing? His breathing
> is the rising and falling of oceans on remote
> stars. The forbidden tree flourishes
> in his garden and he waters it
> with his own blood. (*CLP*, p. 30)

This leads on to wild fears about a maverick spirit of mischievousness, abroad in the life of the universe, that takes possession of human beings and causes them to tamper with the forbidden: 'The combination/ is yielding. What will come forth/ to wreak its vengeance on us/ for the disturbance?'.

Such a vision seems compounded of the stories of both Pandora's Box and the Sorcerer's Apprentice – and the memory of the latter in turn reminds one that the original Gwydion was a wily and resourceful magician whose prodigiously ingenious exploits included, according to the *Mabinogion*, the initially glorious but eventually disastrous act of creating a woman out of flowers. His Blodeuwedd, as she was called, proved to be a veritable Pandora herself, so much so that when Saunders Lewis (R. S. Thomas's great hero) came to reinterpret the story for the twentieth century, he depicted her as a product of human meddlesomeness.[10]

R. S. Thomas's decision to call his son Gwydion is then consistent with his determination to see his son as also a son of Adam, instead of fondly and deludedly believing that he is free of original sin. This is very clear in the following passage from *The Echoes Return Slow*:

The child growing imperceptibly into a boy; the strange plant that has taken root in one's private garden. The apple of the mother's eye. The grudging acknowledgement by the male, so different from the female, that this also is a twig on a branch of the tree of man. The father's share in the promise of fruit and his resentment at canker. (*CLP*, p. 31)

Certain unattractive features of R. S. Thomas's thinking are on view here, such as his tendency to condescend to women and to treat them as the weaker vessels, morally and emotionally. (In this context, there are surely shades of Eve in the ironic reference to the boy as 'the apple of the mother's eye'.) There is also a hint of male jealousy and rivalry between father and son in that description of the garden. But permeating the whole passage is a sense of the father having to come to terms with the fact that his child, just like every other, is growing into the fullness of man's fallen condition. The accompanying poem on the facing page, however, deliberately works in an opposite direction. It begins with the father readily admitting that his son 'was sometimes a bad boy', but then follows a lovely compensatory image of a child's open trust and vulnerability: 'Yet I remember his lips/ how they were soft and// wet, when I kissed him/ good-night' (*CLP*, p. 31).

More important than R. S. Thomas's poems about his son are his poems about his wife. On one reading of his output, these could seem no more than incidental to his primary concerns, those serious subjects that have regularly attracted his consuming interest. At the end of 'Marriage', he seems himself to be ruefully admitting as much, when he regrets that his wife's unassuming qualities have, unlike the brash history of 'kings and queens/ and their battles/ for power', been registered only by 'one man's eyes/ resting on you/ in the interval of his concern' (*CP*, p. 300). The whole piece is, in fact, a tender, humble reversal of that proud convention whereby a poet simultaneously proclaims and demonstrates his power to immortalise his beloved in verse. Of course, Shakespeare it is who provides the most famous and triumphant examples of this convention, notably in his sonnets: 'And all in war with time for love of you,/ As he takes from you, I engraft you new'.[11] But there is surely reason, in the form of Thomas's passionate admiration of Yeats, to suppose that he has the Irishman's great poems to Maud Gonne in mind when he apologises that 'Because there are no kings/ worthy of you; because poets/ better than I are not here/ to describe you . . . you must go by/ now without mention'. In reply to a suggestion made to him by Ned Thomas that he was an underrated but diffident love-poet, R. S. Thomas replied:

Diffident is the word, is it not? We are all afraid of laughter, at being called soft or sentimental; and certainly such states destroy art. Passion seems to have departed from the poetry I am familiar with in English, Welsh or French. I shy at the word 'darling' which was all too current a while ago. It has something to do with linguistic deflation. Surely most of us would like to write a great love poem to God, to Wales, to our betrothed. It would have to be passionate; but we meander and grow shallow, if subtle. ('Probings', 50–1)

It seems that he regards Yeats as one of the few modern poets who could be marvellously impassioned without thereby devaluing his language of love through the use of inflated rhetoric:

> Why should I blame her that she filled my days
> With misery, or that she would of late
> Have taught to ignorant men most violent ways,
> Or hurled the little streets upon the great,
> Had they but courage equal to desire?
> What could have made her peaceful with a mind
> That nobleness made simple as a fire,
> With beauty like a tightened bow, a kind
> That is not natural in an age like this,
> Being high and solitary and most stern?
> Why, what could she have done, being what she is?
> Was there another Troy for her to burn?[12]

It is worth reading this in its entirety, not only because it is so disturbingly magnificent a poem, but also because it brings out for us, so clearly and unmistakably, the connection Yeats's dazzled, tormented mind is moved to make first between beauty and power, and then between this volatile combination and the artistic imagination. In fact, the whole troubling nexus of experiences in this poem reminds us of the arresting remark Hazlitt made at the beginning of his essay on Shakespeare's *Coriolanus*: 'The language of poetry naturally falls in with the language of power. The imagination is an exaggerating and exclusive faculty . . . a monopolizing faculty . . . It presents a dazzling appearance. It shows its head turreted, crowned, and crested . . . Kings, priests, nobles, are its train-bearers . . . Poetry is right-royal.'[13]

In 'Marriage', R. S. Thomas shows an awareness of and a distaste for this right-royal aspect of his own imagination as man, and perhaps most particularly as poet: 'You have your battle,/ too. I ask myself: Have/ I been on your side? Lovelier/ a dead queen than a live/ wife?'. In this sense the poem is written to celebrate and protect, as well as to regret, his wife's anonymity. Her non-appearance in his poem is his tribute to her undemonstrative integrity of being, outside that realm of power that frequently proves such an unhealthy attraction for the historian and the poet. (As Hazlitt noted, 'our vanity or some other feeling makes us disposed to place ourselves in the situation of the strongest party . . . The insolence of power is stronger than the plea of necessity.') At the same time Thomas is saddened by his wife's 'passing', both in the sense of her walking by him almost unnoticed and in the larger, more melancholy sense of her eventual death without proper public or poetic recognition:

> because time
> is always too short, you must go by
> now without mention, as unknown
> to the future as to
> the past, with one man's
> eyes resting on you
> in the interval of his concern.

As usual, Thomas ventures to conclude the poem on a weighty generalisation – a considerable risk, in view of his age's dislike of sententiousness. That last phrase has, though, a notable delicacy about it, critically balanced as it is between two meanings. Since Thomas is writing about how he happened to notice his wife as he raised his eyes for a moment from the history book he was reading, he could be using the word 'concern' ironically to refer to his self-important preoccupation with his studies. On the other hand, the word could mean the very opposite. It could refer to the brief moment when he pays full, conscious, appreciative attention ('concern') to the one person who is *really* important to him, and in the process temporarily (for an 'interval') reorientates his life. What the phrase thus highlights, through its significant ambiguity, is the choice Thomas has to make, between 'concern' (the supposedly important matters of

the world) and 'concern' (a care for that which the world at large ignores).
He has therefore provided himself with a solution to the dilemma with
which his poem opens: 'I have to reconcile your/ existence and the meaning
of it/ with what I read'. No reconciliation is possible, only the realisation
that he is confronted by a test of authenticity, by what Kierkegaard would
call a situation of either/or.

A very different kind of Kierkegaardian situation is brought to mind
by 'Careers', a poem that centres on Thomas's attempt to understand
the relationship between his present 52-year-old self and the boy he once
was: 'How his words/ muddle me; how my deeds/ betray him'. At the
end he laments that

> where I should
> be one with him, I am one now
> with another. Before I had time
> to complete myself, I let her share
> in the building. This that I am
> now – too many
> labourers. What is mine is
> not mine only: her love, her
> child wait for my slow
> signature. (*CP*, p. 181)

The attitude here is reminiscent of Kierkegaard's biting comments about
an individual's attempts to avoid, through 'association', the challenge
and responsibility of his own individuality: 'the association of individuals
who are in themselves weak, is just as disgusting and as harmful as the
marriage of children'.[14] One's reaction to the poem is bound to be as ambivalent as one's reaction to Kierkegaards's assertion. While recognising
the possible validity of such an observation in certain, carefully qualified
circumstances, one is also aware of how it could be used to legitimise
selfish individualism and as a cover for one's fear of intimate, binding
relationships. Perhaps the safest thing one can say about Thomas's adoption of this attitude in 'Careers' is that it seems to be something between
a weakness and a strength. It is only fair to add, however, that he himself
seems to regard it as such. The remark is made in a specific dramatic
context, against a background of mixed feelings. Thomas is being tortured

by the painfully revealing likeness to himself, in all his weakness, that he sees in his son: 'That likeness/ you are at work upon – it hurts'. Accordingly, a part of him wishes that he had never married.

The experience of marriage is explored by him in a number of poems scattered across many of his collections. 'Anniversary' appeared first in *Tares* and it celebrates, in its own 'diffident' fashion, nineteen years spent 'under the same roof/ Eating our bread,/ Using the same air' (*CP*, p. 103). In fact, the present participle dominates the poem, as Thomas tenderly describes a continuous and continuing process in which the care of each partner for the other is grounded in mutual carefulness of one another's separateness: 'Sighing, if one sighs,/ Meeting the other's/ Words with a look/ That thaws suspicion'. This sense of marriage constantly involving delicate negotiations and accommodations (both through and about language) is one that recurs in R. S. Thomas's poetry. It can best be seen in the second of the following stanzas from 'He and She':

> Seated at table –
> no need for the fracture
> of the room's silence; noiselessly
> they conversed. Thoughts mingling
> were lit up, gold
> particles in the mind's stream.
>
> Were there currents between them?
> Why, when he thought darkly,
> would the nerves play
> at her lips' brim? What was the heart's depth?
> There were fathoms in her,
> too, and sometimes he crossed
> them and landed and was not repulsed. (*CP*, p. 459)

Several of the images here partake of the self-consciousness of conceits, thus emphasising the studied nature of the observations made as if by an authoritatively objective or judicious third party standing close to but outside the relationship. An ascetic intimacy of mutual understanding, which is expressed only through stressed negatives ('no need . . . noiselessly') is transformed into sensuously physical-mental rapport through that glorious image of 'gold/ particles in the mind's stream'. As for the last stanza, the series of questions there creates an air of mystery, of indeterminacy, with the point of view of the speaker for the first time being appreciably closer to that of the man than that of the woman. The impression of strange, ungraspable correspondences – of mood and of thought – is enhanced by the ghostly presence of rhyme and internal rhyme. 'Darkly . . . play . . . lips' creates an elusive suggestion of consonantal echo, while 'crossed' in conjunction with 'repulsed' offers the rudiments, but no more, of syllabic end-rhyme. The muted effect is, of course, deliberate.

In fact, 'He and She' reminds one in places of aspects of Donne's poem 'The Ecstasy' transposed to a much lower pitch, to allow for the temperate nature of a settled, habitual relationship, as opposed to the extravagant raptures of courtship. R. S. Thomas's poem is a beautiful meditation on the mystery of a mature married love that 'interinanimates two souls' and 'defects of loneliness controls'. Indeed the speaker in 'He and She' is the ideal witness imagined by Donne: one 'so by love refined/ That he soul's language understood'.[15]

Whereas R. S. Thomas's wife is invoked only as an intensely companionable presence in 'He and She', her character is lovingly detailed in 'The Way of It'. Her talents as a professional painter are Thomas's starting point – 'With her fingers she turns paint/ into flowers' – and her self-effacing dexterity is gently acknowledged to be the domestic art that has sustained their marriage so resourcefully: 'She is at work/ always, mending the garment/ of our marriage, foraging/ like a bird for something/ for us to eat' (*CP*, p. 323). Thomas presents himself as one humbled and chastened by her selflessness, an impression of both partners that is strengthened by the absence of sentimentality in the picture of relationship he paints:

> Her words, when she would scold,
> are too sharp. She is busy
> after for hours rubbing smiles
> into the wounds.

Practical and clear-sighted, his wife is credited at the end with having seen through his early strutting courtship display of his qualities and with accepting him, without even the illusion of romantic love, 'as some-one/ she could build a home with/ for her imagined child'. At that point, Thomas himself seems like one admirably purged of vanity. As we shall see in chapter 9, Kierkegaard once remarked that most of the time we are subjective towards ourselves and objective in our relationship to others, whereas the great Christian achievement is to be objective in relation to oneself and subjective in one's identification with others. In 'The Way of It' R. S. Thomas succeeds very movingly in achieving this reversal.

But the most affecting of all the poems he wrote about, or to, his wife before her death are those where she is addressed as his partner in old age, as together they struggle against the clock, 'the continuing/ prose that is the under-current/ of all poetry'. The phrase comes from 'Countering', a poem that ends with a grand flourish of eloquent defiance, all the more powerful for being so uncharacteristic of the late Thomas:

> Then take my hand that is
> of the bone the island
> is made of, and looking at
> me say what time it is
> on love's face, for we have
> no business here other than
> to disprove certainties the clock knows. (*CP*, p. 499)

This is a passage of expansive plangency, almost comparable with, say, the end of Hart Crane's *Voyages*, V. But it is permeated by a sad knowing-ness much more reminiscent of Donne than of Crane. What Donne and Thomas have in common is a sense of 'the continuing/ prose that is the under-current/ of all poetry'. When Donne, in 'The Good-Morrow', prod-uces a whole exuberant array of images to prove that his new love is unique and indestructible, he does so in the certain knowledge that every-thing mortal is inescapably perishable. The blithe confidence of his last lines is therefore shadowed by secret desperation: 'If our two loves be one, or thou and I/ Love so alike, that none do slacken, none can die' (p. 60). If indeed. And the conclusion of Thomas's poem is surely much more 'poetic' than is usual with him precisely because he wants to hint at the empty rhetoric of bravado even while genuinely placing his faith in the triumph of love over time.

R. S. Thomas's celebration of his wife's 'Seventieth Birthday' is a piece as perfect as any he wrote about their relationship while she was alive:

> Made of tissue and $H_2O$,
> and activated by cells
> firing – Ah, heart, the legend
> of your person! Did I invent
> it, and is it in being still?
>
> In the competition with other
> women your victory is assured.
> It is time, as Yeats said, is
> the caterpillar in the cheek's rose,
> the untiring witherer of your petals.
>
> You are drifting away from
> me on the whitening current of your hair.
> I lean far out from the bone's bough,
> knowing the hand I extend
> can save nothing of you but your love. (*CP*, p. 384)

This is, in its way, a 'language' poem, to use a fashionable term. It offers a contrast between two kinds of discourse, beginning with a pseudo-scientific definition of human being, before proceeding to that other mode of speaking, of which poetry is here self-consciously the supreme example. The exclamation that ushers in this other mode draws attention to its own distinctive peculiarity – the peculiarity of a mode of expression where 'heart' can be synonymous with 'person' in a sense that can be covered by the word 'legend'. The touch of the archaic about the expression is defiantly deliberate, as is the suggestion of old-fashioned courtesy, even gallantry, in the paying of the compliment. And as the poem proceeds, metaphor comes ever more proudly into its own, with the paraphrase of Yeats serving to highlight and to dramatise this process. But the more the writing advertises itself as 'invention', as artifice, the more sincere and authentic a form it seems to become, and the more perfectly suited it undeniably is to the tracing of the inner truth of a human relationship.

In the last poem of *The Echoes Return Slow*, R. S Thomas again attempted a love-poem not only in old age, but also in a sense of old age:

> I look out over the timeless sea
> over the head of one, calendar
> to time's passing, who is now open
> at the last month, her hair wintry.
>
> Am I catalyst of her mettle that,
> at my approach, her grimace of pain
> turns to a smile? What it is saying is:
> 'Over love's depths only the surface is wrinkled'. (*CLP*, p. 72)

Even before this collection had appeared, J. P. Ward had shrewdly noted that Thomas's work was 'suffused with a new sense of the timeless. Poem after poem seems to escape any sense of the present moment, of the pressure of incident, scene or person.'[16] 'I look out' is further confirmation of the move in this direction, and it is surely one of the finest of Thomas's poems in what I have suggested is essentially the genre of epigram. Like many a serious epigram, not only does it conclude with an inscription, it also includes an element of grave wit, which in this case seems to operate as a structural principle. The poem begins with a measured contrast, accentuated by parallelism of phrasing, between the 'timeless sea', and the old lady who is so painfully subject to time. But by the poem's close, the love that the lady continues, in spite of her frailty, to embody is recognised as fundamentally unchanging; and so Thomas ends, through his choice of image, by implicitly associating her with the sea after all.

Since these poems to his wife were published in random fashion over a long period of time, they have never been supposed by commentators to form a significant part of his achievement, being assumed instead to have been written merely in 'the interval of his concern'. His poem 'The Hearth', which has an unassuming place in *H'm*, should, however, have prompted his devoted readers to reconsider:

> In front of the fire
> With you, the folk song
> Of the wind in the chimney and the sparks'
> Embroidery of the soot – eternity

> Is here in this small room,
> In intervals that our love
> Widens; and outside
> Us is time and the victims
> Of time . . . (*CP*, p. 222)

Not, then, merely 'an interval of his concern', but rather 'intervals that our love widens . . .'. *They* are the kinds of intervals that R. S. Thomas's poems to his wife occupy in his poetry. As one reads carefully and thoughtfully through his later work, the influence of those poems seems to 'widen', to spread further and further afield, entering for instance into his poems about painting (his late wife was, after all, a painter). In short, as he admits in the closing lines of the poem that precedes and prepares the way for 'I look out over the timeless sea', he knows himself, and shows himself, to be 'in the debt of love'.

Then, after the passing of Mildred Eldridge, each of Thomas's last two collections, *Mass for Hard Times* and *No Truce with the Furies*, included a poem dedicated to her memory. Delicate in verbal structure as she, so Thomas affectionately recollected, had been of bone structure, and as fastidious in expression as she had been reticent, they seem to lie softly on the page, moving tributes to her continuing power to gentle his fierce spirit. These are not so much 'elegies' as soft exhalations of sorrow, implicit confessions that Thomas still regarded her as the better angel of his own nature:

> And she,
> who in life
> had done everything
> with a bird's grace,
> opened her bill now
> for the shedding
> of one sigh no
> heavier than a feather. (*CLP*, p. 198)

All these poems concerned with close members of his family contribute to, and indeed participate in, R. S. Thomas's disinterested exploration of the mystery of being, not least his own. 'Borges suggested that Shakespeare himself did not know who he was', Thomas once said pointedly to Ned Thomas ('Probings', 36), and he gave his own most celebrated essay in autobiography the provocative title 'Nobody'. Speaking of himself late in life he asked: 'But this one, had he ever been anything but solitary?', only to reply with a sentence that should alert us to the other, little-regarded and under-valued aspect of his imagination, the aspect with which this chapter has been primarily concerned: 'And yet in this coastal solitude, far out on a peninsula, the breaking of which by car or aircraft he so much resented, there came to him at odd moments the wisdom of humans' (*CLP*, p. 71).

## Notes

1   R. S. Thomas, 'Self Portrait', *Laboratories of the Spirit* (London: Macmillan, 1975), p. 27.
2   R. S. Thomas, *Later Poems, 1972–82* (London: Macmillan, 1983), p. 182.
3   William Blake, 'Infant Sorrow', *Songs of Experience*, in David Punter (ed.), *William Blake: Selected Poetry and Prose* (London: Routledge, 1988), p. 132.
4   William Wordsworth, 'Michael', in Philip Hobsbaum (ed.), *William Wordsworth: Selected Poetry and Prose* (London: Routledge, 1989), p. 43.
5   Jason Walford Davies, trans., *R. S. Thomas, Autobiographies* (London: Dent, 1997), p. 82. Hereafter *A*. For a discussion of the implications of the relationship, see Katie Gramich, 'Mirror Games: Self and M(O)ther in the Poetry of R. S. Thomas', Damian Walford Davies (ed.), *Echoes to the Amen* (Cardiff: University of Wales Press, 2003), 132–48. And interesting new information about Thomas's mother is recorded in Sheila Savill, 'The Value of Official Records to Studies of R. S. Thomas's Life and Writings', *Almanac*, 15 (2010–11), 84–111.
6   Ned Thomas, 'Probings: an interview with R. S. Thomas', in *Planet* (80), 28–52.
7   Robert Lowell, 'Commander Lowell, 1888–1949', in *Selected Poems* (London: Faber, 1965), pp. 40–2.
8   It should, however, be noted that the opening sections of 'Salt' are about R. S. Thomas's grandfather, judging by the evidence available in *Neb*, but information about his father's boyhood is at the same time mixed in with this material.
9   E. H. Coleridge (ed.), *Coleridge: Poetical Works* (Oxford: Oxford University Press, 1964), p. 242.

[10] This is a grossly simplified summary of a great and complex play. For an English translation of *Blodeuwedd*, see Joseph P. Clancy, trans., *The Woman Made of Flowers*, in *The Plays of Saunders Lewis*, vol. 1 (Llandybïe: Christopher Davies, 1985).

[11] Sonnet 15, in Stephen Greenblatt, Walter Cohen, Jean E. Howard, Katharine Eisaman Maus (eds), *The Norton Shakespeare* (New York and London: Norton, 2008), p. 1951.

[12] W. B. Yeats, *The Collected Poems of W. B. Yeats* (London: Macmillan, 1971 edn), p. 101.

[13] William Hazlitt, 'Coriolanus', in Christopher Salvesen (ed.), *Selected Writings of William Hazlitt* (New York: Signet, 1972), p. 49.

[14] Søren Kierkegaard, *The Present Age*, trans. Alexander Dru (London: Fontana, 1967), p. 91.

[15] 'The Ecstasy', in A. J. Smith (ed.), *Donne: Complete English Poems* (Harmondsworth: Penguin, 1971), p. 53.

[16] J. P. Ward, *The Poetry of R. S. Thomas* (Bridgend: Poetry Wales Press, 1987), p. 141.

1. Richard Hilder, *Cottages at Litlington* (n.d.). Donated by the Pilgrim Trust. © Victoria and Albert Museum, London.

2. Mildred Eldridge, *Addoldy-y-Bedyddwyr* (n.d.).
© Victoria and Albert Museum, London.

MAES YR ONNEN

Elsie Thomas

3. Mildred Eldridge, *Maes yr Onnen*, reproduced in R. S. Thomas, *Selected Prose* (1982).
© Kunjana Thomas 2001.

SOAR Y MYNYDD

Elsie Thomas

4. Mildred Eldridge, *Soar-y-Mynydd*, reproduced in R. S. Thomas, *Selected Prose* (1982).
© Kunjana Thomas 2001.

5. Mildred Eldridge, *Peat Cutting, Cefn Coch* (n.d.).
© Victoria and Albert Museum, London.

6. Kenneth Rowntree, *Conway Castle and Coracle* (n.d.).
© Victoria and Albert Museum, London.

7. Mildred Eldridge, drawing of R. S. Thomas (n.d.).
Private collection.

8. Mildred Eldridge, drawing of R. S. Thomas (n.d.).
Private collection.

9. Edgar Degas, *Portrait of a Young Woman*, 1867. Musée d'Orsay, Paris;
Giraudon; The Bridgman Art Library.

10. Edgar Degas, *Mademoiselle Marie Dihau at the piano*, oil on canvas, *c.*1869–72. Musée d'Orsay, Paris; Giraudon; The Bridgman Art Library.

11. Edgar Degas, *The Opera Orchestra*, oil on canvas, *c*.1870.
Musée d'Orsay, Paris; Giraudon; The Bridgman Art Library.

12. Ben Shahn, *Father and Child*, painting (n.d.).

13. Toyen, *Hlas Lesa I*, painting (n.d.).

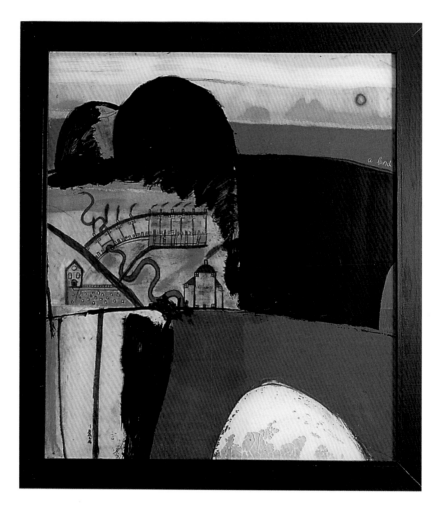

14. Iwan Bala, *Land*, painting (n.d.).

15. Wil Rowlands, *At the End*, painting (n.d.).

16. Christine Kinsey, *Yr Adwy 1 / The Gap 1*,
pencil and charcoal on paper (n.d.).

# The Leper of Abercuawg

Yn Aber Cuawc yt ganant gogeu
Ar gangheu bloduawc.
Coc lauar, canet yrawc.

(In Abercuawg cuckoos are singing/ On blossoming branches/
Loud cuckoo, let it sing long.)[1]

One of the most important books to have been published on R. S. Thomas
is *Gororau'r Iaith: R. S. Thomas a'r Traddodiad Llenyddol Cymraeg*, Jason
Walford Davies's subtle, comprehensive and groundbreaking study of
Thomas's complex indebtedness to the Welsh-language poetic tradition.[2]
Having learnt Welsh as a young adult (one of the many sins he imputed
to his mother was her snobbish discouragement of her son from taking
any interest in the language, despite an upbringing on the overwhelmingly
Welsh-speaking island of Anglesey), Thomas, with the zeal of the linguistic
convert, proceeded to identify so strongly with it that he became a fiercely
militant crusader in support of every attempt to secure its future. But, as
Davies's monograph so arrestingly shows, Thomas also absorbed Welsh-
language poetry into the very substance of his own writing, not least by
adopting strategies of intertextuality that provide some of his poems with
a cultural richness and resonance beyond the ready comprehension of
monoglot English readers. This chapter concerns itself with one example,

small but immensely suggestive, of Thomas's seminal engagements with
the Welsh-language poetic tradition.

* * *

R. S. Thomas confessed a deep passion for Abercuawg. Having delivered
his great lecture on the subject at the National Eisteddfod in Cardigan
(1976),[3] two years later he included a succinct, but rather lame, poetic
version of it in his volume *Frequencies*:

> I am a seeker
> in time for that which is
> beyond time . . .
> always
> about to be; whose duration is
> of the mind, but free as
> Bergson would say of the mind's
> degradation of the eternal. (*CP*, pp. 340–1)

Yet thorough though lecture and poem appear to be in explicating the
uncanny hold that Abercuawg had on the poet's imagination, they seem
to me still to leave something important unstated.

But to begin by recalling the gist of that memorable lecture. To read it
is to become aware that a not insignificant poet is here taking advantage
of an occasion of national importance to make public the essence of his
poetic vision, and to underline the indissoluble dependence of that vision
on his mysteriously intimate relationship with language. While conceding that in its productions the poetic imagination is inherently ambivalent and equivocal, he also insists (avowedly following Coleridge) that
it possesses a core integrity and reliability. Abercuawg, he admits, may
never have existed as a 'real' place, but it nevertheless enjoys a different,
but equally authentic, existence as a hauntingly necessary concept incarnated in a word: the invincible human concept (born of chronic human
need) of a something and a somewhere that, though never fully manifest
in time, forever carries the promise of imminent disclosure. And it is
precisely this concept, a function of the temporal, existential plight of

the eternal soul, which finds its natural home in poetry. Hence Wordsworth's famous invocation of 'something ever more about to be':

> How else does a poet create a poem other than by searching for the word
> which is already in his mind but which has not yet reached his tongue?
> And only through trying word after word does he finally discover the right
> one. This is certainly not an example of emptiness, but of becoming. (*SP*,
> p. 165)

Always sensitive to the fact that the deep meaning of words was inseparable from their sound and texture, Thomas perceptively noted how
the great metric practice of *cynghanedd* (the rules governing the deployment
of sounds that are the root of Welsh practice in the ancient classical *barddas*
tradition) was already implicit in the sonic profile of the word Abercuawg:

> In the poem of Llywarch Hen we are, amongst other things, on the very
> threshold of *cynghanedd*. And at once we see how naturally the word Aber-
> cuawg falls into place in the line. We have heard about *anima naturaliter
> Christiana*. Without a doubt, the Welsh language by its very nature lends
> itself to *cynghanedd*. And this is where the Anglo-Welsh poets, as they are
> called, lose out. (*SP*, p. 155)

Having deliberately set out to remedy that loss in his early English-
language poems by striving to reproduce the effects of *cynghanedd*, Thomas
had eventually given up on the attempt and, by the time he delivered
his eisteddfod lecture, had resigned himself to working exclusively with
the different music of what he persisted in regarding as the 'foreign'
tongue of English.[4]

That remark about *cynghanedd* is underpinned, of course, by Thomas's
awareness of the connection between the medieval *englynion* featuring
Abercuawg and its cuckoos, and the sequence known by the title of *Canu
Llywarch Hen* (The songs of Llywarch Hen). Usually dated to the ninth
or tenth century, this powerful collection centres on the tragic plight of
the aged Llywarch, one of the tribal warlords of 'yr Hen Ogledd' – the
'Old North,' the term applied to that region extending from Stirling to
modern Cumbria, which had remained part of the territory of the Cambro-
British (ancestors of the Welsh) down to its loss at the Battle of Chester in

615. And central to the 'Abercuawg' sequence is the tragic situation of a leper ('claf Abercuawg'), whose infirmity prevents him from taking arms to confront the enemy threatening to despoil his beloved country, with its fair blossoms and mellifluous cuckoos.

But Thomas's remark about the word Abercuawg and *cynghanedd* derived, too, from his awareness as a poet of the powers inherent in, and unique to, the resources of any particular language. His was a poet's peculiar sensitivity to the way in which such potencies and potentialities were inseparable from the distinctive dynamics of sound of each tongue. The Abercuawg lecture therefore constitutes, in important respects, a chapter from Thomas's own 'poetics', and it also includes clear hints, such as the following, about the political convictions underlying some of his poetic practice.

> Wales once had some kind of freedom . . . That freedom depended on force of arms . . . That was the way of those days. The time of armed force is now finished, if civilisation is to survive. If Wales knows those things which pertain to her peace, Abercuawg may come nearer. (*SP*, p. 163)

There is, indeed, a direct connection between this statement and a poem such as 'Welsh History', with its familiar opening line: 'We were a people taut for war' – where 'taut', suggestive as it is of a tightened bow-string, cannot but bring to mind its homonym 'taught'. But as in 'Abercuawg,' the warmongering days of the Welsh are, by the end of the poem, safely consigned to the distant past:

> We were a people, and are so yet,
> When we have finished quarrelling for crumbs
> Under the table, or gnawing the bones
> Of a dead culture, we will arise,
> Armed, but not in the old way.[5]

At least, that was the original ending. But it was later replaced by a very different version: 'we will arise/ And greet each other in a new dawn' (*CP*, p. 36). So why the change? Probably because of the ambiguity of the original, as it seemed to allow for some kind of militant, if not military, struggle in the Welsh present. As a pacifist, Thomas may have been anxious to remove entirely any residual hint of violence, particularly once he had been accused, during the 1970s and 1980s, of being an apologist for the shadowy 'Meibion Glyndŵr' and its arson campaign against holiday homes in the rural, Welsh-speaking heartlands. The original phrasing may nevertheless have registered a genuine, if unacknowledged, equivocation of feeling on Thomas's part about the exercise of violence in support of a just cause. And this largely unconscious ambivalence may, moreover, have been implicated in the complex appeal for him of Abercuawg and the story in which it had been anciently embedded.

From the point of view of modern Welsh scholarship, R. S. Thomas's Eisteddfod lecture is marred by one egregious error. He repeatedly assumes that Llywarch Hen was indeed the author of the sequence of *englynion* that go under his name, whereas modern scholars are now confident that he was not.[6] What is more, they have come to entertain serious doubts as to whether the Abercuawg poems should be regarded as part of the Llywarch Hen corpus at all.[7] In his assumptions, Thomas was guided by the conclusions of an older generation of scholars, the most distinguished of whom, Sir Ifor Williams, further suggested that the Llywarch Hen poems may well be all that has survived to us of a saga about the final tragic fall of the House of Llywarch, that would have originally taken the form of a lengthy prose narrative for public recital, punctuated and enriched by the Llywarch Hen *englynion*.[8] And to this another eminent scholar with whose work R. S. Thomas would also undoubtedly have been familiar, A. O. H. Jarman, added the suggestion that the Llywarch Hen sequence could usefully be contrasted with the great heroic poetry of Taliesin, written several centuries earlier, around the seventh century. The juxtaposition of the two texts, Jarman argued, would make clear the radical shift in values that had occurred during those intervening centuries, because, through its narrative, the Llywarch Hen sequence called into question the cult of military prowess that had been the great glory of the earlier poetry.[9]

In that sequence, Llywarch Hen laments the loss of all but one of his twenty-four sons in the bloody battles to defend his kingdom. While willing to follow his brothers' example, the last son, Gwên, refuses to obey his father's command and swear either to prevail or to sacrifice his life in the struggle. Nevertheless, he too plunges into the heat of conflict and is finally killed, leaving the aged Llywarch, now childless, not only to lament his terrible loss but also consumed by guilt at the part he himself had played in urging his sons on to their fate by taunting them to prove their manly valour. The whole sequence is, therefore, haunted by doubts about the heroic code that would have been inconceivable to the contemporaries of the earlier Taliesin. And it was the cycle's affecting preoccupation with these doubts that made the Llywarch Hen sequence so attractive to T. Gwynn Jones, one of the giants of the twentieth-century Welsh-language Renaissance, who, a pacifist like R. S. Thomas, found himself increasingly disturbed in 1934 by the looming premonition of yet further carnage, so close on the heels of the First World War. It was specifically the bellicose old warlord's bitter gibe that another of his battle-averse sons, Cynddilig, was no true man ('Och, Gynddilig, na buost wraig'/ 'Alas, Cynddilig, that you were not born a woman') that burned its way into Jones's troubled conscience.

> A'r geiriau anhrugarog,
> Yn edliw, gan ryw lusgo'n wawdlyd,
> Iddo ei ofer ddefod,
> A'i adduned yn y dyddiau hynny.

(And the merciless words,/ with their sarcastic drawl, rebuked him/ for his empty rite/ at that time.)[10]

That 'empty rite,' the vow taken by Cynddilig in becoming a monk, chimed with T. Gwynn Jones's own experience, conscience-stricken as he continued to agonise about his decision, during the First World War, to claim exemption from conscription on medical grounds.[11] His long narrative poem about 'Cynddilig' may, therefore, have been his own fantasy of redemption: his saintly prince does, indeed, die a heroic death in the end, when he sacrifices his life in a pacific attempt to save a young girl from the soldiers who are hunting her down.

It is highly probable that R. S. Thomas was aware of this poem from its very first publication in Y Dwymyn in 1944 as, having recently committed himself to learning Welsh, he found himself newly enabled to gain entrance both to the strong pacifist tradition of Welsh-language Wales during the inter-war years (exemplified by 'Cynddilig') and to the rich field of Welsh-language literature that had been one of his reasons for mastering the language. As early as 1946, Thomas specifically aligned himself, as an 'Anglo-Welsh' writer, with the author of 'Cynddilig': 'there are signs now,' he wrote, 'that the mantle of writers like T. Gwynn Jones and W. J. Gruffydd is falling not upon the younger Welsh [language] writers, but upon those of us who express ourselves in the English tongue' (*SP*, p. 31). And familiarity with 'Cynddilig' at this early period would certainly have inclined Thomas to set both T. Gwynn Jones's poem and the Llywarch Hen sequence with which it was intimately connected in the context of the Second World War and the Welsh pacifist tradition with which he himself felt such strong affinities.

\* \* \*

When set in this context, R. S. Thomas's fascination with Abercuawg – the inexplicable hold of which over his imagination he attempts to exorcise by explication in his lecture – may be seen as deeply rooted in a dense complex of feelings, prominent among which is his unease, amounting sometimes to guilt, about the probity of his own pacifist commitments: 'R.S. had been a pacifist on principle ever since finding himself at Chirk directly before the Second World War'.[12] Hence his oblique and probably unconscious, concern with the charged relationship between valour and 'cowardice', explored alike in the Llywarch Hen sequence and 'Cynddilig'. And to begin to suspect this, is to become aware of how frequently this vexed issue surfaces in his writings.

It makes itself most clearly known in the *Abercuawg* lecture in the following passage:

> Whatever Abercuawg might be, it is a place of trees and fields and flowers and bright unpolluted streams, where the cuckoos continue to sing. For such a place I am ready to make sacrifices, maybe even to die. (*SP*, p. 158)

It is the cautiousness of that final phrase ('*maybe* even to die'), qualifying as it does the initial note of heroism, that is worth noting and will need explicating, evocative as it is of the leper of the Abercuawg poems who, much though he would love to face the enemy, is prevented from doing so by his disability. And it is R. S. Thomas's relationship with this leper of Abercuawg, his psychic twin, that invites further reflection.

His remarkable autobiographical volume, *The Echoes Return Slow*, includes the following reminiscence:

> Others were brave . . . What does one do when one does not believe in action, or in certain kinds of action? Are the brave lacking in imagination? Are the imaginative not brave, or do they find it more difficult to be brave? What does a man do with his silence, his aloneness, but suffer the sapping of unanswerable questions? (*CLP*, p. 21)

The poem on the facing page concludes with a devastating self-accusation:

> When volunteers
> were called for to play
> death's part, stood modestly
> in the wings, preferring rather
> to be prompter than prompted. (*CLP*, p. 21)

Whatever their truth, these lines are evidence that Thomas did, at one time, harbour misgivings that his wartime pacifism might have been tainted with a hint of cowardice. Nor is it a lone example of his troubled fascination with courage. There are instances scattered throughout his work of his unease at physical bravery, of his fearful resentment of its manifestation in others, and of his fierce, in some ways self-implicating, contempt for the 'cowardice' of a Welsh nation unwilling to stand up for its rights. And in his obsession with these matters, he possesses a more than passing resemblance to the sick man of Abercuawg.

Thomas's conduct during the wartime years again becomes a subject for concern in his prose autobiography *Neb*. Shortly after his marriage, Liverpool fell victim to a series of devastating attacks from the air that, as was discussed in chapter 1, came disturbingly close to home for the young curate of Chirk and his wife. 'Every night, weather permitting, the aeroplanes would pass overhead on their way in, and they soon started getting on the curate's nerves, not because of fear so much as disgust and despair at the thought that they were on their way to drop their fiendish loads on helpless women and children' (*A*, p. 49). Thus far it is the conscientious objector who is audible. But there follows a reflection that bends the remark in the disconcerting direction of confession: 'At the same time he noticed that he wasn't showing enough confidence and fearlessness in the presence of the girl he had promised to look after.' This self-accusatory misgiving is reinforced a sentence or two later when he reports how, 'One night when he was leaving the church, which was next door to the house, he heard a terrible bang very close by. He ran inside and urged his wife to come and take cover under the stairs, and there they were for hours, while the enemy aeroplanes circled above their heads' (*A*, p. 51). When read in succession, as part of a single paragraph, these sentences, inclining as they do in rather different directions, seem a prime instance of what Thomas had in mind when he described his wartime self as 'suffer[ing] the sapping of unanswerable questions'.

It is of course the 'manliness' of his younger self that Thomas so painfully doubts in these passages of wartime reminiscence, and at the time of writing he would have been fully conscious that in Welsh the word for 'man' (*gŵr*) is actually a constituent of the word for 'valour' (*gwrhydri*) as for 'courageousness' (*gwroldeb*). This, in turn, intensifies the contempt in that phrase of Llywarch Hen's accusing his son Cynddilig of a feminine weakness: 'Och, Gynddilig, na buost wraig'. Indeed, in the original Welsh-language version of his autobiography, his mention of a lack of courage before his wife (*gwraig*) raises the spectre of precisely some such supposed gender role-reversal as is implied in Llywarch's scathing remark. It brings to mind Thomas's lifelong complaint that, by smothering him with love and care, his mother had 'unmanned' him early – a feeling that may well have been enhanced by the knowledge that, as ship's captain, his father was undoubtedly a man among men.

Unfortunately, some of the most prominent parishioners Thomas encountered when he was appointed rector of Eglwys-Fach could boast the kind of distinguished military background most calculated to exacerbate his uncertainties about his own physical valour. This led inescapably to friction and to sour views such as those recorded in *Neb*:

The people of the armed forces wanted you to know that they had been 'someone' in the forces by retaining their rank after retiring . . . A friend of R.S.'s, when he was in Eglwys-Fach would tell of his experience of a cousin of his. When the two men were younger they were friendly, indeed very close to each other. But the cousin, who was in the army, started to get on in the world, reaching the top of his profession and becoming a very important man. R.S.'s friend admitted to him that he could not be doing with him after that. He was so full of his job and importance that he could not remember the affinity that had once thrived between them . . . Wales lost her leaders centuries ago. But there is still a ruling class in England, the product of the public schools and the armed forces. (*A*, p. 74)

Given his strong distaste for the military type, it is hardly surprising that Thomas soon found himself at loggerheads with those from the armed services he encountered at Eglwys-Fach:

The vicar's function is to keep the peace in the parish, not drive people into head-on collision with one another. The worst ones for doing this, perhaps, are officers of the armed forces, and fate plays into their hands, since in the armed forces the chaplain is subordinate to them in rank. It is very difficult for an officer who has retired to convince himself that he has done so. And there is the vicar in front of him to remind him of his superior rank. And since R.S. saw Christ's message as a totally pacifist one, trouble was sure at some time to raise its head. (*A*, p. 75)

His resentments on this score are encapsulated in a sentence in *The Echoes Return Slow*: 'When the English colonise a parish, a vicar's is a chaplain's work.' And this is twinned with a poem sardonically describing his experience of circulating at a cocktail party attended by officers:

> I move
> to a new partner, polishing
> my knuckles, dazzled by the medals
> he has left off. (*CLP*, p. 38)

This is matched by another poem that opens by mentioning 'this one with his starched lip,/ his medals, his meanness;/ his ability to live cheap off dear things' (*CLP*, p. 34). The lack of generosity in these rather cheap gibes has been underlined by Byron Rogers, who has reasonably pointed out that several of the military men Thomas encountered at Eglwys-Fach really had enjoyed a highly distinguished career, including Major-General Lewis Pugh:

> A war hero awarded the D.S.O. three times, a man who could speak German, Urdu and Gurkhali, and had crossed the North West Frontier in disguise, he could have popped out of a Hollywood blockbuster for a breather. And astonishingly this is exactly where he returned twenty years later, to the Hollywood blockbuster *The Sea Wolves*, made in 1980, when he was played by Gregory Peck.[13]

Rogers further interestingly adds: 'physically, he and Thomas were not dissimilar . . . [and] both he and Thomas were intelligent, complex men. Both spoke English with cut-glass accents, yet both took being Welsh very seriously. Pugh, who had spoken Welsh as a child, enrolled in his retirement at a further education class in Aberystwyth, sitting amongst the youngsters, so he could take a GCE in it: this took him four years.' Here, then, is precisely the *alter ego* Thomas would have found psychologically most disturbing, the very embodiment of that physical courage about the presence of which in himself he felt the deepest, most unnerving doubts. This may partly explain the visceral nature of Thomas's recoil from the many Pughs he encountered at Eglwys-Fach and his distaste at the way in which 'People come in their thousands to stare with a mixture of admiration and envy at the winners of medals' (*A*, p. 75).

The context of this last remark is interesting. It occurs when Thomas is ruminating on the distinctive kind of courage that might be more readily found in a creative artist or a priest than in any product of the armed forces – the courage to accept that one's life and one's achievements are of absolutely no note in the face of eternity and thus to admit that one is *neb*, a 'nobody'. The other side of the coin of Thomas's misgivings about his own possible lack of physical courage, then, is the intense interest he shows in distinguishing *other* kinds of courage, of a moral and spiritual kind, to which he might more reasonably lay modest claim. In this again he resembles T. Gwynn Jones, whose 'Cynddilig' concludes with its hero's demonstration of moral courage in an attempt to save a young girl's life without resorting to the force of arms.

\* \* \*

As several commentators have noted, some of Thomas's early poems about Iago Prytherch and his kind have an unexpected heroic ring to them.[14] Sometimes, of course, this is by way of a mock-epic celebration of the upland farmers' feats, as in the celebrated poem 'Cynddylan on a Tractor' (CP, p. 30). In the context of the present discussion, it is worth noticing that the name 'Cynddylan' is, in fact, taken from the same corpus of medieval work to which *Canu Llywarch Hen* belongs. Indeed, it occurs most famously in *Canu Heledd*, a kind of 'companion' sequence to the Llywarch poems, which unforgettably elegises the destruction of Cynddylan's great halls: 'Ystafell Cynddylan ys tywyll heno' ('Cynddylan's chamber is dark tonight'). By implicitly viewing the crude modern hill farmer through the lens of this epic tragic event, then, Thomas is implying the devastating decline of the Welsh from the heroic princes of their past to the servile peasantry of their present. The knight errantry of this vacuously grinning modern hero of the hills takes the self-satisfied form of riding proudly not on horseback but in the seat of a tractor noisily racketing its way down the lane, drowning out the sweet birdsong of Abercuawg as it goes.

But in that seminal poem 'A Peasant', Iago's heroism is more sincerely lauded: 'Remember him, then, for he, too, is a winner of wars,/ Enduring like a tree under the curious stars' (CP, p. 4). Since farmers were at that time being loudly praised by government for their contributions to the war effort by increasing yield through the adoption of new mechanical aids to farming such as Cynddylan's tractor, it would be easy to suppose that this was what Thomas had in mind. But far from it. As 'Cynddylan on a Tractor' demonstrates, he was fiercely opposed to these innovations, destructive as they were of old customs and practices. On the contrary, therefore, Thomas's praise for Iago is, as pointed out in chapter 1, a reaffirmation of the ancient, unchanging pastoralism he represents. And implicit in that praise is Thomas's commendation of Iago for his exemplary Welshness – his stubborn adherence to a way of life that had survived innumerable centuries and their transient conflicts. *This* entailed a kind of moral courage that Thomas highly prized and with which he could passionately identify.

The same concern to identify forms of courage *alternative* to physical valour is manifest in Thomas's poems praising Welsh culture heroes such as Saunders Lewis and D. Gwenallt Jones. In 'The Patriot', Lewis the revolutionary nationalist is admired for insistently voicing an un-compromising and unpopular challenge, addressed as much to the Welsh people as to established authority:

> Those, who saw
> For the first time that small figure
> With the Welsh words leaving his lips
> As quietly as doves on an errand
> Of peace-making, could not imagine
> The fierceness of their huge entry
> At the ear's porch. (*CP*, p. 150)

It was for Thomas a matter of vital importance to establish, to his own satisfaction, that Welsh independence might feasibly be gained by acts of courage not involving armed struggle (such as the non-violent cam-paign of selective law-breaking adopted by Cymdeithas yr Iaith Gymraeg, following the incitements of Saunders Lewis).[15] The whole of history, he well knew, could scarcely provide one example of national liberation that had not entailed bloodshed. In *Neb*, he observed that

The sadness of things is that the only way to freedom is through fighting for it. That is the lesson of history. Though R.S. was a pacifist, as was fitting for a priest, he knew of no example to the contrary, except India . . . He couldn't recommend violence even in the Welsh cause. (*A*, p. 95)

A little later, while connecting his pacifism with his support of the campaign for nuclear disarmament, Thomas adds that 'Tied in with this was the question of Wales, a small peaceful country that each St David's day would broadcast a message of peace to the world' (*A*, pp. 97–8). A memory of this practice would seem to me to be embedded in Thomas's approving mention of that small figure, 'With the Welsh words leaving his lips/ As quietly as doves on an errand/ Of peace-making'. He may well be recalling Lewis's historic radio broadcast of 1962 addressing the fate of the language, which, as was pointed out in chapter 4, had immense consequences indeed, indubitable proof of the 'fierceness of [its] huge entry/ At the ear's porch'. The lecture had been a remarkable Jeremiad, a stark warning that the Welsh language would die out within a generation or so if the most urgent and radical of steps was not taken to win for it the kind of far-reaching social and legal recognition that alone could guarantee its future.[16] The result – unforeseen by Lewis himself – was the formation of the Welsh language society, Cymdeithas yr Iaith Gymraeg, a young people's revolutionary action group dedicated to the kind of law-breaking campaigns that alone, it quickly became apparent, could mobilise opinion in favour of radical remedial actions. And in publicly supporting their campaigns, despite attracting public ignominy for so doing, Thomas did indeed demonstrate precisely the kind of moral courage that he had so pointedly admired in others.

But there is a yet further layer of meaning, directly pertinent to our present concerns, to be excavated from Thomas's likening of the words broadcast by Lewis to the departure of 'doves/ on an errand of peace-making.' The broadcaster's role in the controversial direct action protest at Penyberth in 1936 (discussed in chapter 4) had been celebrated as a memorably subversive act of civil disobedience in a notable poem by R. Williams Parry that opens as follows:

> Disgynnaist i'r grawn ar y buarth clyd o'th nen
> Gan ddallu â'th liw y cywion oll a'r cywennod;
> A chreaist yn nrysau'r clomendy uwch dy ben
> Yr hen, hen gyffro a ddigwydd ymhlith colomennod.
> Buost ffôl, O wrthodedig, ffôl; canys gwae
> Aderyn heb gâr ac enaid digymar heb gefnydd.

(A bright bird lighted in the sheltered yard
Out of another sky and all his colours dazzled
Our native poultry. Above his head
There was consternation in the dovecote, the kind of fuss

You find among the well-fed and the tame.
The bright bird was unwise. He sang his own song
Unaccompanied, on a new scale
Without sympathy or support. Not so much wrong
As solitary. He was bound to fail.)[17]

Saunders Lewis is here imaged as a bird of prey, in terms that recall the baited Coriolanus' bellicose blood-chilling boast: 'like an eagle in a dove-cote, I/ Flutter'd your Volscians in Corioli: Alone I did it.'[18] And there is an appropriateness to the implicit comparison, given that it is the Lewis of Penyberth who is being celebrated – a Lewis, furthermore, who, having served in the Great War, would have no truck with pacifism and accepted that independence for Wales might well involve a period of armed struggle. But it is not the Lewis of Penyberth that is the subject of Thomas's 'The Patriot,' but the pacific yet no less violently revolutionary Lewis of *Tynged yr Iaith*. And it is that same latter-day Lewis who is again celebrated in another poem that Thomas dedicated to him, simply entitled 'Saunders Lewis'. In that poem, too, it is Lewis's genius for turning words into fierce weapons of mental warfare that is being approved: 'He moved among us: would have led/ To rebellion. Small as he was/ He towered, the trigger of his mind/ Cocked, ready to let fly with his scorn' (*CP*, p. 466). Is this passage not reminiscent of the original ending of 'Welsh History': 'We will arise/ Armed, but not in the old way'? In the later Saunders Lewis, then, Thomas had found that compelling embodiment of moral, as opposed to physical, courage for which he had been seeking as antidote to his own feared fearfulness.

Thomas's concern with different concepts of courage again surfaces very clearly in 'Border Blues', a choric work composed out of several different voices representative of the 'Marches', the Wales-England border region. Here, again, his imagination is haunted by memories of the heroic age and its great poetry of loss and lament, represented this time by famous culturally echoic lines from *Canu Heledd*: 'Eryr Pengwern, penngarn llwyt *heno*' (*CP*, p. 11). 'Eagle of Pengwern, grey-crested, tonight/ Uplifted its war-cry/ Avid for Cynddylan's flesh' (*MWP*, p. 91): bloody massacre and its desolate aftermath is again the subject of this bleak sequence of *englynion* about the permanent loss by the Welsh of the region nowadays centred on Shrewsbury. But alongside this passage in 'Border Blues' is set another, keyed to an altogether more pacific pitch:

> As I was saying, I don't hold with war
> Myself, but when you join your unit
> Send me some of your brass buttons
> And I'll have a shot at the old hare
> In the top meadow, for the black cow
> Is a pint short each morning now. (*CP*, p. 71)

A variation on the biblical injunction to turn one's swords into plough-shares, this passage reaffirms the vision of 'The Peasant', of a peaceful pastoralism stubbornly and courageously outlasting all carnage.

* * *

To recap briefly. 'Yn Aber Cuawc yt ganant gogeu': Thomas's fascination with this ancient line of heroic poetry has been traced back to his famil-iarity with the Llywarch Hen sequence, the primary subject of which has been established as the sceptical investigation of the cult of military heroism. Thomas's interest in such a subject has, in its turn, been traced to his doubts, first surfacing during the Second World War, about his own physical courage, and these doubts, it has further been suggested, found expression in his writings in two contrasting but complementary ways: through his attacks on the military heroes he encountered during his sojourn in Eglwys-Fach, and through his sustained attempts to identify impressive instances of courage alternative, and implicitly superior, to physical courage, such as moral courage and spiritual courage.

It remains only to note one or two more of the possible consequences for Thomas's writing of his doubts about his own valour, the first of which is his ferocious attack on his fellow Welsh for their collective cowardice. As has been demonstrated in an earlier chapter, the most numerous and most scathing indictments occur in that remarkable splen-etic little volume *What is a Welshman?*. 'And in Tregaron', he writes, 'Henry Richard/ still freezes, cast in shame to preside/ over the pacifism of a servile people' (*CP*, p. 258). It is a surprising and correspondingly arresting use of the word 'pacifism' in a pejorative sense; the turning of it into a noun denoting the cowardice of the meekly subservient; and, perhaps, an unintended revelation of Thomas's suppressed misgivings about his own pacifism. And in associating it not only with the Welsh people but with Henry Richard, Thomas was adding yet further insinuations to his accusation.

Henry Richard (1812–88) became popularly known as the 'Apostle of Peace' for his work on peaceful coexistence between nations that paved the way for the establishing of the League of Nations (forerunner of the United Nations), before whose former headquarters in Geneva a statue of Richard still stands. Thomas's reference, however, is to the other statue of Richard that stands in the square of the apostle Richard's native village, Tregaron, as a reminder not only of his services to world peace but also of his contributions to key social and political issues of nineteenth-century Wales, including land reform, the disestablishment of the state Anglican church, the establishment of a mature system of popular education, and the future of the Welsh language. His other sobriquet, therefore, as a Liberal Member of Parliament for Merthyr Tydfil, was the 'Member for Wales', and he was regarded as the authoritative political voice of the nineteenth-century 'Nonconformist nation'.

But despite Richard's distinguished record (or rather, because of it), he was viewed by Thomas with some suspicion, as his had at best been a 'contributionist' view of Wales's future within an anglo-British polity to which R. S. Thomas was deeply hostile. Therefore, the Tregaron statue appeared to Thomas, as his remark in *What is a Welshman?* shows, to be a shamefully permanent token of the Welsh people's craven respect for a dominant English establishment. For Thomas, then, Richard's vaunted and lauded pacifism was inauthentic, being merely the mask of his pusillanimity. And in Richard's statue Thomas seems to have discerned the lineaments of his own 'secret shame' – the guilt of uncertainty he felt about the moral status of his own wartime pacifism, in the face of what he feared had been his lack of physical courage at that time. Moreover, those lines about Richard's statue may well be shadowed by Thomas's recollection of one of the landmark poems of the 1960s, Robert Lowell's

'For the Union Dead', which famously takes Saint-Gaudens's statue to Colonel Robert Shaw and his black troops, opposite the State House on Boston Common, as the moral compass by which to judge the moral decline of the city since the Civil War era: 'Their monument sticks like a fishbone/ in the city's throat.'[19] By contrasting means, the statue on Tregaron square also seems to provide Thomas with a mean of orientating his relations both to his nation and to himself.

The heroic poems of the earliest centuries are again brought to mind in *What is a Welshman?*, when Thomas remarks to his fellow-countrymen, 'If I told you that Catraeth/ has always to be refought . . ./ How would that have comforted you?'.[20] The reference is to Aneirin's ur-poem of Welsh nationhood, *Y Gododdin*, composed in around the year 600, with its celebrated opening lines, 'Gwŷr aeth Catraeth oedd ffraeth eu llu' ('Men went to Catraeth, in high-spirits their war-band' (*MWP*, p. 47)). It tells the story of the brave company of one hundred who, after feasting and carousing for a year, sallied forth from the Scottish lowlands (then part of 'Yr Hen Ogledd'/ 'The Old North') to Catraeth (modern-day Catterick) and to certain death at the hands of a huge enemy force. Once again, Thomas's obsession with want of courage is evident, this time in his determination to measure modern Wales against the martial spirit of the men of Gododdin and to find it pitifully wanting.

Thomas was even sufficiently self-aware to sense the dubious provenance and character of his own trumpeted contempt for English military might. Included in *What is a Welshman?* is a poem, bearing the title 'His condescensions are short-lived', spoken in the character of a smugly self-satisfied Welshman:

> I don't know, he said. I feel sorry
> for the English . . .
> 　　　　　All those tanks
> and guns; the processions
> that go nowhere; the medals
> and gold braid . . . (*CP*, p. 259)

Dangling from the lips of the speaker is a cigarette 'supplied, by the way/ as most things in Wales are/ supplied, by English wholesalers'

(*CP*, p. 259). This is the kind of spineless Welshman, opportunistically anti-English rather than commitedly 'nationalist', who may be heard in 'He agrees with Henry Ford' declaring 'Llywelyn? Old hat./ Glyndŵr? A con man' (*CP*, p. 261).

*What is a Welshman?* was R. S. Thomas's exasperated response to what he saw as craven Welsh support for the 1969 Investiture of the Prince of Wales, an event he (as pointed out in chapter 4) regarded as a cynical public relations exercise by the Labour Government (and stage-managed by the 'quisling' Secretary of State for Wales, George Thomas) to drain off the rising popular support for Plaid Cymru. Highly conscious as he was of the key role historically played by the site of the Investiture, Caernarfon Castle, in the Anglo-Norman subjugation of Wales, Thomas was particularly sensitive to the militaristic, as well as the jingoistic, aspects of the modern event. In 'To Pay for His Keep', a speaker who could well be Prince Charles himself, is heard to observe that 'A few medals would do now' (*CP*, p. 257), to complete the work of bringing the Welsh obediently to heel. But imprisoned within his own complacency, the speaker is unable to look beyond the grim shadow cast by the gigantic castle and its keep and see

> that far hill
> in the sun with the long line
> of its trees climbing
> it like a procession
> of young people, young as himself. (*CP*, p. 257)

As noted in chapter 4, the reference is to the protests both of Cymdeithas yr Iaith Gymraeg and of the much more extreme campaigners who had attempted to disrupt the Investiture through the use of explosives (positioned to destroy property rather than people). In their activities, Thomas found instances of the kind of courage with which he could unequivocally identify and which provided him with some hope that the Welsh nation might not be completely lacking in spirit after all.

\* \* \*

The subtle obliquities of Thomas's psycho-textual strategies in many of the bicultural instances considered above are surely indicative of the liminal nature of his anxieties, hovering as they did between his conscious and his unconscious apprehension. 'Is there meaning to a name as such?', he enquires while recalling his deliberate decision to name his son Gwydion rather than William or John. Philosophers, he concedes, might very well argue not, but he begs to differ: 'Nevertheless, a grain of doubt remains in my mind too, because of the inherent power of words. "Now Gwydion was the best story teller in the world"' (*SP*, p. 157) (the quotation comes from that magical store of medieval tales, *Y Mabinogion*). Hence his ruminating at length on the mysterious power the enchanting word Abercuawg has so stubbornly had over his own imagination.

> Yn Aber Cuawc yt ganant gogeu
> Ar gangheu blodeuawc;
> Gwae glaf a'e clyw yn vodawg.
> (*Canu Llywarch Hen*, p. 23)

(In Abercuawg cuckoos are singing
On blossoming branches
Woe to the leper who listens to them contentedly.)

The leper guiltily curses his inability to defend his native paradise. The Abercuawg *englynion* recite his story: he had been one of the strongest and bravest of warriors until felled by leprosy and condemned to the impotency against which he now savagely rails. This chapter has been concerned to try to understand the resonances the leper's situation carried for R. S. Thomas, in particular reawakening as it did his misgivings about his own adequacy as a cultural 'warrior'. Having declined to fight either in the name of Wales or of Britain during the Second World War on the grounds of conscience, he had subsequently been unnerved by the possibility that his action may have been unconsciously motivated in part by lack of physical courage. Thereafter, he became somewhat preoccupied with alternative forms of courage to which he could give his wholehearted assent and attempt to exemplify. However, he may also have gradually come to doubt his efficacy even in these directions. As has already been discussed, his cultural hero was Saunders Lewis, and Lewis himself, at his life's end, had sadly concluded that his own struggles to reawaken pride in the Welsh nation had resulted in nothing but failure. There seem to me to be some grounds for believing that R. S. Thomas ended by sharing Lewis's doubts.

Among the drafts he left behind when he died are several abortive attempts at completing a poem that opens as follows:

> I would have spread my wings over you
> My country, made of you a fortress as impregnable as fair.[21]

It is an attempted translation of 'Caer Arianrhod' (Arianrhod's Fortress), the poem in which Lewis confesses his failure, despite all his lifelong efforts, to rouse Wales to full consciousness:

> Taenais aden fy mreuddwyd drosot ti, fy ngwlad;
> Codaswn it – O pes mynnasit – gaer fai bêr;
> Ond un â'r seren wib, deflir o blith y sêr
> I staenio'r gwyll â'i gwawr a diffodd, yw fy stâd.

(I spread the wing of my dream over you, my country;
I would have raised for you – Oh, had you wished it – a sweet fortress;
But one with the falling star, flung from amid the stars
To stain the gloom with its dawn that soon died, is my state.)[22]

The poem derives from an old tale concerning the dawn meeting between Owain Glyndŵr and the Abbot of Glyn-y-Groes. It tells how one morning Glyndŵr awakened early from the cave where he'd slumbered for long centuries with his men, awaiting recall by his nation in its hour of need, and prepared to resume battle. Happening to meet the Abbot, he remarked that the holy man must be an early riser, only to be advised that it was not the monk but he, the soldier, who was too early afoot – the nation was not yet ready for his services. Disappointed, Glyndŵr returned to his long slumber.

Daniel Westover has perceptively noted two richly suggestive aspects of the terms in which Thomas (as distinct both from Lewis and from the translator of Lewis's work into English, Joseph P. Clancy) chooses his words.[23] By opting to make his fortress 'impregnable' (contrast Clancy's accurate 'fair'), Thomas aligns this late text with his earliest signature poem 'A Peasant': there, in the face of all the militarism of the Second World War, the way of life of Iago Prytherch, pacific like Thomas's own, was defiantly celebrated as an 'impregnable fortress'. And by substituting 'I would have spread my wings over you/ My country', for Clancy's 'I spread the wing of my dream over you, my country' – which is much more faithful to the original – Thomas empowers his text to allude to Jesus's celebrated lament from the Gospel According to Matthew (23: 37): 'O Jerusalem, Jerusalem, thou that killest the prophets, and stonest them which are sent unto thee, how often would I have gathered thy children together, even as a hen gathereth her chickens under her wings, and ye would not!' In the context of the foregoing discussion, it seems important to recall that Christian tradition had always understood the biblical passage to relate to the Jews' expectation of a military deliverer rather than a spiritual and pacific one.

It seems affecting that R. S. Thomas should have so stubbornly persisted in his attempts to translate this poem during his last years. He clearly identified both with Saunders Lewis and with the mythical Glyndŵr. And in sadly confessing by means of 'Caer Arianrhod' his failure to mobilise his fellow countrymen, he seems also to be resignedly recognising his place, at long last, given his inadequacies, alongside that other frustrated Welsh warrior, the leper of Abercuawg, who had so bitterly lamented his inability to defend his beloved patrimony:

> Kynnteuin, kein pob amat.
> Pan vryssant ketwyr y gat,
> Mi nyt af: anaf a'm de.

> (Start of summer, fair every shoot,
> When warriors speed to the fray
> I go not, disease will not let me. (*MWP*, p. 103))

Thomas's self-identification with the leper in the subtext of his Abercuawg lecture marks the pivotal point of the present study. In part, inscribed in that identification is all the guilt and anguish that, as has
repeatedly been demonstrated in the foregoing chapters, Thomas felt at
his inability effectively to protect that distinctive (and of course question-
able) vision of 'Wales' to which he had devoted much of his adult life.
But also folded into that identification is the sense of moral insufficiency
and spiritual bewilderment that was to become the consistent burden
of the poetry of his final decades and to which sustained attention will
therefore have to be paid in the chapters that follow.

## Notes

1 'Claf Abercuawg', in Ifor Williams (ed.), *Canu Llywarch Hen* (Cardiff: Uni-
versity of Wales Press, 1935), p. 23; trans. Joseph P. Clancy, 'The Leper of Aber
Cuawg', *Medieval Welsh Poetry* (Dublin: Four Courts Press, 2003), p. 101.
Hereafter *MWP*.

2 Jason Walford Davies, *Gororau'r Iaith: R. S. Thomas a'r Traddodiad Llenyddol
Cymraeg* (Caerdydd: Gwasg Prifysgol Cymru, 2003); see also Jason Walford
Davies, '"Thick Ambush of Shadows": Allusions to Welsh Literature in the
work of R. S. Thomas', *Welsh Writing in English; A Yearbook of Critical Essays 1*
(1995), pp. 75–127.

3 R. S. Thomas, 'Abercuawg', in Sandrey Anstey (ed.), *R. S. Thomas: Selected
Prose* (Bridgend: Poetry Wales Press, 1983), pp. 153–166. Hereafter *SP*.

4 As Jason Walford Davies has demonstrated, during the 1940s and 1950s
Thomas attempted to import aspects of *cynghanedd* from Welsh into English,
partly modelling his experiments on the work of Austin Clarke. But thereafter
he grew convinced that the English language (and therefore its poetry) was
incapable of sustaining *cynghanedd*.

5 R. S. Thomas, *Welsh Airs* (Bridgend: Poetry Wales Press, 1987), p. 9.

6 'By accepting all the *englynion* as the authentic work of Llywarch Hen, and
as a body of work contemporary with the events it describes, enough material
was assembled to shape the foregoing interesting sketch of the poet's life, and
fully to justify the epithet "Hen" [Old] traditionally attached to his name. A
scrutiny of the poems' style and content, however, leads one to the conclusion
that it is not possible to attribute them either to Llywarch or to his Age.' Ifor
Williams, *Canu Llywarch Hen*, p. x. My translation.

7 'I do not for one minute believe that this unified composition belongs to the
circle of Llywarch at all.' Williams, *Canu Llywarch Hen*, p. lvi.

[8] See also Ceri W. Lewis: 'Nor should it be overlooked that some tales were told in a combination of verse and prose. In most instances only the verse sections have been preserved, as in the celebrated Llywarch Hen and Heledd cycles.' 'The Content of Poetry and the Bardic Tradition', in A. O. H. Jarman and Gwilym Rees Hughes (eds), revised by Dafydd Johnston, *A Guide to Welsh Literature 1282–1550* (Cardiff: University of Wales Press, 1997), p. 79. Also Jenny Rowland, 'The Prose Settings of the Early Welsh *Englynion Chwedlonol*', *Ériu* XXXVI (1985), 29–43.

[9] A. O. H. Jarman and Gwilym Rees Hughes (eds), *A Guide to Welsh Literature*, vol. 1 (Cardiff: University of Wales Press, 1976), pp. 81–97.

[10] T. Gwynn Jones, 'Cynddilig', *Y Dwymyn: 1934–35* (Denbigh: Gwasg Gee, 1944), pp. 25–42, 29. My translation.

[11] See R. M. Jones, *Llenyddiaeth Gymraeg, 1902–1936* (Llandybie: Barddas, 1987), p. 139.

[12] R. S. Thomas, *Autobiographies*, trans. Jason Walford Davies (London: Dent, 1997), p. 95. Hereafter *A*.

[13] Byron Rogers, *The Man who went into the West: the Life of R. S. Thomas* (London: Aurum Press, 2006), pp. 192–3.

[14] Anthony Conran, *The Cost of Strangeness: Essays on the English Poets of Wales* (Llandysul: Gomer, 1982), pp. 220–62.

[15] 'And the more he took to noticing it, all the more English he saw; . . . On reflection, R. S. had no doubt that it was Cymdeithas yr Iaith Gymraeg that had woken him up to the situation' (*A*, p. 93).

[16] A translation of the text by Gruffydd Aled Williams, under the title of 'The Fate of the Language', may be found in Alun R. Jones and Gwyn Thomas (eds), *Presenting Saunders Lewis* (Cardiff: University of Wales Press, 1973), pp. 127–41.

[17] R. Williams Parry, *Cerddi'r Gaeaf* (Dinbych: Gwasg Gee, 1971), 76. Translation by Emyr Humphreys, in Menna Elfyn and John Rowlands (eds), *The Bloodaxe Book of Modern Welsh Poetry* (Tarset: Bloodaxe Books, 2003), p. 63.

[18] *Coriolanus*, 5.6, lines 115–17.

[19] Robert Lowell, 'For the Union Dead', *Collected Poems* (New York: Farrar, Straus and Giroux), pp. 376–8.

[20] R. S. Thomas, *What is a Welshman?* (Swansea: Christopher Davies, n.d.), p. 8.

[21] I am grateful to Gwydion Thomas and family, and to Professor Tony Brown and Dr Jason Walford Davies at the R. S. Thomas Research Centre at Bangor University, for permission to quote unpublished material.

[22] Saunders Lewis, *Selected Poems of Saunders Lewis*, trans. Joseph P. Clancy (Cardiff: University of Wales Press, 1993), p. 30.

[23] Private correspondence. I am very grateful to Dr Westover for these significant insights.

# 7

# Irony in the Soul:
# R. S.(ocrates) Thomas

To those avid for variety, R. S. Thomas's preoccupation, over a quarter of a century, with a very limited number of spiritual issues may seem about as exciting as marking time by marching on the spot. But what appears at first to be an immobility of imagination can turn into its very opposite, if one understands Thomas to be producing an art intensely reflective of the modern condition, as once defined by Maurice Blanchot:

> But where has art led us? To a time before the world, before the beginning. It has cast us out of our power to begin and to end; it has turned us toward the outside without intimacy, without place, without rest. It has led us into the infinite migration of error. For we seek art's essence, and it lies where the nontrue admits of nothing essential. We appeal to art's sovereignty: it ruins the origin by returning it to the errant immensity of an eternity gone astray.[1]

Thomas's production of innumerable religious poems on ostensibly the same subject may then be seen as a confession of incorrigible 'errancy'; an admission that, as a human being dealing in friable language with supra-human matters, he can at best but endlessly demonstrate the paradox that, the more convincing the authority of his phrasing and the finality of his formulations, the greater is the error committed; an error that may, moreover, be undone only by being repeated. As the theologian Mark C.

Taylor has expressed it, every verbal attempt at revealing the mystery of divinity turns into a reveiling of it.[2] And yet, granted its built-in obsolescence, every poetic sortie may also be a passing and passable success; a recovery of spiritual truths in a perpetual spirit of provisional discovery; of re-*new*-ing one's understanding of them. Thomas was a lifelong student of Kierkegaard's writing, and the Dane clearly brings out the spiritual significance of processual thinking in his *Concluding Unscientific Postscript*, when explaining what it means to become a full individual:

> An existing individual is constantly in process of becoming; the actual existing subjective thinker constantly reproduces this existential situation in his thoughts, and translates all his thinking into terms of process. It is with the subjective thinker as it is with a writer and his style; for he only has a style who never has anything finished, but 'moves the waters of the language' every time he begins, so that the most common expression comes into being for him with the freshness of a new birth.
>
> Thus constantly to be in process of becoming is the elusiveness that pertains to the infinite in existence . . . The incessant becoming generates the uncertainty of the earthly life, where everything is uncertain.[3]

In such a state of awareness, Kierkegaard adds, it is possible for someone to 'have a rendezvous with the Deity, who is present as soon as the uncertainty of all things is thought infinitely' (*CUP*, p. 80). It is this fundamental aspect of Thomas's situation as a religious poet – his immutable fixity in, or infinite fixation on, error/repetition/renewal/uncertainty – that tends to be overlooked by commentators eager to see him as involved in a spiritual 'search', and accordingly anxious to distinguish between the different 'stages' of his development.

This is not, however, to deny that different aspects of spiritual existence have concentrated Thomas's mind at different periods. For instance, he followed Kierkegaard in recognising narcissism as a defining feature of spiritually alienated mankind, and this emerges as a particular concern in the volumes he published in 1972, *H'm* and *Young and Old*, where Thomas evolves forms of writing that are concerned with the disestablishment of the self. Indeed, the former opens with a poem, 'Once', in which the biblical account of the creation of mankind is rewritten, in almost

Behmenist fashion, in the form of a narrative of the birth of selfhood. In this revisionist version, the intrusion of a human being (of deliberately unspecified gender) onto a primeval landscape still molten from the subsiding fires of what was clearly a ferociously elemental process of creation, implies a human encounter with an almost savagely awesome divinity. According to Thomas's heterodox account, it was in fearful reaction against this disconcerting exposure to the raw power of the sacred, and not by greedily eating of the fruit of the forbidden tree, that man chose to refashion himself in his own image, creating in the process a 'paradisal' environment in which a subordinated nature becomes demurely deferential. Rather than listen to a disconcerting God speaking in a 'fire sermon' (the phrase, of course, recalls *The Waste Land*), man prefers 'the mingled chorus/ Of weeds and flowers'. Humanity's increasing assurance is registered in the syntax and pattern of the verse, as it moves towards a confident conclusion in which line and phrase are eventually marshalled into almost complacent alignment:

> I held my way
> To the light, inspecting my shadow
> Boldly; and in the late morning
> You, rising towards me out of the depths
> Of myself. I took your hand,
> Remembering you, and together,
> Confederates of the natural day,
> We went forth to meet the Machine. (*CP*, p. 208)

In this passage, Thomas uses both intertextual strategies and symmetries of syntax to produce 'echoes' of meaning and judgement at odds with the confidence of stated meaning. The shape 'rising towards me out of the depths/ Of myself' – with that last phrase (glancing sideways at *The Waste Land*) cunningly held back, changing the whole nature of the experience – is obviously reminiscent of Narcissus' self-infatuation. Moreover, the syntax, aided by the lay-out of the lines, quietly points us to the possibility that the 'you' is no more than the product of the speaker's inspection of its shadow, and therefore an aspect of it. So, when Milton is invoked in the closing lines ('Some natural ears they dropped . . .', as his Adam and Eve left Paradise), he is invited by the text to bring with him all the tragic irony compressed into his celebrated use of that word 'natural' to denote not man's true ('natural') but his fallen and familiar ('natural') state. 'Confederates of the natural day' implies an unholy alliance not only between humans but also between them and a perverted state of narcissistically manipulated, or man-managed, existence that is mistaken for an objective 'natural' order. The very last line, in which mankind goes forth to keep its assignment with the 'Machine' (Thomas's short-hand description of the products of the state of mind that gave rise to what F. R. Leavis used to call 'technologico-benthamite civilization') is therefore a kind of parodic echo of the opening line of the poem: 'God looked at space and I appeared'.

Reading 'Once' alerts us, then, to the way in which Thomas's theology may be inscribed in every aspect and at every level of his writing – from lexicon and syntax to formal patterning. When interpreting his work, we need constantly to be aware of the theology of his style. And in *H'm* that style is often used to explore the self-absorbed, and self-referential, character of ordinary human existence. The nexus of tropes relating to perception in/of space is particularly apt in this connection, and the first 'paragraph' of 'The River' instances this beautifully:

> And the cobbled water
> Of the stream with the trout's indelible
> Shadows that winter
> Has not erased – I walk it
> Again under a clean
> Sky with the fish, speckled like thrushes,
> Silently singing among the weed's
> Branches. (*CP*, p. 226)

Vision is here born of re-vision, which is in turn the result of the (syntactically registered) dethroning and displacing of the self, the replacing of it *in media res*, the returning of it to the world of which it is a part. So the 'I walk it' is a phrase placed physically, as it were, within the stream. The syntax is one of humble subordination to an encompassing, pre-established reality, which the language respectfully endows with a diffused life of its own. 'And the cobbled water. . .' implies a delayed verb, but does not stipulate whether 'water' should be its subject or its object. In retrospect, 'cobbled water' (which, of course, can mean either cobbles in water or water that is itself [like] cobbles) can be seen as the *feet's way* of 'seeing' their world. Indeed, by walking [in] the water, Thomas takes his stand, so to speak, against the great tradition of Romantic poetry where dominion is given to the controlling eye/I. In 'The River', the eyes cease to offer a fixed point of view. In those last lines of the passage, 'above' and 'below' bewilderingly but exhilaratingly exchange places, with 'fish, speckled like thrushes,/ Silently singing among the weed's/ Branches.'

In 'Earth', Thomas, in Swiftean mood, explicitly warns against the human sin, exacerbated by modern technological invention, of false perspective:

> We are misled
> By perspective: the microscope
> Is our sin, we tower enormous
> Above it the stronger it
> Grows. (*CP*, p. 228)

As this makes clear, an obsession with power and control is for R. S. Thomas, as it was for Blake, one of the most malign symptoms of narcissism. And as the opening lines of 'Earth' indicate, such an obsession is as evident in human (mis)constructions of the divine as in human (ab) uses of science: 'What made us think/ It was yours? Because it was signed/ With your blood, God of battles?'. Several poems in *H'm* are satiric exercises in the semiotics of 'religion', disclosures of those pseudo-religious systems of signification by which man dignifies his will-to-power by pleading divine precedent and sanction. Kierkegaard had mischievous things to say about this in his *Concluding Unscientific Postscript*. He spoke witheringly of the sort of 'religiosity' that 'entertains a notion of God that makes Him a jealous and stupid despot . . . That a tyrannically-minded human being might be imbued with the idea that the world should be brought to realize how much power he has over others by means of an ostentatious subjection on their part, surely proves nothing with respect to God.' Kierkegaard sees this as analogous to supposing 'that God in the last analysis came to be in need of the world's admiration, and of an "awakened" individual's queer gesticulations, attracting the world's wonder and thereby directing the world's most august attention to the fact that God exists – poor God, who in His embarrassment at being invisible while still so dearly desiring that public attention should be focused upon Him, must sit there and wait for someone to do it for Him!' (*CUP*, pp. 441–2).

One of the most highly evolved examples of R. S. Thomas's exploration of this theme is 'Echoes', a poem in which lucid satire, along the lines indicated above, nevertheless leaves an after-image of tragic agony, just as the dazzled eye, turning away from the light, is bespotted with throbbing darkness. A parable, the poem depicts a (narcissistic) god who, enraged by the dumbness of the originally uninhabited earth, and resentful of its serene beauty, vengefully endows it with life so that it can offer up to him its praise, compounded of fear, wonder, and anguish:

> Where are you?
> He called, and riding the echo
> The shapes came, slender
> As trees, but with white hands,
> Curious to build. On the altars
> They made him the red blood
> Told what he wished to hear. (*CP*, p. 211)

On one level, this is strong, direct satire of man's fearful desire to appease the almighty. By feminising mankind ('slender / As trees'), Thomas brings out the strongly masculine, patriarchal, macho character of this particular conception of the divine and 'his' power. By invoking the image of sacrificial altars, Thomas seems to focus his satire on the 'primitive' Old Testament version of god, which is still such a presence in Christian faith, and which may even be said to influence (and distort?) the traditional Christian understanding of the New Testament crucifixion as atonement. But on another level, crude and narcissistic though this kind of 'faith' may be, it also powerfully bespeaks man's deepest need: the agonising need to find a 'language' of wonder and suffering for existence. Indeed, so understood the poem is very much about the origins of language, and the motive for poetry, in this human imperative to 'address' its own pain.

A pondering of a poem such as 'Echoes' brings us to an appreciation of the radical doubleness of Thomas's discourse; his secret passion for equivocation. In this respect, of course, he is close to Kierkegaard, for whom devices of indirection were the indispensable means both of keeping the elusiveness of authentic spiritual insight alive for oneself and of bringing it home to others. In *H'm* this forked tongue approach becomes a forked rod for divining even the most hidden and sympathetic forms of narcissism, as instanced in the powerful poem, 'Petition'. The speaker (whose opening words echo those of Tiresias in *The Waste Land*) is one so experienced in the atrocities of life as to have been struck dumb by them, resigned merely to witness that for which there can be no redress. Out of his tragic vision of the human situation there emerges just the one request:

> One thing I have asked
> Of the disposer of the issues
> Of life: that truth should defer
> To beauty. It was not granted. (*CP*, p. 209)

Yet, searing in their sincerity though these lines are, there is about them a hint of almost comic presumption. What sort of 'god' would it be who could be conceived of as entertaining, let alone granting, human petitions? Presumably the sort of 'god' who could grandiosely be referred, and deferred, to as 'the disposer of the issues/ Of life'. The inappropriateness of all this lies not in God's being, in His supreme power, 'above' all such arrangements and negotiations, but in His not having power, in this sense, over the world at all. Yet, in this case, Thomas is not satirising the petitioner, since his one cry is allowed to come feelingfully and persuasively out of the very heart of the human dilemma. Rather, Thomas views him in a double perspective; that of sympathetic identification and of ultimate disassociation. Through a speaker plainly *in extremis* he enables us to see that, as Kierkegaard put it, 'all existential problems are passionate problems, for when existence is interpenetrated with reflection it generates passion' (*CUP*, p. 313). 'For existence generates passion',

Kierkegaard continued, 'but existence paradoxically accentuated generates the maximum of passion.' To the passion of the speaker in 'Petition',
R. S. Thomas adds the accent of paradox, and thus maximises that passion.
In other words, he shows that an understanding of the divine starts at
the point at which man is brutally thwarted in his attempt to hold God
simply accountable to human standards of reason, decency and justice.
Poems like this are powerful examples of the way Thomas temporises,
in the root sense of the word: that is, he procrastinates in order to represent the baffling character of human life as engaged in time and yet
engaged to eternity.

This temporal temporising is strikingly instanced in the cluster of
fantastical poems, scattered throughout *H'm*, in which R. S. Thomas
variously imagines what sort of God might be held responsible for the
creation. In this particular, as we shall see in chapter 9, he resembles
Jorge Luis Borges, whose work he came to appreciate and who wrote of
the metaphysicians of Tlön that 'They seek neither truth nor selfhood;
they seek astonishment. They think metaphysics is a branch of the literature of fantasy.'⁴ And, again like Borges, Thomas is an (unrecognised)
humorist, dealing as he does with an inscrutable God, who signs Himself
only in ciphers. There is a sense in which for this poet the price of serious
pursuit of a chronically deviant and devious deity is eternal levity. No
wonder he adopted the modes of writing of a Kierkegaard who 'learned/
his anonymity from God himself', and whom he described in his final
volume as 'the first/ of the Surrealists' (*CLP*, p. 220), just as Borges
viewed him as the precursor of Kafka. No wonder, either, that Thomas
payed homage to Wallace Stevens as one of the 'trapeze artists of the
language' (*CLP*, p. 266), or that he admired in Paul Klee a ludic artistry
to which he himself partly aspired.

Thomas's fantastical wit could be complex and sharply multifaceted,
as has already become apparent from our consideration of 'Echoes'. In
'Making', a God who produces a world to His 'taste' and for His own
'diversion' is awakened from his narcissism only when he fashions a
being in His own likeness, and discovers Himself to be 'in love with it/
For itself, giving it freedom/ To love me; risking the disappointment'
(*CP*, p. 221). The full nature and terrible cost – to man and to God – of

that 'love' is considered in such extraordinary poems as 'Cain' and 'The Coming'. In the former, a baffled Cain seeks an explanation as to why God has been strangely roused by the spilt blood of Abel, whereas He had previously been indifferent to the offer of flowers and vegetables, 'things that did not publish/ Their hurt, that bled/ Silently'. He receives a reply in language that verges disturbingly on the grotesque:

> The limp head,
> The slow fall of red tears – they
> Were like a mirror to me in which I beheld
> My reflection. I anointed myself
> In readiness for the journey
> To the doomed tree you were at work upon.[5]

The poignancy of this passage – a vision of God accepting responsibility for the world's pain, a pain which He then sacrificially prepares to share – derives ultimately from the way in which it affirms what it denies and denies what it affirms. Human beings cannot use a language that is not rooted in self-consciousness, a fact that makes it impossible for the self ever to be completely self-less. However scrupulously and sincerely we phrase the sacrifice made in the crucifixion, the taint of God's narcissism, of His subtle self-regard and self-satisfaction, will inescapably attach to our mortal phrasing. Thomas shows us, shatteringly, how utterly necessary and utterly impossible it is to 'understand' the crucifixion.

In his meditations on this 'crux' he seems at times to be spiritual kin to the Dietrich Bonhoeffer who, while awaiting butchering by the Nazis, so calmly persisted in urging believers to renounce religion's comforting concept of an all-powerful, Providential God:

So our coming of age forces us to a true recognition of our situation vis à vis God. God is teaching us that we must live as men who can get along very well without Him. The God who is with us is the God who forsakes us (Mark 15.34). The God who makes us live in this world without using Him as a working hypothesis is the God before whom we are ever standing. Before God and with Him we live without God. God allows Himself to be edged out of the world and on to the cross. God is weak and powerless in the world, and that is exactly the way, the only way, in which He can be with us and help us.[6]

This, as I understand it, is what R. S. Thomas is saying when he writes so beautifully of the Christ who 'Comes to us in his weakness,/ But with a sharp song.'

Bonhoeffer associates the traditional Christian worship of an omnipotent God with the modern human obsession with power over the natural environment. This illuminates for us the dual aspect of R. S. Thomas's attacks on 'the Machine' – a symbol that obviously signifies man's corrupt use of science as a tool for technological dominion, but which also signifies a Christianity that has, as Bonhoeffer put it, turned God into a *deus ex machina*, a theatrical god who steps out of a machine at moments of crisis to provide 'the answer to life's problems, the solution of its distresses and conflicts' (*LP*, p. 114). It is over against this image of God that Thomas, like Bonhoeffer, puts the cancelling emblem of the cross, in which 'man is challenged to participate in the sufferings of God at the hands of a godless world' (*LP*, p. 122). As I read it, the volume *H'm*, the first of R. S. Thomas's great collections of religious poetry, is centred on the conflict between myths of power (both secular *and* Christian) and the profound mystery of powerlessness, as symbolised by the Cross. Indeed, for the last three decades of his life the cross consistently commanded the full attention of Thomas's spiritual imagination. Almost a quarter of the poems in *Laboratories of the Spirit* (1975) involve some kind of meditation on the cross, while *Counterpoint* (1990) and *Mass for Hard Times* (1992) offer a series of remarkable conceits on the same subject, including one representing it as the ultimate figure of selflessness: 'We close/ our eyes when we pray/ lest the curtain of tears/ should come down on a cross/ being used for the time to prove/ the correctness of a negation' (*CLP*, p. 107).

What the cross 'means' to R. S. Thomas is, I believe, suggested by his vertiginous phrase about 'a mystery/ terrifying enough to be named Love'.[7] However, to try to piece together a 'doctrine' of the crucifixion from his poetry would, I feel, be catastrophically inappropriate, since for him doctrine was the death of spiritual truth. No magisterially definitive statements can be made about a God who 'is the shape in the mist/ on the mountain we would ascend/ disintegrating as we compose it' (*CLP*, p. 83). These words are in themselves a perfect example of what Thomas is talking about – they disintegrate even as we compose them into meaning. First we read them as meaning that the shape disintegrates as we compose it. But then we realise that it could be the mountain that disintegrates as we compose it. And finally, we are thoroughly disorientated by the discovery that it could be we who are composed of the shape, and of the mountain – and perhaps of God too. Having thus begun with what seemed a perfectly simple statement, we end in the realisation that such simplicity is the innocent face of profoundly duplicitous ironies.

This brings us face to face with the fact that, for R. S. Thomas, the profundities of the spirit can only be adumbrated in ironical terms. To use Kierkegaardian language, irony is the inescapable mode of spiritual understanding, since it is only on these terms that existence can relate to essence, and the mortal can mediate the divine. God will always have the last laugh, and we need to be able to take the divine mirth to heart – R. S. Thomas is therefore an inveterate joker, because the relationship of the infinite to the finite is inherently ironical. Take, as a simple instance, the structure of the 'Credo' in *Mass for Hard Times*, with its running commentary of snide, sniping, undercutting remarks:

> I believe in God
> the Father (Is he married?)
> I believe in you, the almighty,
> who can do anything
> you wish. (Forget that irony
> of the imponderable.) Rid, therefore
> (if there are not too many
> of them), my intestine
> of the viruses that against
> (in accordance with? Ah, horror!)
> your will are in occupation
> of its defences. (*CLP*, p. 136)

Here the irony cuts many ways. It mocks the glibness of flip, knowing, modern, rationalist sarcasm, even as it employs such sarcasm to unsettle the solemnities of the creed. And it ironises the creed not only by exposing its vulnerability to the cross-analysis of the enlightened contemporary mind, but also by showing that *any* human attempt to formulate statements about God is bound to be internally inconsistent, is bound to collapse under its own weightiness – *gravitas* cannot withstand the pull of the force of an otherworldly gravity.

It is that last point I want to emphasise, by pointing out that this 'Credo' approximates in form to that of the old 'Echo' poems, where Echo regularly mocks, reduces and distorts every statement that is made, so that no statement means only, or exactly, what it says. Echo, as Kierkegaard pointed out, is the key figure for the workings of irony. The human mind *is* an echo chamber, because all consciousness involves self-consciousness that mocks the authority of every conscious thought. Beginning (in a crypto-Derridean way) by being attracted to the nihilism of such a condition, Kierkegaard ended by seeing it as the form eternity takes when translated into the productions of time. The Truth is always more than, and other than, any particular expressions of it we are able to offer – in other words, even the deepest truths we can utter fall ironically short of the Truth. Even human consciousness itself proceeds through constant change that makes every moment redundant, even as it passes. As Kierkegaard put it, lived life is 'a history wherein consciousness successively outlives itself'.[8] R. S. Thomas's poetry is, in a way, a record of the endlessly unstable, mutating terms on which such a consciousness understands ultimate existence. He writes poems precisely because they are provisional, existential, reports; he writes religious poems precisely because they are *disposable* theology.

Moreover, at any and every moment we are always more than, and other than, any of the self-images we are capable of producing – an aspect of Thomas's interest that will be explored much more fully through a reading, in the next chapter, of *The Echoes Return Slow* as a spiritual autobiography. Here again, Kierkegaard saw each of us as a dangerously self-obsessed Narcissus, deaf to the saving ministrations of Echo. He recommended that we deliberately cultivate Echo – that we develop a double relationship to ourselves, so that we are at once subjectively involved in our experiences *and* objectively reflecting on them from another point of view. Irony is a salutary disciplinarian in this regard: 'It limits, renders finite, defines, and thereby yields truth, actuality and content' (*Concept*, p. 338). And it assists us in developing a stereoscopic vision of ourselves.

Thomas's most extended and mature exercises in spiritual autobiography, *Neb* and *The Echoes Return Slow*, are developments of those ironic
self-portraits with which his volumes of poetry are studded. Take, for
instance, his 'Self-portrait' in *Laboratories of the Spirit*:

> That resigned look! Here I am,
> it says; fifty-nine,
> balding, shirking the challenge
> of the young girls. Time running out
> now, and the soul
> unfinished. And the heart knows
> that it is not the portrait it posed for. (*LS*, p. 27)

Here the mirror acts the part of echo, ironically returning to the looker
a look very different from that which he intended to see. The ironies here
are at once simple, beautifully playful, and poignantly complex. For
instance, the poem plays with the cliché difference between heart and
head. What the heart wants is contrasted with what the head literally
looks like: 'All that skill/ life, on the carving/ of the curved nostril and
to no end/ but disgust'. But the poignancy is in the fact that in spite of
this face, the heart lives on – indeed, in a sense the poem is a dialogue
between heart and head. The self that emerges from this portrait is a self
ironically compounded of the interaction between the heart's self-image
and the mirror's image of the self.

If the mirror is a form of echo, then art in its turn is a kind of mirror
– offering an image of a person at variance with the person's image of
himself or herself. R. S. Thomas's painting poems – to which sustained
attention will be paid in chapter 12 – repeatedly bring out the ironies
of the painted biographies he contemplates. So Van Gogh's 'Portrait of
Dr Gachet' is a picture of 'a doctor/ becoming patient himself/ of art's
diagnosis' (*CP*, p. 371). Gauguin's 'La Belle Angèle' tellingly juxtaposes
a woman and cat:

> Beside her
> in bronze is her other
> self, the cat-like image
> that causes her to sheathe

> her fingers and try looking
> as demure as the small
> cross on her bosom tells
> her she ought to be.[9]

In this painting, therefore, the cat's features become a telling echo of the feline human face. Even when the painting is of landscape, Thomas reads it as a revealingly ironic composition. Consider, for example, 'Gauguin: Breton Landscape, the Mill'. Here, 'The eye is to concentrate/ on the tree gushing/ over the bent-backed woman/ with her companion and/ dog. But there is so much/ besides' – besides in both the sense of apart from this and alongside this. And what Thomas shows is not just what else is in the painting, but how, in providing other foci of attention, all those other elements assert their existence as alternative centres of life. The narcissistic human concern with the human is ironically commented upon by the other elements in the painting which, in the process, turn into an ironic parody, or echo, of human features: 'the house/ asleep in its counterpane/ of colour; and beyond/ them all the whey-faced cloud/ agog as at a far sill' (*BHN*, p. 57).

This discussion has now moved away from the religious poetry to consider the other major forms of writing – autobiography and painting-poems – favoured by R. S. Thomas over his last quarter of a century. Such a move is deliberate, because I think it is time (as I shall emphasise in several later chapters) we appreciated, and explored, the cast of mind that is common to *all* these kinds of writing: they are all of them exercises in spiritual irony, and should be seen as complementing one another in this radically important respect. Taken as a whole, they illustrate what Kierkegaard would call R. S. Thomas's 'contemplative irony', deriving from his 'ironic stance'. 'Irony in the eminent sense directs itself not against this or that particular existence . . . It is not this or that phenomenon but the totality of existence which it considers *sub specie ironiae*' (*Concept*, p. 270).

To bear this in mind is to be better prepared to appreciate the great repertoire of ironies Thomas deploys in his religious poetry. Take, for instance, his treatment of the technological age. The grand joke, for him, is that in the name of enlightened secular reason man has enslaved himself to the crudest superstition. 'They will come to understand', he writes of the men and women of the future, 'our folk-tale was the machine./ We listened to it in the twilight/ of our reason, taking it as the hour/ in which truth dawned' (*CLP*, p. 124). All his poems about the machine have, therefore, been attempts to expose the crudely mythical cast of modern imagination that prides itself on having outgrown the (true) myths of religious belief. The irony of such self-deception is often seen by him as grotesque, or comic, but he is not blind to its tragic essence:

> And the cross
> that was set up was the rod
> and the crankshaft man's body
> was nailed to with no power
> to atone. And a voice
> taunted him in passing:
> 'If you were so clever
> as to invent me, come down
> now so that I may believe.' (*CLP*, p. 92)

This particular poem ends with a searing image of visionary irony: 'On the skylines I have seen gantries/ with their arms out awkwardly/ as love and money trying to be reconciled' (*CLP*, p. 93).

Such hallmark passages have led to Thomas being characterised as chillingly inhumane and craggily dour. To describe his notoriously attenuated poems as beautiful, tender, compassionate or playful would certainly seem to be as perverse as describing Giacometti's figures as plump or Beckett's characters jolly – after all, Thomas was celebrated for hauteur, even in his humility. And yet, many of the finest pieces of his old age confound our prejudiced expectations of bleakness and harsh spiritual austerity. The pitiful horror of the mental disintegration that may accompany ageing is equivocatingly counterbalanced, in 'Geriatric', by a compensatory hope that falls movingly short of certain belief: 'I come away,/ comforting myself, as I can,/ that there is another/ garden, all dew and fragrance' (*CLP*, p. 213). There, the 'as I can' is precariously balanced between certainty ('as I have the spiritual assurance to do'), pragmatism ('best I can'), and self-indictment for the convenient rationalising away of a devastating truth about man's mere mortality ('as I am practised at doing'). Then, in 'Remembering', 'No Time' and 'Still', Thomas adds to the impressive series of delicate elegies for his first wife mentioned in chapter 5:

Last night, as I loitered

where your small bones had their nest,
the owl blew away from your stone cross
softly as down from a thistle-head. I wondered. (*CLP*, p. 231)

In this, surely one of his most perfect poems, a tributary gentleness (inscribed in the minutest readjustments of sound: small/ bones/ owl/ stone/ down/ wondered) accrues to this image of the owl in a collection (*No Truce with the Furies*) in which otherwise the bird habitually figures as one of nature's fiercest 'raptors' (a recurrent term here for the predatoriness both of Nature and of God). Nor is such gentleness at variance with Thomas's ironic vision. Rather, it is a function of it; the expression of a mind chronically tormented by the irreconcilable antinomies of the human condition.

And if R. S. Thomas takes an ironic view of the modern secular world, because he sees it as the opposite of what it proudly supposes itself to be, he also (perhaps more strikingly) takes an ironic view of the world of modern faith, either (following Bultmann, Tillich and Bonhoeffer) because it clings to its untenable myths and dogmas; or, most profoundly (and again following Bonhoeffer and Tillich), because any human attempts to apprehend the suprahuman *can* be articulated only in ironical terms. This was an aspect of his work touched on above when considering the 'Credo' from *Mass for Hard Times*. But his poetry abounds in examples. There are those audacious instances of his conceiving of God not only as a master of irony, but as a *victim* of irony. An arresting instance is found in 'Rough', where God is the cynically appreciative creator of a world of mutual cruelty between all living things. As he admires his handiwork, 'There was the sound/ of thunder, the loud, uncontrollable laughter of/ God, and in his side like an incurred stitch, Jesus' (*CP*, p. 286). This whole poem is a movingly ironic demonstration of the baffled impulse that underlies Christian theology – the impulse to square the circle, to construct a narrative that will bring evil into a meaningful relationship with love. Yet the poem's myth conveys a powerful sense of the primacy of love – of an almost consciously evil universe being ultimately helpless before its own instinctive reflexes of love – even as the myth is saturated with irony at the impossibility of proving, or 'explaining', such a conviction.

Indeed, as I read them, R. S. Thomas's religious poems are frequently self-ironising, even at their most affirmative. Irony is so close to the very heart of his vision, that it often seems to be the very form an authentic vision must take. Consider the poem 'Suddenly', which records a rare moment of revelation: 'I looked/ at him, not with the eye/ only, but with the whole/ of my being, overflowing with/ him as a chalice would/ with the sea'. But the very next sentence is: 'Yet was he/ no more there than before,/ his area occupied/ by the unhaloed presences' (*CP*, p. 283). Here, it is not the insight that is ironic; rather, the irony *is* the insight itself. Man expects transfiguration to involve change; but it is when, in a sense, there is *no* change that transfiguration occurs, so that revelation is at once irrefutable and unverifiable. In 'Ffynnon Fair', the bottom of Mary's well is littered with rusting coins thrown in by the hopeful faithful. But their offering is ironically inappropriate to the pure spirit

> that lives there, that has lived there
> always, giving itself up
> to the thirsty, withholding
> itself from superstition
> of others, who ask for more. (*CP*, p. 292)

There the ironies are obvious, elsewhere they are more hidden. This is how that same poem begins: 'They did not divine it, but/ they bequeathed it to us'. It is only after we see where the poem is headed – that is on rereading – that we begin to realise how the word 'divine' here accommodates three ironically juxtaposed meanings: to discover, as by using a divining rod; to divinise it, by endowing it with divine power; and to understand it. These meanings have power in direct proportion to our *failure* to divine them at first reading. Our discovery of these meanings, therefore, hits us as a precious revelation, involving not just the appreciation of a local verbal trick, but a revaluation, and heightened evaluation, of the (previously hidden) tenor of the whole poem. This is what Kierkegaard calls 'maieutic' irony; maiuetic meaning 'pertaining to intellectual midwifery; i.e. to the Socratic process of helping a person to bring into full consciousness conceptions previously latent in the mind' (*OED*). R. S. Thomas is a master of maieutic irony – indeed, I am tempted to say that that is not only how he writes his poetry but *why* he writes it. It is his very raison d'être as a poet; because poetry is for him the maieutic structure par excellence.

It is so because of the hidden concentrations of meaning that inhere in the actual formal patterning of a poem. And R. S. Thomas is particularly good at taking advantage of the ironic fact that modern poetry, when it doesn't rhyme or conform to metre, actively encourages us in our modern habit of reading for mere sense; that is, reducing everything to glib prose. Take the following versions of the 'same' passage:

> Here on my knees in this stone church, that is full only of the silent congregation of shadows and the sea's sound, it is easy to believe Yeats was right. Just as though choirs had not sung, shells have swallowed them; the tide laps at the Bible; the bell fetches no people to the brittle miracle of the bread.

Here
on my knees in this stone
church, that is full only
of the silent congregation
of shadows and the sea's
sound, it is easy to believe
Yeats was right. Just as though
choirs had not sung, shells
have swallowed them; the tide laps
at the Bible; the bell fetches
no people to the brittle miracle
of the bread. (*CP*, p. 282)

In the poem, the line break firmly separates 'stone' from 'church', even as it attaches 'stone' to 'only' – an attachment through parallel form that is actually reinforced by the rhyme. 'Stone' is thus enabled to function independently as a self-sufficient noun as well as a qualifying adjective. The line break insists that we give equal weight to the two words, and therefore to the full strangeness of the phenomenon. This is stone that is also a church – a strange, ironic, combination, which either signifies the mystery of faith (that stone can also be holy); or the absurdity of faith (the church is 'only' an arrangement of stone). And it is also a kind of internal rhyme, caught and emphasised by the line unit, that places the word 'only' into a peculiarly intimate relationship with the preceding word 'full', so that through the interaction of the two words we hear echoes of 'lonely' and 'forlornly'. Then a later line break again sensitises us to the quiet intercourse of sounds that breeds hidden meanings: 'sea's/sound' [makes it] 'easy to believe': the line literally enacts, or sonically emblematises its meaning, as the 'sound' of the word 'sea' leads the mind naturally, if insidiously, to think of words like 'easy' and 'believe'.

It would be possible to go on. But the point has, I hope, been made. As we reread, the passage begins at once to grow in poignancy and plangency (it is a lonely *cri de coeur*) but it also begins to ironise itself; to show us what it's up to; to make us see how self-indulgently easy it is to believe that the church is nothing but the stone that the knees tell us it is; and that it is full of nothing but the sea's sound. The more we read, the more touched we are by the emotion (or motion) of loneliness in the very phrasing, and yet the more suspicious we become of fully 'believing' that emotion, as it were. Indeed, as we reread we are led to recognise the irony of that last line break occurring where it does: 'it is easy to believe/ Yeats was right'. Christians are often mocked by remarks suggesting that their faith is a comfortable and comforting one. Here, Thomas calls up the shadow of the memory of such condescension – 'it is easy to believe' – before he completes his phrase and ironically reverses the whole thrust of its meaning. Here, it is easy to believe there is no God. All this is not something Thomas tells us, of course; it is something his poetry gradually does to us – the maieutic way in which it brings a new understanding to birth in us. It is what Kierkegaard called the Socratic method.

Socrates was a heroic figure and role model for Kierkegaard. 'His whole existence is irony', he wrote in his late *Journals*, 'and it was this: while the whole contemporary population of farm-workers, businessmen, and so on, in brief, all these thousands were all perfectly sure that they were men and that they knew what it meant to be men, Socrates was at a lower level (ironically) and occupied himself with the problem, what it means to be a man. And what he really says is that all the activity of these thousands is an illusion, mere juggling, tumult, noise, and bustle, which from the standpoint of the idea are nothing, or less than nothing, in so far as these men could have used their life to ponder the ideal.'[10] Kierkegaard goes on to say that thanks to a 'progress in nonsense' since Socrates' time, people in Christendom now believe that they know what it means to be a Christian, with a certainty that cries out for the ironic scrutiny of Socrates. Thomas, in his turn, is constantly ironising, not without a hint of rue- fulness, the impulse to simplify faith that he finds as unavoidable as the next Christian: 'Father, I said, domesticating/ an enigma; and as though/ to humour me you came' (CLP, p. 121). Yet deep down he knows other- wise: 'But there are precipices// within you. Mild and dire,/ now and absent, like us but/ wholly other – which side/ of you am I to believe?' (CLP, p. 121).

Since only Christ can, of course, be the way, the truth and the life, Socrates by contrast, and of human necessity, follows the negative way, the *via negationis*. His method is indeed an appropriate method of ap- proach to that God beyond the God of traditional Christendom, who is the God of Bonhoeffer, Tillich, and R. S. Thomas. As Thomas wrote in 'Via Negativa', a poem that takes its title from the famous negative approach to God defined by the Scholastics:

> Why no! I never thought other than
> That God is that great absence
> In our lives, the empty silence
> Within, the place where we go
> Seeking, not in hope to
> Arrive or find. He keeps the interstices
> In our knowledge, the darkness
> Between stars. His are the echoes
> We follow, the footprints he has just
> Left. (CP, p. 220)

The 'Via Negativa' was the celebrated way of the great mystics, and R. S. Thomas repeatedly and properly denied that he was a mystic. But perhaps – allowing, naturally, for the irony of the description – he could properly be designated the Socrates of Wales. Because, through his writings over the last quarter century and more of his life, he consistently showed himself to be a master of irony, a virtuoso of the negative way. Steadfastly refusing the refuge of certainty, either in the form of authoritative negation or in the form of authoritative affirmation, he was one in whom, as Kierkegaard marvellously put it, 'the wounds of possibility always remain open'.[11]

## Notes

1   Maurice Blanchot, *The Space of Literature*, trans. A. Smock (Lincoln: University of Nebraska Press, 1982), p. 244.
2   Mark C. Taylor, *Tears* (Albany: State University of New York, 1990), p. 110. See also the same author's *Erring: a Postmodern Theology* (Chicago: University of Chicago Press, 1981).
3   David F. Swenson and Walter Lowrie (eds), *Concluding Unscientific Postscript* (Princeton: Princeton University Press, 1944), p. 79. Hereafter *CUP*. The most subtle discussion of Thomas's debts to Kierkegaard is Rowan Williams, 'Suspending the Ethical: R. S. Thomas and Kierkegaard', in Damian Walford Davies (ed.), *Echoes to the Amen* (Cardiff: University of Wales Press, 2003), 206–19; see also, by the same author, '"Adult geometry": Dangerous Thoughts in R. S. Thomas', in M. Wynn Thomas (ed.), *The Page's Drift: R. S. Thomas at Seventy* (Bridgend: Poetry of Wales Press, 1993), 82–98. The radically unsettling character of Kierkegaard's irony has recently been given illuminating emphasis in Jonathan Lear, *A Case for Irony* (Cambridge, MA: Harvard University Press, 2011), and in the same author's 'A Lost Conception of Irony', *www.berfrois. com/2012/01/jonathan-lear-lost-conception-irony/* (accessed 18 July 2012).
4   Jorge Luis Borges, *Labyrinths*, eds. Donald A. Yates and James E. Irby (Harmondsworth: Penguin, 1970), p. 34.
5   R. S. Thomas, *H'm* (London: Macmillan, 1972), p. 15.
6   Dietrich Bonhoeffer, *Letters and Papers from Prison*, ed. Eberhard Bethge (London: Fontana, 1959), p. 122. Hereafter *LP*.
7   R. S. Thomas 'Scenes', *Laboratories of the Spirit* (London: Macmillan, 1977 [1979 edn]), p. 44. Hereafter *LS*.
8   Søren Kierkegaard, *The Concept of Irony*, trans. Lee M. Capel (London: Collins, 1968), p. 341. Hereafter *Concept*.

[9] R. S. Thomas, *Between Here and Now* (London: Macmillan, 1981), p. 61. Hereafter *BHN*.

[10] Søren Kierkegaard, *The Last Years: Journals, 1853–5*, trans. Ronald Gregor Smith (London: Fontana, 1968), pp. 282–3.

[11] That Thomas was aware of this quotation is suggested by an apparent allusion to it in his late poem to 'SK': 'The game was perilous/ to them both, though her// wound was for stanching/ as his own was not' (*CLP*, p. 219).

# 8

# 'Time's Changeling'

Although *The Echoes Return Slow* is, at least in my estimation, one of R. S. Thomas's most impressive collections, it has received relatively little attention. In overlooking it, readers are, unawares, discounting individual poems of exceptional quality, as well as missing an opportunity to familiarise themselves with aspects of Thomas's background and personal history that shed considerable light on his work as a whole. But the matter is more complex than that. *The Echoes Return Slow* is an innovative work, and is so in ways that even seasoned, let alone casual, readers of Thomas could not have foreseen. It is an exercise in autobiographical writing, but of a highly unusual kind.

Indeed, so unusual a text is it that it seems especially resistant to categorisation. Once one has got beyond the stage of excitedly regarding it (in conjunction with *Neb* and the many extended interviews he gave) as an invaluable quarry of materials relating directly to Thomas's life, and of consequently exploiting it as a rare resource (since he had always been so notoriously reticent about himself),[1] one is likely to begin noting the peculiarity of the terms in which Thomas has chosen to construct his narrative of the self, and to ponder the significance of the methods he has adopted. In the original edition his text, for instance, consists of a series of pairings of prose and poetry, the former invariably printed on the left-hand page and the latter facing it on the right, with each pair jointly devoted to a consideration of the 'same' period, or occasion, or experience in his life. Frequently, the prose is beautifully crafted and cunningly moulded, so that in some cases it is difficult for a reader to understand in what respect precisely, except for the style of its layout, the prose discourse differs from the poetic discourse. There are many instances, particularly in the prose, when Thomas speaks of himself in the third person (as he does throughout his 'official' autobiography, *Neb*). And although the complete text comprises a chronological narrative tracing the whole course of Thomas's life, from the womb (literally) down to the period of his composing the book, the materials included are selective in ways that are sometimes disconcerting: for instance, very little is revealed about his marriage or his family life, until those enchanting sections very late in the collection that, as noted in chapter 5, constitute such a wonderfully loving tribute to his first wife.

Any serious attempt, then, to address the autobiographical character of *The Echoes Return Slow* has carefully to consider, and to account for, key features such as these. And it would also be advisable to resist the pressing invitation to offer a purely psychological reading of the text. My suggestion, to be developed in this chapter, is that crucial to our understanding of *The Echoes Return Slow* is the realisation that Thomas conceives of the self as essentially a spiritual rather than a psychological category. Consequently, the true history of one's self is bound, for him, to take the form of spiritual autobiography. But just as his religious poems reflect, in their every aspect, the problem of finding an authentic contemporary means (involving language, style and form) of conveying the complex conditions and the distinctive 'style' of modern belief, so too does his autobiography address the problem of how to develop a contemporary discourse appropriate for exploring the concept (so alien and unsympathetic to modern minds) of the intrinsically spiritual character of the self. It is true that spiritual autobiography is an ancient, sophisticated and distinguished 'literary' genre, and that as such it would seem to provide modern writers with a great variety of models and templates. But the same is true of the great genre of religious poetry and yet, as we know, Thomas (although highly appreciative of past achievements) felt compelled by the very uniqueness of the contemporary situation to depart from precedent and to embark on a course of radical innovation. And it is the same compulsion, deriving from the same circumstances, that caused him to experiment with unconventional means of narrating the self.

What he is particularly concerned to register – by ensuring it is inscribed in his very discourse – is the way that any valid modern conception of the spiritual self is bound to take very substantially into account those aspects of the development of personal identity that have been so notably identified by such ostensibly 'secular' modern disciplines as psychology and sociology. Thus *The Echoes Return Slow* is careful, for instance, to explore those earliest relations with mother, father and nurturing environment that, it has now become accepted, significantly influence the development of selfhood. Moreover, these relations are, in turn, understood as having been specifically influenced by the specific time and place (the historical culture) within which they operated. This interpenetration of the personal and the extra-personal, an interaction that produces the historical and social components of individual existence, is subtly registered in the prose when Thomas recalls his young parents' first home in Cardiff:

> A scrubbed doorstep, clean enough to be defiled by the day's droppings, circulars, newspapers. A threshold of war, unbeknown to the young couple, the child-planners . . . (*CLP*, p. 13)

Here the doubling process, by means of which Thomas keeps the radical dualities of existence in sight throughout the volume, takes the form of a sort of extended pun, to which our attention is drawn by a pointed parallelism of phrasing. The scrubbed doorstep is also the threshold of war: the new home, and the marriage it houses, is about to be 'defiled', and redefined, by world conflict. The poem that 'corresponds' to this prose passage contrasts almost violently with it in tone. The foreboding that is controlled by irony in the passage about Cardiff is transposed into a very different key in a poem that recalls the rawness of a primal scream:

> The scales fell from my eyes,
> and I saw faces. I screamed
> at the ineffectuality
> of love to protect me. (*CLP*, p. 13)

This change in key corresponds to a change in the very category of the experience being 'recalled'. Whereas the prose is concerned with violence as an aspect of history, the poem is concerned with violence as the naked 'face' of existence per se; a view of life as consisting of what Thomas powerfully calls 'Pain's climate'. And in 'seeing' this, the child (or rather the baby) ironically sees more, and sees further, than do the 'child-planners' themselves.

Prose and poetry are brought together, and used in tandem, here as throughout the volume, in order to explore the multi-dimensional character of a self that relates to time in an extremely complex fashion. 'Time's changeling' is Thomas's own arresting phrase for this. 'I have no name:/ time's changeling . . .' (*CLP*, p. 12); the phrase thus grammatically circumstanced *becomes* the name (that is, identity) he gives himself, as already noted in chapter 5. It has several ramifications of meaning, which are rendered both as styles of living and as styles of writing in *The Echoes Return Slow*. 'Changeling' can obviously be understood as the noun-form of an adjective such as 'changeable' or 'changeful' – that is, as expressing the mutability to which the self is 'subject', both in the sense of its being helplessly affected (if not existentially effected) by change, and in the opposite sense of the self's being itself the author of its own restless changes. Therefore, the pejorative meaning of 'changeling' (as the *OED* reminds us) is a waverer, or turncoat – a name for himself Thomas contemptuously adopts at several points in *The Echoes Return Slow* ('A will of iron, perforated/ by indecision' (*CLP*, p. 41)). And as the dictionary further confirms, 'changeling' can also mean 'half-wit', a construction that Thomas seems to be recalling when, in the very poem that follows the one in which he characterises himself as 'time's changeling', he speaks of his infant self as exhibiting in a photograph

A dislocation of mind:
love photographed
the imbecility of
my expression and framed it. (*CLP*, p. 13)

Of the many equivocations of meaning in these lines (as in virtually every passage in *The Echoes Return Slow*) it is the play in the opening phrase that at this point repays attention. 'Dislocation' means, of course, to 'displace', as well as to wrench out of joint, and as such it points up the sense in which the dislocation of mind (like the 'imbecility' with which it has been made cognate) may be understood as the result of the violent removal of the self from its true place and its re-siting in a bewilderingly, painfully alien situation. This conveniently brings us to the final meaning of the word 'changeling', namely that of a fairy baby surreptitiously exchanged for a human child. Used in that sense, 'time's changeling' implies that the self may be understood as not really belonging in, or to, the temporal order – that is, as being rather the child of eternity foisted onto, and abandoned to the care of, unsuspecting time.

Understood in these several senses, 'time's changeling' is a wonderfully suggestive, compressed definition of the 'existential' self, that concept whose currency in modern ideological discussion still owes so much to the profound experimental work undertaken by Kierkegaard, a thinker known to have been important for Thomas.[2] And although *The Echoes Return Slow* is by no means to be understood as systematically Kierkegaardian in its approach to the life-history of the self, our reading of it is, I would suggest, likely to be enhanced by an awareness of certain of the Danish thinker's modes of apprehending personal existence.

In the opening passage of *The Sickness Unto Death*, Kierkegaard writes as follows: 'Man is spirit. But what is spirit? Spirit is the self. But what is the self? The self is a relation which relates itself to its own self.'[3] This concept of the spiritual self as actually existing only in and as a process of self-relating seems relevant to the very way in which *The Echoes Return Slow* emerges out of the interrelating of prose and poetry. Kierkegaard has partly in mind the kind of incessant internal conversations, infinitely recessive in character, that constitute human consciousness even as

understood in exclusively secular terms. Yet, in that connection, his definition of 'relation' differs from the ordinary, as has been noted by H. A.
Nielsen:

> the underlying relation to myself that constitutes me as a human self is not
> the presence or potential of inward dialogue per se, much less any of the
> transitory relations we noted before, but rather those parts or threads of
> the dialogue which deal with matters of what I really think it is worth to
> have a human life, what I privately judge it is worth to me to have *this* one.
> The rest of my self-dialogue will doubtless concern some important matters
> amongst the trivial, but the part of the dialogue Kierkegaard seems to want
> to isolate and later X-ray concerns in a rather narrow sense how I in my
> uttermost privacy feel about being the one I am. (pp. 3–4)

Some such concept of the kind of self-relating which truly constitutes
the self seems to me to underlie R. S. Thomas's chosen mode of proceeding
in *The Echoes Return Slow*, and to account for such features as its manifest
selectivity, its compression of style (in the prose almost as much as in the
poetry) and the *kind* of privacy to which it so movingly gives us access.
Thomas successfully devises strategies for 'committing his silence to
paper' (*CLP*, p. 35), as he puts it, and for thus safeguarding the integrity
of his inwardness even in the process of making it public. But then his
best poetry is not infrequently felt to be a kind of precipitate of silence.

Kierkegaard specifically denies that the self, in his sense of the term,
is susceptible of purely secular definition. For all its subtleties, such a view
of the self is bound, for him, to remain a simplistic one – a view he characterises as so blithely one-dimensional as to amount to no more than the
redundant definition of the self as the 'I-am-I'. Such simplification may
include immense complexities of psychological (and psychoanalytical)
analysis revealing the multi-layered, multi-faceted and virtually unfathomable nature of the self. But simplification it nevertheless remains,
since the self viewed in secular terms – even the radically fractured and
dispersed self of postmodernist writers – is considered as essentially
homogeneous, that is, as wholly belonging to a single category of existence. Kierkegaard, by contrast, sees the self as profoundly paradoxical
in its ontological character, precisely because its very existence is a logical

impossibility, an oxymoron compounded of those two mutually incompat-ible states, eternity and time. And the compound self truly discovers itself (that is, discovers this fundamental aspect of itself) only when it enters into the relationship with God that brings it into being as an 'individual'.

Viewed in this context, *The Echoes Return Slow* might appropriately be subtitled 'an autobiography of an individual', since the book has been constructed in the very image of a self that knows itself as belonging simultaneously to the temporal and the eternal. It is with the self as the continuous, and necessarily paradoxical, product of *this* 'relation' that the volume is primarily concerned. As Wyschogrod has pointed out, this state of 'relating', which is the inescapable existential state of the com-pound self, generates pathos precisely 'because of the basic incommensur-ability of [its] ontological ingredients'.[4] In order to reproduce that pathos, Thomas needs faithfully to render the temporal conditions that, para-doxically, provide the spiritual self with the very terms of its existence. In eternity, all will be reconciled, but not in time, which is the realm not of being but of existence:

> When all things are accomplished providence rests in consummation; when all things are accomplished the atonement comes to rest in equilibrium, but they do not *exist*. Faith is therefore the anticipation of the eternal which holds the factors together, the cleavages of existence.[5]

So, in *The Echoes Return Slow*, birth itself is imaged as a reluctant coming to life: 'The marks in the spirit would not heal. The dream would recur, groping his way up to the light, coming to the crack too narrow to squeeze through' (*CLP*, p. 12). But are we offered historical fact here, or existential myth? Specialists assure us that babies in the womb have no capacity for recording experience in the form of memory. And, after all, one of the inescapable aspects of life in time is that time present denies us full and immediate access to time past. The deliberate acts of recollection that constitute the act of 'life-writing', of writing the life of the self, are themselves inevitably compromised as to their 'truth' by this fact. Or perhaps we should say that in Thomas's view, autobiography's only legitimate *raison d'être* is its search (however ultimately self-defeating) for the kind of 'truth' about the self (a 'myth of the self') that is available only on these equivocal existential terms.

Accordingly, he finds ways of dramatising these very terms, in order to foreground the paradoxical nature of his undertaking. So, for instance, the 'interference' of present with past, the positive aspect of which is maturity of judgement, is part of the point Thomas has 'in mind' when recalling an early occasion of 'Gathering mushrooms by the light of the moon':

> The clouds towered. Their shape was prophetic, but there were no prophets. Through long hours, inhaling the dust that was not injurious, he was prepared with a minimum of effort on the part of himself to 'satisfy the examiners'. (*CLP*, p. 16)

Here, the way in which the detonation of the atom bomb irrevocably altered mankind's whole way of seeing the world, including personal memory of a past ostensibly wholly unconnected with that event, is shown also to have involved an alteration of language itself: 'mushroom' and 'dust' are words that can no longer be used in the ways they once could when Thomas was that child. (Such an emphasis is cognate with Geoffrey Hill's observation that etymology is the record of language's fall from innocence, and a synecdoche of humanity's fall from grace.) Thus inscribed in language itself is the fact that recollection is, unavoidably, retrospection. Similarly, when Thomas writes at one point, while remembering the early phase of the Second World War, 'The innocent [that is, himself] could not believe the robin could whistle in deaf ears. Its breast should have been his warning' (*CLP*, p. 20), he is seeing the robin retrospectively in the light of the bombing of Liverpool, when 'Skies [became] red where no/ sun had ever risen/ or set' (*CLP*, p. 20). Again, when he recalls his eventual move to Manafon, and thus to the hill country he had previously viewed only from a nostalgic distance, he writes as follows:

> What had been blue shadows on a longed-for horizon, traced on an inherited background, were shown in time to contain this valley, this village, and a church built with stones from the river, where the rectory stood, plangent as a mahogany piano. (*CLP*, p. 23)

In this context – that of a prose which is constantly advertising its doubleness of meaning – the phrase 'were shown in time' seems to imply not only 'were shown in due course' but also 'were shown in truth, that is, in that aspect which was theirs in time'. The implication is that the human mind, constantly yearning for escape from the limits and limitations of the temporal (Kierkegaard's 'despair of finitude') is always liable to dream of some place, somewhere, where the operation of such conditions may virtually be suspended. For Thomas, as for Kierkegaard, true existence becomes possible only when such a dream is abandoned ('the despair of infinitude'), and the self is not only awakened but reconciled to its paradoxical state as 'shown in time'.

Elsewhere in *The Echoes Return Slow*, the hybrid nature of memory is considered under the more general rubric of the relativity that inescapably characterises all human acts of comprehension. This is given simple parabolic expression in a poem (deliberately written in the form of a children's story) about the sailors' view of shore from ship and of the children's view of ship from shore (*CLP*, p. 15). Pondering his own relation to his childhood self as he stands on the Llŷn peninsula, gazing over and back at his native Anglesey, Thomas ruefully notes that 'One headland looks at another headland. What one sees must depend on where one stands, when one stands' (*CLP*, p. 47). And the accompanying long poem brings out the pun in that ostensibly innocent geographical expression, 'headland':

> How shallow the minds
> they played by! Not like mine
> now, this dark pool I
> lean over on the same
> headland, knowing it wrinkled
>
> by time's wind, putting my hand
> down, groping with bleeding
> fingers, for truths too
> frightening to be brought up. (*CLP*, p. 47)

If the prose appears, however briefly, to be leaving a door open to belief in the mere relativity, and equal (in)validity of all judgements, then the poem very firmly closes it. Emphasise relativity though Thomas may as a textual strategy for highlighting the self-limiting character of the existential self, he does not mean to imply that all judgements are thereby rendered essentially nugatory. Indeed, from the beginning of *The Echoes Return Slow* he is very particularly concerned to establish the difference between the true and the false, and throughout the volume he remains deeply troubled by the inexhaustible resourcefulness of human beings (including himself) when it comes to practising deception and self-deception. It is an issue beautifully imaged in the picture of himself as a child aboard his father's ship during the First World War, whiling away his time while his parents enjoyed themselves:

> I lay in a bunk while they feasted, turning and turning the glossed pages. The cockroaches should have been a reminder. The shadows from which they crawled were as dark as those where the submarines lurked. (*CLP*, p.14)

Those pages he read were therefore more than 'glossy'; they were 'glossed' in the sense that they were specifically designed to deflect the attention away from the truth by providing the mind with a false textual gloss on events. Thomas's sceptical view of the world – particularly the adult world – recurs throughout the volume, and he frequently focuses on the way language is routinely used to mislead. 'The war to end all wars! After "the hostilities were over" the return to cross-channel' (*CLP*, p. 15).

What is becoming clear from the above considerations is that, for Thomas, the act of personal recollection is truly legitimate only when it involves a considered act of understanding, which in turn involves the fullest possible judgement of the self by the self, conducted in the light of its existential experience of its paradoxical state and of its acknowledgement that human apprehension (even the self's apprehension of itself and its history) is, in every instance, fundamentally flawed and narrowly circumscribed. For him, memory is most consequential when it is deliberate, not least in the sense of being the product of those profound acts of deliberation that the paradoxes of existence demand. And it is this measured, considered mode of remembering that Thomas emphasises through the deliberateness of the composition of his text, regardless of whether it is prose or poetry. Yet in order for it to retain its existential integrity and authenticity, such deliberateness must be constantly qualified, and redeemed, by the humility of uncertainty, an uncertainty with regard both to the finality of judgement, and to the (unreliable) language in which that judgement has to be couched. So, Thomas's writing is constantly destabilising itself, taking rigidity out of its firmness, and taking the simple firmness out of its affirmations. This is done both through the interplay between the sometimes contrasting discourses of prose and poetry, and through the play of meaning within each of these discourses taken singly. As a simple example, consider parts of the early passage in which Thomas recalls his family's move from England, and the various ports at which his father had been based, to live permanently in Holyhead:

> After the 'hostilities were over' the return to cross-channel. So many hours at sea, so many more on shore. The salt waters were spat into from Welsh mouths. (*CLP*, p. 15)

What sort of estimation is being made, in that last sentence, of Holyhead? It is surely ambiguous. There may be wry affection in it, as Thomas notes with amusement that *every* aspect of 'home', including the most banal or unattractive, is liable to have its charms. But the sentence may also be read as comical, since it is comical to suppose that the sea could care what nationality was the mouth that was self-importantly spitting into it. Thus understood, the sentence may be regarded as a comment on the presumptuousness of human beings, who make so much of distinctions that are meaningless in a cosmic perspective. But the sentence may also be felt to be sardonic, and satirical in tone; what do the Welsh do to the sea but spit into it with the ineffectuality that in Thomas's frequently voiced opinion typifies the nation? Even the slightly unusual readjustment of customary phrasing ('from Welsh mouths' rather than 'by Welsh mouths') seems to have been determined by a wish to hint at the distance a Welsh spitter is careful to place between himself and the sea. Or is it rather intended to emphasise the self-conscious separation of the human from the realm of the non-human?

Such equivocations of meaning, or multiple suggestiveness, abound in both prose and poetry in *The Echoes Return Slow*. Indeed, they may safely be said to be part of the *raison d'être* of the text, and to be what the text is carefully composed to produce. The results can be disturbingly powerful, as when Thomas speaks of his first curacy:

> So he was ordained to conduct death, its shabby orchestra of sniffs and tears; the Church renowned for its pianissimo in brash scores. (*CLP*, p. 19)

The puns here on 'ordained' and 'conduct' are many, and between them the meanings range with profound resonance over such issues as fate and free will, authorisation and its relations to authority, the human being in the priest and the priest in the human being, ritual and its potential for both revelation and deception.

It is, then, in these potent terms that the text in *The Echoes Return Slow* is always very evidently a studied composition, not least in being a careful composite of past and present, of feeling and judicious reflection. As has been seen, in order for it to be genuinely responsive to both the elements that constitute these, and other, dualities, the text needs to take double-ness upon itself, and it is to this end that Thomas avails himself of both prose and poetry. His use of these modes is, however, extremely flexible. They can be interchangeable in function, and sometimes he deliberately minimises the difference between them, as if to stress that what they have in common – their compositional character – is more important than what separates them. At other times he capitalises on the different effects of which they are respectively capable, since that allows him to maintain his double vision.

For Thomas, as for Kierkegaard, double vision is all when one is deal-ing with the human, spiritual, self. After all, his God is intelligible only as 'the double agent/ of life, working for/ the continuance of it/ by its betrayal' (*CLP*, p. 68). And just as doubleness is inscribed everywhere in his text (as pun, parallelism, contrast, dialogue, dialectic, and so on), so too is it explicitly addressed by the text as a psycho-spiritual phenom-enon. No wonder Thomas is attracted to the little owl, 'Athene noctua', who may be 'too small for wisdom' (as, in a sense, Thomas feels himself to be), but who, unlike the grander barn owl, is active both by night and day: 'at night it was lyrical, its double note sounded under the stars in counterpoint to the fall of waves' (*CLP*, p. 51). In such an act of counter-pointing, doubleness dizzyingly redoubles itself. But what is playfully affectionately touched upon here is considered altogether differently elsewhere. So, for instance, the agony of human consciousness, which derives from its awareness of itself – that consciousness of self that con-stitutes the very being of the human self – is rendered in a poem depicting man as dancing to the music of time played by 'The piper with the thin lips':

> I only
>
> look at him as I dance,
> shaming him with the operation
> on the intelligence of
> a creature without anaesthetic. (*CLP*, p. 61)

Even in an instance as anguished as this, however, Thomas might be understood by some as being essentially concerned only with the secular aspects of human doubleness. For those concerned to identify the specific-ally spiritual aspects of that condition as registered in *The Echoes Return Slow*, certain comments by Kierkegaard may again prove useful. In the following passage from his *Journals*, he is considering the kind of double-mindedness that for him characterises the highest mode of self-conscious-ness:

Most men are blunted I's. What was given to us by name as a possibility of being sharpened to an I is quickly blunted to a third person (like Baron Münchhausen's dog, a greyhound which wore down its legs and became a daschund).

It is quite a different matter to be related objectively to one's own subject-ivity.

Take Socrates: he is not third-personal in the sense that he avoids danger of exposing himself and risking his life, as one would do if one were third-personal and not I. Not at all. But in the midst of danger he is related object-ively to his own personality, and at the moment when he is condemned to death he speaks of the condemnation as though he were a third person. He is subjectivity raised to the second power, he is related to objectivity as

a true poet wishes to be related to his poetic production: this is the objectivity with which he is related to his own subjectivity. This is a work of art.
Otherwise one gets either an objective something, an objective stick of
furniture, which is supposed to be a man, or a hotch-potch of casual and
arbitrary happenings. But to be related objectively to one's own subjectivity
is the real task.[6]

Modern psychoanalysis might, of course, see in this only a misinter-
pretation of the phenomenon of dissociation (which, taken to extremes,
characterises psychotic states). But Kierkegaard is speaking not of a
psychological state but of a spiritual condition and it is to this, it seems
to me, R. S. Thomas is attempting to approximate as closely as possible
in *The Echoes Return Slow* as he multiplies textual strategies for relating
objectively to his own subjectivity. He can only do so dialectically, that
is by ensuring that both the move towards objectivity and the equal but
opposite impulse towards subjectivity are held together in tension, thus
preventing the objective from becoming dangerously impersonal and the
subjective from becoming familiar self-indulgence. The coexistence of
both, maintained by an interaction between them, guarantees the authentic
spiritual qualities of each. And the alternation between prose and poetry
is one (but not the only) essential textual means by which this dialectic
is created and preserved.

The way in which prose and poetry interact to this end constantly
changes. Any example must, therefore, be a partial one. Allowing for
that, however, the following instance may give some indication, at least,
of the way in which the process seems to work. Both texts are printed
complete, so that the full effect of juxtaposing/ combining/ contrasting
them may be judged:

Memento mori! But he was young for death. Was the sea calling him on
or back? It was a false voice in the trees. Bad days were when three herring-
gulls cried above the valley; or when a shepherd in the high moors said:
You can almost smell the sea today. From different motives he assumed a
cure, where that same sound was no longer a trick of the wind, but real
waves on the bar a few miles to the west. He was reminded all too soon
that journeying is not necessarily in the right direction.

206

The wrong prayers for the right
reason? The flesh craves
what the intelligence
renounces. Concede

the Amens. With the end
nowhere, the travelling
all, how better to get
there than on one's knees? (*CLP*, p. 33)

The prose in this instance is deliberately discursive in style, the poem
deliberately elliptical. The prose plays with the idea of sententiousness
– at first rejecting it, through its ironic discounting of 'Memento mori',
but then quietly assuming the very manner of moralising, of emblematis-
ing the personal and blazoning it as representative, that it had begun by
repudiating. And, of course, the past self is spoken of, rather than for, in
the third person. It is thus re-viewed in the perspectives of both morality
and eternity, its significance thereby being both diminished and enlarged;
diminished by its being reduced to a 'case', and set in a context that
denies it centrality, yet enlarged, or amplified, by its being connected to
universals. The poem, by contrast, is written in the language and grammar
of actual existential experience, and gives us the self agonistes, through
lines that seem to be bent and buckled at their right-hand margins by the
pressure of feeling to which they are almost palpably subject. The curt
phrases, like those in Emily Dickinson's poems, belong to an urgently
compressed and curtailed style of mental notation, the poetic equivalent of
the stammered morse code of a mind in the midst of spiritual emergency.

The main point is that for Thomas autobiography becomes spiritually
authentic only when the history of the self is written simultaneously in *both*
these styles, in a fashion that is consequently both objective and subjective. And in allowing him to write like this, the prose-poetry combinations
also allow him to explore a related concern, namely the inexhaustibly
mysterious question of the origins of poetry, and of its status as both
a cognitive and an ontological instrument. Indeed, it would not be too
much to claim that as well as being specifically a spiritual autobiography,
*The Echoes Return Slow* is also necessarily, and not merely incidentally or

contingently, a *poet's* autobiography, one of the subjects of which must be the distinctive modus vivendi of a poet's mind. As we read the book, this subject is likely to take the form of a whole nexus of interrelated comments and questions: how on earth did the circumstances and experiences recorded for this period in the prose give rise to *this* poem? Who would have thought that *this* poem would find its point of origin *there*? In what way, if at all, does it make sense to claim that this poem is commensurate with that experience? Is it the prose that, in this instance, is a sort of afterthought, a doubtfully appropriate gloss on the experience of the kind with which Thomas was particularly taken in the marginal comments to Coleridge's 'The Ancient Mariner'? Or could it be that the poem belies the actual experience, in the interests of intensifying it?

These questions and many, many more are likely to come to mind as one reads. And the result is not only that one discovers what a penetrating autobiography of a poet *The Echoes Return Slow* is, but also that one appreciates how, for Thomas, the mystery of poetry is a significant aspect of the mystery of the existential spiritual self. It reveals, once more, the strangely compound character of that self, the ways in which it is, as it were, radically inconsistent with itself, and consists of experiences that coexist yet are incommensurate with each other. One of the sections based on his period at Eglwys-Fach brings this out with particular sharpness:

> The highway ran through the parish. The main line ran through the parish. Yet there were green turnings, unecclesiastical aisles up which he could walk to the celebration of the marriage of mind and nature. Otters swam in the dykes. Wild geese and wild swans came to winter in the rush-growing meadows. He hummed an air from Tchaikovsky quietly to himself. Yet on still days the air was as clerestories in which the overtones of gossiping voices would not fade. (*CLP*, p. 41)

Several of these sentences seem already to be aspiring to the condition of poetry. There seems to be a poem here struggling to get out, so that it would seem natural for it to be allowed to materialise, to realise itself, on the adjoining page. Instead of which, the prose is followed by one of the most blistering of Thomas's poems of self-accusation, 'A will of iron, perforated/ by indecision. A charity/ that, beginning at home,/ ended in domestication', and so on in a bitterly witty litany of self-indictment. What has happened is that those 'gossiping voices' that made themselves heard in the concluding sentence of the prose have taken full, malevolent, possession of that part of Thomas's mind and self from which poems come. But then, through the response to those voices that is the poem itself, Thomas turns destructive criticism into a devastatingly creative act of self-evaluation. It is a striking example of how poetry does not necessarily originate in the 'poetic', and of how, in Thomas's case, it is most likely to emerge from the most spirit-haunted recesses of himself. That the result may as often be a poetry of radiance as of darkness is beautifully illustrated in the conjunction of texts that relate to his period in Manafon:

> How far can one trust autumn thoughts? Against the deciduousness of man there stand art, music, poetry. The Church was the great patron of such. Why should a country church not hear something of the overtones of a cathedral? As an antidote to Ancient and Modern, why not Byrd and Marcello? But was winter the best time? (*CLP*, p. 26)

The poem comes as an answer to that question, and may even be read as Thomas's distinctive response to Wallace Stevens's famous observation that 'one must have a mind of winter':

> It was winter. The church shone.
> The musicians played on
> through the snow; their strings sang
> sharper than robins in the lighted interior.
>
> From outside the white
> face of the land stared in
> with all the hunger of nature
> in it for what it could not digest. (*CLP*, p. 26)

In this case, the poem becomes a means of revealing a potential in 'winter' that had previously been hidden, and in the process comes to stand for a state of mind, or condition of self, that can scarcely be made available

209

in, or by, prose. Poetry here powerfully instances the kind of insights that, as the prose concedes, are possible only in art. And art is shown to speak to art, and to inspire it, as the poem becomes the only form of words that can, in any adequate sense, conform to music.

The poem also, in this instance, becomes an affecting example of that spiritual effect which Kierkegaard characterised as 'repetition'. By this he meant a special kind of sameness in difference; the recovery of the past in a way that transfigures the present and transposes it to an entirely different pitch of understanding. Or rather, to use the terms Thomas himself chooses to employ in these passages, 'repetition' is the way in which the mind – for instance, in great art – can miraculously acquire the kind of permanence of insight that the very 'deciduousness' (impermanence, mutability) of man paradoxically makes possible.

'Repetition' is, then, an experience of the self which is both the opposite and necessary complement of what I earlier called 'deliberation'. Whereas 'deliberation' is likely implicitly to value the present above the past, and thus to view the self's progress through time as growth and development, 'repetition' instead views the self as ceaselessly working in effect to stand still, to stand by what was, and is, best. These, along with several other models of the self's existence in time – models that represent a portfolio of possibilities for autobiographical writing, variant ways of writing the self – are consciously entertained and implemented in *The Echoes Return Slow*. (These include instances where the metaphor of space is used for exploring man's situation in time.) And the very title itself, if we refer back to the poem in the volume that gives rise to it, carries several very interesting connotations in this connection. It occurs in a moving poem about visiting the elderly:

> They keep me sober,
> the old ladies
> stiff in their beds,
> mostly with pale eyes
> wintering me.
> Some are like blonde dolls
> their joints twisted;
> life in its brief play

was a bit rough.
Some fumble
with thick tongues for words,
and are deaf;
shouting their faint names
I listen;
they are far off,
the echoes return slow.

But without them,
without the subdued light
their smiles kindle,
I would have gone wild,
drinking earth's huge draughts
of joy and woe. (*CLP*, p. 43)

The need for patience when listening for what life – one's own and that of others – has got to say about its past; the slowness of the self to answer to any single name, however intimate; the need to use the past as a kind of tuning fork to keep the present in a sober key; these, and other meanings important for our understanding of Thomas's way of practising autobiography, emerge from the poem. But there is also more, which appears if one takes this poem in conjunction with the prose passage that accompanies it, where Thomas bleakly notes: 'There is no cure for old age. And the old tend to be sick. When one should be leading them on to peer into the future, one is drawn back by them into the past' (*CLP*, p. 43). Echo, then, has its got its distinctly narcissistic features. Autobiography may mean no more than an orgy of remembering indulged in so that, replete with the past, the self may complacently sleep out that future which leads to eternity. In his pseudonymous work on *Repetition*, Kierkegaard has Constantine Constantius observe:

When existence has been circumnavigated, it will be manifest whether one has the courage to understand that life is a repetition and has the desire to rejoice in it. The person who has not circumscribed life before beginning to live will never live; the person who circumnavigated it but became satiated had a poor constitution; the person who chose repetition – he lives. He does not run about like a boy chasing butterflies or stand on tiptoe to look for the glories of the world, for he knows them. Neither does he sit like an old woman turning the spinning wheel of recollection, but calmly goes his way, happy in repetition.[7]

It is against the 'spinning wheel[s] of recollection', those other, familiar versions of autobiography – narrating the progress of the self, or confidently recalling its experiences – that *The Echoes Return Slow* is written. Attention has already been drawn to some of the means by which Thomas deliberately avoids falling into this pattern, but there are many others that, were there space, could be considered. Of these, some of the most obvious – such as his keeping death constantly in mind, and his extended exploration, through the image of the sea, of life as the neighbourhood of eternity – are also probably the most important.

The figure of time that particularly fascinated R. S. Thomas was that of the circle, as one might perhaps have expected, given that his poetic career had turned (monotonously, as some would have it) around his own seemingly obsessive return not only to particular subjects (Iago Prytherch, the hidden god) but to the repertoire of phrases and tropes that were, for him, inseparable from those inescapable concerns. *The Echoes Return Slow* is in many ways modelled on that figure, with Thomas even reflecting on the way his career as priest had brought him circling back to near his original point of departure ('For some there is no future but the one that is safeguarded by a return to the past'). It is appropriate, therefore, that his last published essay should have taken the form of a meditative circling around the epigraph to David Jones's *The Anathémata*: 'It was a dark and stormy night, we sat by the calcined wall, it was said to the tale-teller, tell us a tale, and the tale ran thus: it was a dark and stormy night'. And as epigraph to that essay he printed a poem that itself echoes (or redoubles) many of the concerns of *The Echoes Return Slow*:

> We asked our questions and passed
> on. The answer, discovered
> by others, was to a different question.
> Yet they, too, had the feeling
> of having been here before.
> We are our own ghosts, haunting
> and haunted. We live out a dream,
> unable to equate the face

> with the owner, the voice
> with the speaker, the singer
> with the song. Ah, how we thought
> science would deliver us, when
> all it has done is to set us
> circling a little more swiftly
> about a self that is an echo.[8]

The phrases correspond to, and in a sense with, those in *The Echoes Return Slow*, when Thomas speaks of how 'The spirit revolves/ on itself and is without/ a shadow', before proceeding to twin that spiritual movement with the biological movement of the 'twin helix/ where the dancing chromosomes/ pass one another back/ to back to a tune from the abyss' (*CLP*, p. 66). It is in the echoing coexistence of those two movements – the one seemingly self-determined, the other seemingly determining the 'self' – that Thomas sees the paradox of 'existence', and it is on this paradox that he meditates both in *The Echoes Return Slow* and in the David Jones essay.

In the latter, he notes the fatalism of writers such as Hardy and Yeats, and historians such as Spengler and Toynbee, who believe that 'the same elements, the same characters recur and must go on doing so in accordance with some mysterious but inexorable law' (*DJ*, p. 155). Although Thomas is in so many ways very deeply drawn, by his own inclination towards pessimism, to such a conclusion himself, he nevertheless resists it, fortified by the observation that exact repetition – of the kind that is significantly called 'mechanical' – is totally impossible for human beings. By way of illustration he invokes examples such as Borges's celebrated story of Pierre Ménard's rewriting of *Don Quixote* and the alteration of meaning by 'repetition' of identical phrases in Beckett's *Krapp's Last Tape*. Of particular significance, though, is the way in which a case of 'repetition' may involve not just an alteration of meaning but a change to a completely different category of experience, a completely different order/ conception of 'reality'. Repetition thus becomes radically recreative, and profoundly revealing of the truth that a human being is, in Sir Thomas Browne's celebrated phrase, a great amphibian, existing (simultaneously) in several entirely different elements.

In being recreative, repetition is necessarily a fiction (even when it goes under the name of 'history', or even, perhaps 'science'), but then fiction, as the Latinist in Thomas knows and points out, comes from 'Fingo, fingere – to fashion, to form' (*DJ*, p. 158). At root, therefore, it does not mean 'falsehood', but rather a particular 'form' of understanding and truth. And in this 'form', human beings may not only gain access to their own paradoxical nature as existing beings, time's changelings, but may also, as Coleridge famously put it, echo the creative act of the primary imagination. While very willing to admit that, in his time, it is science that has proved the most revelatory of our 'fictions', our creative acts, Thomas ends his essay by doubting whether 'the only truth in life is that which can be repeated by experiment' (*DJ*, p. 159). He is therefore attracted to the scientific 'truth' 'that as the electrons whirl about their nucleus at dizzying speeds, one will suddenly leap into a new orbit' (*DJ*, p. 159). This – reminiscent of Harold Bloom's interpretation of the Heraclitean notion of the 'swerve' – is, one might suggest, also a metaphor for that leap of faith undertaken by Thomas, the move towards a belief that God's grace can shift a human life 'into a new orbit'. And, as recent commentators have stressed, Kierkegaard's conception of 'repetition' was itself a version of that very same belief.[9]

If, then, the Thomas of *The Echoes Return Slow* is 'time's changeling', he is also, to adopt his own phrase for 'D.J.' (David Jones), 'time's disc jockey', commenting through his 'fictions', his compositions of prose and poetry, on the many revolutions of his own life. Repetition – in the ordinary sense of the word – is, as *The Echoes Return Slow* illustrates, the 'form' that autobiography must inevitably take, but Thomas's work obviously emphasises, and fetishises, that structural characteristic of recall and recollection, not least by repeating, in poetry, the 'prose' version of a past period or event. He thus underlines the fact that autobiography is always a self-fashioning, always ('Fingo, fingere') a fiction. The existential implications of this rhetorical strategy have already been explored earlier in this chapter: it is an attempt to conceive of the self as an 'individual', in Kierkegaard's sense of that term. What now, finally, remains to be suggested is that the strategy can also be understood as signifying the central drama of Thomas's effort at self-understanding, the struggle within him between a fatalistic acknowledgement of the law of recurrence and a belief in the redemptive possibility of 'repetition', in the Kierkegaardian sense.

'Towards the end of one's life, towards the end of the century; worse still towards the end of the millennium, the tempter approaches us as desperation' (*CLP*, p. 67). The temptation to despair of any possibility, in his own representative case, of the amendment of self was always strong in Thomas, and in the last phase of his life was powerfully expressed through the fateful metaphor of the furies. Not only was *No Truce with the Furies* the title of his last published collection, but the furies recur as an avenging metaphor in several of the late poems that remain in manuscript. No wonder he had been so drawn to Coleridge's 'The Ancient Mariner' that he had in significant part modelled *The Echoes Return Slow*, in its twinning of poetry and prose 'glossary', on that poem about a lost soul condemned to the endless repetition of his terrible autobiographical story.[10] But he concluded his last published essay with an affirmation of the Christian promise 'of an [*sic*] new sphere for the purified soul', recalling Christ's salvific words: 'let him that heareth say "Come". And let him that is athirst come; And whosoever will, let him take the water freely' (*DJ*, p. 159). Perhaps the most rapturous image in *The Echoes Return Slow* of Thomas taking that water is that in which he registers the experience of offering, and receiving, communion:

> He lifted
>
> > the chalice, that crystal in
> > which love questioning is love
> > blinded with excess of light. (*CLP*, p. 46)

But if that is the most intense of those moments when life is transfigured by grace, the most moving and sustained occur in the final pages of *Echoes* when the word 'love' (so notoriously rare in Thomas's vocabulary) is repeated, not simply within a single line as in the above quotation, but in each of the last two poems, in which Thomas registers that he also is 'in the debt of love'.

One of the books which R. S. Thomas particularly admired was George Steiner's *Real Presences*, in which the following passage occurs:

Serious painting, music, literature or sculpture make palpable to us, as do no other means of communication, the unassuaged, unhoused instability and estrangement of our condition. We are, at key instants, strangers to ourselves, errant at the gates of our own psyche. We knock blindly at the doors of turbulence, of creativity, of inhibition within the *terra incognita* of our own selves.[11]

*The Echoes Return Slow* is compelling because it is serious in exactly this way, and so possesses the precious strength that Steiner definitively recognises:

Beyond the strength of any other act of witness, literature and the arts tell of the obstinacies of the impenetrable, of the absolutely alien which we come up against in the labyrinth of intimacy . . . It is poetics, in the full sense, which informs us of the visitor's visa in place and in time which defines our status as transients in a house of being whose foundations, whose future history, whose rationale – if any – lie wholly outside our will and comprehension. It is the capacity of the arts . . . to make us, if not at home, at least alertly, answerably peregrine in the unhousedness of our human circumstance. (139–40)

But it is Kierkegaard who, perhaps, best captures the challenge Thomas sets himself in *The Echoes Return Slow* and thus best enables us to appreciate the measure of his achievement in this, one of his most remarkable volumes:

For . . . existence paradoxically accentuated generates the maximum of passion. To abstract from existence is to remove difficulty. To remain in existence so as to understand one thing in one moment and another thing in another moment, is not to understand oneself. But to understand the greatest oppositions together, and to understand oneself existing in them, is very difficult.[12]

# Notes

1  For an interesting discussion of the volume from this point of view, see Barbara Prys-Williams, '"A Consciousness in Search of its own Truth": Some Aspects of R. S. Thomas's *The Echoes Return Slow* as Autobiography', *Welsh Writing in English 2* (1996), 98–125.

2  The significance of Kierkegaard for Thomas is discussed in William V. Davis, '"At the foot of the Precipice of Water . . . Sea Shapes Coming to Celebration"': R. S. Thomas and Kierkegaard', *Welsh Writing in Engish 4* (1998), 92–117. In addition to the works cited below, I have found the following particularly useful: Mary Finn, *Writing the Incommensurable: Kierkegaard, Rossetti and Hopkins* (Pennsylvania: Pennsylvania State University Press, 1992); Patrick Gardiner, *Kierkegaard* (Oxford: Oxford University Press, 1988); David Law, *Kierkegaard as Negative Theologian* (Oxford: Clarendon Press, 1983); and Graham Ward, *Barth, Derrida and the Language of Theology* (Cambridge: Cambridge University Press, 1995). It should, however, be noted that throughout this chapter I have assumed (on the basis of my own discussions with the poet) that his deeply pondered understanding of Kierkegaard was not systematic or scholarly, and so I have not respected the distinctions scholars draw between the different periods of Kierkegaard's writing career, nor have I had regard to the complex issue of his use of personae, as examined so profoundly, for instance, in Roger Poole, *Kierkegaard: the Indirect Communication* (Charlottesville and London: University of Virginia Press, 1993). Finally, I am grateful to Professor John Heywood Thomas for his advice on interpreting Kierkegaard.

3  Quoted in H. A. Nielsen, 'The Anatomy of Self in Kierkegaard', *Essays on Kierkegaard and Wittgenstein*, ed. Richard H. Bell and Ronald E. Hustwit (Ohio: College of Wooster, 1978), p. 1.

4  Michael Wyschogrod, *Kierkegaard and Heidegger: the Ontology of Existence* (London: Routledge, 1954), p. 132.

5  Søren Kierkegaard, *The Journals of Kierkegaard, 1834–1854*, ed. and trans. Alexander Dru (London: Collins, Fontana Books, 1967), p. 110.

6  Søren Kierkegaard, *The Last Years: Journals 1853–1855*, ed. and trans. Ronald Gregor Smith (London: Collins, Fontana Books, 1968), p. 235.

7  Søren Kierkegaard, *Fear and Trembling/ Repetition*, ed. and trans. Howard V. Hong and Edna H. Hong (Princeton, NJ: Princeton University Press, 1983), p. 132.

8  Quoted in R. S. Thomas, 'Time's Disc Jockey: Meditations on Some Lines in *The Anathémata*', in *David Jones: Diversity in Unity*, ed. Belinda Humfrey and Anne Price-Owen (Cardiff: University of Wales Press, 2000), p. 153. Hereafter *DJ*.

9  There are interesting discussions in Alastair Hannay and Gordon D. Marino (eds), *The Cambridge Companion to Kierkegaard* (Cambridge: Cambridge University Press, 1998), p. 273 and pp. 282–307.

10  During his discussion of *The Echoes Return Slow* with me, R. S. Thomas repeat-edly noted that 'The Ancient Mariner' had served him as a model.

11  George Steiner, *Real Presences: Is there Anything in What we Say?* (London: Faber & Faber, 1989), p. 139.

12  Søren Kierkegaard, *Concluding Unscientific Postscript*, trans. David F. Swenson and Walter Lowrie (Princeton, NJ: Princeton University Press, 1941), p. 316.

# 9

# 'The fantastic side of God'

On 14 March 1943, as night was drawing in, a man named Jaromir Hladik was arrested by the Nazis in Prague. His 'crime' was being a Jew, sufficient for him to be sentenced to death by firing squad on the morning of 29 March. Terrified by his imminent execution, Hladik devoted much of his brief remaining time to imagining every dread detail of his fate, in the vain belief he would consequently be spared, as reality never exactly corresponds to what is imagined. He was only forty years old, and apart from the occasional friendship, his entire life had been devoted to creative writing. Yet, staring extinction in the face, it seemed to him that of all his unfinished works only one promised to be satisfactory, a play about Baron von Roemerstadt, an obsessive who did nothing except repeat himself. Now, during his final hours, Hlaldik beseeched God to allow him just sufficient time to complete that play. And his prayer was answered. Just as the execution squad raised their guns to a deadly level on 29 March, time was arrested. But Hladik's mind remained active, allowing him to perfect his Roemerstadt play. Then, exactly at the end of a miraculous suspended year, he fell limply to the ground under the hail of bullets from his executioners.

The story is one told by Jorge Luis Borges,[1] and the inclusion of a poem entitled 'Jaromir Hladik' in *Mass for Hard Times* (*CLP*, p. 197), is intriguing proof of the interest taken in the great Argentinian writer by

R. S. Thomas during his later years. Indeed in one important respect, the poem may be read as Thomas's elegy for the blind visionary:

> What genealogy
> has the self other
> than the wisdom gathered
> from standing so often
> before time's firing
> squad, computing its
> eternity in the triggered interval
> before the command to shoot?

But like several of his late poems – and like that magnificent volume *The Echoes Return Slow* throughout – there are autobiographical dimensions to the writing. Isn't Hladik rather like R. S. Thomas in old age? – a lonely solitary whose sole/soul identity is bound up with the impossible attempt to capture something of the mysterious truth about God in language? Thomas was agonisingly aware of endlessly 'elucidating' the same old insoluble riddle of existence; and, as he grew older, he became ever more conscious of standing 'before time's firing/ squad' as he did so. He also came to fear he was becoming befuddled as a poet, repeating himself endlessly, just like Roemerstadt. And both during his time and after his death critics have been divided between seeing him positively as a metaphysically entranced and poetically entrancing Hladik, and viewing him negatively as a sad obsessive whose talents were narrowed to the point of insignificance over the last three decades.

And what was his final 'obsession'? It was well identified by R. S. Thomas in one of the last interviews he gave:

I wouldn't say that I'm an orthodox Christian at all and the longer we live in the twentieth century the more fantastic discoveries are made, the more we hear what the universe is like I find it very difficult to be a kind of orthodox believer in Jesus as my saviour and that sort of thing. I'm more interested in the extraordinary nature of God. If there is God, if there is deity, then He, even as the old hymn says, He moves in a mysterious way and I'm fascinated by that mystery and I've tried to write out of that experience of God, the fantastic side of God, the quarrel between the conception of God as a person, as having a human side, and the conception of God as being extraordinary.[2]

There the word "fantastic" attracts him like a magnet, yet it is a word rarely used by critics to help orientate them through Thomas's later writings. It is, though, the very word used (in English translation) by the pseudonymous author of Borges's story 'Tlön, Uqbar, Orbis Tertius': 'The metaphysicians of Tlön do not seek for the truth or even for verisimilitude, but rather for the astounding. They judge that metaphysics is a branch of fantastic literature' (SS, p. 34). Consistent with the high value Borges placed on ambiguity, this statement is double-edged. In part an indictment of the totalitarian ideological systems elaborated by the idealist culture of Tlön, the sentences also point in the opposite direction, towards Borges's own love of playfully inventing universes to demonstrate the unsettling possibility that truth may perhaps be elusively glimpsed only through the strangest, or most fantastical, of fictions. And it is through this convergence of Welsh and Argentinian vocabularies, this coincidence of 'fantasies', that we may best begin to understand such affinities as the later, metaphysically challenged, Thomas may have felt with the outrageous and outlandish fables of Borges.

The basic premise of Borges's vertiginous tall tales was one shared by Thomas, and it is ingeniously displayed in the Argentinian's story 'The Immortal'. This concerns a man from the late Roman Empire so obsessed with the rumour of an Eternal City that he dedicates himself to locating it. Eventually discovered in the remotest parts of the burning North African desert, it turns out to be an elaborate, deserted structure of crazy disorder. In its shadow lives a bestial tribe of troglodytes, and it eventually dawns on the traveller that these are the original inhabitants of the city – human Immortals who had razed the beautifully symmetrical metropolis they originally built in order to construct this mad labyrinth, before abandoning it to live solitary lives of pure speculation in nearby burrows, eventually losing all capacity for speech. All this they had done in a desperate attempt to comprehend the ways of the 'irrational gods, who govern the world and of whom we know nothing, save that they do not resemble man' (SS, p. 144). At once an instance of, and a satire on, Borges's own writerly infatuations, the tale exposes the single generative principle underlying all his extravagant fictions. He, too, loves the exotica of theological learning, adventures widely in the wild zone of philosophy, and finds particularly rich food for his own mentally exuberant 'speculations' in the writings of the Gnostics and heresiarchs. And, true to his aphorism that every important writer creates his own precursors, Borges is ever ready to reinvent Gnostic teaching in the image of his own fantasies. When an interviewer teasingly remarked that 'it's always good to have an obscure Gnostic saint', Borges replied 'Oh, yes, of course. They're very handy, eh? They're available at any moment', before going on to elaborate on his reading in authentic Gnostic texts.[3] Likewise, when R. S. Thomas fully emerged as a metaphysical poet with the publication of the enigmatically entitled *H'm*, he did so partly in the guise of a latter-day Gnostic or Rabbinical Cabalist, turning away from orthodoxy to engage with the riddle of a universe whose nature was, he realised, grotesquely incompatible with the neat platitudes of conventional religious belief. 'Alas, we are heretics/ all', he ruefully noted in *No Truce With the Furies* (*CLP*, p. 233), in a poem in which he highlights the speculative nature of all religious orthodoxies. 'Man has to believe/ something. May as well invest/ in this creed as in that' – the Nicean and Chalcedonian dogmas being scarcely more likely than the previous belief in 'Parthenogenesis'.

'In the beginning,' wrote Borges, 'God was the Gods (Elohim), a plural which some call the plural of majesty and others the plural of plentitude; . . . [but in the Hebrew] Elohim takes a single verb . . . [and] despite the vagueness suggested by the [English] plural, Elohim is concrete and is called the god Jevovah'.[4] It is this concept of God as a baffling plurality of contradictory qualities – Elohim, Jehovah – that is shockingly explored in Thomas's *H'm*, where he deliberately alternates between reference to 'God' and 'the God,' the latter being suggestive not only of the plural form of the Hebrew Elohim but also of the Gnostic belief in a multiplicity of divinities. As Borges observed, when questioned about his own view of the human body, 'I suppose the best solution is one given by the Gnostics: the idea of a rather clumsy God, God not doing very well his own job' (*Barnstone*, p. 109). This notion of a bungling God is evident in the set of nine extraordinary poems about Creation that so singularly punctuate

222

*H'm.* In response to the desperate petitions of human prayer, the God of 'Soliloquy' sardonically observes of his Creation, 'Pray away,/ Creatures; I'm going to destroy/ It', adding lugubriously 'The mistake's mine,/ If you like. I have blundered/ Before' (*CP*, p. 230). Such blundering turns into open malignancy in several of the other poems in the set, starting with the opening poem of the volume in which Adam wakes to consciousness of a sulphurously smoking earth, and subsequently manifest in the petty anger of the God in 'Echoes' at the muteness of the soil, an anger satisfied only by creating beings who build him altars and offer living sacrifices so that 'the red blood/ Told what he wished to hear' (*CP*, p. 211). In 'Making', creation is animated to the God's satisfaction only once it has been set teeming with bacteria; in 'The Island', a gleefully inventive God plans first to torment humankind into the impotent pleading of prayer and then callously to dispose of the most saintly; the lament of poetry is what the God of 'Repeat' sadistically 'blesses' humankind with, having initially turned away from his Adam 'as from his own/ Excrement';[5] and, as for the satanic God of 'The Other', he is furiously jealous of every gentle instance of human love and virtue.

In these, as in all the metaphysical poems of Thomas's last thirty years, may be felt something of that pure, intellectual and aesthetic delight that Borges felt in the fabrication of fantastic fictions. But there is a difference. Agnostic that he avowedly was, Borges could convincingly declare himself happy with the 'guesswork' he imagined all forms of human explanation (including religion, the arts, philosophy, history and science) to be (*Barnstone*, p. 110). When asked what the word 'god' meant to him, and whether he believed in a transcendent order, he replied 'Of course I do. I believe in the mystery of the world. When people use the word *god*, I think of what George Bernard Shaw said. He said, if I remember rightly, "God is in the making." And we are the makers. We are begetting God. We are creating God every time that we attain beauty' (*Barnstone*, p. 102). Thomas, though, could never be so contentedly or unequivocally a humanist. If *H'm* is full of a sense of God the Elohim, it is also deeply haunted by Thomas's belief in the Christian God of self-sacrifice and love. Any flinching from the painful paradox of the co-incidence of such irreconcilables seemed to Thomas an unconscionable

223

evasion. And, for him, the ultimate symbol of the 'mystery' was the cross.

How appallingly difficult such a 'faith' in self-sacrificial love was to sustain is movingly evident in *H'm*. There is the example of the title poem itself. Attempting to explain the concept of love, a preacher unexpectedly finds himself uttering the word 'god', only to realise helplessly that he is imprisoned within the circularity of language. Turning instead to physical gesture, he tries to enact Christ's injunction to suffer little children to come unto Him, only to discover that they, with 'bow/ legs that were like/ a razor shell/ were too weak to come' (*CP*, p. 232). What his every, failed, attempt therefore shows is that faith can never find consolatory validation in reality – and it is this stark, brutal truth that Thomas insists on confronting in all his metaphysical poetry. The word 'H'm' may itself be read as a letter short of a confident identification of God, as if a copula were missing that connected words up to form a meaningful sentence. Hence, too, his image of a cross whose arms point puzzlingly in opposite directions. If *H'm* includes the vision of one who 'holds out his two/ Hands, calloused with the long failure/ Of prayer' (*CP*, p. 224), it also includes a vile, scorched landscape where 'people/ Held out their thin arms': 'The son watched/ Them: Let me go there, he said' (*CP*, p. 234). As these examples suggest, Thomas can sometimes use line-breaks to problematise the construction of meanings, to dramatise the contingency of his grammatical connectives, as if he were uncertainly, or stutteringly, piecing together his statements about faith's perception of a broken world. His baffled theology is thus inscribed in the movingly baffled syntax of his poetry.

Not that his signature line-breaks always form the broken-backed sentences of a perplexed faith; they can also suggest the rapt meditative mind holding its breath as mystery deepens. As has already been shown in a previous chapter, *H'm* provides one of the most compelling instances of this in 'Via Negativa' which itself opens with an incredulous negative: 'Why no! I never thought other/ Than that God is that great absence in our lives' (*CP*, p. 220). As Borges observed in his essay on 'From Someone to No One', Christian conceptions of God have veered between two extremes. 'In the first centuries of our era, the theologians renovated the

prefix *Omnia* . . . and supplied the words *omnipotent, omnipresent, omnisci-
ent,* which make God into a respectable chaos of unimaginable superla-
tives.' But then, towards the end of the fifth century, 'the unrevealed
author of the *Corpus Dionysiacum* declares that no affirmative predicate
is seemly for God. Nothing should be affirmed about Him, everything
can be denied, Schopenhauer dryly notes: "This theology is the only true
one, but it has no content"' (*PA*, p. 119).

Much of R. S. Thomas's religious poetry is devoted to the necessarily
impossible attempt of resolving this dilemma of how to speak meaningfully of a God whose essential nature is the negation of speech. 'What
language', he rhetorically asks, 'does the god speak?' (*CP*, p. 360). Knowing the answer, he nevertheless persists in fashioning poems that keep
reframing the question, somewhat, it sometimes seems, in the mad spirit
of those creators of Borges's Library of Babel, who assemble an infinitely vast collection of books, using every conceivable combination of
every letter in every conceivable language, in the hope that some chance
arrangement or other might approximate to an ultimate truth. Another
of Borges's stories introduces us to a prisoner, an Aztec priest, engrossed
in the Cabalistic conviction that on the skin of a jaguar confined in an
adjacent cell is written a magical sentence of divine revelation: 'the concrete enigma' of deciphering it, he recognises, 'disturbed me less than
the generic enigma of a sentence written by a god. What type of sentence
(I asked myself) will an absolute mind construct?' (*SS*, p. 205). As Borges
further noted in an essay, 'All language is of a successive nature; it
does not lend itself to a reasoning of the eternal, the intemporal' (*SS*,
p. 260). Just as for him (and as for Ted Hughes)[6] the imprisoned jaguar
itself suggests the tragic futility of the human attempt to cage the un-
confinable, to domesticate the feral, so for R. S. Thomas the white tiger's
body is 'too huge/ and majestic for the cage in which/ it had been put'.
'The colour of the moonlight/ on snow', it breathes 'as you can imagine
that/ God breathes within the confines/ of our definition of him, agon-
izing/ over immensities that will not return' (*CP*, p. 358).

'I modernise the anachronism// of my language, but he is no more
here/ than before' (*CP*, p. 361). Like Borges, Thomas was chronically
fascinated by the paradox of the futile yet incessant human attempt

to confine God within the definitions of language. 'For the failure of language/ there is no redress', he lamented (*CP*, p. 291). He was therefore repeatedly moved to meditate on the unseen sentence that, according to Scripture, Christ once stooped to inscribe in sand. It surfaces first in *Between Here and Now*, in a poem that begins with a typically beautiful equivocation: 'He grew up into an emptiness/ he was on terms with'.[7] Suggesting that any coming to terms with the lack of any concrete evidence of God's presence is, for Thomas, dependent on getting on the best possible speaking terms with Him – finding terms appropriate for expressing a rationally groundless but nevertheless continuing faith – the sentence leads to an affirmation of 'the duplicity/ of language, that could name/ what was not there'. Poetry, for Thomas, is a tabernacle built out of 'the duplicity of language'. And it is this duplicity that is, for him, the best human response to the literal inscrutability of Christ's personal scripture, his sandy signature: 'He was content, remembering/ the unseen writing of Christ/ on the ground, to interpret/ it in his own way.'

He returns to the same enigmatic biblical episode in *Mass for Hard Times*, in the intensely moving poem 'The Reason', via a meditation on the famous opening sentence of the Johannine Gospel: 'In the beginning was the Word.' Fearing that the Word is irretrievably buried 'under the page's/ drift', and that 'not all our tears,/ not all our air-conditioning/ can bring on the thaw', he accepts that 'Our sentences/ are but as footprints arrested/ indefinitely on its threshold' (*CLP*, p. 151). Poetry is also, therefore, the self-confessing language of liminality. As in the lines quoted, the deliberately unpredictable line breaks (try second-guessing Thomas by writing one of his poems out in prose and then reconstructing the breaks without reference to the original) suggest the arrests, the fatal fissures, in our ordinary, confidently explanatory and declaratory, rational statements. And poetry's ability to allow us to 'get the drift' of all this is entirely dependent, of course, on its abandonment of the reason's arrogant aim of touching bedrock. As for humanly speaking the Word, it may be that 'our letters for it/ are too many' (*CLP*, p. 151) – a possibility that Borges's Aztec priest also entertains: 'A god, I reflected, ought to utter only a single word and in that word absolute fullness' (*PA*, p. 205). When, at the end of the story, he succeeds in deciphering the jaguar's 'God script' he therefore chooses silence over disclosure. Thomas could like-wise imagine that for Christ, during his period of withdrawal into the wilderness, 'the true fast/ was abstention from language' (*CLP*, p. 239). Thus in 'The Reason' he speculates that the unearthly cry of the Delphic oracle might have come closest to articulating divine truth, or perhaps 'the cipher the Christ/ wrote on the ground, with no one/ without sin to peer at it/ over his shoulder' (*CLP*, p. 151).

The third and final mention of that 'cipher'occurs in 'Symbols,' in *No Truce With the Furies*, the last volume for Thomas to publish: 'Always in my dream/ he kneels there silently/ writing upon the ground/ what I can't read – signs/ and diagrams; and his accusers/ have withdrawn' (*CLP*, p. 242). Silence is Christ's invincible defence against the assaults from the 'old-fashioned artillery'of language, trained 'to inflict on him woe'. So, too, is his crucifixion, as it baffles even the poem's attempt to translate it into humanly comprehensible terms. Thus, Thomas returns, at the very end of his life, to an interpretation of the crucifixion he had first hazarded in *Frequencies*, over twenty-five years earlier. There, a God harassed by the ever-rising Babel's tower of language that inexorably closes the gap between him and his human creatures, solves the problem by letting his own blood 'to make the sign in the space/ on the page, that is in all languages/ and none; that is the grammarian's/ torment and the mystery/ at the cell's core' (*CP*, p. 324).

In his turn, Thomas writes poems that are self-confessedly doomed to be swallowed up by silence as instantly as Christ's cipher was erased by sand. The white margins of the pages on which these slim poems ephemerally rest seem spatial signifiers of that omnivorous silence, just as the endless return of his poems to the same paradoxes for some thirty years enacts an infinite process of recuperation and loss – that incessantly futile 'raid on the inarticulate' of which T. S. Eliot had spoken. And yet, the poems do represent a gain of a sort over the ways in which human beings normally deploy language. In 'Emerging', 'the mind, sceptical as always/ of the anthropomorphisms/ of the fancy, knew he must be put together/ like a poem or a composition/ in music, that what he conforms to/ is art' (*CP*, p. 355)). Thomas here acknowledges that the poem of the spirit 'emerges/ from morphemes and phonemes' 'under the mind's tooling'. In the very word 'morphemes' may be heard the ambiguous echo of that previous condemnatory word 'anthropomorphism', as if Thomas were implicitly qualifying the spiritual reach of a poem's linguistic power in the very act of affirming it. After all, just two poems previous to 'Emerging' in *Frequencies*, he had used the word 'tool' to very different effect: 'The mind's tools had/ no power convincingly to put him/ together' (*CP*, p. 353). In reading his poems, whether singly or in sequence, it is accordingly always important to pay attention to the 'morphemes and phonemes', to the interplay of sounds and syllables and all the related music of what textually happens. Only then can we begin to appreciate language's liminal powers to point beyond itself. Take the following lines:

> It is this great absence
> that is like a presence, that compels
> me to address it without hope
> of a reply. (*CP*, p. 361)

The compulsion of which the passage speaks is felt in the dead weight of the repeated syntax ('that is like . . . that compels'); the Siamese twins of polysyllabic abstracts ('absence' and 'presence') turn the monosyllabic word 'hope' into a negligible lightweight, even as the conspiracy of agreed sounds between 'absence', 'presence' and 'address' not only surround 'hope' but also drown out the sonically isolated word 'reply'. In his early years as a poet, Thomas had after all been fascinated by the challenge to reproduce the intricate alliterative and assonantal patterns of Welsh-language *cynghanedd* poetry in English, and his experiments had helped sharpen his sensitivity to 'morphemes and phonemes'.[8] Over a century earlier, Gerard Manley Hopkins had likewise evolved an incarnational theory and praxis of poetic language in the wake of his own remarkable study of Welsh-language poetry.

The redemption of language is, therefore, one of Thomas's conscious aims, as it had been for the seventeenth-century George Herbert, whose poetry Thomas edited and greatly admired. As he writes in 'After Jericho':

> There is an aggression of fact
> to be resisted successfully
> only in verse, that fights language
> with its own tools. (*CP*, p. 356)

Borges was likewise concerned to resist 'the aggression of fact', but his main tool was the story, by means of which he constructed the 'labyrinths' that unravelled the familiar, established world of common sense into a dizzyingly different pattern. In 'The Garden of Forking Paths', the protagonist searches out the fabled garden of his illustrious ancestor, Ts'ui Pen, that 'labyrinth in which all men would become lost' (*SS*, p. 48), only to discover the maze is the 'chaotic' manuscripts of the book to which Pen had devoted thirty years of solitary labour. The family had wished to consign it to the flames, but it is rescued by a perspicacious Taoist or Buddhist monk. So, when R. S. Thomas opens a poem with the lines 'A maze, he said/ and at the centre/ the Minotaur/ awaits us' (*CP*, p. 382), he may well have had partly in mind the Borges with whom he specifically identifies the figure of the labyrinth in his late essay on David Jones (*DJ*, p. 157). For Thomas, the dead-ends of the maze 'are no through road/ to the fearful', and as for the 'brave men', whose 'invisible portraits' he imagines as hanging on the walls, their deeds were no more than 'the dust we throw/ in the eyes of the beast'. For Borges, in dizzyingly mirroring return, it is the monstrous Minotaur at the very centre of the labyrinth that obsesses him in 'The House of Asterion'. He imagines the creature's impatience with the bric-à-brac of quotidian details, his scorn for the empty pretensions of literacy, and above all his yearning for a redeemer who will take him to 'a place with fewer galleries and fewer doors' (*SS*, p. 172). It is as if the encounter with the monster epitomises Borges's wish for a release from both the petty 'aggression' of the mundane order and the mirroring (dis)order of his own grandiose mental and fictional labyrinths. As the narrator of 'Tlön, Uqbar, Orbis Tertius' wearily concludes: 'Tlön is surely a labyrinth, but it is a labyrinth devised by a man, a labyrinth destined to be deciphered by man' (*SS*, p. 42). There is no way through by these means, either, to ultimate reality.

Nevertheless, those labyrinths were, for Borges, central to his exploration of enigmas, of riddles, one of the foremost of which he bluntly identified in a late interview: 'I think that the problem of time is *the* problem' (*Barnstone*, p. 110). It was also a major problem for R. S. Thomas, and one he explored most subtly through his work in a genre his contribution to which he felt – with considerable justice – had been overlooked; the ekphrastic poems collected in *Between Here and Now* and *Ingrowing Thoughts*. In a late interview, he ventured to reveal that 'I thought they were quite good myself', pointing out that they were concerned with 'God and reality and time and all these things' (*DJJ*, p. 100). Distinguishing between the poems that addressed works by the Impressionists and those that were concerned with the Surrealists, he explained that 'when you look at some of the Impressionist paintings and you see a village street with a pedestrian plodding on his way, I think it's a natural question to ask what is a road for, where does it go to, what's its direction, do we have to go anywhere?'; and when you 'get some of those Magrittes, a cannon pointing out into space – to me they're really evocative images'. So they are, and to examine the two collections is to be struck, as will be demonstrated in detail in chapter 11, by how well suited not only were the paintings but was the art form of painting itself to Thomas's purposes.

It was so, of course, because in the very nature of its being it miraculously incarnated the familiar paradox so definitively identified by Keats in 'Ode on a Grecian Urn', of a fixity forever immanent/imminent with movement, and of an instant forever helplessly pregnant with its own future ('The moment/ is history's navel' (*CP*, p. 383)). For a poet chronically haunted by Wordsworth's great phrase about 'something ever more about to be', painting naturally proved irresistible. And the theological potential of its paradox – its capacity to suggest the intersection of eternity with time – is clearly brought out in 'The Annunciation by Veneziano', a painting poem included not in either of the two major collections but rather in *Laboratories of the Spirit*. He is responding to a tempera painting on wood completed by Domenico Veneziano around 1445. One of five predella panels, it is an elongated horizontal at the two extremities of which are positioned the kneeling Angel and Mary respectively, the latter gravely standing with bowed head. Between them, as they stand lucidly bathed in the cool light of morning, there stretches a distance, at once physical and spiritual, that poignantly conveys the human loneliness to which the unique singularity of this experience will condemn her. Both painting and poem are predictably enthralled by that instant, which is both in and out of time, when angel and virgin are suspended between here and now, to borrow Thomas's later phrase, 'a distance/ between them/ and between them and us' (*CP*, p. 288). This kind of liminality is unique to painting, but finds its counterpart, as we have seen, in Thomas's approach to language. His poems and artists' paintings were therefore exceptionally well met: as with language, what fascinated him about art was its paradoxical capacity to convey that which was absent.

An Impressionist painting in *Between Here and Now* of the kind to which Thomas alluded in his interview is Monet's 'The Bas-Bréau Road', and his tribute to it opens with the question, 'Who bothers/ where this road goes?' (*BHN*, p. 17). For him, the picture is an arresting comment on the oppressive modern model of time as progress towards a goal – a model to which Thomas was viscerally opposed, and to which he found what he believed to be a definitive answer in Einstein's special theory of relativity, that demonstrated the space-time complex was curved. Hence he loved Pissarro's 'The Louveciennes Road' for 'not bothering to arrive; exchanging/ progress without a murmur/ for the leisureliness of art' (*BHN*, p. 33). Hostile as he was to the present's confident prediction of the direction of its future, he naturally revelled in time's little ironies, the revenges brought in by its unpredictable whirligig. Thus, examining Bazille's 'Family Reunion', he notes the complacency of the 'well-dressed, well-fed' bourgeoisie, ignorant as they are that 'their servants/ are out of sight/ snatching a moment/ to beget offspring/ who are to overturn all this' (*BHN*, p. 19). But whereas the force of this picture derives partly from the observer's knowing something that the painted figures do not, Manet's 'The Balcony' suggests the opposite. Here the gazers in the painting have the advantage of us:

> We watch them. They watch
> what? The world passes,
> they remain, looking
> as they were meant to do

at a spectacle
beyond us. (*BHN*, p. 31)

'Art is recuperation/ from time', notes Thomas in 'Pissarro: Kitchen Garden, Trees in Bloom' (*BHN*, p. 41), and his meditations on Impressionist paintings in *Between Here and Now* consistently circle around this perception. 'It would be good to live/ in this village with time/ stationary and the clouds/ going by' (*BHN*, p. 45), is how 'Pissarro: Landscape at Chaponval' opens. Similar moments, repeated throughout the sequence, confirm how 'Art is a sacrament in itself', and that 'brush-strokes go on/ calling from the canvas's/ airier belfries/ to the celebration of colour', long after 'the angelus is silent' (*BHN*, p. 59). This sense of art as providing a healing spiritual equipoise repeatedly surfaces, as when he notes how, in a 'Portrait of Madame Gaudibert', Monet keeps himself 'on an even keel' not with an oar, but with 'a fast-dipping brush' (*BHN*, p. 23).

An entirely different aspect of art's revelations about time, however, informs *Ingrowing Thoughts*, the collection that includes examples of the Surrealist paintings also mentioned by Thomas in his interview. Here we seem to be dealing with the bewildering alternative logic at work in Borges's story 'The Lottery of Babylon'. 'I come', the narrator there explains, 'from a dizzy land where the lottery is the basis of reality' (*SS*, p. 55), a land run by a lottery in which each chance outcome is itself made subject to other chance outcomes, and so on to eternity. If Einstein famously protested that his God did not play dice, then Borges's god does nothing else. Thomas was likewise very open to the possibility that life 'is the play of a being/ who is not serious in/ his conclusions' (*CP*, p. 346). A recurrent theme in his poetry is that of God as a kind of joker – benign and malign by bewilderingly unpredictable turns. And on occasions he felt the only appropriate human response was that of the Jester, the poet's role being in essence that of Feste: 'Heigh-ho that the universe/ through over-rehearsal/ should become farcical' (*CLP*, p. 290). What has not yet been noticed is that his final volume, *No Truce with the Furies*, concludes with a suite of poems ('Words', 'Play', 'Anybody's Alphabet') of reckless levity and of anarchic gaiety, as if he were choosing to sign off with trifles of verbal shreds and patches, the parti-coloured costume of the Clown or Fool. Already in *Between Here and Now* he had sought out, beyond the blurred radiance of the church façade in Monet's 'Rouen Cathedral, Full Sunshine' (*BHN*, p. 73), the gargoyles 'deep inside', 'the chipped figures/ with their budgerigar faces', 'a sort of divine/ humour in collusion with time'. Who, he had asked, but God 'can improve/ by distortion?'

Improving our understanding of temporal existence by distortion is exactly what Thomas came to feel the Surrealists did. That he saw their work as approximating to that of the subtlest theologians is clear from the fine poem about Kierkegaard he included in his final volume, *No Truce with the Furies*, where Thomas's favourite theological thinker is characterised as 'the first/ of the Surrealists, picturing/ our condition with the draughtsmanship// of a Dalí' (*CLP*, p. 220). In entitling his poem 'S.K.', a Thomas whose own identity, both personal and public, had become inseparable from the two initials 'R.S.' was implicitly acknowledging the Dane to be his spiritual twin. And Thomas's appreciation of a mocking laughter in Kierkegaard's work that comes from 'the asylum of genius' finds an echo in the splendid 'Homage to Paul Klee' in the same volume. Thomas celebrates the eggs with spectacles and the full moon on a trapeze in Klee's work, loving 'such insouciance/ in art' and sardonically remarking on 'how easily/ the ridiculous establishes itself/ as existing without end' (*CLP*, p. 279). Believing this sense of the ridiculous to be a prophylactic that protects us from mistaking mere human earnestness for authentic spiritual seriousness, he exults in seeing Klee 'scribbling,/ where once there was crucifixion,/ those crotchets and semiquavers/ with which levity begins'. For Thomas, the inexplicable mystery of the crucifixion could be conceived of only as existing beyond reason and therefore as humanly absurd.

Some of the absurdities that speak most powerfully to him through the Surrealist paintings in *Ingrowing Thoughts*, though, are those produced by the violent history of his own times. The volume opens with the 'imagination's wandering/ of the smashed city' in Picasso's famous elegy for the Guernica barbarously levelled in 1936 by Franco's bombing. In the visual anarchy of grotesquely maddened horse, cruelly glaring light bulb and mutely screaming heads Thomas sees 'love in reverse', painted by one who had 'been down at the root/ of the scream' (*CP*, p. 437). The disaster of war is revisited in 'Father and Child, Ben Shahn' and in Paul Éluard's 'La Nuit Venitienne', where background buildings 'suppurate' with smoke, while an ageing man and woman, dressed in sombre, respectable bourgeois black, sit at a desk in the foreground, scanning what seems to be a ledger in the face of what the poem starkly states is 'a future . . . without assets'.[9] No wonder, therefore, that Thomas reads Magritte's 'On the Threshold of Liberty' as he does. For him, the cannon pointing at empty sky, an image recalled in his interview, signifies a futile attempt to prevent mankind from putting advances in technology to the most lethal of uses. In the absurdity of the painting, Thomas therefore discerns the absurdity of any such hope and the consequent violent lunacy of human history. It is accordingly understandable that, faced with Max Ernst's 'Two Children Menaced by a Nightingale', he warns the children against accepting the invitation 'into a house/ haunted by a clock/ on the wall' (*CP*, p. 445). Instead, he directs their attention to an open gate, pointing towards eternity. Their protector, like that of the babes in the wood, must be the bird that will sing to them, 'pressing sanguinely/ its breast against time'. The nude torso enclosed within a globe made of curved interconnecting rods in Roland Penrose's 'Captain Cook's Last Voyage' becomes, for Thomas, an allegory of the human condition: 'On eternity's background/ is the shadow/ of time's cage, where nautically/ we are becalmed' (*CP*, p. 447).

When interviewed at eighty, Borges not only remarked that 'the problem of time is *the* problem', but added that 'The problem of time involves the problem of ego for, after all, what is the ego? The ego is the past, the present, and also the anticipation of time to come' (*Barnstone*, p. 110). The riddle of the ego was one to which Borges repeatedly returned in his work, as did Thomas, for whom the mysterious otherness of the self to itself was the counterpart, or corollary, to the otherness of God. In 'S.K.', his late elegy for Kierkegaard, he commended the Dane on his strategy of adopting a bewildering variety of pseudonyms in his writings. Approvingly noting that this leaves the reader 'to grope', as in the book of life itself, 'for the meaning/ that will be quicksilver in the hand' (*CLP*, p. 219), he reflects that Kierkegaard 'learned/ his anonymity from God himself'. Thomas himself had learnt a similar lesson, and also adopted rhetorical strategies closely allied to those of Kierkegaard. When he came to write *Neb*, his autobiography in Welsh (the title translates literally as 'no one', but the published English translation is titled *Autobiographies*), he chose to refer to himself throughout in the third person, as 'R.S.', with implications and results that commentators have been pondering ever since – as Thomas no doubt intended they should. Chapter 8 noted how possible interpretations have ranged from the psychoanalytical to the metaphysical and back again but, whatever paradigm of explanation one adopts, the text seems to make one disconcertingly aware it has obediently, yet only provisionally, become a mirror to such an assumption. As for ultimate 'meaning', it is given in the form of an authoritative grip on the essence of Thomas's personality, that has conspicuously turned to 'quicksilver in the hand'.

Borges played precisely the same games of elusive self-presentation, not least in the interests of being true to his sense of being an enigma to himself. Unsurprisingly, this was an aspect of the Argentinian's writing to which Thomas was particularly susceptible:

> The leaves fall
> from a dark tree, brimming
> with shadow, fall on one who,
> as Borges suggested,
> is no more perhaps than the dream God
> in his loneliness is dreaming. (*CLP*, p. 165)

The most celebrated example of self-alienation comes in the brief essay 'Borges and I'. It opens with 'The other one, the one called Borges, is the one things happen to' (*Barnstone*, p. 282), and ends teasingly with 'I do not know which of us has written this page'. Thomas might well have identified with such a confession of self-bafflement. Usefully explored of late by commentators under the rubric of the 'uncanny', [10] his work, like that of Borges, abounds in a sense of self-alienation, of being lost in the labyrinth of his own being. And as has repeatedly been noted by commentators, the image of the mirror is one that recurs throughout his poetry in this connection. [11]

In his final elegy to Kierkegaard, the trope of the mirror is used to forge a connection between the experience of the divine, the experience of the self, and the experience of reading:

> Is prayer
> not a glass that, beginning
> in obscurity as his books
> do, the longer we stare
> into the clearer becomes
> the reflection of a countenance
> in it other than our own? (*CLP*, p. 221)

In both his poetry and his prose, Thomas worked to create precisely this kind of ultimately enabling, spiritually obstetric, 'obscurity', again instructed by a Kierkegaard who, writing 'under/ a pseudonym always', had succeeded, as Thomas penetratingly noted, in ensuring that 'The limpidity of his prose//had a cerebral gloss/ prohibitive of transparence'. No better description could possibly be found of Thomas's own method of composition – approximating, as the passage above indicates, to prayer – most memorably instanced in that strange autobiography, that mirror to self, *The Echoes Return Slow*, where again the self is referred to in the third person throughout. Whenever Thomas, or Borges, wrote about himself it was always with a sense of writing about a stranger, and with the understanding that the claim to privileged, full self-possession that was implicit in the genre of autobiography was a complete illusion. Yet Thomas was never taken in by his own strategy of dealing with himself as if he were a person separate from the one writing. As he noted in the late poem 'Fathoms', this time using the pool as a trope cognate to the mirror, when he looked at his reflection he saw nothing but 'the self/ looking up at the self/ looking down, with each/ refusing to become/ an object' (*CLP*, p. 214). There was never any getting beyond that paradox – that the self can never become objective to itself and so can never become the 'subject' of self-understanding.

The puzzle of the self's location was, for both Thomas and Borges, bound up with the uncertain status of the 'reality' of the world the self actually occupied. 'We (the undivided divinity operating within us) have

236

dreamt the world', wrote Borges. 'We have dreamt it as firm, mysterious, visible, ubiquitous in space and durable in time; but in its architecture we have allowed tenuous and eternal crevices of unreason which tell us it is false' (*Barnstone*, p. 243). Borges located himself, and his work, in these crevices, as did a Thomas who recognised in himself, as in all others, 'one who,/ as Borges suggested/ is no more perhaps than the dream God/ in his loneliness is dreaming' (*CLP*, p.165). What Thomas found so useful in such an image was its power to call into question the unexamined hierarchies of reality that customarily governed human thought and action. 'What is life?', he asks in his essay on David Jones: 'Are art, love and society its main features, with war, money and the machine in parenthesis? Or are war, industry and money its main realities, with art and love in parenthesis?'[12] He ends his paragraph with the familiar Shakespearean quotation that 'We are such stuff/ As dreams are made on'.

In his story 'Circular Ruins', Borges tells of a man who painstakingly dreams another young man into 'real' existence, only to realise at the end that he himself is the creature of another's dream. Thomas could likewise conceive himself to be part 'of the universal mind that reflects/ infinite darkness between points of light' (*CP*, p. 347), and both he and Borges were accordingly attracted to aspects of Buddhist and Hindu teaching. Such a deep sense of being, in his otherness to himself, the being of another, could lead Thomas to such statements as 'All art is anonymous' (*CLP*, p. 292). At the root of language he detected the cry 'of human anguish, aftermath/ of the alibis of God'; and in his celebrated essay 'Everything and Nothing', Borges, too, imagined human life in terms of its relation to such a deity:

> There was no one in him; behind his face . . . and his words, which were copious, fantastic, and story, there was only a bit of coldness, a dream dreamt by no one. (*SS*, p. 284)

The sentence is Borges's singular description of Shakespeare, that most popular, populous, yet anonymous of authors, who had been fascinated by 'the fundamental identity of existing, dreaming and acting' (*SS*,

p. 285). In living a life of 'controlled hallucination', Shakespeare lived out the truth of Borges's own aphorism that artistic creation is 'a voluntary dream' (SS, p. 220). Finally face to face with god, this Shakespeare, craving release from prodigious multitudinousness into self-possession, into singleness of identity, hears only the Lord's answer from a whirlwind confessing that 'Neither am I anyone; I have dreamt the world as you dreamt your work, my Shakespeare, and among the forms in my dream are you, who like myself are many and no one' (SS, p. 284).

Thomas would undoubtedly have recognised himself in this Shakespeare and in this god, and yet there remained in him, unlike Borges, a more Christian yearning for ultimate resolution. As was explained in chapter 8, in his essay on David Jones he concentrates on an issue that is central to Borges's whole oeuvre, namely the eternal return of all experiences and phenomena, the closed circle of existence, in an attempt at the end to imagine an escape, through eternity, from such infinite repetition. One suspects that the issue had taken on a new and desperate urgency for a Thomas who, at the end of his life, was repeatedly heard to affirm in conversation that he, unlike Yeats, had no wish to re-enter flesh after death and experience it all again. So, too, in his final volume, he pointedly warns the 'departed' against the 'hunger . . . to come back': '"Stay where you are," I implore' (CLP, p. 267).

Vulnerable as he was to a sense of belatedness, to a feeling of déjà vu in relation not least to his own later poetry, Thomas found comfort in Borges's famous story 'Pierre Menard, author of Don Quixote'. Menard decides to 'anticipate the vanity awaiting all men's efforts' (SS, p. 70) by reproducing Cervantes's novel word for word purely from recollection, while never in the process excluding the experience of being Pierre Menard. The result, says Borges, is something 'more subtle than Cervantes', because of the patina of different meanings and values that has accumulated over the centuries since the original was written. As Thomas approvingly notes, Menard 'is recreating in the act of telling' (DU, p. 154) and such a perception offers us an exit from the fear of eternal, pointless repetition. By this means, Thomas finds what is an acceptable alternative not only to the deadening model of eternal recurrence but also to modernity's obsession with progress predicated on a false

understanding of the new. And at the end of his essay, Thomas finds
further confirmation, this time in subatomic physics, for his own spiritual
belief in release from time into eternity. He 'wrings a truth' out of the
fact that 'as electrons whirl about their nucleus at dizzying speeds, one
will suddenly leap into a new orbit' (*DU*, p. 59). In this he finds a great
trope for Christianity's 'promise of a new sphere for the purified soul'.
It is a trope that is unlikely to have appealed to Borges.

Of the cry of a whale, R. S. Thomas memorably wrote, 'It is pain searching for/ an echo' (*CLP*, p. 238). Such a description applies more exactly,
and harrowingly, to his poetry than it does, perhaps, to the work of Borges.
In the end, the writings of poet and of fiction writer are keyed to a somewhat different pitch. In his poem on Baltasar Gracian, Borges imagined
the Jesuit as so 'doped on' his bleak 'labyrinths, quibbles, emblems' that,
when he died, perhaps 'he never noticed heaven' (*Barnstone*, p. 85). There
is surely more than a hint in such a speculation of Borges's fears for
himself, and it would be difficult to substitute Thomas in this connection
either for him or for Gracian. But that Thomas nevertheless found the
great Argentinian's work deeply appealing is certain, as are the suggestive parallels between both writers. 'Jorge Luis Borges is most poignantly
and hauntingly interested in what men have believed in their doubt',
wrote Anthony Kerrigan, introducing an anthology of his writings (*PA*).
In that respect, at least, Borges was undoubtedly wholly at one with the
R.S. who was, in his incomparable poetry, one of the most sublime of
modernity's doubting Thomases.

## Notes

1 Jorge Borges, *Labyrinths: Selected Stories and Other Writings*, trans. David A.
Yates and James E. Irby (Harmondsworth: Penguin, 1970), pp. 118–24. Here-
after *SS*.
2 'R. S. Thomas in conversation with Molly Price-Owen', *The David Jones Journal:
R. S. Thomas Special Issue* (summer/autumn 2001), 93–110, p. 93. Hereafter
*DJJ*.
3 William Barnstone (ed.), *Borges at Eighty* (Bloomington: Indiana University
Press, 1982), p. 80. Hereafter *Barnstone*.

[4] Anthony Kerrigan (ed.), *Jorge Luis Borges: a Personal Anthology* (London: Jonathan Cape, 1968), p. 118. Hereafter *PA*.

[5] R. S. Thomas, *H'm* (London: Macmillan, 1972), p. 26.

[6] Ted Hughes, *Selected Poems 1957–1981* (London: Faber, 1986).

[7] R. S. Thomas, *Between Here and Now* (London: Macmillan, 1981), p. 98. Hereafter *BHN*.

[8] See Jason Walford Davies, *Gororau'r Iaith* (Caerdydd: Prifysgol Cymru, 2003), pp. 163ff.

[9] R. S. Thomas, *Ingrowing Thoughts* (Bridgend: Poetry Wales Press, 1983), p. 41

[10] Tony Brown, *R. S. Thomas* (Cardiff: University of Wales Press, 2006); Fflur Dafydd, '"[A] shifting/ identity never your own": The Uncanny and the Unhomely in the Poetry of R. S. Thomas' (PhD dissertation, University of Wales Bangor, 2004).

[11] Katie Gramich, 'Mirror Games: Self and M[O]ther in the Poetry of R. S. Thomas', in Damian Walford Davies (ed.), *Echoes to the Amen* (Cardiff: University of Wales Press, 2003), pp. 132–48.

[12] Belinda Humfrey and Ann Price-Owen (eds), *David Jones: Diversity in Unity* (Cardiff: University of Wales Press, 2000), p. 154. Hereafter *DU*.

# 10

# Transatlantic Relations

In 1995, the city of Swansea was enabled, by government funding, to hold a year-long festival of writing that featured authors from many nations working across the whole range of 'literary' genres. One of those participating was the noted American-British poet Denise Levertov (conspicuously proud of her Welsh mother and distant forebear Angel Jones of Mold), whose visit coincided with a campaign in Wales to secure R. S. Thomas's nomination for the Nobel Prize for Literature. During my own discussions with Levertov on that occasion, her admiration for Thomas's poetry became apparent. I therefore briefly considered attempting to arrange a meeting between the two poets, a possibility that Levertov viewed with a mixture of anticipation and apprehension – she seemed to regard Thomas as a 'grand, grim, passionate old hero' (to quote her own memorable description of Cézanne).[1] Sadly, no such arrangement proved possible but, following her return to Seattle, I received a copy of a letter she had addressed, in her capacity as a prominent member of the American Academy of Arts and Letters, to the Nobel Committee of the Swedish Academy. There, in stating that she would like to nominate Thomas for that year's prize, Levertov not only noted his 'grief for the erosion of Welsh culture', and his 'strong sense of the beauty of mountains and fields, and of individual lives of integrity lived among them', but commented that 'His intimate and often Job-like dialogues with God

(God's voice of silence being present by implication) engage both sceptics and believers'.[2]

Since she mentioned *No Truce with the Furies* – the collection published the very year of her letter – it was obvious that Levertov had kept abreast of his writing. That she herself, as troubled believer and poet, 'engaged' with Thomas's late, religious poetry became apparent to me when, during that same period, she kindly sent me a copy of several of her late collections. There I was startled to find passages such as the following, familiar, I felt, from my acquaintance with Thomas's poetry:

> Lord, not you,
> It is I who am absent.
> At first
> belief was a joy I kept in secret,
> stealing alone
> into sacred places:
> a quick glance, and away – and back,
> circling.
> I have long since uttered your name
> but now
> I elude your presence.[3]

With its fine capture of the subtle flows and eddies of the meditative impulse, and its sensitivity to the fugitive nature of human relationship to the divine, this seemed almost uncannily similar to Thomas's writing. But reading further, I quickly realised that, while from time to time similarly reminiscent passages intriguingly occurred, they were part of a body of poetry that suggested not so much the influence of Thomas as an unconsciously intimate kinship of concerns between two ageing poets – concerns, occasionally converging, to evolve a poetic discourse authentically answerable to the spiritual crises of late twentieth-century civilisation.

How to relate God to the universe, the natural world, human beings and historical events? – these were profound perplexities common to both poets, reluctant heirs as they were to Darwinian science and appalled witnesses to the cataclysmic social and political events of their century (Levertov's father was a 'Jewish Christian' and her parents had been active during the thirties in assisting refugees from Hitler's Germany). Both struggled with the temptation to hold God culpable for His implacable silence and His incorrigible absence, although Levertov did so only occasionally, whereas for Thomas it was a piercing obsession. Her poem, 'Psalm Fragments (Schnittke String trio)', begins by railing against a 'Tyrant God./ Cruel God./ Heartless God./ / God who permits/ the endless outrage we call History', but concludes by acknowledging the beneficent all-sustaining Lord who 'provide[s]'.[4] Even in that opening litany of indictments, the childishly absolute tone suggests this is a premature, petulant, intemperate, unconsidered response. It is the irrepressible benedictions of life that are Levertov's constant impulsive theme, and when she places herself 'Again before your altar, silent Lord', the sound of rushing waters and crooning doves bespeak for her 'your hospitable silence' (*SW*, p. 126).

Not so Thomas, a chronically bereft soul who, while sometimes ready like Levertov to blame God's invisibility on his own spiritual inadequacy, was habitually altogether more intransigent in his accusatory pursuit of an inaccessible deity. Much of the writing of his last thirty years took the form of poetic strategies for addressing (but never resolving) this moral and metaphysical conundrum. Their range and resourcefulness are already apparent in the pivotal volume *H'm* (1972), which contains the celebrated 'Via Negativa' (*CP*, p. 220), its classic formulation of the existential consequences of a godhead apparent only as 'that great absence/ In our lives' prefaced by an impatient dismissal ('Why no! I never thought other . . .'), in advance of the poem's subsequent moving affirmations ('He keeps the interstices/ In our knowledge'). Elsewhere, the volume offers that Gnostic version of the monstrous god of creation already considered in chapter 9, and a believer's chilling experience of the alterity of the natural world: 'And the dogfish, spotted like God's face,/ Looks at him, and the seal's eye-/ Ball is cold' (*CP*, p. 224). That second line-break, effectively reducing 'eye' to 'ball', brilliantly underwrites the unnerving absence of human reciprocity in the creaturely world – what he called 'this blank indifference . . . the neutrality of [nature's] answers' (*CP*, p. 206). His description of the seal parallels Emily Dickinson's description of a bird's eyes as 'frightened beads'.[5] Most piercing of all is the title poem 'H'm' (*CP*, p. 232), with its disturbingly grotesque account of the way a preacher's attempt to speak of God turns into a would-be gesture of all-inclusive love that is appallingly thwarted by the inability of starving children, rendered helplessly weak by hunger, to stagger to the sanctuary of his arms. Not the least disturbing aspect of this, surely one of the most powerful poems Thomas ever wrote, is its punning reference to Christ's famous injunction, 'Suffer the little children to come unto me'. Rarely could the word 'suffer' in that celebrated biblical passage have been tortured (by human anguish) into such a terrifying parody of its intended meaning. But to such bleak, black disavowals of divine concern Thomas, paradoxical as ever, juxtaposes extraordinary affirmations. 'The Coming' (*CP*, p. 234) offers one of those comparatively rare instances of his focusing on the crucifixion, in this case read in terms of the incomprehensibly selfless act of a Father and Son moved by the scene of human sufferings to the ultimate sacrifice. And in 'The River' (*CP*, p. 226), Thomas produced another relative rarity, a love poem to God's nature, magical as a Chagall painting, in which fish, 'speckled like thrushes', are seen as 'Silently singing among the weed's/ Branches'. In this case, with the line break we turn the corner into a world of wonder.

Chagall was a very important painter for Denise Levertov. In *Tesserae*, the marvellous memoir she constructed out of shards of memory to capture 'the wraiths and shifts of time-sense',[6] she associates Chagall with her Russian-Jewish father. And in her early poetry, her sense of spiritual immanence in the natural world is sometimes mediated through the mystical Hasidic Jewish theology that was her patrimony. The result is Chagall-like moments, such as when, in 'A Happening' (*SP*, p. 27), birds metamorphose into people, or, in 'Come into Animal Presence', 'The lonely white/ rabbit on the roof is a star/ twitching its ears at the rain' (*SP*, p. 35).

Around the time of her conversion to Catholicism (*c.*1992), Levertov became enthralled by the work of Catholic thinkers such as Maritain, and began to draw on Christian orthodoxy for her language of immanence. But throughout her life, the crux of her spiritual poetic was an insistence that the transcendent had to be mediated through what Blake termed the 'minute particulars' of mundane, concrete experience: it was her distinctive version of her mentor William Carlos Williams's celebrated maxim, 'no ideas but in things'. Her signature poem, 'The Jacob's Ladder' (1961), is her most complete and memorable establishing of this cornerstone of her faith and her poetry. In it, she insists that the stairway is 'not/ a thing of gleaming strands/ a radiant evanescence', but rather full of 'sharp angles' (the line-break turning the text itself into such) on which 'a man climbing/ must scrape his knees' (*SP*, p. 40). And her early poetry, in particular, is full of wonderfully sharp-angled observations, surprising the reader with its unexpected perceptions, mixed registers and lexicons – such as when, exhorting us to 'taste and see' (*SP*, p. 55), she urges 'the imagination's tongue' to savour 'grief, mercy, language,/ tangerine, weather'. She convinces us of the authenticity of her relish by that succulent insertion of a humble citrus fruit into exalted abstract company. In the best of the poetry of these early decades, her poetry goes 'much as that dog goes, intently haphazard/ . . . dancing/ edgeways, there's nothing/ the dog disdains on his way' (*SP*, p. 19). In her late decades, her poetry lost some of that vivacity of perception and of language. Thus the late poem corresponding to the early 'The Jacob's Ladder' is 'On Belief in the Physical Resurrection of Christ', a poem that, characterising her new baptised poetic, unintentionally signifies her settling (at some cost to her poetry) for a calmer, more muted rapture. It accepts that 'people so tuned/ to the humdrum laws' can't accept a symbol 'unless convinced of its ground,/ its roots/ in bone and blood'. Hence the significance of the meal at Emmaus, where the bread was broken by 'warm hands' (*SW*, pp. 115–16).

All her life, Levertov was a believer in what Hopkins called 'inscape' (the indwelling spiritual-material form that gives a thing its quiddity) and 'instress' (human imaginative perception of that informing *telos*.[7] Indeed several of her brief late praise-poems to the universe of sense resemble the rapid notations of such perceptions found in Hopkins's notebooks:

> Pearlblossom bright white
> against green young leaves that frame
> each tuft, black
> pinewoods, graybrown buildings. (*SW*, p. 32)

This typical, painterly, viewing of a scene in terms of juxtapositions of colour and texture reminds one not only that the young Levertov went on a pilgrimage to Cézanne's studio but also of her account, in *Tesserae*, of her period of training as a youngster to be a painter. What she was primarily taught was to see 'the complex interaction of three-dimensional objects in space, and their transmutation into compositions; forms and colors on a flat surface' (*T*, p. 79). In passages such as the above, her poetry performs an analogous miracle, and in the process conveys her sense of the intricate interdependence of otherwise highly individualised phenomena, making material 'the indivisible / shared out in endless abundance' (*SW*, p. 37). She characteristically glosses Hopkins's concept of 'inscape' as involving 'intrinsic form, the pattern of essential characteristics both in single objects and (what is more interesting) in objects in a state of relation to each other' (*PW*, p. 7).

Accordingly, Levertov particularly prized poetry born of what she terms 'the ecstasy of attention' (*PW*, p. 97), no doubt, given the interest in etymology evident in her prose writings, being fully aware that the root meaning of the word is 'to stand outside of oneself'. In one of the finest of her later poems, she hymns the heightening of the faculty of sight: 'I look and look. / Looking's a way of being' (*SW*, p. 91). Elaborating on the actively investigative power of the excited eye, she appropriates to it the powers of several of the other senses, as if it were a synthesis of them all:

> The eyes
> dig and burrow into the world.
> They touch
> fanfare, howl, madrigal, clamor. (91)

Even in her late poetry she remained capable of such powers of perception, albeit in relatively muted form. Treasuring throughout her life Albert Schweitzer's doctrine of 'Reverence for Life', she insisted it involved 'the recognition of oneself as *life that wants to live* among other *forms of life that want to live*. This recognition is indissoluble, reciprocal, and dual' (*PW*, p. 53), and her poetry is usually a loving acknowledgement of those 'other forms of life'.

Of course, on a few memorable occasions, R. S. Thomas did match Levertov's excited awareness of 'a beauty not to be denied' (*SW*, p. 35), but he always seemed chary of presenting them as anything but rarities to be circumspectly cherished. Contrasted to the prodigality of natural epiphanies in Levertov, it is not only the parsimony but the conditionality of revelation in Thomas that strikes one. Although 'The Bright Field' is routinely instanced as one example of radiant immanence, few have noted the spiritual self-misgiving that so characteristically lies at the very heart of the poem. He may well briefly have glimpsed 'the pearl/ of great price, the one field that had/ the treasure in', but viewing this ephemeral wonder as he does through the lens of biblical phrasing, Thomas knows full well 'that I must give all that I have/ to possess it' (*CP*, p. 302). That's the rub. He is honestly human enough implicitly to admit that he is not Moses enough to turn aside 'to the miracle/ of the lit bush'. He is really of the company of those farmers in 'Hill Christmas' who attended the festival's communion service, 'felt it sharp/ on their tongue, shivered as at a sin/ remembered, and heard love cry/ momentarily in their hearts' manger', only to go back to 'their poor/ holdings, naked in the bleak light/ of December' (*CP*, p. 290). To Levertov's 'The Jacob's Ladder', Thomas tartly retorts with a question – 'Are there angels or only/ the Furies?' (*CLP*, p. 268) – and, in the face of European history, sceptically enquires 'Where is/ the ladder or that heavenly/ traffic that electrified Jacob?'

In such instances, the blame may be said to reside with humans, but there were also many occasions when, as suggested in chapter 9, Thomas typically viewed nature's joyous revelations as 'God's roguery' (*CLP*, p. 249), a divine jape to detract attention from the evil that is naturally inherent in the divinely created world. A neat – perhaps over-neat – way of distinguishing his vision in this regard from that of Levertov is to compare their respective treatments of the owl. Her belief in the fundamental 'innocence' of all creatures apart from the human encompasses acceptance that they kill, because they do so only to satisfy 'natural' needs such as hunger. Accordingly, she can capture with equanimity the dual aspect of an owl that, while 'the terror of those he must hunt' (the innocence is in that 'must' – an imperative of nature), sounds his 'mournful notes [in] tone[s] much like the dove's' (*SW*, p. 13). For Thomas, though,

> The owl has a clock's
> face, but there is no time
> on it. No raptor ever
> is half-past its prey. (*CLP*, p. 272)

In the same volume, God Himself becomes the supreme raptor, 'brushing me sometimes/ with his wing so the blood/ in my veins freezes':

> I have heard
> him scream, too, fastening
> his talons in his great
> adversary, or in some lesser
> denizen, maybe, like you or me. (*CLP*, p. 256)

Decades earlier, and his vision had been equally steady, equally uncompromising. In *The Way of It* (1977), he noted that the barn owl 'happens/ like white frost as/ cruel and as silent'; over the 'bleached bones' of its victims echoes its 'night-strangled cry' (*CP*, p. 319). For Thomas, it is the fact that God-made nature lives, moves and has its being in a process to which pain and cruelty are endemic that is perennially disturbing. As he repeatedly insisted, the painful question was not 'Is there a God', but rather 'what sort of a God *is* He?', given the accusatory witness not only of human history but also of the history of creation itself. 'Stoats, weasels, ferrets/ have evil reputations, and are indeed/ without mercy', Levertov too admits, but goes on imperturbably to note as a fact of nature that only human beings, for all their cruelty, have the potential of mercy for a species other than their own. She ends up charmed by a tame ferret that nuzzles up to her as if 'willing to try out/ the Peaceable Kingdom' (*SW*, p. 47). It is a moment indicative of the conciliatory character of her own vision of nature: not for her Thomas's anguished sense of a natural world at once unbearably beautiful and unbearably ferocious, 'a self-regulating machine/ of blood and faeces' (*CP*, p. 286). She is inclined to see nature as existing in the sunlight of God's constant love: he, on the other hand, is at best conscious only of a sky 'shot/ with the rainbow of [God's] coming and going' (*CP*, p. 280).

Where both are, however, in full agreement, is in passionately protesting human assault not only on other human beings but also on the
environment. Thomas and Levertov were indefatigable campaigners and
protesters. Her activism was a strong family trait, characteristic not only
of her parents but also of her wayward older sister, Olga, whose lifelong
devotion to radical causes led to 'years of humiliation,/ of paranoia and
blackmail and near-starvation' (*SP*, p. 73), as well as alienation from all
who loved her, culminating in her death at fifty. As for Levertov herself,
she came to prominence in the US, her adopted country, during the 1960s
and early 1970s, as one of the leading poets publicly protesting against
the Vietnam War. Later conflicts such as the Gulf War similarly provoked
her to desperate, impassioned public statement:

> The choice: to speak
> or not to speak.
>
> We spoke.
>
> Those of whom we spoke
> Had not that choice.
>
> At every epicenter, beneath
> roar and tumult,
>
> enforced:
> their silence. (*DHET*, p. 173)

Every stanza in this poem consists of two lines, with the exception of
the one which starkly states 'We spoke': the form itself thus enacts the
act of stepping out, of exposing and isolating oneself, that was the price,
and challenge, involved in the unpopular act of voicing outrage. As a
'speaker' against social evils, Levertov was as indefatigable as she was
impassioned, always insistent that 'the days of separating war, and racism,
and pollution of natural resources, and social injustice, and male chauvin-
ism, into neat little compartments are over' (*PW*, p. 122). Thomas would
have been sympathetic to such a radically holistic approach. An objector
to the Second World War, he went on to protest against the military's
appropriation of Welsh land, the building of nuclear power stations, the
violent degrading of the environment (particularly in his local Llŷn),

and, of course, the colonisation of Wales, and the undermining of the Welsh language and culture. Of these causes, it was these last only that were addressed explicitly in his poetry, whereas Levertov was incomparably more politicised, producing works that attempted (mostly unsuccessfully) to translate her outrage at a range of US imperialistic military adventures into poems.

As her late poetry makes clear, such an imperative as she felt to speak on such issues was, for her, mandated by God: *'The earth is the Lord's,*we gabbled,/ *and the fullness thereof –/* while we looted and pillaged, claiming indemnity' (*DHET*, p. 168). For her, man is a travesty of his original Adamic self, created as he was 'to have been/ earth's mind, mirror, reflective source./ . . . to be those cells of earth's body that could/ perceive and imagine' (*DHET*, p. 168). Whereas Thomas might have balked at phrasing it exactly in these terms, his poetry, too, engages with the fall of man, insofar as that has increasingly taken the form of falling for 'the Machine'. The image became, for him, a convenient shorthand for what F. R. Leavis used to call a 'technologico-Benthamite' civilisation, one dominated by the doctrine of functionality. For both, this meant a nexus of evil, involving the arrogant and violent subjugation of the natural world to the service of gross, demanding human needs: human reason was (ab)used to turn scientific discoveries into technological tools for exploiting the environment. This was the apotheosis of knowledge as power. Very conscious of being the heir to the great English Romantic tradition, from the time of Blake to that of Lawrence, critiquing such a malign philosophy of life, Thomas repeatedly made 'The Machine' the subject of his most acid poetry in his later years. This Urizenic monster is born of the temptation Thomas clearly identified in *H'm* as the human temptation to take the material world as its own invention. For him, then, the fall happened when 'the mind climbed up into the tree/ of knowledge, . . . and began venting its frustration/ in spurious metals, in the cold acts of the machine' (*CP*, p. 287). Ubiquitous in Thomas's volumes for three decades, the indestructible Machine epitomised everything he feared, hated and despised about a modern world forcibly maintained by destruction: 'The machine appeared/ In the distance, singing to itself/ Of money. Its song was the web/ They were caught in, men and women/ together' (*CP*, p. 235).

For Levertov, it is the poet who now performs the duty God originally envisaged the whole of mankind as performing, the Adamic duty of 'perceiving and imaging' the earth, of serving as the consciousness of the created world. In the process, the poet also brings mankind to full, spiritually awakened consciousness – Levertov was haunted by a phrase from one of Rilke's letters, where he referred to 'the unlived life of which one can die' (e.g. *PW*, p. 20): she understood it to refer to the unfulfilled potential of a largely secularised human existence. One of the strongest sections of her last collection, *Sands of the Well*, was devoted to reflections on poetry, and it included a poem on the loss of one of the branches that had given a tree the shape of a lyre. She ends with a prayer to be blessed with the power to hymn the tree's 'unlived life':

> O Orpheus,
> lend me power to sing
> the unheard music of that vanished lyre. (*SW*, p. 93)

The head of the Orpheus whom she addresses had itself, of course, continued to sing even after it had been torn from its trunk by the voracious Maenads (referred to in *PW*, p. 68), and Levertov was vividly conscious of herself as an Orphic poet.

In the same section of *Sands of the Well*, she is also tormented by the futility of continuing to write in old age, when all that seems possible is a repetition of earlier achievements. She is comforted in part by memories of the old Cézanne, 'doggedly *sur le motif*', persisting in painting and repainting Mont Sainte Victoire, 'his mountain/ a tireless noonday angel he grappled like Jacob,/ demanding reluctant blessing' (*SW*, p. 96). But a more urgent and therefore compelling motive for persisting is the need to register wonders that would otherwise go unnoticed, their lives, so to speak, 'unlived':

> it's the way
> radiant epiphanies recur, recur,
> consuming, pristine, unrecognized –
> until remembrance dismays you. And then, look,
> some inflection of light, some wing of shadow
> is other, unvoiced. You can, you must
> proceed. (*SW*, p. 96)

Levertov passionately believed that the arts were precious 'expanders of consciousness', a revolutionary medium whose implicit message was always that which Rilke seemed to hear when viewing the 'Torso of an Archaic Apollo': 'You must change your life'. She cherished Wallace Stevens's maxim that a poem 'stimulates the sense of living of being alive' (*PW*, p. 101).

Thomas was less exercised by the issue of language's relation to the created world than by its relation to the divine, and although he produced innumerable poems sceptically pondering this relationship, he also persisted in affirming that only through the arts could man imaginatively apprehend ultimate spiritual realities. In his last collection, he was still epigrammatically asserting that 'Not electricity/ but the brush's piety/ affords divinity' (*CLP*, p. 289). And the very last poem in that last collection was 'Anybody's Alphabet' (*CLP*, p. 292), at once a gamesome bagatelle, a linguistic tour de force, and a final homage to the inexhaustible human but also spiritual potential of the poet's medium, language. It is also a witty meditation on the profound implications of the primary human need to play – throughout his career, Thomas retained a sense, already identified in chapter 8, that the relation between man and God was inescapably ludic, and that poetry was the best game for apprehending it. This – a central aspect of his writing that tends to pass unremarked – finds no real echo in Levertov's work. It stems directly from his deep fascination with the 'mysterious way' of God. 'I'm fascinated by that mystery', he penetratingly observed in a revealing late interview, 'and I've tried to write out of that experience of God, the fantastic side of God, the quarrel between the conception of God as a person, as having a human side, and the conception of God as being so extraordinary'.[8]

Where Thomas and Levertov do agree is that poetry is the redemption of language – that 'normal' human language is defaced and debased by the diminishing, degrading and sometimes evil uses to which it is routinely put. 'There is an aggression of fact', wrote Thomas in 'After Jericho', 'to be resisted successfully/ only in verse, that fights language/ with its own tools' (*CP*, p. 356). He therefore exhorts the poet to smile 'among the ruins of a vocabulary/ you blew your trumpet against'. 'It is the poet', wrote Levertov, 'who has language in his care, the poet who more than others recognizes language also as a *form* of life and a common resource to be cherished and served as we should serve and cherish earth and its water, animal and vegetable life, and each other' (*PW*, p. 53).

Levertov's late poem 'Mysterious Disappearance of May's Past Perfect' ponders the disappearance of the verb form 'might' from common vocabulary, beginning with the example of a report about an oil spillage from a tanker at sea. She speculates first that fear – of facing the fact that 'causes do/ produce effects' – might account for this, but then widens her field of explanation into an indictment of modern discourse with particular reference to political discourse:

> Or, in these years
> when from our mother-tongue some words
> were carelessly tossed away, while others hastily
> were being invented – chiefly among them, *overkill* –
> has the other meaning, swollen as never before,
> of *might* thrust out of memory its minor
> homonym, so apt for the precise
> nuance of elegy, for the hint of judgement,
> reproachful clarities of tense and sense? (*DHET*, p. 167)

The passage is both a reflection on, and an instance of, the nature of a poet's social responsibilities.

Given the high value both Levertov and Thomas place on the role of poetry (and the other arts) as an unique form of human understanding, a medium for exploring man's spiritual being, it is not surprising that when, in old age, they attempted an audit of the mystery of their own lives (Glyn Jones's valediction to his life, *Goodbye, what were you?*,[9] would have appealed to them both) they produced spiritual autobiographies that, as such, inevitably traced in each of their cases the distinctive growth of a poet's life. *Tesserae* is a remarkable volume, a self-portrait in a crazy mirror. The daughter of a scholarly Russian Jewish father who became an Anglican priest, and an ebulliently imaginative Welsh mother who relished the adventure of living, Levertov could scarcely fail to regard her life as a maze of conjunctions as vividly amazing as her own parents' unlikely meeting in Constantinople. In *Tesserae*, she writes as the oracle of her own past, producing her own Sibylline leaves as memory multiplies its enigmas. The strange coincidences seem to represent what, in 'The Jacob's Ladder', she called 'profound/ unanswer, sustained/ echo of our unknowing'. The book is about our profound unknowing of ourselves, the hidden interconnections between people, the secret collusion between fact and fiction, the inalienable mystery of origins – and of signs.

She is also aware of herself as one whose native language is art quite as much as 'nature' – there is for her the important example of Magritte, a master of 'magic transformation, *entre chien et loup'*. It is not the fierce political campaigner for civil rights, and against the bomb and the USA's sinister involvement in Latin America, who appears in this portrait, but that different self which dwells with ambivalence and which trusts to metamorphoses. In *Tesserae*, personal recollection hovers between 'memories and suppositions'. As for the poet in her, its memories are of ambivalent status in a further way. 'I have remembered it always', Levertov writes of thrilling to a nun's spectrally sensuous voice rising high, in an 'intensity of beauty', out of a hidden choir, 'or have remembered at least what words and images might have described it' (*T*, p. 101). In registering experience, words also displace it. Transfiguring or disfiguring, either way they perhaps distort. Whenever Levertov submits to an audit of memory – when she checks her recollections against those of others – she is invariably entranced by the disparities that emerge. This is a feature of an artist's imagination she highlights in 'The Heron', a poem from her last collection. Noting of a poet friend that 'the Great Blue Heron' 'turned white in your mind,/ conflated with regrets', she notes that this is how symbols form. They are thus the product of

> experience feeding
> the mind's vision, that moves
>
> with beating wings
> into and over
> the page, the parable. (*SW*, p. 101)

*Tesserae* is both a collection of a poet's involuntary parables (born of vision's intercourse with experience) and a reflection on her life as a process of parable-making.

But for her, such parables are not arbitrary, nor are they merely of personal, psychological provenance and significance. Rather, they are means of revelation – of revealing the otherwise hidden spiritual contours of mundane existence. They are the divining rods that map the subterranean forces and energies of the spirit just as, in her signature poem 'A Map of the Western Part of the County of Essex', she wrote as cartographer of the native region that was also her special imagined place (*SP*, pp. 34–5). No wonder that in *Tesserae* she mourns the loss of a childhood treasure, the torn copy of Peter Heylyn's 1665 'Cosmography in four books. Containing the choreography and history of the whole world, and all the principal kingdoms, provinces, seas and isles thereof' (*T*, p. 111). Her poetry was, in a way, the creation of her own special substitute cosmography, her own wonders of the invisible world, her own record of her adventures in the realm of the spirit.

Although he wrote two valuable prose memoirs, one of them particularly idiosyncratic, the 'writing of self' by R. S. Thomas that most interestingly corresponds to *Tesserae* is *The Echoes Return Slow*. The twin-track structure studied in chapter 8 is as thought-provoking as it is singular, with the poems paired throughout with 'prose' that is, in fact, something far more crafted and refined than anything that normally passes for such:

> Minerva's bird. Athene noctua: too small for wisdom, yet unlike its tawnier cousin active by day, too, its cat's eyes bitterer than the gorse petals. (*CLP*, p. 51)

This is not ordinary workaday prose, rather it is prose concentrate, prose compressed into what might surely not inaccurately be described as prose poetry. The question is why? What is going on here? In chapter 8 this practice was understood primarily as a textual strategy for encompassing the dualities of human existential being. But, as was also passingly implied in that discussion, it may also be understood as a demonstration of the way in which a poet's memory selects and shapes experience in a fashion that turns it into rich soil for poetry. 'The creative mind', it is observed in *The Echoes Return Slow*, 'judges, weighs and selects, as well as discarding, in the act of composing' (*CLP*, p. 42). A useful comparison might be made with Jeremy Hooker's practice in his *Welsh Journal*. There he punctuates his journal entry with poems that seem to arise out of, and obliquely to illuminate, the experiences being recorded. As he notes in his foreword, 'Instead of an exact temporal "placing" [i.e. the exact allocation of poems to a supposedly specific time and place of origin] my aim has been to relate poems to the imaginative and experiential ground-ing – the life – from which they evolved.'[10] The same, after a somewhat different fashion, seems to be true of Thomas's practice in *The Echoes Return Slow*. He is, of course, writing retrospectively, and knows that recollection is also palimpsest – the overwriting of the past by subsequent experience, so that the result is a richly layered deposit, a multi-faceted and creatively stimulating imaginative construct. The crafted 'prose' passages in *The Echoes Return Slow* foreground the fact that what we are being given is not the unmediated past, but the past as mediated by the present, a present in which a memory that is specifically that of a poet is at work carving out materials suitable for present purpose. And, for a poet, that 'purpose' is poetry – a poetry that, in turn (or so *The Echoes Return Slow* implies), is the best instrument for accessing, grasping, comprehending and articulating the otherwise hidden spiritual *gestalt* of an individual life. Poetry reaches the parts of a life that prose, however beautifully crafted, can never fully reach.

So what is the poem towards which the prose poem quoted above may be said to 'aspire', or of which it may be said to be the forerunner and enabler? It opens as follows:

> There are nights that are so still
> that I can hear the small owl calling
> far off, and a fox barking
> miles away. It is then that I lie
> in the lean hours awake, listening
> to the swell born somewhere in the Atlantic
> rising and falling, rising and falling
> wave on wave on the long shore
> by the village, that is without light
> and companionless. (*CLP*, p. 51)

In being so evidently a different order of writing from the prose, embryonically 'poetic' though that may be, this is a manifestation of the multi-dimensionality of human existence that was also Levertov's theme. It underscores the belief Thomas many times professed in his prose writings and interviews: poetry was the natural idiom of the spirit, a language of image and of symbol – appropriately enough, for his was the belief succinctly voiced by Yeats's dictum that 'the truth cannot be known, it can only be symbolised'. It therefore made sense for Thomas bluntly to state (with characteristic tactlessness) that 'Jesus was a poet' (*CLP*, p. 56). Elsewhere, he remarks that 'against the deciduousness of man there stand art, music, poetry. The Church was the great patron of such' (*CLP*, p. 26). What is more, Thomas suggested that the New Testament itself was a work of poetry, so scandalising the faithful who did not understand what he meant by the phrase. This explains why he so witheringly objects in *Echoes* to the replacing of the majestic King James Bible by the new revised version. 'What committee', he enquires with reference to the latter, 'ever composed a poem?' (*CLP*, p. 60). It is as if, in some of the prose-poems in *Echoes,* he were consoling himself for this desolating loss by composing his own alternative spiritual meditations – rather as his compatriot Henry Vaughan had famously composed *Silex Scintillans* when the victorious Puritan reformers and iconoclasts had effectively closed the doors to him on the ancient festivals, rituals, sacraments and symbols of the Established Church in Wales.

Even in *The Echoes Return Slow*, R. S. Thomas includes poems that address 'the deafness of space', that speak of the one 'who has not come', that pursue the endlessly recessive 'being' 'who is called "God"'. 'I lift my face', he poignantly records, 'to a face, its features dissolving/ in the radiation out of a black hole' (*CLP*, p. 30). There is no real equivalent in Levertov's writing to Thomas's poetry of the *Deus Absconditus*. The nearest to it is the sequence of late poems reflecting on the way a mountain distantly visible from her Seattle home varies greatly in clarity depending on light and weather: 'The mountain comes and goes/ on the horizon' (*DHET*, p. 112). What she comes to accept is the mountain's otherness, that its power 'lies in the open secret of its remote/ apparition' (*DHET*, p. 122), and even when it is shrouded in mist she knows that it is always solidly there, 'obdurate, unconcerned'. It is an image of her faith, which is never remotely rooted, like Thomas's, in anguished uncertainties. We equate, she writes,

> God with these absences –
> Deus absconditus.
> But God
> is imaged
> as well or better
> in the white stillness
> resting everywhere,
> giving to all things
> an hour of Sabbath[.] (*DHET*, p. 113)

The constancy of God's presence, whether manifest or not, was itself a solid constant of Levertov's faith in the world, whatever form experience might take. That is what made her a sacramental poet – somewhat unorthodoxly so in the decades of her youth and maturity, but orthodox in expression in her late, final years after her conversion. One of the poems in the same section of *The Evening Train* as the mountain sequence begins with a vivid registering of the quiddity of bird life:

> A gull far-off
> rises and falls, are of a breath,
> two sparrows pause on the telephone wire,
> chirp a brief interchange, fly back to the ground[.] (*DHET*, p. 121)

All is prelude, though, to the poem's conclusion; '*This is the day that the Lord hath made,/ let us rejoice and be glad in it*'.

The religious poetry of Denise Levertov and R. S. Thomas does, however, have one feature in common: they are both contemplative poets, in the sense of the term suggestively outlined by Levertov herself. She is discussing the origin of 'this demand: the poem':

The beginning of the fulfillment of this demand is to contemplate, to meditate; words which connote a state in which the heat of feeling warms the intellect. To contemplate comes from '*templum*, temple, a place, a space for observation, marked out by the augur.' It means not simply to observe, to regard, but to do these things in the presence of a god. And to meditate is 'to keep the mind in a state of contemplation'; its synonym is 'to muse', and to muse comes from a word meaning 'to stand with open mouth' – not so comical if we think of 'inspiration' – to breathe in. (*PW*, p. 8)

How this translates into the movement and form of a poem on the page is what she makes clear in an interview entitled 'Line-breaks, Stanza-spaces, and the Inner Voice', and what she has to say also affords valuable insight into the way that a late, religious poem by R. S. Thomas also works – a lesson of which many contemporary critics unfortunately still seem in urgent need. For Levertov, form, rhythm, spacing, line-breaks are all means of transcribing the 'inner voice' onto the page. She thinks of the end of a line as equivalent to 'half a comma'; in other words, she uses it as a subtle way of punctuating her text, so that it seems to capture and convey the very breath and pulse of her contemplating intelligence. And for her the 'inner voice' is the poet 'talking to himself, inside of himself, constantly approximating and evaluating and trying to grasp his experience in words . . . The written poem is then a record of that inner song' (*PW*, p. 24).

A good example of such 'inner song' is provided by 'What One Receives from Living Close to a Lake', a poem that concludes with the following passage:

> a clearing amid the entangled
> forest of forms and voices,
> anxious intentions, urgent
> memories: a deep, clear
> breath to fill
> the soul, an internal
> gesture, arms
> flung wide to echo
> that mute generous outstretching
> we call *lake*. (*SW*, p. 108)

The layout maps the movement of mind, the line-breaks repeatedly suggesting the brief searching for the right noun to follow the qualifying adjective ('entangled/ forest', 'urgent/ memories', 'clear/ breath', 'internal/

gesture'), for the precise verb for its purpose ('arms/ flung wide'), for the object that exactly complements the verb ('to fill/ the soul'). The result is the conveying not of thoughts but rather of the act of concentrated thinking – in other words, of 'contemplation' sufficiently sustained so as to become 'meditation'. It is a fine example of what Wallace Stevens famously called 'the poem of the act of the mind'.

And there are exact counterparts aplenty to such a passage to be found in the later poetry of R. S. Thomas. A notable instance is provided by that exceptionally fine poem 'Sea-watching':

>       Nothing
> but that continuous waving
>    that is without meaning
> occurred.
>     Ah, but a rare bird is
> rare. It is when one is not looking
> at times one is not there
>     that it comes.
> You must wear your eyes out,
> as others their knees. (*CP*, p. 306)

All the line breaks are potent conveyors of the process of focusing both the outer and the inner eye. It highlights the pun in 'waving', the chiming of that word with 'no meaning' so that the perfect, trite, rhyme establishes the bland pointlessness of the sea's incessant motions. The deliberate repetition of the word 'rare' brings out the tautology in the statement; the stating of the self-evident that dramatises the mind's arrival at a dead end; the implicit confession that a miracle is a miracle is a miracle. And the holding back of the second use of the word reinforces this by suggesting that the mind's labours of intensive thought, allowed for in the timing that's recorded in the spacing, lead only back into repetition and not forward into revelation.

The late poetry of both Levertov and Thomas affords a powerful example of what might be called the poetics of contemplation and of meditation. No wonder that Thomas was fascinated by poets such as Herbert, Wordsworth and Edward Thomas, all of whom were masters of this particular art. But in the end, the American poet and the Welsh were naturally and spiritually inclined to practise this poetics to rather different ends. Levertov entitled the penultimate poem she ever wrote 'Thinking about Paul Celan'. Recalling that genius's suicide, brought on in part by his appalling experience of the Nazis' death camps, Levertov prays for his forgiveness of those, such as herself, who 'flourish/ . . . exceed/ our allotted days':

> Saint Celan,
> Pray for us
> that we receive
>
> at least a bruise,
> blue, blue, unfading,
> we who accept survival.[11]

She herself certainly exhibits such bruises in her poetry, most notably when she engages with the obscenities and atrocities of war. But unlike Thomas she did not suffer from a chronic 'hernia/ of the spirit' (*CLP*, p. 60). All his greatest poetry may perhaps have derived from that. Not so hers. She once recalled that her father, when on his deathbed, got up and danced an ecstatic Hasidic dance in celebration of life. Levertov was herself, to the very end, her father's daughter. In her poem 'Joy', she recalled Rilke's dying words, 'Never forget,/ dear one, life is magnificent!'. 'I looked up "Joy" in a dictionary,' she goes on:

> and came to
> 'Jubilation' that goes back
> to 'a cry of joy or woe' or to 'echoic
> *iu* of wonder.' (*SP*, p. 65)

Her greatest poetry is the record of that echo. And Thomas? From what does his poetry proceed? From, perhaps, that other very different primal sound of human being he identified in the final poem of his final collection:

> All art is anonymous.
> Listen: *Ai, ee; ai, ee,*
> the unaspirated sound
> out of a cave in anticipation

of human anguish, aftermath
of the alibis of God. (*CLP,* p. 292)

## Notes

[1] Denise Levertov, *Tesserae: Memoirs and Suppositions* (Newcastle: Bloodaxe Books, 1997), p. 106. Hereafter *T.*

[2] I am grateful to my friend and colleague Nigel Jenkins for providing me with a copy of this letter.

[3] Denise Levertov, 'Flickering Mind', in *A Door in the Hive/ The Evening Train* (Newcastle; Bloodaxe Books, 1993), p. 68. Hereafter *DHET.*

[4] Denise Levertov, 'Psalm Fragments (Schnittke String Trio)', in *Sands of the Well* (New York: New Directions, 1996), pp. 117–18. Hereafter *SW.*

[5] Emily Dickinson, 'A Bird Came Down the Walk', in Thomas H. Johnson (ed.), *The Complete Poems of Emily Dickinson* (London: Faber, 1977), p. 156.

[6] Denise Levertov, 'Olga Poems', in *Selected Poems* (Newcastle; Bloodaxe Books, 1994), p. 73. Hereafter *SP.*

[7] This is discussed in Levertov's important early essay, 'Some Notes on Organic Form', collected in *The Poet in the World* (New York: New Directions, 1973), pp. 7–13. Hereafter *PW.*

[8] Molly Price-Owen, 'R. S. Thomas in Conversation', *The David Jones Journal; R. S. Thomas Special Issue* (Summer/ Autumn, 2001), p. 97.

[9] Glyn Jones, *Goodbye, What Were You?* (Llandysul: Gomer Press, 1994).

[10] Jeremy Hooker, *Welsh Journal* (Bridgend: Seren, 2001), p. 5.

[11] Denise Levertov, *This Great Unknowing* (Tarset: Bloodaxe, 2001), p. 58.

# 11

# 'The fast dipping brush'

'In the past forty years, the production of ekphrastic poetry has become nothing less than a boom', a modern commentator has noted, alongside a definition of ekphrasis as 'the verbal representation of visual representation'.[1] That boom shows no sign of moderating, since striking poems about paintings continue to be published by a host of notable poets, including Seamus Heaney, Derek Mahon, Charles Wright, Charles Simic, Jorie Graham, Louise Gluck, Dave Smith and Rita Dove. Over the last century, several of the most enduring poems have, in fact, been of this kind – from the famous responses to Brueghel's painting by W. H. Auden, John Berryman and William Carlos Williams, to the extraordinary musings of a John Ashbery fruitfully bemused by Parmigianino's 'Self-Portrait in a Convex Mirror'. The attractiveness of this poetic genre to publishers as well as to poets has resulted in the profileration of anthologies of painting-poems – with three collections, for instance, being published in Britain in a single year (M, p. 135). In America, the Ecco Press launched some years ago a series of 'Writers on Art', to which the poet Mark Strand contributed a remarkable collection of prose 'poems' on the work of Edward Hopper. And in Strand's native Canada, complete sequences on art have been written by poets like Don Coles, whose 'Edvard Munch poems' take the Norwegian's paintings as their 'point of departure'.

This boom has also been evidenced in the many painting-poems produced over the last few years in Wales, a development common to both
Welsh-language culture (witness the work of Euros Bowen, Bryan Martin
Davies, Christine James) and English-language culture (as exemplified
by the poetry of John Ormond, Gillian Clarke, Tony Conran, Tony Curtis,
Dannie Abse and Pascale Petit).[2] So, when R. S. Thomas devoted first
a key section (of *Between Here and Now*) and then a whole collection of
poems (*Ingrowing Thoughts*) to the searching scrutiny of paintings, he
was participating (no doubt unawares, and most uncharacteristically)
in a popular, even fashionable, modern trend.[3] He was also, however
belatedly, doing what came naturally, since from the beginning his own
poems had been manifestly strong in graphic and painterly qualities, as
film-makers (like Emyr Humphreys and John Ormond) had been quick
to realise, and as was recently recognised by a group of artists who collect-
ively paid visual tribute to Thomas's poetry by producing a book of paintings based on a selection of his work.[4]

As has been implied in earlier chapters of this study, Thomas's painting poems have not, however, received very much critical attention, a
relative neglect which is understandable enough given that his serial
obsession, first with Iago Prytherch and then the divinity, is liable to
make any other interest seem passing and slight. In addition, the whole
manner of his approach to pictures is likely to seem old-fashioned and
conservative, still governed by an ideology of art that originated in
Renaissance and Neo-Classical aesthetics, was given definitive expression by Lessing, and eventually resulted in the influential Modernist concept of 'spatial form'. This concept, most memorably articulated by the
theoreticians Joseph Frank and Murray Krieger, is based on the trope of
painting as 'time spatialized', the temporal stilled by form. Such a trope
certainly acted as a magnet for Thomas who, as Anglican priest, was
naturally drawn to a treatment of visual art as iconic and sacramental
in character, an epitome of paradoxical human co-existence in existential
time and timeless eternity. As Thomas further recognised, literature seeks
to approximate to this effect by means of rhetorical and formal devices
that seem to suspend the linear movement of language (which for Lessing
constituted the irreducible difference between the verbal and the visual

arts), resulting in a poem (or even a novel) that invites intellectual scrutiny as 'verbal icon', or a 'well-wrought urn'.

The poem 'Pissarro: Kitchen Garden, Trees in Bloom' provides a concise example of one of Thomas's devices for creating the illusion of the suspension of time.[5] Contemplation of the painting leads him to conclude that it typifies a particular kind of location. And what is that kind? It is, for Thomas, the kind of place where the passage of time is simultaneously felt and suspended. On the one hand, the 'clock's insect/ aggravates the hour'. The image captures the cricket-like chirping of a clock as it disturbs our peace of mind by gratingly insisting that we register every passing second. On the other hand, the room is full of 'the dry smell/ Of sunlight'. This suggests the way the warmth of the sun brings out, say, the perfume of leather furniture in a kind of synaesthetic experience – the sense of sight metamorphosing into the sense of smell. The result is the opposite of the clock's time, in that it heightens awareness of the room's spatial as opposed to its temporal existence. As it fills with the 'dry smell/ of sunlight', it turns into a time capsule, a sealed jar of sensation. Hence Thomas's next conclusion, based on this experience the painting has just produced in him: 'Art is recuperation/ from time'. Viewing the painting has, for him, became a 'convalescence', a leisurely 'prospect' – the word is, of course, a pun, since it means both 'prospect' in the sense of 'spatial view' and 'prospect' in the sense of temporal anticipation. And that pun fuses space and time together to create a single, time-freezing, experience.

However, as Michael Davidson has very clearly demonstrated, many of the best post-war poems about painting have been energised – and their aggressively processual style and rhetoric have been determined – by a restless dissatisfaction with the orthodox aesthetics of spatial form.[6] They constitute a deliberate attack on what, with reference to Lessing, has been described as the 'extreme laocoonization of modern criticism'. Philosophers such as Heidegger have enabled postmodernist writers to substitute a 'hermeneutics of existential temporality' (Davidson, p. 71) for the hermeneutics of closure they perceived as inscribed in the characteristic practices of Modernism. The result has been a radically new kind of 'ekphrasis', a mode of writing about painting pioneered in the

1950s by Frank O'Hara and the poets of the New York School, and later perfected by the great survivor of that group, John Ashbery.

Closely related to developments such as Abstract Expressionism, open field poetry and the work of the Black Mountain poets, the 'contemporary painterly poem' (to borrow Davidson's designation) is characterised by features that radically distinguish it from traditional poems about paintings:

> Instead of pausing at a reflective distance from the work of art, the poet reads the painting as a text, rather than as a static object . . . poetic reflection refuses to constitute the painting in an act of linguistic recovery. Realization implies dematerialization; the instability of the object, its extensions in a larger world of signs, is exposed by the poem's verbal play, its dislocation of speaker/viewer, and its apprehension of stylistic and formal codes. Painting and poems are, as John Ashbery says, 'stable within/ Instability'. (p. 72)

Viewed against the background of such developments, R. S. Thomas's poems about works by the Impressionists, Post-Impressionists and Surrealists may seem anachronistic; no more than conventional exercises in the outmoded tradition of what Davidson calls 'the Classical painterly poem'. But then, as James Heffernan has fairly noted (pp. 2–3), classical ekphrasis was, and is, capable of accommodating much more flexible responses to painting than are dreamt of in Davidson's rather rigid postmodern philosophy. The aim of this chapter is to explore something of the variousness of R. S. Thomas's painting-poems and to uncover the rationale of his practices.

\* \* \*

There are thirty-three poems on painting in *Between Here and Now,* and a further twenty-one printed in *Ingrowing Thoughts.* In this instance, as is the case with his religious poetry, Thomas seems intent not on repetition but on rendering the process (but emphatically not the progress) of experiences that are speculative in both senses of that word. It is a process that gives rise to an assortment of reflections on art that, for all the firmness with which each is formulated, mutually reveal each other to have only limited, compromised, validity. In its very gravity, each sententious utterance is thereby revealed to be gravid with hyperbole. Nevertheless, a brief listing of these *sententiae*, lifted out of their context in *Between Here and Now*, may serve as a crude index of the wide spectrum of Thomas's interest in art:

(i)          exchanging
progress without a murmur
for the leisureliness of art. (33)

(ii)   Art is recuperation
from time. (41)

(iii)              this is art
overcoming permanently
the temptation to answer
a yawn with a yawn. (53)

(iv)       Art is a sacrament
in itself. (59)

(v)        a doctor
becoming patient himself
of art's diagnosis. (63)

(vi)              The red kerchief
at the neck, that suggests
blood, is art leading
modesty astray. (69)

These are, of course, instances only of Thomas's most explicit reflections on the nature of art, but even this very limited sampling allows us to note how, depending on the occasion, art may variously be understood as refuge, solace, unsparing truth, seductive artifice, sacred, spiritual, sensual, soothing, invigorating, not to mention other more vertiginous possibilities allowed for, and even mischievously encouraged by, the ambiguous phrasing. (In that last example, is the 'art' that leads modesty astray the art of the painter or of the subject herself? And – even more disturbingly from the epistemological point of view – how can one tell?)

In fact, if one chooses to measure Thomas's painting poems against the extensive list of *topoi* contemporary criticism has accustomed us to expect in sophisticated modern examples of the genre, then one is likely to be suitably impressed. For instance, no self-respecting practitioner could nowadays afford to overlook the fact that in writing about painting what is being addressed is the representation of a representation, which inescapably involves the production of art about the art of art. So, in 'commenting' on Matisse's 'Portrait of a Girl in a Yellow Dress', Thomas begins by establishing the formally self-contained and self-referential character of painting – 'Windows in art/ are to turn the back/ on' – before proceeding to register an awareness of this human portrait as 'purely' a matter of colour:

> The draught
> cannot put out
> her flame: yellow
> dress, yellow
> (if we could come close
> enough) eyes; (CP, p. 438)

In turn, these lines are conspicuously presented to us as a design of words that both designates the compositional features of the painting and (like the painting's arrangement of colour) has designs upon us. There is the artfulness that places a gulf of distance (measurable by the eye) between 'draught' and 'flame'; appropriately so since of course the draught (which in this instance has the status of (imagined) fact) cannot exist on the same plane as the 'flame' (which is purely a metaphor suggested by the way that colour works in this particular case). In turn, 'flame' and 'yellow' share a line, from which 'dress' is excluded although it, and not 'flame', is the noun qualified by 'yellow'. This is because, in the topsy turvy world of art, a metaphor (yellow flame) may legitimately be given priority over the duly subordinated 'fact' (yellow dress) for which in 'real' life it is merely a figurative substitute. That window which *is* art is like Alice's looking-glass, through which we step into a magically disordered and rearranged world. But then, art may be strangest of all precisely when it conceals its strangenesses – when, in short, it is illusionist enough to allow us to believe that we can get as close to the painted image of a person as we can to real flesh and blood, only to nonplus us with the revelation that within the painting there can be only paint and more

paint. So, too, in Thomas's poem, the promise of intimacy and inwardness, conventionally signified in print by the beckoning recessiveness of
bracketed parentheses, is revealed to be a hollow one. We are left with
a kind of redundancy of verbal iteration: yellow dress, therefore yellow
eyes, since in a yellow painting everything is by definition going to be
tinged with, or keyed to, yellow.

Yet, emphasise though he may the formal spatial properties of which
visual art is in a sense exclusively constituted, Thomas also likes to em-
power it to tell a story – a preference no doubt deriving in part from his
lifetime experience, as preacher, of delivering regular homilies. So he
concludes 'Portrait of a Girl in a Yellow Dress' by turning stasis into
story, image into imagined history:

> hands
> that, after the busyness
> of their migrations between cheek
> and dressing-table, lipstick
> and lip, have found in the lap's
> taffeta a repose
> whose self-consciousness the painter
> was at pains not to conceal.

None of this is, strictly speaking, in the painting – a discrepancy to which
the poem implicitly, and wittily, admits when through the interplay of
'lipstick/ and lip', extended to include 'lap', it draws attention to the
'artistic' effects possibly only in textual compositions. Similarly the way
in which, by characterising it as 'self-conscious', Thomas silently reminds
us that 'repose' contains the word 'pose' is another instance of the way
his poetry pointedly takes advantage of words in the name of lending
voice to silent images.

One of the most notable, and hermeneutically profitable, features of
recent discussions of the poetry of ekphrasis has been the alert attention
paid by commentators to the rich variety of ways in which it is possible
to figure the relationship between poems and paintings. A poem may
be about, to or for a work of art. Language may be treated as obediently
serving the image or as jealously rivalling it. One or other medium may

even suddenly find itself represented as weak precisely where it thought it was invincibly strong. So, in his powerful poem on Picasso's 'Guernica', Thomas succeeds in suggesting that the ostensibly 'silent' picture is possessed, in unexpected reality, of an unrivalled power to express those raw primary sounds of anguished human existence that language actually inhibits:

> The painter
> has been down at the root
> of the scream and surfaced
> again to prepare the affections
> for the atrocity of its flowers. (*CP*, p. 437)

Even when Thomas more conventionally conceives of his poem as envoicing a painting, he can use the potentially authoritative rhetorical technique of prosopopeia in a playfully self-subverting kind of way. Turning the telling exchange of looks between man and woman in Gustave de Smet's 'The Meeting' into imagined conversation, Thomas first of all produces a multi-media pun by turning the hedge that separates the one person from the other into the symbolic edge of their respective personal space: 'You are using my edges/ to look over'.[7] Then, after two stanzas of invented verbal exchange, he abruptly breaks off:

> I translate the encounter.
> But the flag at attention
> at the house corner prefers
> the original: Vive la France.

The poem is, of course, not so much about the foreign language of painting as about the foreignness to language of painting. The French ('Vive la France') is about as illuminating of the painting as was the English. If the flag in the painting is a tricolour, then the flag being implicitly flown by the poem at its conclusion is the white one of surrender, as signified by the blank page at the point where the inadequate black text comes to an abrupt full stop. The very playfulness of tone indicates that, relative to the painting, the text is a veritable *jeu d'esprit* of language, and little more.

* * *

One is, then, frequently reminded in reading Thomas's painting poems that 'the relation between literature and the visual arts [may be represented as] *paragonal*, a struggle for dominance between the image and the word' (*M*, p. 1). Something of the tentativeness, even the unease, of a poem's approach to a picture is indicated by the fact that a third of the painting poems in *Between Here and Now* begin with a question. The tone thus generated is often quizzical, even wary; 'An agreement between/ land and sea, with both using/ the same tone?', wonders Thomas, while contemplating Jongkind's 'The Beach at Sainte-Adresse' (*BHN* 15). But for the question mark, this could as easily function as a statement as a question, and this shadow of grammatical ambiguity is surely important in this instance. What we say about a painting may be figured either as a comment which, however firmly made, can never be more than questionably appropriate; or it may be figured as a suggested interpretation to which, however hesitantly phrased, we are in fact secretly committed and attached, since it provides us personally with the only possible grounds for making sense of the picture. The rest of Thomas's poem therefore treats the opening question as the answer to the painting's meaning, and proceeds to elaborate an interpretation of it on these terms.

This is a technique he repeatedly employs, as when his poem on Degas's 'Mademoiselle Dihau at the Piano' opens with 'Asking us what she shall play?', and then proceeds to 'key' all the comments that follow to that initial self-questioning assumption. By such means, Thomas also explores another aspect of the complex relationship between the two art forms, namely the way in which paintings, when verbalised, tend to turn into stories. This is a truism which, once again, is open to many different kinds of interpretation. Is narrative in this connection a case of word triumphing over image, or of word acting as midwife to image? Does a picture indeed tell a story, or is a story told, willy nilly, about a picture? Could it even be that some pictures are hospitable sites for story-telling

271

– that they put one in mind of stories, in the plural? Such a possibility is nicely entertained, not to say enacted, in Thomas's poem on Pissarro's 'The Louveciennes Road':

> So beautiful it hurts;
> yet nothing for tears
> to exploit. April afternoon?
> A village into which
>
> two walk, from which another
> departs, and a horse
> with its burden in the middle
> of the road. Going home?
>
> Yes, but not bothering
> to arrive; exchanging
> progress without a murmur
> for the leisureliness of art. (*BHN*, p. 33)

The poem becomes the verbal embodiment of that leisurely reflectiveness of which it finally speaks, and which has been enabled by the painting. In this instance, the grammatical questions mark those points where other possibilities, of which the poem at present chooses not to avail itself, are invisibly present. From those points of possible alternative departure, and through these possibilities, other stories may materialise and very different routes through the painting may open up.

For Thomas, a painting may itself take the form of a question, as when Cézanne's 'The Bridge at Maincy' is understood to ask: 'Has a bridge/ to be crossed?' (*BHN*, p. 49). Thus the poem gives the familiar topos of the stillness of painted images – a theme to which Thomas is predict-ably attracted – a vigorous new twist. What follows that abrupt opening question is, however, a strangely paradoxical passage of extended rumin-ation:

> Has a bridge
> to be crossed? Better empty
> this one, awaiting
> the traveller's return

> from the outside
> world to his place
> at the handrail to
> watch for the face's
>
> water-lily to emerge
> from the dark depths
> as quietly as the waxen
> moon from among clouds. (*BHN*, p. 49)

Why does Thomas proceed perversely to supply the very image of human presence whose absence from the painting he began by celebrating? It is, perhaps, a reminder of the centrality of the human in Thomas's world. This empty bridge is significant not in itself, but for the quality of *human* experience it signifies, and which indeed it helps produce. To view the picture is – as was perhaps the act of painting it – to be brought into being in a new way; to see our own face emerging like a water-lily out of its depths. And through the long momentum of a syntax that slowly yields to the painting, and thus slowly yields its meaning, that measures its length across three stanzas, and which turns on a centrally placed rhyme (place/face), the text itself seems physically to enact the process of merging into the painting and thus emerging from it; as if the poem, too, had grown anew out of that painted water.

Yielding to a painting, entering the picture, being sensually seduced by it, these and related tributary tropes are repeatedly explored and exploited in Thomas's painting poems, and in turn they provoke a host of opposite reactions reasserting the power of word over image. In considering 'Portrait of a Young Woman' (fig. 9), he impatiently brushes aside (the pun seems appropriate) Degas's supposed intentions:

> I imagine he intended
> other things; tonal
> values, the light and shade
> of her cheek.
>                     To me innocence
> is its meaning. (*BHN*, p. 21)

Such airy impatience is, however, its own undoing – it raises in the reader's mind a variety of objections on which Thomas as poet actually seems to calculate, turning the poem into an unspoken argument between aesthete and moralist, the painter and the poet, the latter seeming to be very deliberately figuring himself here as an almost primly proper Protestant priest ('If the lips/ opened a little, blessings/ would come forth', he coyly observes). Seeming to, that is, until the priest in turn exposes himself in all the avidness of his male sensuality:

> Her young being
> waits to be startled
> by the sweetness in roughness
> of hands that
> with permitted boldness
> will remove her bark
> to show under how smooth a
> tree temptation can shelter. (*BHN*, p. 21)

It is evident how ambiguously gendered, in this particular instance, is the image of the power of sensuousness (inextricably entangled with the temptations of sensuality). The unawakened sexuality of the girl understood both as a stimulus to the male and as an unconscious desire in the female herself; the girl's body as therefore unwittingly instinct with temptation for herself as well as for the man; the man in turn as constituting temptation in the smoothness of his exposed body as well as responding to temptation in the different smoothness of hers he has exposed – the lines construct this intricate sense of interactive and inter-dependent male-female sexuality by deliberately blurring the roles trad-itionally assigned to the actors in the original story of the Fall. In Thomas's modern version of that story, it is difficult to say, as between man and woman, who exactly is the serpent, what is the tree, and which is Eve, as it is equally difficult to determine the exact character of the Fall into knowledge of the fully sensate flesh.

By thus turning Degas's supposed study in tonal values into a site for violently committed exploration of the sensual tension between male and female, Thomas is implicitly raising questions about how the female figures in images painted by males are looked at by males. These are questions to which he repeatedly returns. 'Could I have loved this?', is his frank response to a 'Portrait of Madame Renou' by André Derain, and the first stanza of the resulting poem is given over to his attempt to read the mind's complexion in this female face. Only in the second stanza does he bring himself to register the title of the painting, and thus reluctantly faces up to the fact that the woman is already married:

> Yet now the disclosure:
> Madame Renou! While the mind
> toys with the title, the
> rest of me has no time
> for the spouse. Art like
> this could have left her tagged surname out. (*IT*, p. 14)

Read in the light of gender concerns, these lines are a frank exposé of the male's wish to make free with the image of a female subject – not to be inhibited by conventional restraints, but to be entirely at liberty to possess or reject her precisely as he wills. That, after all, is the very desire to which so many paintings of women by men have explicitly pandered. Judged in the light of such traditional practices, the Derain painting has already disappointed, since it offers an image of a lady so self-possessed, so fore-armed with knowledge of life, that the male is discouraged by the very look of her, and retreats into cold censure:

> A tendency to disdain
> our requirements promises
> she has nothing to give.
> It is not the observer
> she pouts at, but life itself.

But piqued though he is, the viewer continues to find a piquancy in this image, hence the annoyance at discovering from the 'tagged surname' that this woman has been rendered further unapproachable by marriage. However, he remains undaunted: 'While the mind/ toys with the title, the/ rest of me has no time/ for the spouse'. The phrasing is wittily suggestive: it manages to imply that the (nicely unspecified) 'rest' of the speaker 'toys' with this female image in ways the mind would not consciously like to countenance. Taken as a whole, then, this poem may be read as a disclosure of the covert assumptions and expectations governing the way in which males have customarily approached the female image.[8]

There is, though, another way in which the poem may be interpreted. Thomas's annoyance with the title may be understood as deriving not from (deliberately assumed?) gender prejudice but rather from a conviction that a work of art is entitled to a life of its own, free of the interfering will of the artist. Derain's portrait needs no impertinent title to describe it, or to speak for it. So understood, the poem may be seen as one of a set, scattered across two collections, in which Thomas rebels against both the verbal dictates and the visual directives by means of which the artist seeks to maintain ideological control over his work. Thus, after noting how, in Gauguin's 'Breton Landscape, the Mill', 'The eye is to concentrate/ on the tree gushing/ over the bent-backed woman/ with her companion and/ dog', he stubbornly goes on to insist 'But there is so much/ besides' (*BHN*, p. 57). In responding to 'Composition' by John Selby Bigge, he goes so far as to supply the painting's perceived deficiencies:

> Painter,
> with your impressed brush,
> you forgot the look-outs
> peering fore and aft from the hurtling
> wind-jammer, both lamenting. (*IT*, p. 38)

And, when confronted by Monet's 'Rouen Cathedral, Full Sunshine', he goes even further. The poem begins by stepping *through* the painting, and entering the actual cathedral itself:

> But deep inside
> are the chipped figures
> with their budgerigar faces,
> a sort of divine
> humour in collusion
> with time. Who but
> God can improve
> by distortions? (*BHN*, p. 73)

This rhetorical strategy is tantalisingly reminiscent of the approach to images and texts advocated, and practised, by those influential modern theorists (including Marxists, feminists and postmodernists) who are ever alert, in their reading, to the secret signs (in the form of gaps, contradictions, elisions, silences, omissions) of what has been ideologically suppressed. But whereas such analyses are designed to expose the secret *social* agenda of 'aesthetic' productions, Thomas's analysis of Monet is *metaphysical* in its thrust. It uncovers – with calculated (c)rudeness – the 'natural' human tendency, so amply evidenced in art, to equate the sacred exclusively with the sublime and the beautiful, with the serious and the radiantly intense. Faced once more by the evidence of this in Monet's glowing 'façade', Thomas responds much as Anna so memorably does in Lawrence's novel, *The Rainbow*, when Will tries to coerce her into admiring the soaring nave of Lincoln cathedral. She fixes on the leering, mocking gargoyles: 'These sly little faces peeped out of the grand tide of the cathedral like something that knew better. They knew quite well, these little imps that retorted on man's own illusion, that the cathedral was not absolute.'[9]

Thomas's impulse to read a painting 'against the grain' may on occasion arise from a desire to challenge the all-too-human perspective of the image, to register the sometimes absurdly different scale of values that applies once eternity is brought into the picture. Since this is a radically important aspect of his approach, it is worth glancing again at his impulse to 'people' John Selby Bigge's painted wind-jammer with distraught lookouts. He does so by way of protest against the proffered image of a schooner that 'urges the horizon/ to admit the fallacy/ of its frontiers' (*IT*, p. 38). In other words, he views Bigge's painting as a silent endorsement of the modern world's abandonment of the wreck of the old, and of its hubristic will to transgress the limits of what has traditionally been regarded as humanly possible. The painter's 'impressed' brush has been press-ganged, pressed into serving the ideology of the modern. The painting presents us with a Post-Impressionist image in the sense that, for Thomas, the technique of the Impressionists was the signature, or the imprint, of a more humble, pre-modern age.

Alongside the impulse to supply the unsettling perspective of the eternal (to be considered further in the next chapter), there exists in Thomas's poems of 'corrections' of the painted image a complementary wish to effect the restitution of what he would regard as the *authentic* image of the human. If this is manifest in one way in his wish to turn Selby Bigge's painting into one of modern existential angst, it is manifest in another way in his moving response to Carl Hofer's painting 'Still Life':

> The chianti has escaped
> from the mandolin, from the bottle
> the music. Only the black
> grapes are untouched on the table.
>
> They were not too high. With those
> gone who had begun their meal
> the sourness is in the work
> of art's claim to be still life. (*IT*, p. 18)

Here Thomas deliberately, and wittily, misreads the familiar grammar of such paintings. And in so doing he again deliberately imputes a sinister modern ideology to a long-established convention, the convention of presenting a 'mere' arrangement of objects as an aesthetically complete and satisfying image. Thomas chooses to read this ostensibly harmless modern example of the genre as a cold exercise in dehumanisation, which he then protestingly converts into an elegy for the departed human life (the meal has been left, abandoned rather than finished). Through a quietly playful transference of terms (chianti from the mandolin, music from the bottle) he first establishes a sense of relaxed intimacy and magical interfusion which, it is then implied, has been allowed to escape. And that magic is tinged with the sacred to the extent that we are aware, as hovering in the background, of a sense of communion, and its near homonym, community. Moreover, a poem that could almost be said to proceed by multiplying puns ('high', 'sour', 'still') must surely encourage us to discover the otherwise lost syllable, or last trace, of the human in the word 'mandolin'.

That familiarity with painting genres, which is obliquely evident in 'Still Life', is directly apparent in other poems by Thomas. Indeed, his striking interpretation of 'Father and Child' (fig. 12) by Ben Shahn depends

entirely on his perceiving the painting as a modern re-vision of the iconography of the Madonna and Child:

> Times change:
> no longer the virgin
> ample-lapped; the child fallen
> in it from an adjacent heaven. (*IT*, p. 13)

Alert to the semiotics of painting, Thomas is aware of how a whole religious cosmology was signified by the way in which holy figures were
'placed' in picture space. And he is equally aware of how the ordering
of space was in turn a metaphor for a spiritually coherent concept of
teleological time. In fact, Thomas regularly reads modern paintings in
terms of the secularisation of religious iconographical practices. His initial
response to Bazille's 'Family Reunion' is to see this revealing image of
the bourgeoisie proudly parading its finery as a kind of visual palimpsest;
beneath all the luxury he perceives the barely erased traces of the 'original'
garden scene:

> In groups
>          under the tree,
> none of them sorry
> for having partaken
>          of its knowledge. (*BHN*, p. 19)

Eden, and the Fall, are again discovered to be lurking presences of meaning in Rousseau's mysterious painting of 'The Snake Charmer':

> A bird not of this
> planet; serpents earlier
> than their venom; plants
> reduplicating the moon's
>
> paleness. An anonymous
> minstrel, threatening us
> from under macabre
> boughs with the innocence

279

> of his music. The dark
> listens to him and withholds
> till tomorrow the boneless
> progeny to be brought to birth. (*BHN*, p. 75)

Even as he succeeds in capturing the disturbing ambivalence of the image – curiously compounded as it is of menace and of mellifluous mystery – Thomas turns the painting into a meditation on our dreamy desires for a prelapsarian innocence. Such dreams may bear strange witness, after all, to the dark sides of our natures, since for instance sentimentality and sadism are the oddest, and yet most common, of bedfellows.

Thomas's pronounced tendency to find sermons in painted stones and running brooks may, no doubt, seem no more than a tedious and regrettable diversion to some; another instance of the moralising, allegorising priest in him triumphing over the creative artist. But another response is surely permissible. He may, for instance, be seen as concerned to point out unexpected signs in modern art of the return of the repressed. His spiritualised, and spirited, readings often have a dry wit and a sardonic point to them. It is as if he were, at least on occasion, gleefully inciting the painting to bear witness against the ostensibly modern, secularised, mind of both the painter and his painted subject. In like spirit, he can also indulge in fantasies of the social revolutions that can be unknowingly incubated by paintings. His response to the smugness of the French bourgeoisie's self-presentation in Bazille's 'Family Reunion' is to observe that 'their servants/ are out of sight,/ snatching a moment/ to beget offspring/ who are to overturn all this' (*BHN*, p. 19).

\* \* \*

When it comes to relishing the duplicities of the painted image, however, Thomas is most appreciative of it when it exposes the artifices of women. He loves it when Monet's 'Lady with a Parasol' exposes its subject as a sturdily fertile peasant studiedly veiling herself in mystery (*BHN*, p. 13). Although he acknowledges, in his treatment of Monet's study 'Portrait of Madame Gaudibert', that it is to her wealthy merchant husband that the painter is demeaningly indebted for keeping him afloat, it is Madame who attracts Thomas's scathing censure. She, in his eyes, is an actress, 'Waiting for the curtain/ to rise on an audience/ of one – her husband' (BHN, p. 23). That this splenetically sexist response is rooted in Thomas's own sense of vulnerability as artist is clear from the poem's conclusion, where he rejoices how, 'for a moment/ at least, Monet on even/ keel paddled himself/ on with strokes not/ of an oar but/ of a fast-dipping brush'.

Thomas's visceral mistrust of women went much deeper, however, than his identification with his art, and involved unmistakeable sexual tensions. As Griselda Pollock has pointed out, the work of the Impressionists is very much a record of 'scenes and locations almost exclusively available to men – bars, cafes, brothels, behind scenes in the dance'.[10] These are locations suitable for catching women unawares – off their guard, a male cynic such as R. S. Thomas might say. In his set of poems responding to the work of the Impressionist, Thomas takes full advantage of their preoccupation with the female and her intimate spaces – women are the subject of almost half his texts (fifteen poems out of thirty-three). And it is to their supposed duplicity, both conscious and unconscious, that he is repeatedly, obsessively attracted. The poor derelict street-walker captured in Degas's 'Absinthe' is censured for wearing clothes 'out of the top drawer', suspected as she is of putting 'them on in order/ to have something good she could take off' (BHN, p. 43). As for Mary Cassatt's beautifully intimate and sympathetic picture of 'Young Woman Sewing' – a painting full of that sense of sisterly inwardness with the scene that, as Pollock has pointed out, sets Cassatt's depiction of women apart from that of the male Impressionists – it becomes, for Thomas, full of the pre-monition of puberty with its sudden onrush of a sexuality about which he clearly feels queasily ambivalent. The redness of the flowers by which the young girl is surrounded is decoded as 'an indication of the arrival/ of her period to come/ out now and spread her wings' (BHN, p. 55). That pun on 'period' captures a more than verbal equivocation; it fuses sexual excitement and disgust.

It is the feline character of female predatoriness that Thomas believes to have been emblematically represented in Gauguin's 'La Belle Angèle'

(*BHN*, p. 61). The bronze cat to her right is a warning to the male viewer not to be deceived by her 'sheathed' fingers or her demure look. And while thoroughly approving the ostensibly docile passivity of Toulouse-Lautrec's slim-waisted 'Justine Dieuhl' (*BHN*, p. 69), Thomas's poem finds provocative suggestiveness in her demure self-composition. Indeed, there is scarcely a poem in which he addresses a female subject when Thomas is not sexually troubled in one way or another. Temptation is ever present, as it is for the dance-master in Degas's 'The Dancing Class' (*BHN*, p. 37), studiously raising his eyes no higher than the feet of the young girls who flutter, like flightless exotic birds, all around him. Hence the poet's ambiguous response to the high-kicking dancer Jane Avril, depicted in Toulouse-Lautrec's painting (*BHN*, p. 67) as 'showing the knees/ by which some would gain entrance to heaven'. In her disregard for the social and moral conventions so conspicuously being observed by the onlooking couple behind her, she is the subject at once of Thomas's approval (as the blithely embodied spirit of sexual liberation) and of his disapproval (there is a prim distancing of himself from those others, the 'some' who would cheerfully enter heaven between her legs).

While R. S. Thomas liked to dismiss his painting-poems as mere five-finger exercises for the imagination, those in which women feature suggest the contrary. His exercises in the genre were no mere bagatelle. They are psychically charged to a powerful degree, probably reflecting Thomas's own complex relationships with the two women most prominent in his life – his (s)mothering mother and his wife. About his tortured relationship with the former he had much to write, and his frigidly affectionate relationship with his wife seems to have been little less complicated. Mildred Eldridge had already established a reputation for herself as an accomplished artist by the time of their first meeting when Thomas was a curate on the English border at Chirk. And she continued to consolidate that reputation throughout those early years of their marriage. As has been noted previously, Eldridge was sufficiently well-known by the early 1940s for her to be invited to participate in an important wartime national project, to Record the Changing Face of Britain. This was a scheme administered by the Committee on the Employment of Artists in Wartime, created by the Ministry of Labour and National Service, a Committee chaired by Kenneth Clarke.

All this, then, before R. S. Thomas had published a single original poem of note. And yet, over the half-century and more of their marriage, the balance of fame between them steadily shifted, until it was he rather than she who was much the better known artist, albeit an artist in words. Nor did he ever publicly acknowledge her achievements, as if he were driven always to eclipse them, to silence her art with his increasingly dominant words. His work could, then, be seen as in some obscure part powered by intimate marital rivalry. Initially powered by a desire to emulate the achievements of his wife, his poetry eventually became the proof of his own surpassing talents. In other words, painting could be said to have been a silent, challenging, unsettling and inescapable presence in R. S. Thomas's poetry throughout his long career. If so, then no wonder that he was so magnetically drawn to it yet uncertain what to make of it. No wonder he favoured paintings, and therefore poems, that imaged what he regarded as the enigmatic power of the eternal feminine. And no wonder, either, that from time to time he was tempted to master images by words, as he composed his painting-poems. Hence the many 'paragonic' poems that, as has been shown, feature so prominently in his collection about the Impressionists. [11]

While all this may be little more than speculation, what is more certain is that it was from the young Mildred Eldridge that R. S. Thomas first began to learn what it really meant to be an artist – in any medium, including language. And it was from her, too, that he slowly learnt the vocabulary and grammar of painting and became literate in visual art. Most important of all, perhaps, his growing admiration of the mute, non-verbal, silent eloquence of visual art reinforced his steadily maturing determination that his own poems should be as verbally spare as possible, so as to save words from their own glib garrulity.

When confronted by Degas's 'Mademoiselle Dihau at the Piano' (fig. 10), Thomas's instinct is once again is to turn this seductive image into monitory narrative. Only on such occasions as have been noted does he make the actual composition of a painting the subject of his paint ing poems. Unlike William Carlos Williams, for instance, he doesn't consistently dwell on a painting's disposition of shapes, textures and colours; its leading of the eye through a staged, complex process of gradual apprehension; its aesthetic integrity as a shaped object. Instead, from the beginning R.S. personalises the engagement between viewed and viewer: 'Asking us what she shall play?'. It's as if the presence of the piano in the image immediately triggers the response not just of R.S.'s eyes, but of his ears. The painting seems to him to aspire to the condition of speaking image. 'Asking us what she shall play?' The question form is an admission, of course, that such a response is merely speculative, as any and every attempt to account verbally for the 'meaning' of paintings can never be more than redundant speculation. But conversely, the function of art might be said to enable and encourage speculation, ruminative reflection. And, as if to underline this, the whole middle section of Thomas's poem turns out to be a leisurely, ruminative digression into a comparison, a simile: 'We listen to her/ as, on an afternoon/ in September, the garden listens/ to the year ripening' (*BHN*, p. 25). Not for the first time, to view a painting is, for R. S. Thomas, to have a door opened onto a particular kind of experience, and so to prompt the viewer to bring parallel instances to mind from the depths of his unconscious. Paintings, one might say, are depth charges; they bring suppressed dimensions of our natures, of our existence, up to the surface of our consciousness, thus changing the perspective we have on our individual and human being.

But if the poem, and the painting, thus once again turn out to have spiritual implications for Thomas the priest, he is also stirred by its sensuous power and thus by the sensual allure of Mademoiselle Dihau. She seems a 'mellow-fleshed,/ sun-polished fruit'. Yet, 'her eyes are the seeds of a tart apple'. As so often elsewhere in these disconcerted engagements with woman's image, his is decidedly a 'male gaze', to employ a term that has been much in vogue these many years particularly among feminist analysts of the way females tend to be imaged by male image-makers and regarded by male viewers.[12] In this case that notoriously detached, objectifying and appropriating male gaze is at once confidently devouring and also fearfully wary. Thomas's complex, conflicted feelings about women resulted not infrequently in misogynistic treatment of them as cunning, calculating actresses, threateningly unfathomable in their motives and actions. But, at least in this instance, he grants the female subject of his examination the power to turn him into the unexpected subject of her own. The tables for once are turned, as the gazing male becomes the unnerved object of a female gaze.

Yet even when they involve a female subject, Thomas's painting poems are liable to carry the tell-tale marks of a priest accustomed to delivering regular sermons. The homiletic habits of mind thus formed are clearly evident as, in the manner of a modern-day emblem book, the viewing of an image is turned into an occasion to learn a moral lesson. A clear example comes in the form of his textual representation of Degas's 'Musicians in the Orchestra' (*BHN*, p. 27) (fig. 11), where women are once again the main source of trouble.

> Heads together, pulling
> upon music's tide –
> it is not their ears
> but their eyes their conductor
>
> has sealed, lest they behold
> on the stage's shore
> the skirts' rising and falling
> that turns men into swine. (*BHN*, p. 27)

Those last phrases are an obvious reference to the episode in Homer's Odyssey when Ulysses, returning home by ship from Troy, narrowly avoids being seduced by the witch Circe, whose beguiling beauty literally turns all men into swine. Thomas's father was a ship's captain, who worked on the Holyhead–Dun Laoghaire ferry route. And, as was noted in chapter 5, Thomas came to see him as eventually lured away from the freedom of the open sea to be shipwrecked on his wife's home comforts. This poem, therefore, has its roots in Thomas's early family background.

And in this text, Thomas fuses the Circe episode with another, again from the Odyssey, when Ulysses orders his sailors to seal their ears with wax when they are passing the Sirens, lest they be so attracted by the sweet singing that they allow their ship to drift fatally onto the rocks. However, in the case of Degas's painting, 'it is not their ears/ but their

eyes their conductor// has sealed'. There is an ancient tradition of allegorising the Odyssey, and Thomas is here consciously evoking it. There
is also an ancient Christian tradition of treating the eye as one of the
most dangerous organs of sense, because it is the gateway through which
evil is most liable to enter. Hence, it is more important to protect the eye
from temptation than it is to protect the ear. And upon which organ of
sense is painting totally dependent per se? Well, it is of course the eye.
Thomas's poem is, therefore, a witty reading of Degas's painting as a
warning against the Circean power and Siren song of visual art itself.
Hence, it is implied, the picture's strange composition: the effect the image
gives of being awkwardly off-centre. The real, and usual, centre of attraction is the female flesh here relegated to the background, and to the upper
margin of the painting. But this painting is disorientatingly aligned
instead with the horizontal band of heads, all fixedly concentrating on
a focal point somewhere outside the painting's right-hand border. The
effect is to make the painting seem awkwardly lop-sided, aesthetically
deformed. In that sense, it is an example, we might say, of visual art
voluntarily castrating itself.

\* \* \*

It is not, however, in those texts directly concerned with women that
the psychic crises underlying his painting poems surface most powerfully and arrestingly. Rather, it is manifested in his choice of 'Drawing
by a Child', a work by the Surrealist artist Diana Brinton Lee, as the last
one to be subjected to his poetic examination in *Ingrowing Thoughts*. As
he reads it, Lee's image, anarchically crammed with feverishly scribbled
doodles of people and animals, is a child's revenge on its parents 'for
bringing me to be'. Toys are equipped with claws, dolls snarl and a kit-
ten's tail is converted into a serpent by the child's maliciously gleeful
imagination:

> And horns, horns for everything
> in my nursery, pointing to the
> cuckold I know my father to be. (*IT*, p. 49)

286

As noted in a previous chapter, all through his career Thomas produced searing poems of self-disgust, most of which implicated his parents in his self-hatred. Time and again he stressed he'd never asked to be born, and that for him living was a torture. Included in his greatest volume, *The Echoes Return Slow*, is the following account of his own birth: 'Pain's climate. The weather unstable. Blood rather than rain fell. The woman was opened and sewed up, relieved of the trash that had accumulated nine months in the man's absence. Time would have its work cut out in smoothing the birth-marks in the flesh. The marks in the spirit would not heal.'[13] No wonder he was drawn to Lee's raw, uninhibited, savagely infantile drawing. And in choosing to grant this poem the last word in *Ingrowing Thoughts*, Thomas is underlining that collection's concern with the psycho-social crisis that is the legacy of modernity.

Although published only four years after *Between Here and Now*, *Ingrowing Thoughts* nevertheless marks a decisive and irreversible shift in Thomas's taste for paintings. Thereafter, he was to grow steadily dissatisfied with representational images and to complain bitterly when his publishers insisted on choosing such images for the covers of his books. Insight into his new passion for the Post-Impressionists, Surrealists and others is perhaps best available in the form of the 'Homage to Paul Klee', included in the last collection published during his lifetime, *No Truce with the Furies* (1995), its cover a strikingly abstract image of Thomas's own satisfied choice for once by the young Welsh artist Wil Rowlands. For Thomas, Klee's work epitomises 'the insouciance/ in art' appropriate to a modern age alive to 'how easily/ the ridiculous establishes itself/ as existing without end'.[14] And, like the non-human God that the Thomas of the later poetry envisages as the endlessly elusive and enigmatic presiding spirit of modern reality, Klee's composition teases the anthropo-morphising observer by hinting at incipient human forms that never fully materialise. 'I imagined/ an expression,' writes the approvingly exasperated Thomas, 'only to find/ it was the concern/ of angles with their degrees.' The artist, he concludes, is concerned only with

> scribbling,
> where once there was crucifixion,

> those crotchets and semiquavers
> with which levity begins. (*CLP*, p. 279)

Klee's work is very much in the style and to the taste of the joker God whose blithely incomprehensible ways are endlessly pondered in Thomas's late religious poetry.

And it was because modern art had found a new aesthetic adequate to the representation of the metaphysics of modernity that Thomas, during his last decades, found himself ever more steadily drawn to it. As its placing at the very beginning of *Ingrowing Thoughts* suggests, he discovered in Picasso's 'Guernica' the first Medusan muse of this modernity and its arts. Thomas never loses his composure when responding to the work of the Impressionists. There he is always the self-collected viewer, sufficiently detached to act the commentator. But he is thoroughly discomposed by his encounter with 'Guernica'. He writes as if his mind were still in shock. It's as if his imagination has been eviscerated, and as if he has been jolted into 'reassembling' the 'bones' jigsaw' of his own poetry. His poem captures the way his distressed mind distractedly wanders the smashed image of traditional painting that is Picasso's 'painting' of modernity. The result is a poem that strains to produce the extravagant, explosively compressed phrases urgently needed to comprehend the senseless force that turned the whole human world upside down and back to front: 'The whole is love/ in reverse' (*CP*, p. 437). The pithiness of epigram is Thomas's textual equivalent of Picasso's attempt to strip reality back to its bare basics, to burrow down to the root of the scream, to identify the critical single point of origin of the atrocity of modernity. And when he concludes by grimly praising Picasso for preparing 'the affections/ for the atrocity' of the flowers that blossom from that root, he is in part acknowledging that any art, whether painting or poetry, that wants to be authentically modern, has to find ways of recording those *fleurs du mal* that grow in the rubble of a world of belief and value.

'Guernica' sets the post-religious scene for Thomas's contemplation next of Ben Shahn's 'Father and Child' (fig. 12). In this new reality, to be human is to be a permanent refugee, forever expelled from our original home in sacred space, and therefore forever lost wanderers through meaningless time. Heaven is back of us. Like the figures in the painting, we are nothing but dis-placed persons pressing on towards a future that is itself chronically dis-placed, because it has no destination, no goal. Time can no longer be understood teleologically. So the figures slant restlessly but pointlessly across the picture space, inclining towards that endless, unbounded space that awaits them beyond the picture frame. And in a gesture that is emblematic of what has happened to art itself, the woman carries her mother's portrait upside down. It is reminiscent of that phrase describing the world of 'Guernica' as one in which love is reversed. Thomas's poem not only offers this interpretation of the painting, it deliberately mimics it, as he finds textual means of reproducing these key features of the visual image. The bleak repetition of brief sentences is his way of suggesting that modern life can be nothing more than one damned thing after another. Once the teleological, end-directed experience of time is lost, all that is left is mere chronology.

This modern landscape of moral bankruptcy and spiritual dereliction is revisited in his response to 'La Nuit Venitienne', by Paul Eluard: 'In the background fire,/ buildings suppurating/ with smoke, the ruins/ of an idea' (IT, p. 41). As can be seen, his instinct whenever faced with this kind of prospect is not, as is the case with more radically post-modern ekphrastic practice, to mirror its instabilities and indeterminacies, but rather to stabilise it through allegory. So the elderly, composed, couple seated at a table in the foreground, apparently poring over a book, are, he deduces, pondering a 'future [that] is without assets'. While behind their backs the past goes on 'filling the prams/ full with the consequences/ of its indirections'. Thomas is repeatedly drawn to those Surrealist images whose grotesque absurdities seem to him expressive of those twisted, distorted realities of existence that the post-religious mind has uncovered. So, for him, part of the meaning of Ernst's 'Two Children Menaced by a Nightingale' is its fantasticating confession that 'insects/ . . . are required to produce its sweetness of tone' (CP, p. 445). And so much, he adds, for the sweet Romantic dreams of Keats. Similarly, Magritte's 'On the Threshold of Liberty' is read as emblematic of the hideously hubristic delight of modern man in the omnipotence of his inventions. While his poem in response to 'Captain Cook's Last Voyage', by Roland Penrose, crammed grotesquely full of clashing metaphors in a manner corresponding to the weirdly disorientating style of its subject's juxtapositions of objects, ends by registering 'the echoes/ in the nerves' rigging/ of that far-off storm/ that is spirit blowing itself/ out in the emptiness at the Poles' (*CP*, p. 447).

Attention has been drawn in this chapter to the richness and (relative) variety of R. S. Thomas's poetic response to paintings in the hope that the poems he produced may cease to be slighted and ghettoised, as they hitherto have tended to be. While it is true that he himself was ready enough to disown them in public, seeming content to dismiss them as mere doodles designed to occupy his mind until it became persuaded again to bend its efforts to more serious subjects, in private he was not unwilling (at least in my limited experience) to shyly own they possessed their own distinctive point and power. On the basis of such evidence as has been afforded here, I should myself be inclined to go further and suggest not only that many of these poems have presence enough to hold their own in the company of Thomas's other poetry of Iago and of God, but that this body of work as a whole represents a significant contribution to the realisation of Thomas's central and deepest concerns as an artist. They need to be included in, and properly integrated into, any attempt at a comprehensive evaluation of his achievement. To overlook them, or deliberately to marginalise them, is to lose sight of a significant means by which, as a poet, he advanced his consuming visions.

## Notes

[1] James A. W. Heffernan, *Museum of Words: the practice of ekphrasis from Homer to Ashbery* (Chicago: University of Chicago Press, 1993), pp. 135 and 3. Hereafter *M*.

[2] One important manifestation of this was the *Meta* exhibition (2005), organised by Christine Kinsey, a collaboration between poets and artists that visited five locations, including Vilnius (Lithuania); see *Meta: Delweddu'r Dychymyg/ Imaging the Imagination* (a Queens Hall Gallery Narberth/Arts Council of Wales publication, n.d.).

[3] He also included occasional painting-poems in other collections.

[4] *R. S. Thomas Inspiration: A Book to accompany an Exhibition, 1995* (Plas Glyn-y-Weddw: Cyfeillion Oriel Glyn-y-Weddw, 1995). Attention will be paid to this volume in the next chapter.

[5] R. S. Thomas, *Between Here and Now* (London: Macmillan, 1981), p. 41. Hereafter *BHN*.

[6] Michael Davidson, 'Ekphrasis and the Postmodern Painting Poem', *Journal of Aesthetics and Art Criticism*, XLII: 1 (Fall, 1983), 69–79.

[7] R. S. Thomas, *Ingrowing Thoughts* (Bridgend: Poetry Wales Press, 1985), p. 25. Hereafter *IT*.

[8] For Thomas's highly complex relation to women, see Fflur Dafydd, '"There were fathoms in her too": R. S. Thomas's Love Poems to his Wife', *Renascence*, LX: 2 (Winter, 2008), 117–30.

[9] D. H. Lawrence, *The Rainbow* (Harmondsworth: Penguin, 1962), p. 204.

[10] Griselda Pollock, *Vision and Difference: Feminity, Feminism and the Histories of Art* (London: Routledge, 1988), p. 52. See also Griselda Pollock and Roszika Parker (eds), *Old Mistresses: Women, Art and Ideology* (London: Pandora, 1981); Roszika Parker and Griselda Pollock (eds), *Framing Feminism: Art and the Women's Movement, 1970–1985* (London: Pandora, 1987); Norman Broude and Mary D. Garrard (eds), *Feminism and Art History: Questioning the Litany* (Berkeley and Los Angeles: University of California Press, 1982); Norman Broude and Mary D. Garrard (eds), *The Expanding Discourse: Feminism and Art History* (Berkeley and Los Angeles: University of California Press, 1992); Norman Broude and Mary D. Garrard (eds), *Reclaiming Female Agency; Feminist Art History after Postmodernism* (Berkeley and Los Angeles: University of California Press, 2005); Richard Kendall and Griselda Pollock (eds), *Dealing with Degas: Representations of Women and the Politics of Vision* (London: Pandora, 1992); Jane Hedley, Nick Halpern and Willard Spiegelman (eds), *In the Frame: Women's Ekphrastic Poetry from Marianne Moore to Susan Wheeler* (Newark: University of Delaware Press, 2009).

[11] For the 'paragonic' aspect of painting-poems, see, for instance, W. J. Mitchell, *Picture Theory: Essays on Verbal and Visual Representation* (Chicago: University of Chicago Press, 1994).

[12] One *locus classicus* of discussion of 'the female gaze' is Griselda Pollock, 'The Gaze and the Look: Women with Binoculars – A Question of Difference', in *Dealing with Degas*, pp. 106–30. The binary opposite of 'the male gaze' is set out by Laura Mulvey in her landmark essay 'Visual Pleasure and Narrative Cinema', written in 1973 and first published in 1975.

[13] R. S. Thomas, *The Echoes Return Slow* (London: Macmillan, 1988), p. 2.

[14] R. S. Thomas, *No Truce with the Furies* (Tarset: Bloodaxe, 1995), p. 75.

# 12

# 'The brush's piety'

Among the poems left unpublished by R. S. Thomas at his death in 2000 were some thirty-nine responding to paintings.[1] They were tucked into the pages of two art books, each poem placed adjacent to the painting with which it was in dialogue. Both books related to Surrealist art, and both were edited by Herbert Read, at one time probably the best-known British advocate of Surrealism. Neither book was new. *Art Now: An Introduction to The Theory of Modern Painting and Sculpture* was first published in 1933, with a second edition following in 1968: the painting poems published in *Between Here and Now* included responses to several of the images featured in this volume. *Surrealism* was published in 1936 and, in this case, too, Thomas had already quarried some images for the 'paintings' section of *Between Here and Now*.[2] As for the collection of unpublished poems, the fact that some of the personal correspondence intermingled with the texts is dated 2000 suggests that some, if not all, of the poems were the product of the poet's very last months. At the least, the lateness of these letters suggests he continued to be concerned with this body of work virtually down to the time of his death.

As always, when responding to paintings, Thomas seems to have taken very little notice, if any, of the artists' known biographies and visions, of the historical milieu of the works themselves, or even of their titles.[3] What is less clear is whether he consulted any of the interpretative commentaries

and personal credos by Read and others (including prominent practitioners such as André Breton) that are gathered in the two art books.
There are, though, certain intriguing coincidences between some of these
discussions and the approach adopted by Thomas to the paintings. In
*Art Now*, for example, Read argues that modern post-representational art
is, like the cave art of 'primitive' man, a product of crisis, a consequence
of the collapse of those comprehensive explanatory models of existence
on which humans had traditionally depended. That collapse has produced a kind of 'political, economic and spiritual chaos' (*AN*, p. 81), to
which modern art attempts to respond by creating a radically new vocabulary of symbols, 'fixed conceptual images' designed 'to subdue the torment
of [unmediated] perception' and restore some sense of meaningful order
(*AN*, p. 81).[4] Read's interpretation corresponds to the belief implicit in
Thomas's posthumous painting-poems, that the primary responsibility
of the modern arts is not to perpetuate familiar conventions of expression
in a vain attempt to restore past certainties but rather to reorientate
humanity by grounding it anew in permanent spiritual realities. This
necessarily involves snatching 'things from the security of their normal
existence', as Read puts it (*AN*, p. 97), and the production of an alternative art 'appealing less to the eye and more to the soul' (*AN*, p. 110).
This art, Read further argues, employs 'archetypal forms', animistic
products of the collective unconscious instinct with 'a mysterious potency
that is super-real and non-aesthetic' (*AN*, p. 119). He characterises this
potency as a kind of numinous 'presence', such as Thomas is often concerned to convey in his co-responding poetry.

As for the other volume, *Surrealism*, it features an extended discussion
(*S*, pp. 77ff.) by Herbert Read that privileges 'image' over 'metaphor',
in which he sees the former – described as fundamental to the internal
economy of both paintings and poems – as the pure product of an intuitive
apprehension whose source is deep in the human unconscious. Throughout his long career, Thomas adhered to precisely such a conception as
this of the essential source and value of poetry. As, too, he subscribed to
another of Read's tenets:

Art is more than description or 'reportage': it is an act of renewal. It renews vision, it renews language; but most essentially it renews life itself by enlarging the sensibility, by making men more conscious of the terror and the beauty, the *wonder* of the possible forms of being. (*S*, p. 90)

As is repeatedly evident in *Surrealism*, many of the practitioners freely acknowledged an indebtedness to the Romantic cult of the imagination, especially as that had been articulated by Coleridge, whose discussion of the subject in the *Biographia Literaria* so deeply and lastingly influenced R. S. Thomas's ideas about poetry. Hugh Sykes Davies, a prominent English Surrealist, goes so far as to boast that 'In general method, in fact, we can claim to be a direct continuation of Coleridge's work – we are its prehensile tail' (*S*, p. 139). What Sykes Davies particularly values is Coleridge's conclusion that 'poetry, far from being regarded as a rejection or distortion of reality, comes to embody the only complete approach to reality' (*S*, p. 147). 'Surrealism', Sykes Davies adds, 'might employ almost the same words to describe its conclusions.' And with such avowals of a deep debt to English Romanticism, R. S. Thomas would fervently have agreed.[5]

\* \* \*

But the influence on Thomas, if any, of these discussions by Read, Sykes Davies and others, could only have been slight. His poetic engagements with the works of the Surrealists are stubborn records of his own distinctive vision, and thus expressive of his aboriginal concerns as man and as artist. Prominent among these, in the case of the poems in question, is a brooding fascination with the mystery of selfhood, to which attention has repeatedly been paid in this study. Put simply, he seems to have been interested in Surrealism primarily as a solvent of 'normal' identity, and therefore as an art that might loosely be termed 'post-humanist' in its representational practices. In this connection, his attention is sufficiently caught by André Derain's 'Portrait of the Artist', for not one but two poems to result. The first registers the way in which Derain 'defaces' his subject, in a deliberate erasure of the familiar lineaments of identity.

295

Having come 'face to face' with his own anonymity, Derain attempts, through his painting, to provide this alien 'self' with an appropriate 'name', or legible form. In a bold image, Thomas imagines the resulting application of paint to involve first an immersion of the brush 'in the coloured excrement/ of [the] palette', followed by a 'defecation' onto the canvas. The result, he concludes, is not a recovery of lost familiar self-hood, nor even a definitive discovery of some other, deeper, 'nameable', alternative self, but simply an illegible countenance, 'tantalising him with/ the memory of a recognition'.

Here, then, is the aged Thomas once again restlessly confronting one of the darkest obsessions of his later years and grappling with the recalci-trant mystery of personal identity. It is an abiding concern of his, which is addressed elsewhere in this study, insofar as it had a shaping influence on *The Echoes Return Slow*. And it is a concern further aspects of which have been fruitfully explored by critics who have variously concentrated on the recurrent image of mirrors in Thomas's work and on the traces of the 'uncanny' in his writings.[6] He seems to have conceived of this psychic crisis of identity in two different ways, potentially contradictory yet for him overlapping. First as a kind of psychological 'wound' or dis-ability, from which he personally suffered – one of the many deficiencies of personality he was always inclined to attribute to his early upbringing under the dominantly supervisory care of his mother (see chapter 5); and, secondly, as religious or spiritual in character, a kind of unnerving exposure to the deep 'otherness' of one's own self, of one's 'alien' identity as soul as opposed to social being (see chapter 8). He made the dual aspect of this discovery of the 'nothingness' of one's quotidian being into a central subject of his long autobiographical essay, pointedly entitled *Neb*. In order to ensure that the 'not-me' of his own most intimate being made itself fully known to his readers, Thomas controversially elected to write of 'himself' in the third person throughout. Readers have accord-ingly been divided between those irritated by the presumption of a 'self-lessness' they shrewdly point out may function paradoxically as a form of self-advertisement (and a means of avoiding unpleasant home-truths), and those who, whatever their reservations about many of the implications and consequences of Thomas's outrageous rhetorical strategy, remain fascinated by its potential for producing a genuinely unorthodox 'auto-biography of a soul'.

In his response to Derain's painting, Thomas is obviously revisiting the area of psychic tension he had previously attempted to map in *Neb* and in *The Echoes Return Slow*. And, in this instance, he is further concerned to align art itself with this research into the mystery of selfhood, by representing the quest as a key motive for painting (and, by extension, for poetry). Derain's picture is, Thomas surmises, a response to an imperious and indeed irresistible prompting from his anonymous 'self': 'Name me, name me'. But in imaging the result as 'defecation', Thomas treats paintings as symptoms of 'abjection',[7] obviously wanting to underline how disturbing (and even, to conventional tastes, disgusting) this process of 'self-discovery' actually is. It is raw, it is visceral, it involves the working of the artistic equivalent of what in religious contexts used to be called 'the bowels of compassion'. Since it implies the violation of the social norms by which the everyday self is constrained, and thus defined, it involves the breaking of conventional bonds, the transgression of boundaries, the breaking of taboos. And the result? It is a kind of troubling anticlimax, because it is inconclusive, disturbingly unfinished business.

Accordingly, the poem itself ends by implying the need for a sequel; and this second, sibling, poem produced by Thomas addresses the painting not as a portrait of a 'self', but as very specifically the self-portrait of an artist, 'posing to his palette'. The last phrase makes it clear that paint is not merely the medium of this picture, it is actually its only begetter: the picture is literally a paint-[th]ing. R.S., however, shrewdly registers that the painting is officially described as a self-portrait, and understands the motive for this. An artist knows that, for him or her, there is a strange selfhood inseparable from the act of producing art: in this connection, art is the very *raison d'être* of one's deepest existence. Hence, 'self-knowledge', Thomas concludes, was responsible for Derain's deliberately 'muddying the distinction' between a self-portrait and a portrait of an artist.

That art has a mind and a life of its own to which the artist becomes answerable in a depersonalising way is another of the reflections on the subject that Thomas addressed in the Derain poem, which assumes the form of a painting poem. This time, the subject is Jankel Adler's 'David', which gives a disturbing twist to the story of the young harpist's soothing performances for the distraught Saul. Viewing this player with muscular forearms, a comically startled look on his stylised face as he grapples with a harp that looks more like a sinister instrument of torture than a stringed instrument, Thomas is reduced to suggesting that the evil spirit that had supposedly possessed Saul must have migrated to the painter, prompting him to become a 'mock[er]' of a David confronted by an instrument 'that was getting the better of him'. Given his familiarity with the Bible and his inwardness with artistic experience, Thomas would certainly have been aware of the way in which Jacob's Old Testament wrestling with the angel had been interpreted by many painters and writers as a kind of parable of their own struggle with whatever spirit or 'daemon' was the barely controllable source of their own creative gift. Responding to Adler's image, therefore, he revisits this ancient and perennial mystery of artistic creation, again emphasising that in originating somewhere totally other than the sources available to an artist's ordinary socialised self, it too witnesses to dimensions of individual being that are irreducibly, and at times alarmingly, alien to that self.

Thomas's interest in the self-reflexive but self-disintegrative images produced by Surrealism prompts him to focus on Gabriel Robin's 'The Hearth'. Typically, he reads the painting as a subversion of the domestic idyll implicit in its title. Despite the long association of the hearth with the comfortably centred, even cosily ordered, life of the fully 'domesticated' self, the painting's effect is to turn the familiar experience of dreamy ember-gazing into a reorientating encounter with an unsuspected inner alterity. Even while the glowing coals radiate a reassuring warmth, they also reflect back to the gazer her own disconcerting 'anonymity', and thus hint at her essential strangeness to her 'self'. Here the traditionally nurturing image of the feminine 'spirit of the hearth', and therefore of the nourishingly familiar, is turned into an inscrutable sphinx, as the light from the fire completely erases that vital common source of expression (and index of personality), the mobile mouth.

Thomas's radically deconstructive approach to human selfhood as 'normally' experienced and conceived is everywhere evident in his reading of the Surrealists. It is again manifest in his interpretation of William Roberts's 'Dressmakers', although this time his emphasis is not on metaphysical recalibration but rather on a treatment of the human being – as much as the human body – as a vector of impersonal energies and desires. In the painting three chunky ladies, with 'avid faces', fuss around a customer, busily brandishing scissors as they trim the dress she is wearing to mould her slim figure. In rather cumbersome fashion, Thomas discerns a hint of the Classical Fates in this image, but more interestingly (if typically) he conceives of it also as representing the preparation of a garment 'towards which/ the muscular lover/ helplessly is being drawn'. The poem belongs, therefore, with those considered in the previous chapter, which feature the threatening power of the female; but it is also another means of articulating Thomas's concerns, in his Surrealist 'suite', with disaggregating the socially experienced self into the mysterious processes of which it is ephemerally composed.

One of the strategies of human self-estrangement Thomas was prompted by Surrealist paintings to adopt involved the merging of the human subject into the material world. In Magritte's 'La gravitation universelle', a soldier, rifle slung over his shoulder, reclines nonchalantly against a wall surmounted by pillared windows. Thomas read this as an emblem of the comic futility of 'self-defence' in the fundamental sense of that term – an attempt to defend a solid self, which was no more than a fictive construct. For him, the image clearly implied that the soldier was 'part/ of what he resists', the thronging molecules of his body being as material as the bricks out of which the wall was built. And, taking his clue from the title of the painting for once, Thomas noted how exactly the same forces were operative on the soldier as on the wall. As for what lay beyond the wall, in his estimation it was not any human enemy, only rabbits that, however 'perilously' they browsed, would always be sufficiently numerous to ensure ultimate 'immunity' for the species, whatever local havoc a rifle might wreak.

Thomas was attracted to the idea of the ultimate survival only of rabbits and their kind in a human-free world as an aid to focusing on the ephemerality of the human species. Hence his approving response to Edvard Munch's 'House under the Trees', largely consisting of a landscape bare of any living figure, humans being confined to a group of people in the bottom right hand corner of the picture. They huddle together as if, suggests Thomas, they were waiting for the 'Gestapo' of time to hurry them underground. His sympathy, though, is not so much with his human fellows as with the empty landscape quietly rejoicing in their absence. Similarly, he is appreciative of the deserted square in Le Sidanie's 'Au Café', because the artist has resisted all importunings to 'complete' the painting with figures. Instead, he is content that the carafes on the tables are full of neither water, nor wine, but simply of light. Both these poems are, then, meditative exercises in viewing the life of the human self *sub specie aeternitatis*. They remind us of one of Thomas's key tenets:

> Not electricity
> but the brush's piety
> affords divinity. (*CLP*, p. 289)

The savage attack mounted by Thomas in his mature religious poetry on the anthropomorphic character of conventional Christian belief is complemented in these late painting poems by his attack on humankind's infantile preference for an anthropocentric view of creation. As a corrective, and in order to discipline the human imagination into recognition of how it really is circumstanced, he reflects on the post-human landscapes he encounters in Surrealist art, some of which are post-apocalyptic in character. Such, for instance, are two paintings by Yves Tanguy, 'The Flight of the Dukes', and 'The extinction of the species'. Thomas values these for the weird emptiness of landscapes stretching to horizons that 'suggest// further horizons'.

> The appearance
> is of a landscape God
> looked at once and from which
> later he withdrew his gaze.

Even more evocative is Tanguy's 'Terre d'ombre', which is nothing but 'an undulating plain/ silent as/ a graveyard'. Nonplussed by the tree stumps that litter the landscape like headstones and disconcerted by the

300

anonymity of it all, even the Almighty doesn't know where to start on the business of resurrection.

'Mankind,' Eliot had once famously observed, 'cannot bear very much reality.' But Thomas is determined that at least more of that reality should be brought to the attention of his reluctant contemporaries, in the name of advancing their spiritual comprehension. In a fine poem of reflection on a Henry Moore sketch of a figure asleep in the shelters of the London Underground during the Second World War, Thomas sympathises with the mind's wish to escape in sleep the 'crackling meadows' of a city aflame above, but nevertheless ends by noting that in those blazing streets and among the levelled buildings survivors of the Blitz are already 'poking/ among the remains of others/ who were too brave to dream'. 'Too brave to dream': in its immediate context the phrase is, of course, a moving tribute to those dead fire-fighters and their comrades who had braved the bombing. But by legitimate extension it may be applied to Thomas's concern, throughout these poems, to demonstrate to those dreamers who in his view constitute the mass of his self-centred, and correspondingly self-deluded, contemporaries what it might mean to discover the courage to stay awake to the spiritual truths of their human condition.

What Thomas values about Dalí's 'Suburbs of the paranoiac-critical Town' is the reassuring impression it gives that 'despite the intimacy/ of the heartbeats from the church/ belfry, there are distances still'. The comment is typical of him. He hated the cosiness of conventional religious belief, believing it simply confirmed man in his infantile supposition that not only was this a universe in which to make oneself comfortably at home but also that the Almighty was a thoroughly domesticated and amenable deity at heart. And his attachment to the arts derived from a conviction that, at their greatest, they possessed a unique power to register that to live was to dwell among metaphysical 'distances' not even to be measured let alone to be crossed. Hence his appreciation of the impenetrability of Picasso's 'Painting', and the resistance of its constituent forms even to translation into identifiable objects. 'They are', he approvingly writes, 'as contraceptives/ allowing familiarity/ while incapacitating/ from breeding contempt.'

It is a convenient coincidence that the concern with the troubling 'otherness' in which all existence is rooted, and that is the deepest, most consistent, and most urgent strain to be detected in Thomas's painting poems, should find its most powerful symbol and expression in the very last of his responses to the Surrealists, when he is confronted by 'Hlaslesa' (fig. 13), an enigmatic image painted by Toyen based on a Czech legend about its subject, 'The Voice of the Wood'. Disconcerted by confronting an image unmistakeably resembling an owl, but lacking the raptor's identifying talons, beak and eyes, Thomas wonders what name to give 'something that has nothing/ but existence to deserve/ tenure'. (This last poem in the 'series', therefore, circles back to the first, in which Thomas imagines the artist Derain as painting in a vain response to his self's plea, 'Name me, name me'.) And although recognising in himself a strong, self-protective instinct to disown, by ignoring, this 'being' captured by Toyen, Thomas is compelled chillingly to confess that

> an echo
> far down in us
> responds to what
> as Stevens would remark
> looks at me without eyes
> and without a mouth speaks.

In this image, then, Thomas discovers, as his poem implies, a revelation of the perfect coincidence of the mystery of God and the ultimate, irreducible mystery of the 'self'. And in that image, too, he reaches the limits of all art. How can a being without eyes relate to a painting? And how can a mouthless being relish the art of language? Beyond limits there is only the everlasting finality of eternal silence. It is what Thomas meant when, deeply appreciating a brace of paintings by Tanguy, he concluded they were so saturated with silence that 'entrance' to the images could be 'by the eye only'. 'Amidst/ so much absence,' he concluded, meaning must 'appear/ as an absence of mind.'

Structuralism, post-structuralism, post-modernism, discourse theory – over the last few decades they have revolutionised understanding of interactions between image and text, consistently tending to the conclusion that the gap between the verbal and visual arts should be narrowed, if not eliminated, because both are semiotic structures, derivatives of merely provisional human systems of signification.[8] And although R. S. Thomas had no interest in such theories, there is a broad analogy between their conclusions and his own practice in his painting-poems. While his indifference to the separate 'integrity' of paintings – their moments and circumstances of origin, their 'foreign' language of form and colour, and their otherness to verbal forms of expression – may readily be taken as evidence of his ruthlessly 'appropriative', 'colonising' (and, some would doubtless add, 'masculine') approach to the visual arts, it is also susceptible of a different interpretation. Thomas's reading of most of these Surrealist paintings may be understood as based on the conviction that they have the same *raison d'être* as poems: being 'works of art' both are, in his view, necessarily concerned with the fundamental metaphysical truths about mankind's existential situation. That is why he shows no concern to understand paintings on, say, their painters' terms, because such terms are in his opinion irrelevant to their 'real' meaning. That, too, is why he is ready to ignore titles, those traditional signposts of meaning. It is, similarly, why he seems so often to read a painting 'against the grain' of what he would dismiss as the surface details cramming the canvas, distracting the eye and confusing the intelligence. His poems are spiritual X-rays, that look through all this in order to detect and expose the essential forms of the paintings in which their true, 'deep' meaning reside.

\* \* \*

In a pioneering study published thirty years ago, Wendy Steiner noted how modernist art had already anticipated many of the conclusions of post-modern theories of ekphrasis, by abandoning any claim to be 'mimetic'. Instead, artists began to emphasise 'the programmatic tension between artistic medium and represented world'.[9] For all his relatively conventional poetics, Thomas shared this scepticism about art's 'mirroring' capacities. As has already been seen, what he steadily came to value was art's power to interrogate what might be termed the 'reality

303

consensus' of modern, largely secularised society and to problematise human understanding of the established 'norms' of existence. Hence his steady decline of interest, as pointed out in the previous chapter, in the representational art with which he had been primarily concerned during his earlier career. And hence, too, his particular late interest in the work of the Surrealists, although not for their self-advertising claim of having penetrated to the securely locatable 'alternative reality' of the 'unconscious', with its bizarre sexual grammar. In his dissenting poems, he deliberately reads the Surrealists 'against the grain' of the movement's official agenda. While agreeing that their images are, indeed, rigorous inquisitors of constituted 'reality', he believes that their consciousness-bewildering strategies result in metaphysical disclosures. This 'metaphysical turn' is repeated, of course, in the work of many modernist artists, from Kandinsky to Rothko, but secular critics have frequently been too shy or embarrassed to confront it.

Thomas's journey from representational painting to post-representational painting was interestingly mirrored in *Ysbrydoliaeth/ Inspiration*, a striking exhibition held at Plas Glyn-y-Weddw, near Pwllheli, of work by nineteen Welsh-resident artists paying homage to his poetry.[10] Roughly half of these might be classified as representational in idiom, reflecting, perhaps, the many conventionally 'painterly' features and references to be found in Thomas's own early poems. These extend from his way of framing a scene in words, through his repeated reference to various kinds of art ('a water-colour's appeal/ To the mass') to his complex awareness, alluded to previously, of the way in which Wales was depopulated and deculturated through being reduced entirely to landscape in the colonising art of English Romantic painting. An early poem such as 'The Welsh Hill Country' is, in a sense, a savage critique of a picturesque Wales, its 'sheep. . ./ Arranged romantically in the usual manner', where the grim realities of economic and cultural decline have been prettily landscaped out of existence (*CP*, p. 22). And with its warning of how easily a beautiful land may be despoiled by an infestation of visitors, 'The Small Window' is obviously relevant to the picture-postcard Wales of the tourist industry:

> Those who crowd
> A small window dirty it
> With their breathing, though sublime
> And inexhaustible the view. (*CP*, p. 202)

Appropriately enough, therefore, *Inspiration* includes a Gwyneth Tomos painting that, with explicit reference to 'The Small Window,' places an arc of caravans slap in the middle of what is otherwise a parodically beguiling, chocolate-box image of stone cottages scattered across rough country overlooking a bay. The prettified image is highly coloured to enhance its glossy appeal. And if this is one case where a literalism of response by painting to poem seems highly appropriate and effective, another is Donald McIntyre's 'Winter'. Its *point d'appui* is a passage from Thomas's long poem 'The Minister', emphasising the fate of any dweller in Welsh hill-country as the seasons pass: to be fated to remain 'summer and winter through,/ Rooting in vain within his dwindling acre' (*CP*, p. 53). McIntyre, a confirmed disciple of the 'Scottish Colorists', confronts us with a thickly paint-laden canvas central to which is the massed form of the pine-end of a remote farm, one wing of its outbuildings roofless and exposed to the elements. This is set against a landscape in which substantial areas of earth and rock, formidable in their blackness, withstand the smothering whiteness of snow. Although it bulks large, a black-and-white cow, also viewed sideways-on, is virtually indistinguishable from its wintry surroundings, while, blackly silhouetted, a farmer cuts a bleakly solitary figure. Whether he is gazing towards us or away from us is impossible to tell. If the former, then he is staring at a building that, far from signifying refuge, seems to lie starkly across his way as if blocking his exit, turning the path on which he is standing into a dead end. If the latter is the case, then the farmer's humanity has been completely muted by his anonymity, and he has been reduced simply to a figure that seems a function of its landscape. McIntyre has, therefore, found a powerful visual equivalent for the plight of the poem's upland farmer, who looks out like the chapel minister 'on a grey world, grey with despair' (*CP*, p. 53).

An inappropriate concern with 'resemblance' of image to text can, however, produce the kind of unsatisfactory result we associate with literal translation. So, seemingly hypnotised by Thomas's invocation in 'Out of the Hills' of the hill farmer, 'dreams clustering thick on his sallow skull', working among 'Clouds of cattle breath, making the air heady' (*CP*, p. 1), Selwyn Jones ends up producing a painting melodramatic with dark, brooding, colours and depicting rather lamb-like cows being quizzically studied by workaday figures in no way corresponding to the semi-mythologised being of the poem. Vaughan Bevan's rendering of 'The Welsh Hill Country' seems likewise in no way to capture the ferocious anger of Thomas's attack on the visiting sight-seer, a town-dweller conveniently blinded by distance to the cruel truths about country living – the 'fluke and the foot-rot and the fat maggot' (*CP*, p. 22); the devastated farming communities, where nettles grow through cracked doors; and the farmers themselves, their health undermined by the harshness of their existence, once-sturdy frames wasting 'under the ripped coat[s]'. Bevan's painting of quietly crumbling farm buildings seems altogether too understated to match the focused fury of Thomas's poem. But it does prove more accountable to the text in another, unexpected way: the medium of watercolour is used to address the un-picturesque truth about what Thomas called 'the depopulation of the Welsh hill-country'. Thus, Bevan's painting effectively subverts a genteel medium invincibly (and no doubt unfairly) associated, in Thomas's mind, with the misrepresentations of Wales typical of the English Romantic topographical tradition. It eschews what Thomas had so scornfully called 'the watercolour's appeal/ To the mass', choosing instead to honour 'the poem's harsher conditions'.

Another example of watercolour being put to unexpected use is Peter Prendergast's 'Foothills of Tryfan', one of three images generated by 'Welsh Landscape', a poem that seems to act as a magnet for art. Prendergast is able to achieve effects in this medium normally associated with the oils of an artist like Kyffin Williams. By limiting his painting to thick daubs of purply blacks, densely dark browns and muddy greens, he moulds a landscape of chunkiness and cragginess, seemingly sunk in everlasting night appropriate to the poem's gloweringly atmospheric opening: 'To live in Wales is to be conscious/ At dusk of the spilled blood/ That went to the making of the wild sky,/ Dyeing the immaculate rivers' (*CP*, p. 37). Prendergast has commented that 'we should all know what Wales is about, for Wales does have a culture, a language and the roots of a visual language that simply needs encouraging in order to grow. I have always believed that the visual language in Wales should be a way of uniting and expressing the spirit of Wales.'[11] While specifically a painting of a famous mountain in the Snowdonia range of north Wales, Prendergast's 'Tryfan' is also infused with his memory of the hilly landscape of his different native region of south-east Wales, and is thus a deliberately composite 'Welsh Landscape', generic rather than local in character, just like the landscape invoked in Thomas's poem.

Emrys Parry, another artist drawn to the same poem, is attracted by a passage later in the text, marking its shift into gothic mode as it conjures up a paralysed land, haunted by the ghosts of its livid past: 'There is only the past,/ Brittle with relics', the 'thick ambush of shadows', and notoriously 'an impotent people,/ Sick with inbreeding,/ Worrying the carcase of an old song' (*CP*, p. 37). By restricting the palette of his oil painting to slatey purples darkening in places to a brownish hue, Parry captures the poem's angrily helpless sense of limited potential; while, by allowing an uprooted tree, its bark the pallor of dead bones, to lie laterally across the picture and blocking the 'view', he establishes the impression of a skeletally gaunt landscape. On the horizon looms a single mountain, miniaturised by distance, the flattened cone of its dark silhouette resembling that of an extinct volcano. Gwilym Pritchard also dyes his oil painting the purple of the spilled blood of 'Welsh Landscape', while a dark central image rises upwards and spreads outwards like a stain, or gash, or tree, or flowing river ghosted by a purplish white moon. In its powerful indeterminacy, this nexus of images corresponds to Thomas's sense of confronting an illegible landscape, full of mysterious hints, and whispers and sounds: 'There are cries in the dark at night/ As owls answer the moon,/ And thick ambush of shadows,/ Hushed at the fields' corners' (*CP*, p. 37).

All these images are painterly tone-poems; free, expressionist 'equivalents' of Thomas's work; mood-music to accompany his poetry. They testify to the painter's having been put into a way of feeling and seeing by the text, thereby affirming the extraordinary evocative power of the writing and the sensuousness of its effects. What they do not address, however, is the electrifying charge of cultural concern in 'Welsh Landscape', as in all of Thomas's poems relating to the condition of his own country. It is Iwan Bala whose highly sophisticated visual idiom, deliberately developed to enable a cartographical rendering of a people's cultural identity, is perhaps best suited to capture this seminal aspect of the poetry. Bala has always been interested in what might be termed the 'symbolic geography' of such identity, including the plethora of visual signifiers of which it is partly composed, and he resembles the early R. S. Thomas in particular in his dedication to what he has termed a 'custodial aesthetics' – the creation of images dedicated to the maintenance of an historically informed national consciousness. Rather, however, than adopt what might be termed traditional, Romantic means of promoting cultural awareness, Bala often employs eclectic post-colonial and postmodernist methods, suffused with a playfully sceptical humour, to dismantle barren and inappropriate national stereotypes. In this respect, too, his enterprise bears a certain resemblance to R. S. Thomas's undertaking in a volume such as *Welsh Airs* – a work whose very title (as noted in chapter 4) is a corrosively playful multiple pun, incorporating 'Welsh heirs', 'Welsh [musical] airs', and reference to the 'airs and graces' of Welsh self-conceit. Poet and artist thus share the campaigning aim of creating an 'alternative iconography' for their nation.[12]

Iwan Bala's interest in dismantling the gallery of images that have long been instrumental in perpetuating his nation's cultural subordination derives, of course, from his alertness to modern Wales's 'post-colonial' condition. And he has been guided in his search for an alternative visual vocabulary, expressive of his country's true, authentic distinctiveness, by the work of artists from such other post-colonial nations as Cuba, Zimbabwe, the Basque Country and Ireland. His participation during the 1980s in the agit-prop activities of the group of Welsh artists that constituted Beca was consistent with an admiration for the radically deconstructive work of another influential Welsh artist of that period, the militantly Europhile Ivor Davies, whose commitment to the calculated derangements of a liberation Surrealism found literally explosive expression in his practice of a 'Destruction in Art'.[13]

The condition of a people chronically depressed by long colonial suppression is the subject of R. S. Thomas's poem 'A Land'. And this is a subject that resonates powerfully for Iwan Bala. The poem is full of the brooding ferocity of Thomas's repressed rage at a population of valley-dwellers, anaemically pale figures cowed by the shadow cast by their steep mountains, spindly with spiritual in-breeding – 'winding themselves about each other/ inhibiting growth' (*CP*, p. 465). This is a death-haunted scene, whose occupants 'look at it through the eternal downpour of their tears', while the inevitable 'chapel crouches,/ a stone monster, waiting to spring' (*CP*, p. 465). Yet from such an unpromising building, the emblem of a nation's captivity, rises 'not music/ so much as the sound of a nation/ rending itself, fierce with all the promise/ of a beauty that might have been theirs' (*CP*, p. 465).

And Iwan Bala's response? True to his interests in naïve art, he abandons perspective to give us mountains, river, terraced houses and chapel, rendered in the simplified, short-hand forms of a child's scrawlings, and all placed on the same single visual plane (fig. 14). The beehive hills are rendered in a black that spills down and out over a large section of lowland and is then repeated in the thick black outlines of the rudimentary forms of the houses, chapel and river lurking down in the valley, that are set against a background of darkish pinky brown. That colour in its turn is repeated in the band of blank sky and bland stretch of land lying athwart the top of the picture as if viewed at a distance beyond a simple expanse of water, its unrelieved deep cobalt blue again repeated as a great slab of colour at the bottom of the picture out of which is cut a pinky brown arc (mirroring the beehive shape of the hills above), variously suggesting half an egg, or the slightly distorted half of a flattened globe. In the overall monotony of its effect, the work (emulsion perspex) is perfectly faithful to the depressed spirit of the poem.

But, as with the poem, the 'subconscious' of the painting seethes with thwarted potentialities. As Iwan Bala has remarked, his avowed aim has always been to 'regain painting [from modernist formalism] and bring it back from the abstract level to the narrative' (*WPT*, p. 194), and so it is to ancient legends and myths that he has repeatedly found himself drawn in his search for national story. Those rounded hills in his painting suggest the 'twmps', or ancient burial mounds, around which legends have accrued throughout Wales. But they also feminise the landscape, in stylised iconic tribute to the powerful goddesses of the Celtic and pre-Celtic past. For the artist, 'the fertility of this landscape woman' is suggestive of 'the birth of Welsh consciousness' (*WPT*, p. 197). His scene is therefore full of images instinct with potential but drawn from the ancient, ancestral memory not only of a people but of the land itself. It is the 'land [that] remembers', as one historian has put it, a concept memorably captured by the great artist-poet David Jones in several of his classic composite images and texts, and hence Iwan Bala's interest in installations and other projects of landscape art. In his painting, the squiggled form of the river, too, brings with it not only suggestions of the birth canal but memories of the snake and its mysterious, arcane powers of eternal self-renewal, while into that strange arc that suddenly invades the painting from the bottom are compressed suggestions of the cosmic egg of creation. This indeterminate shape also seems to float into view like an island, which Iwan Bala connects with the ancient Greek idea of 'Omphalos, the Greek word that now has universal meaning as island in a sea of chaos' (*WPT*, p. 197). And read in the light of these ancient emblems, the crudely delineated forms of houses and chapel begin to take on another aspect: with their thick black outlines, they resemble the shapes drawn on walls by burned sticks in the great cave art of prehistory (*WPT*, p. 197).

So closely aligned in their politico-aesthetic convictions are R. S. Thomas and Iwan Bala it comes as no surprise that, in this case, there is such a suggestive correspondence between image and text. A like affinity is evident in two other images from the exhibition, both employing a minimalist idiom in keeping with the stripped-down bareness of Thomas's late religious verse. Austerity of palette and of form is the feature of Alice Mroczkowska's 'Trust'. Restricting her colours to limited shades of brown and off-white, she places the radically simplified shape of a grubby white church at the centre of her design. With its tower surmounted by a modestly plain cross and buttressed by two sloping wings, it strikingly resembles a space rocket poised for lift-off. Out of one of these wings a simple door is abruptly cut, against which a miniature figure is crudely silhouetted. The whole design works in effective counter-point to Thomas's poem 'Tidal'. 'Counterpoint', because Mroczkowska's image is by no means a visual trace of the line of thought of a poem in which Thomas uses tropes from the natural world to convey the fluctu-ations of his prayerful spirit. Like the waves as they come ashore, 'I run/ up the approaches of God/ and fall back'; despair is his 'ebb-tide'; and by the poem's ending he trusts to 'discovering somewhere/ among his fissures deposits of mercy' (CLP, p. 167). Instead, Mroczkowska's oil painting functions like a silent simile, as it calls to mind the resemblance between 'Tidal' and other poems by Thomas in which he likens his hopeful prayers to probes sent out in search of a 'God-space'. Thus, she confirms the impression left implicit in 'Tidal' that, far from being a passing mood, what Thomas is here describing is for him a settled state of soul; a chronic uncertainty of spiritual belief, albeit differently troped in different poems. And additionally, there may lurk another allusion behind her rocket-like image of the church; a reference to Thomas's im-placable hostility to the arms race and its stock-piling of long-distance nuclear missiles. Finally, deeply appreciative as Thomas was of the po-tency of puns, so there may be a pun on 'rock' in this painting of a church in the form of a rock-et, just as buried beneath the concluding image of 'Tidal' ('discovering/ among his fissures deposits of mercy') may lie the memory of 'Rock of Ages, cleft for me'.

After the death of his first wife, Thomas's hermit instinct intensified, resulting in such poems of systematic dis-possession as 'At the End'. included in the last collection published before his death, where he is left only with

> a chair,
> a table, a bed
> to say my prayers by,
> and, gathered from the shore,
> the bone-like, crossed sticks
> proving that nature
> acknowledges the Crucifixion.[14]

This is the setting he finds most conducive to meditation:

> All night I am at
> a window not too small
> to be frame to the stars
> that are no further off
> than the city lights
> I have rejected. (*NTF*, p. 42)

It is to this scene that one of Thomas's favourite artists, Wil Rowlands, is drawn (fig. 15). Choosing card, not canvas, as an appropriately humble base for his oil painting, he places bed, chair and table on an inclined plane that also accommodates wall and ceiling. The viewer is thus disconcerted as each object, carefully detached from every other to cancel any sense of cosy communal occupancy, seems not so much free standing as free floating in zero gravity. The resultant impression is of what might be termed undomesticated space – space that is feral, like outer space itself, the 'background' colours (although there is no sense of spatial depth) being a watery whitish blue and an off-white (echoed in the chillingly pristine bed-linen) that creates the effect of a dust-cloud similar to a cosmic nursery of the stars. The tiny window, pinpricked with the yellow of stars, is partly obscured by this cloud as if, cosy domesticity having leaked out, this narrow aperture had admitted an outer space and was now being omnivorously engulfed by it. This is no ordinary bedroom but a monastic cell conceived of as a spiritual space capsule.

* * *

Painting-poems and painting poems: there is an interesting history to this inter-art practice in twentieth-century Wales that has been well documented in such volumes as *Imaging the Imagination*.[15] Poets writing both in English and in Welsh have been attracted to paintings. Among the latter are Euros Bowen, Bryan Martin Davies, Alan Llwyd, R. Gerallt Jones, Mererid Hopwood, Christine James, Damian Walford Davies Menna Elfyn, along with the many poets who have been invited by the National Eisteddfod over recent years to respond to the paintings on display in its art exhibition. And among the former may be numbered Dannie Abse, Gillian Clarke, Tony Conran, Tony Curtis, Jeremy Hooker,

Glyn Jones, Nigel Jenkins, Rowan Williams, Pascale Petit and John Ormond, whose virtuosic 'Certain Questions for Monsieur Renoir' is an inexhaustible cascade of tributary improvisations, a riff on all the modalities of blue that constitute 'La Parisienne':

> She has been dead now nearly a century
> Who wears that blue of smoke curling
> Beyond a kiln, and blue of gentians,
> Blue of lazurite, turquoise hauled
>
> Over the blue waves[.][16]

This is a hymn of praise in the form of a sensual love poem to the medium of paint such as the verbal ascetic R. S. Thomas (of whom Ormond made a superb film study) could never conceivably have written. It is hard to imagine Ormond being contented, as Thomas was, with black-and-white colour reproductions of the 'paintings' about which his poems were written.

Welsh painters, in their turn, have reciprocated the interest of the poets. Two of the closest friends of the fledgling Dylan Thomas were Alfred Janes and Mervyn Levy, while another Swansea artist, Ceri Richards, found in Thomas's 'process' poems, full of the violent dialectic of life and death, biomorphic images electrifyingly similar to those that restlessly invaded his own canvasses. The result was the famous set of lithographs for Tambimuttu's *Poetry London* (1945) based on 'The force that through the green fuse'. Richards subsequently went on to produce luminous visual responses to Vernon Watkins's majestic 'Music of Colours' poems and in 1965 commemorated the poet's work in the form of a series of quietly vibrant prints.[17]

The contemporary artist Ivor Davies has drawn on the creative work of Waldo Williams and Saunders Lewis to construct major mythopoeic canvasses dedicated to the theme of what he has characterised as 'the memory of an ancient culture', which are his attempt at 'retrieving from cultural theft' (*WAT*, pp. 145, 147). And his tribute to R. S. Thomas – a visual meditation on his poem 'Senior' – is very much in the same vein. Above a woman's sleeping head, confined to the painting's bottom right corner, rises a mysterious night landscape, its ancientness suggested by a shadowy druidic figure whose miniature trident gestures towards a vast sky, darkening from a cumulus white to a deep blue. Into this night-scape rises the spire of a tall obelisk, surmounted by a faint crescent moon balanced on the other side of the picture by a much larger, fuller but fainter crescent moon, visibly pregnant with its own mature shape. Insofar as all this is a woman's dream, it could be said to be a tribute to the formidable creative power of goddesses in Celtic mythology, as if the modern sleeper were the unwitting muse of a sleeping land. But that land, in turn, although Welsh, is for Davies one in its ancientness with the lands of Egypt and of Africa. The work both of the Surrealists and their predecessors the Symbolists clearly haunt Davies's canvas, and if Jung has been one influence, then Freud has been another – the phallic trident and upwardly thrusting obelisk are both obvious signifiers of the ancient intercourse between earth and heaven from which all life pro-ceeded according to the primal fertility religions.

And the relation of this to Thomas's poem? It has a double aspect. First, Davies's oil painting is a visual invocation of the vastness of time and space and their eternal indissoluble unity as captured in Thomas's lines:

> The stars relay to the waste
> places of the earth, as they do
> to the towns, but it is
> a cold message. (*CP*, p. 387)

And, second, the painting is a realisation, in tonal colour and image, of the concluding lines of 'Senior':

> A man's shadow
> falls upon rocks that are
> millions of years old, and
> thought comes to drink at that dark
> pool, but goes away thirsty. (*CP*, p. 387)

Also of interest, in the present context, is the inter-art work of painter-writers like Brenda Chamberlain and David Jones. By not only alternating between writing and painting but periodically choosing to fuse the two into a single complex composite medium, Chamberlain seems to have found a mixed form of creative expression exactly matching her own indeterminate, liminal – and possibly trans-gendered – personality. And by transfiguring word itself into image, the devout Catholic Jones was able to produce iconic objects deeply suggestive of the mystery of transubstantiation central to the sacrament of the Eucharist.

With its roughly formed lettering – 'the tree of poetry that is eternity wearing the green leaves of time' – circling around the central stylised design of a tree whose foliage encloses the silhouettes of an ark, a fish and a downward plunging dove, Tony Goble's acrylic, 'The Prayer', recalls David Jones's set of prints imaging the Flood. The whole corresponds well to a recurrent trope in Thomas's later work, of poetry as the modern equivalent of the salvatory Ark which, in Christian typographical tradition, had always been seen as an emblem of the Church. But the whole design is given a bizarre Gothic twist, connecting it to medieval mortuary tradition, since the tree arises out of a bone in a skeletal figure complete with death's head skull. It is through the introduction of this macabre element that Goble succeeds in paying tribute simultaneously (as his dedication confirms) both to R. S. Thomas and to the Baudelaire of *Fleurs du Mal*. The whole design constitutes an ingenious comment on a poem ('The Prayer') in which a Thomas, who is experiencing a crisis of seeming spiritual death, feels a final desperate prayer welling unexpectedly up in him: 'Let leaves/ from the deciduous Cross/ fall on us, washing/ us clean, turning our autumn/ to gold by the affluence of their fountain' (*CP*, p. 270).

Literature and the visual arts are each a distinct semiotic system, self-enclosed and self-regulating. Only within such a system could a connection between R. S. Thomas and Baudelaire, such as Goble's image signals, be meaningfully made. And by tacitly acknowledging that poems circulate within an economy of interdependent signs that is closed to paintings, that circulate within a similar economy of their own, his work confirms the partial truth of a comment made by Saunders Lewis – one of the major creative and political figures of twentieth-century Welsh intellectual life and a profound influence on Thomas's outlook as noted in chapter 4 – in a 1954 review of a Cardiff exhibition entitled 'Thirty Welsh Paintings of Today':

> But one cannot translate from paint to language [or, conversely, from language to paint]. One must stare meditatively and eagerly to receive what the picture says. Perhaps one can discover an akin-ness between M. Eldridge's Corris pen and the poetry of R. S. Thomas, but what is told the eye and what is told the ear are two different things.[18]

Leslie Jones's work, by contrast, exposes the limitations of Lewis's comment. By fashioning a single, composite image of double tribute, he manages to acknowledge both the internal economy of poetry and the internal economy of painting simultaneously. Thereby he succeeds in succinctly implying that both signifying systems can be treated as cognate and their products accordingly as interchangeable. By entitling his work in wax and crayon '"Nocturne by Ben Shahn" and "Ah!" by R.S.T. Homage to both', he manages a further fusion of the two art forms, since 'Nocturne' is a celebrated Shahn poster-painting of 1970, while 'Nocturne by Ben Shahn' is the corresponding poem by Thomas from *H'm*. In Jones's title, therefore, a graphic image is enfolded within a poem title and, in addition, his painting is in part about a poem's version of a painting.

As for his work itself, it subdivides into an upper and a lower half. The former is filled by a reproduction of Shahn's 'Nocturne', featuring two black figures in conversation, one of whom cradles a guitar. In the lower section, a cartoon image of a thoughtful R. S. Thomas, one hand raised to mouth, the other resting on the inverted texts of the two poems mentioned in the title, is placed against a blue and white background of stylised swirling smoke and flame. The tendrils of an arterial 'tree', running from bottom to top, provides the design with its blood-red right-hand margin. What this complex composite image highlights is the way in which the metaphor of fire binds together both of the R.S. poems, as it also binds together image and poems, and provides the means of linking Jones's art-work to Shahn's poster. And the metaphor performs this function partly through the inherent multivalence of its meaning. In 'Ah!', fire is a trope for the cruel torturing life-energy of flesh-and-blood existence; while in 'Nocturne for Ben Shahn', it is a figure for the charged source of artistic creativity, and its perilous power to arouse and capture the dangerous energies of the self – to electrify the arteries with coursing blood. These two different uses of fire arise, of course, from a single root, a common assumption: that the artist is one who composes (word, or music, or image) by riskily laying herself open to the terrible consuming wonder of life. And this is what Jones's design seeks to signify, making of Thomas's contemplative figure a bridge between written text and performed music and showing poet and musicians alike surrounded by the smoke and flames of raging internal fire that metamorphoses, beyond a notionally sketched window frame, into a latticework of red suggesting both a network of veins and a tree of life. This synthesis of three different art forms (literature, painting and music) is the appropriate production of a painter who was inspired by a poet who took inspiration from a painter and is thus in itself proof of the partial translatability (*pace* Saunders Lewis) of one art form into another. Or rather, perhaps, it exposes the narrow limits of Lewis's concept of 'translation'.

Contrasting with Jones's empathetic response to the more tortured aspects of the work of Thomas and Shahn is Alex Campbell's witty visual commentary both on Cézanne's famous painting 'The Card Players', and Thomas's corresponding poem. Thomas reads this as a picture of boredom, seeing in the lugubrious intensity of the participants nothing but the solemn ritual of killing time: 'their minds/ lazily as flies/ drift/ round and round the inane/ problem their boredom/ has led them to pose' (*CP*, p. 369). By isolating the word 'drift' and thus insisting that it alone absorbs as much of our attention, and therefore time, as longer phrases as 'round and round the inane . . .', Thomas has his poem warp time to a temporary standstill, as Cézanne seems to do in his painting. Campbell, however, will have none of this. Mockery can sometimes be the sincerest form of flattery, and his lively depiction of four smug-looking transport workers (bus or railway) enjoying – or so their sly expressions seem to suggest – a sneakily unofficial rest-break is a work very much in the spirit of such irreverent poetic tributes to R. S. Thomas's monumentally morose 'Iago Prytherch' as those delicious ones by Bryn Griffiths or Harri Webb.[19] Like Webb, Campbell manages to back-light Thomas's work, his jaunty painting with its clean blocks of colour emphasising by contrast the brooding disenchanted intensity that Thomas's frequently lugubrious painting-poems share with the main body of his secular and spiritual work.

\* \* \*

What the Plas Glyn-y-Weddw exhibition demonstrated was that some of the most thoughtful, imaginative and perceptive interpretative commentaries on Thomas's poems have come in the form of paintings. It also testified to the fact that his hold on the mental landscapes of Welsh artists was as strong as his hold on the minds of Welsh creative writers (to which attention was drawn at the beginning of this study). And, given the liberties taken by some of the artists, and the felicitous infidelities that could result, one might perhaps be a little more inclined to forgive R. S. Thomas for the cavalier way with paintings – if not the wilful blindness to colour – that understandably dismayed his artist-wife. Many of these painters employ strategies similar to those adopted by Thomas. In particular, instead of adopting an holistic approach to a poem by creating a visual image intended to incorporate the complex totality of the chosen text's signifying structure, they treat one particular phrase, or line, or image, as germinal – as if it included the whole poem in embryo – and allow that to generate the proliferating visual imagery of their painting. This method of textual interpretation is suggestively similar to that pioneered by Coleridge in the *Biographia Literaria* and elsewhere – and Coleridge's concepts of literature had a longstanding influence on the thinking and creative practice of R. S. Thomas. There is, then, an interesting correspondence of method between this body of poem-paintings and Thomas's painting-poems, and between them they exemplify the fruitful possibilities of a conversation between art forms.

And artists have continued to be drawn to Thomas's work, developing an interest in it almost as obsessive, in some cases, as his own notorious concerns. Over the past dozen years, for instance, Christine Kinsey has produced several series of images acknowledging Thomas as her spirit-guide through 'an interior "odyssey" of self discovery'.[20] Her creative intimacy with Thomas dates back to 2000, when she recognised an uncanny coincidence between his own preoccupations and hers. Reading *Collected Poems, 1945–1990*, she found in 'The Gap' (*CP*, p. 287) intimations, uncannily similar to her own, of being at once existentially 'unhoused' and yet creatively at home with some greater presence (fig. 16). Then came a further shock of recognition. Turning the page, she discovered Thomas's poem on 'The Annuncation by Veneziano' (*CP*, 288), a painting instancing compositionally the mysterious gap between 'the spiritual and the material worlds' that she had spent the previous five summers pondering in Siena by looking at a series of Annunciation paintings. Kinsey felt certain that Thomas, like herself, had recognised that this 'gap is where the artist could become himself', and her work over the past dozen years has been devoted to the intensive working through of this conviction. Her resultant work, like that of the Plas Glyn-y-Weddw group, constitutes compelling evidence that some contemporary artists feel a kinship with Thomas, sensing perhaps that the poet's interest in visual images was lifelong, intelligent and deeply serious, and that it had occupied his imagination as profoundly as, albeit less conspicuously than, those *idées fixes* – Iago, Wales, the self, his mother and, of course, God – conventionally acknowledged to be the great obsessive subjects of his poetry.

## Notes

1. I am very grateful to Gwydion Thomas and family, and to Tony Brown and Jason Walford-Davies at the R. S. Thomas Research Centre (Bangor University) for permission to quote from this body of material.

2. Herbert Read, *Art Now: an introduction to the theory of modern painting and sculpture* (London: Faber and Faber, 1933 (*AN*); quotations from second edition, 1968); Herbert Read (ed.), *Surrealism* (London: Faber and Faber, 1936 (*S*)).

3. Thomas's careless way with paintings is exposed and censured in Robert Rehder, 'R. S. Thomas's Poems about Paintings', *Renascence: Essays on Value in Literature*, LX: 2, Winter 2008 (special R. S. Thomas edition), 83–102. Contrast Helen Vendler, 'R. S. Thomas and Painting', in M. Wynn Thomas (ed.), *The Page's Drift: R. S. Thomas at Eighty* (Bridgend: Seren Books, 1993), pp. 57–81; Dennis O'Driscoll, 'R. S. Thomas and the Poetry of Paintings,' *Agenda: A Tribute to R. S. Thomas*, 36: 2, 38–48.

4. Read is at this point quoting from Wilhelm Worringer, *Form in Gothic* (London: Putnam's, 1927), p. 29.

[5] Read adopts a lengthy passage from Coleridge's *Miscellaneous Criticism* (celebrating the 'strange . . . self-power of the imagination') as epigraph for *Surrealism*. And he also incorporates several quotations from Coleridge about the powers of the imagination into the body of his discussion (pp. 124ff.). He then follows up with extended discussion of Coleridge's key concepts (pp. 133ff.).

[6] Tony Brown, *R. S. Thomas* (Cardiff: University of Wales Press, 2006); Katie Gramich, 'Mirror Games: Self and [M]Other in the Poetry of R. S. Thomas', in Damian Walford Davies (ed.), *Echoes to the Amen; Essays After R. S. Thomas* (Cardiff: University of Wales, 2003), pp. 132–48.

[7] Kristeva's theories of abjection are applied interestingly to Welsh writers in Harri Garrod Roberts, *Embodying Identity; Representations of the Body in Welsh Literature* (Cardiff: University of Wales Press, 2009).

[8] See, for instance, Jane Hedley, 'Introduction: The Subject of Ekphrasis', in Jane Hedley, Nick Halpern and Willard Spiegelman (eds), *In the Frame: Women's Ekphrastic Poetry from Marianne Moore to Susan Wheeler* (Newark: University of Delaware Press, 2009), pp. 15–40.

[9] Wendy Steiner, *The Colors of Rhetoric: Problems in the Relation between Modern Literature and Painting* (London: University of Chicago Press, 1987), p. xi.

[10] *Ysbrydoliaeth R. S. Thomas Inspiration: A Book to accompany an Exhibition, 1995* (Plas Glyn-y-Weddw: Cyfeillion Oriel Glyn-y-Weddw, 1995).

[11] *Welsh Painters Talking to Tony Curtis* (Bridgend: Seren Books, 1997), p. 112. Hereafter *WPT*.

[12] R. S. Thomas, *Welsh Airs* (Bridgend: Poetry Wales Press, 1987).

[13] *Welsh Artists Talking to Tony Curtis* (Bridgend: Seren Books, 2000), p. 116. Hereafter *WAT*.

[14] R. S. Thomas, 'At the End', in *No Truce with the Furies* (Tarset: 1995), p. 42. The cover of this volume, a detail of a painting by Wil Rowlands, was that rarity for his books, an image of Thomas's own choosing.

[15] Christine Kinsey and Ceridwen Lloyd-Morgan (eds), *Imaging the Imagination: An Exploration of the Relationship between the Image and the Word in the Art of Wales* (Llandysul: Gomer, 2005). Hereafter *II*.

[16] John Ormond, *Selected Poems* (Bridgend: Poetry Wales Press, 1987), p. 75.

[17] See Tony Curtis, '"Life's miraculous poise between light and dark": Ceri Richards and the Poetry of Vernon Watkins', *Welsh Writing in English 9* (2004), 80–101.

[18] Quoted in Kinsey and Lloyd-Morgan, *Imaging the Imagination*, p. 127.

[19] Harri Webb, 'Ianto Rhydderch: Tch Tch', in Meic Stephens (ed.), *Harri Webb: Collected Poems* (Llandysul: Gomer, 1995), pp. 140–1.

[20] All quotations from Christine Kinsey that follow are taken from private correspondence, reproduced with her kind permission.

# Index

Aberdaron 90, 107
Aberystwyth 54, 95
Abse, Dannie 264, 312
'Absinthe' (Degas) 281
Abstract Expressionism 266
Act of Union (1536) 101, 103
'Addoldy-y-Bedyddwyr,
    Glyndyfrdwy' (Eldridge) 46–7
Adler, Jankel 298
aerial warfare 18, 19, 20, 21–2, 43
American Academy of Arts and
    Letters 241
*Anathémata, The* (David Jones) 212
'Ancient Mariner, The' (Coleridge)
    208, 215
Aneurin 164
Anglesey 37, 38, 57, 95, 107, 147, 201
Anglican Church 47, 112, 163, 253,
    264
Anglo-Irish literature 94–5, 97
Anglo-Welsh literature 93–4, 95, 95,
    97, 109, 149, 153
*Architectural Review* 47
Arnold, Matthew 1, 40, 44–5
*Arolwg* 89

*Art Now: An Introduction to the Theory
    of Modern Painting* (Read) 293,
    294
*Art Quarterly* 50
Arthur 84
Ashbery, John 263, 266
'Au café' (Le Sidanie) 300
Auden, W. H. 263

Bala, Iwan 308, 309–10
'Balcony, The' (Manet) 231–2
Bangor 123
*Barddoniaeth y Chwedegau* (Llwyd)
    85
Barnie, John 130
'Bas-Bréau Road, The' (Monet) 231
Basque Country, the 308
Baudelaire, Charles 315
Bazille, Frédéric 231, 279, 280
BBC Radio Cymru 8
'Beach at Saint-Adresse, The'
    (Jongkind) 271
Beca 308
Beckett, Samuel 185, 213
Behmen, Jacob 173

'Belle Angèle, La' (Gauguin) 183–4, 281–2
Berenson, Bernard 42
Bergson, Henri 148
Berryman, John 263
*Beti a'i Phobl* 8
Betjeman, John 47
Bevan, Vaughan 306
Bianchi, Tony 109
Bible, the 112
Bigge, John Selby 276, 277, 278
*Biographia Literaria* (Coleridge) 295, 318
Black Mountain poets 266
Blake, William 120–1, 175, 244, 250
Blanchot, Maurice 171
Blodeuwedd 134
Bloom, Harold 214
Boas, Franz 23
Bonhoeffer, Dietrich 179–80, 186, 190
Borges, Jorge Luis 9, 145, 178, 213, 219–20, 221–2, 223, 224–5, 226–7, 229–30, 232, 234, 235, 236–9
'Borges and I' (Borges) 235
Borrow, George 44, 46
Boston 164
Bosworth, battle of 82
Bourne, Mark 50
Bowen, Euros 264, 312
Brecon 55
Breconshire 24
Breton, André 294
'Breton Landscape, the Mill' (Gauguin) 276
'Bridge at Maincy, The' (Cézanne) 272–3
*Britain and the Beast* 40
British Museum 41
Brown, Tony 9
Browne, Sir Thomas 213
Brueghel, Pieter 263
Bultman, Rudolf 186

Byrd, William 209

Cader Idris 31
'Caer Arianrhod' (Saunders Lewis) 167–8
Caernarfon 105, 106, 107, 165
Campbell, Alex 317–18
Canada 263
*Canterbury Tales, The* 41
*Canu Heledd* 158, 161–2
*Canu Llywarch Hen, see* Llywarch Hen sequence
Capel Celyn 87, 102
'Captain Cook's Last Voyage' (Penrose) 234, 290
'Card Players, The' (Cézanne) 317
Cardiff 8, 38, 94, 102, 195, 316
Cardiff Free Library 48
Cardigan Bay 54, 90
*Caseg Broadsheets* 15
Cassatt, Mary 281
Catholicism 244
Catraeth, battle of 164
Ceiriog (John Ceiriog Hughes) 81
Ceiriog Valley 38
*Celtic Heritage* (Rees and Rees) 28
Ceredigion 48
'Certain Questions for Monsieur Renoir' (Ormond) 313
Cervantes, Miguel de 238
Cézanne, Paul 51, 241, 246, 251, 272, 317
Chagall, Marc 244
Chamberlain, Brenda 13, 14, 15, 314–15
chapels 43, 46–7, 112
Charles, prince of Wales 105–6, 165
Chaucer, Geoffrey 41
Chester, battle of 150
Chirico, Giorgio de 56
Chirk 38, 45, 153, 154, 282
Christianity 189, 190, 215, 220, 224–5, 239, 244

'Circular Ruins' (Borges) 237
Clancy, Joseph P. 168
Clarach 54
Clarke, Gillian 264, 312
Clarke, Sir Kenneth 39, 283
Claudel, Paul 117
CND 107, 159
Cnicht, the 54
Coleridge, S. T. 40, 133–4, 148, 208,
    214, 215, 295, 318
Coles, Don 263
Collected Poems, 1945–1990 319
colonialism 40, 45, 49, 52, 53–4, 55, 56,
    58, 59, 60, 309
'Come into Animal Presence'
    (Levertov) 244
Committee on the Employment of
    Artists in Wartime 39, 282–3
Commons and Footpaths Protection
    Society 40
'Composition' (Bigge) 276, 277
Concluding Unscientific Postscript
    (Kierkegaard) 172, 175–6
Conran, Tony 15, 264, 312
conscientious objectors 13–14, 155
Coriolanus (Shakespeare) 136
Corpus Dionysiacum 225
Corris 316
'Cosmography in four books'
    (Heylyn) 255
Cotman, John Sell 41
Council for the Preservation of Rural
    England 40
Cowper, William 45
CPRW annual report (1967–8) 42
Crabbe, George 45
Crane, Hart 141
Cumbria 149
Curtis, Tony 264, 312
Cymdeithas yr Iaith Gymraeg 80, 90,
    96, 104, 105, 107, 159, 160, 165
'Cynddilig' (T. Gwynn Jones) 152–3,
    157–8

cynghanedd 68, 125, 149, 150, 228

Dafydd ap Gwilym 28
Daily Telegraph 3, 7
Dalí, Salvador 233, 301
Damnés de la Terre, Les (Fanon) 52
'Dancing Class, The' (Degas) 282
'David' (Adler) 298
David, saint 100
Davidson, Michael 265, 266
Davies, Bryan Martin 264, 312
Davies, Damian Walford 312
Davies, Hugh Sykes 295
Davies, Idris 15, 16
Davies, Ivor 308, 313–14
Davies, Jason Walford 147
Davies, Pennar 13
Davis, William Virgil 8
Degas, Edgar 27, 273–4, 281, 282, 283,
    285–6
Denbigh 14
depression, the 15, 16, 56, 99–100
Derain, André 275–6, 295–6, 297, 302
Derrida, Jacques 182
devolution referendum (1979) 108;
    (1997) 108
Dickinson, Emily 68, 124, 207, 243
'Dilyw, 1939, Y' (Saunders Lewis)
    99–100
Donne, John 140, 141
Dove, Rita 263
'Drawing by a Child' (Lee) 286, 287
'Dressmakers' (William Roberts) 299
Dun Laoghaire 85
Dwymyn, Y (T. Gwynn Jones) 152

Eastwood, Clint 50
Ecco Press 263
'Ecstasy, The' (Donne) 140
'Edvard Munch poems' (Coles) 263
Edward I 106
Eglwys-Fach 155, 156, 157, 162, 208
Einstein, Albert 231, 232

ekphrastic poetry 183–4, 230–4, 264–90, 293, 294, 295–6, 297–303, 312–13, 316, 317
Eldridge, Mildred (Elsi) 38–9, 41–2, 43, 44, 45, 46, 47–9, 50, 51, 53, 56, 60, 282–3, 316, 318
Elfyn, Menna 312
Eliot, T. S. 6, 21, 73, 93, 227, 301
Elizabeth I 48
Éluard, Paul 234, 289
England 5, 24, 26, 39, 40, 41, 43, 44, 49, 51, 53, 55, 71, 80, 94, 103, 106, 108, 156, 203
English, the 5, 23, 26, 42, 43, 45–7, 73
English language 5, 15, 80, 83, 85, 87, 88, 95, 96, 97
English topographical tradition 41, 49, 53, 54–5, 56, 60
*englynion* 149, 151, 162, 166
environment, the 41, 42, 47, 107, 133, 180, 249, 250
Ernst, Max 234, 289
Eryri 107; *see also* Snowdonia
Etheridge, Ken 14
evacuees 15, 26–7
Evans, Caradoc 95, 96
Evans, Derry 125
Evans, Gwynfor 90
*Evening Train, The* (Levertov) 258
'Everything and Nothing' (Borges) 237–8
'Extinction of the species, The' (Tanguy) 300

Faber, publishers 13
'Family Reunion' (Bazille) 231, 279, 280
Fanon, Frantz 46, 52, 53
'Father and Child' (Shahn) 234, 278–9, 288–9
Faulkner, William 10, 127
Finch, Peter 11
First World War 13, 14, 15, 21, 31, 37, 151, 161, 202

'Fisherman, A' (Yeats) 59
Fleure, H. J. 23–4, 25
*Fleurs du Mal* (Baudelaire) 315
'Flight of the Dukes, The' (Tanguy) 300–1
'Foothills of Tryfan' (Prendergast) 306–7
'For the Union Dead' (Lowell) 163–4
'Force that through the green fuse . . ., The' (Ceri Richards) 313
*Four-Walled Dream, The* (Heseltine) 14
Frank, Joseph 264
Freud, Sigmund 314
'From Someone to No One' (Borges) 224–5
Frost, Robert 10, 78
'Frost at Midnight' (Coleridge) 133–4
Futurism 21

'Garden of Forking Paths, The' (Borges) 229
Garlick, Raymond 4, 10
Gauguin, Paul 183, 276, 281–2
Geneva 163
Giacometti, Alberto 2, 185
Gluck, Louise 263
Glyn-y-Groes, abbot of 167
Gnostics, the 222, 243
Goble, Tony 315
*Gododdin, Y* 164
Gonne, Maud 135
*Goodbye, What Were You?* (Glyn Jones) 253
'Good-Morrow, The' (Donne) 141
*Gororau'r Iaith: R. S. Thomas a'r Traddodiad Llenyddol Cymraeg* (Jason Walford Davies) 147
Gracian, Baltasar 239
Graham, Jorie 263
'Gravitation universelle, La' (Magritte) 299
*Great Hunger, The* (Kavanagh) 59
Greece 30–1

*Green Heart, The* (Chamberlain) 14
Gregynog 27
Griffith, Wyn 14
Griffiths, Ann 112–13
Griffiths, Bryn 317
Gruffydd, W. J. 96–7, 153
Guernica 21
'Guernica' (Picasso) 233–4, 270, 288, 289
Gulf War 249
Gwenallt (David James Jones) 83, 110, 159
*gwerin* 70, 98
Gwydion 134
Gwynedd 107

Hackney 26–7
Hafod Lom 111
Hanmer 18–19, 24, 26, 45
'Happening, A' (Levertov) 244
Hardy, Thomas 5, 10, 27, 71, 213
Hartman, Geoffrey 74, 87
Hay Literature Festival 6
Hazlitt, William 136, 137
Heaney, Seamus 130, 263
'Hearth, The' (Robin) 298
Heffernan, James 266
Heidegger, Martin 265
Hen Ogledd, yr (the Old North) 149–50, 164
Heraclitus 214
Herbert, George 228, 260
Herod 101
'Heron, The' 254
Herrick, Rober 45
Heseltine, Nigel 14
Heylyn, Peter 255
Hill, Geoffrey 130, 200
Hitler, Adolf 243
'Hlaslesa' (Toyen) 302
Hodgkins, Frances 42
Hofer, Carl 278

Holyhead 37, 38, 58, 60, 76, 95, 123, 132, 203, 285
Homer 285
Hooker, Jeremy 256, 312
Hopkins, Gerard Manley 228, 245, 246
Hopper, Edward 263
Hopwood, Mererid 312
'House of Asterion, The' (Borges) 229
'House under the Trees' (Munch) 299–300
Hoylake 37
Hughes, John Ceiriog, *see* Ceiriog
Hughes, Ted 225
Humphreys, Emyr 15, 95–6, 264
Hyddgen 111

'I make this in a warring absence' (Dylan Thomas) 13
I Tatti 42
'Image of Wales in R. S. Thomas's poetry, The' (Dafydd Elis Thomas) 105
*Imaging the Imagination* (Kinsey and Lloyd-Morgan) 312
'Immortal, The' (Borges) 221–2
Impressionists, the 230, 232, 266, 277, 281, 283, 288
'In the Vale of Glamorgan' (Huw Menai) 22
'In Time of the Breaking of Nations' (Hardy) 27
'Infant Joy' (Blake) 121
'Infant Sorrow' (Blake) 120–1
inscription verse 74–5
investiture of prince of Wales (1969) 105–7, 165
Ireland 97, 308

'Jacob's Ladder, The' (Levertov) 245, 247, 254
James, Christine 264, 312

'Jane Avril Dancing' (Toulouse-Lautrec) 282
Janes, Alfred 313
Jarman, A. O. H. 151
Jenkins, Nigel 313
Joad, C. E. M. 40
Job, Book of 33, 34
Jones, Angel 241
Jones, David 14, 212, 214, 229, 237, 238, 310, 314, 315
Jones, David James, see Gwenallt
Jones, Dic 68–9
Jones, Glyn 13, 253, 313
Jones, Gwyn 53–6
Jones, J. R. 103
Jones, Leslie 316–17
Jones, R. Gerallt 312
Jones, Selwyn 306
Jones, T. Gwynn 14, 84, 96–7, 152, 153, 157–8
Jones, T. Harri 14
Jones, Thomas 54
Jongkind, Johan 271
Jonson, Ben 125
Journals (Kierkegaard) 189, 205–6
'Joy' (Levertov) 261
Judaism 244
Jung, Carl 314
'Justine Dieuhl' (Toulouse-Lautrec) 282

Kafka, Franz 178
Kandinsky, Wassily 304
Kavanagh, Patrick 59
Keats, John 45, 230, 289
Kerrigan, Anthony 239
Keynes, J. M. 40
Kierkegaard, Søren 77–8, 79, 80, 138, 141, 172, 175–6, 177–8, 181, 182, 188, 189–90, 191, 197–9, 201, 204, 205–6, 210, 211–12, 214, 215, 233, 234–5, 236

Kinsey, Christine 318–19
Kipling, Rudyard 40
Klee, Paul 178, 233, 287–8
Krapp's Last Tape (Beckett) 213
Krieger, Murray 264

'Lady with a Parasol' (Monet) 280
'Lamentation' (Lynette Roberts) 15
landscape 10, 11, 15, 40, 44, 48–9, 51, 54, 55–6, 60, 74, 87–8, 103, 107, 110, 111, 184, 299–301, 304, 305, 306, 307, 310, 313–14, 318
Lawrence, D. H. 128, 250
Lawrence, T. E. 40
Le Sidanie, 300
League of Nations 163
Leatherhead 42
Leavis, F. R. 174, 250
Lee, Diana Brinton 286, 287
Leicester 24
Lessing, Gotthold Ephraim 264–5
Levertov, Denise 9, 241–3, 244–7, 248, 249, 250, 251–5, 257–61
Levertov, Olga 249
Levy, Mervyn 313
Lewis, Alun 13, 14, 15, 17, 18, 30
Lewis, Saunders 2, 9, 57, 78, 79, 80, 85, 90–1, 93, 94–5, 96, 97, 98, 99–100, 103–4, 105, 108, 112–14, 134, 159, 160–1, 167, 168, 313, 315–16, 317
Life Studies (Lowell) 129–30
'Line-breaks, Stanza-spaces and the Inner Voice' (Levertov) 258
Liverpool 37, 67, 87, 102, 154, 200
Listener 73, 85
Llanberis 14
Llanddewi-brefi 100
Llanrhaeadr-ym-Mochnant, 111–12
Llan-y-bri 14
Llwyd, Alan 68, 85, 312
Llyn Celyn 102
Llŷn peninsula 1, 54, 90, 107, 201, 249

Llywarch Hen sequence (*Canu Llywarch Hen*) 149, 151–2, 153, 155, 158, 162
London 82
'Lottery of Babylon, The' (Borges) 232
'Louveciennes Road, The' (Pissarro) 231, 272
Lowell, Robert 129–30, 163–4

*Mabinogion*, the 3, 30, 54, 134, 166
MacDiarmid, Hugh 51, 57, 74, 93
McIntyre, Donald 305
Maddison, John 42
'Mademoiselle Dihau at the Piano' (Degas) 271, 283–4
Maentwrog 8
Maes-yr-Onnen, chapel 47–8
Magritte, René 230, 234, 254, 289, 299
Mahon, Derek 263
Mametz Wood 14
Manafon 18, 20, 24, 26, 29, 30, 34, 45, 69, 70–1, 73, 76, 82, 83, 86, 95, 98, 200, 209
Manet, Edouard 231
'Map of the Western Part of the County of Essex, A' (Levertov) 255
Marcello, Benedetto 209
Marches, the 161
Maritain, Jacques 244
Marxism 277
Massacre of the Innocents 101
Mathias, Roland 14, 72
Matisse, Henri 268
May, Derwent 3
'Meeting, The' (Smet) 270–1
Meibion Glyndŵr 151
Menai, Huw (Huw Owen Williams) 15, 16, 22
Menai Straits 107
Mersey, the 37

Merseyside, bombing of 18, 19, 20, 21, 30, 34, 154–5, 200
Merthyr Tydfil 163
Methodists 112
'Michael' (Wordsworth) 75–6
Minera 19
*Modern Welsh Poetry* (Rhys) 13–15, 17, 22, 33, 34
Modernism 41, 264, 265
Moel Famau 19
Monet, Claude 231, 232, 233, 276–7, 280–1
Montgomeryshire 24, 48, 70
Moore, Henry 42, 301
Morgan, Bishop William 112
Mroczkowska, Alice 310–11
Munch, Edvard 263, 288–300
'Music of Colours' poems (Vernon Watkins) 313
'Musicians in the Orchestra, The' (Degas) 285–6
*My People* (Caradoc Evans) 95
'Mysterious Disappearance of May's Past Perfect' (Levertov) 253

'Nant y Mynydd' (Ceiriog) 81
Nash, Paul 42
National Assembly for Wales 108
National Eisteddfod 312; Denbigh (1939) 14; Cardigan (1976) 83, 148
National Museum of Wales 42
National Trust 40
nationalism 5, 90, 94–5, 97, 102, 104, 107, 108–9, 159
native intellectuals, resident natives 46, 48, 52, 53, 56–7, 58, 59, 62, 63
Nazism 24, 41, 179, 261
Neo-Romanticism 41, 44, 53
New York School 266
Newton, Isaac 40
Newtown 24, 25

Nielson, H. A. 198
'Nocturne' (Shahn) 316
'"Nocturne by Ben Shahn" and "Ah!"
    by R. S. T. Homage to both'
    (Leslie Jones) 316–17
Nonconformity 40, 47–8, 94, 95, 112,
    113, 163
'Nuit Vénitienne, La' (Éluard) 234

Oakley Arms (Maentwrog) 8
Oates, Captain Lawrence (Titus) 8
'Ode on a Grecian Urn' 230
Odyssey, the 285–6
Offa's Dyke 73
O'Hara, Frank 266
'On Belief in the Physical
    Resurrection of Christ'
    (Levertov) 245
'On my son' (Jonson) 125
'On the Threshold of Liberty'
    (Magritte) 234, 289–90
On Trust for the Nation (Williams-
    Ellis) 40
Ormond, John 69, 264, 313
'Out of the Cradle' (Whitman) 128
Owain Glyndŵr 45, 167, 168

pacificism 150–1, 152, 153, 161, 162–3
'Painting' (Picasso) 301
Palmer, Arnold 42–7, 48
Paradise Lost (Milton) 21
'Parisienne, La' (Renoir) 313
Parmigianino, Girolamo 263
Parry, Emrys 307
Peacock, Thomas Love 44
'Peat Cutting, Cefn Coch,
    Montgomeryshire' (Eldridge) 48
Peate, Iorwerth 25, 54, 85
Peck, Gregory 157
Pembrokeshire 110
Penguin Modern Painters series 42
Penrose, Roland 234, 290

Penyberth, burning of bombing
    school 93, 160–1
Petit, Pascale 264, 313
'Piano' (Lawrence) 128
Picasso, Pablo 233–4, 270, 301
Picturesque, cult of 49
'Pierre Ménard, author of Don
    Quixote' (Borges) 213, 238
Piper, John 41, 47, 48
Pissarro, Camille 231, 232, 272, 288
Plaid Cymru 90, 93, 104, 105, 165
Plas Glyn-y-Weddw 304, 318, 319
'Poem from Llanybri' (Lynette
    Roberts) 15
Poetry in Wartime (Tambimuttu) 13
Poetry London (Tambimuttu) 313
Poetry Wales 90
Pollock, Griselda 281
'Portrait of a Girl in a Yellow Dress'
    (Matisse) 268–9
'Portrait of a Young Woman' (Degas)
    273–4
'Portrait of Dr Gachet' (Van Gogh) 183
'Portrait of Madame Gaudibert'
    (Monet) 232, 280–1
'Portrait of the Artist' (Derain) 295–6,
    297
post-colonialism 49, 53, 56, 59, 74, 308
Post-Impressionists, the 266, 287
'Post-Script for Gweno' (Alun Lewis)
    30
Powys, John Cowper 25
'Prayer, The' (Goble) 315
Prendergast, Peter 306–7
Preseli mountains 54
Present Age, The (Kierkegaard) 77
Pritchard, Gwilym 307
Prospect of Wales, A (Rowntree) 47, 53–6
Pryce, Malcolm 10–11
'Psalm Fragments (Schnittke String
    Trio)' (Levertov) 243
Pugh, Major-General Lewis 157

Rabbinical Cabalists 222
Radnorshire 24
*Raiders' Dawn* (Alun Lewis) 17
Read, Herbert 293, 294–5
*Real Presences* (Steiner) 216
*Recording Britain* 39, 40–1, 42, 44, 46,
    49, 51, 52, 53, 55, 56, 60, 282
Rees, Alwyn 28
Rees, Brinley 28
'Reluctance' (Frost) 78
Renoir, Pierre-Auguste 313
*Repetition* (Kierkegaard) 211–12
*Responsibilities* (Yeats) 59
Revelation, Book of 28
Rhys, Keidrych 13, 14–15, 17, 22, 33,
    34
Richard, Henry 162–3
Richards, Ceri 313
Rilke, Rainer Maria 251, 252, 261
*Rite of Spring, The* (Stravinsky) 28
Roberts, Lynette 13, 14, 15
Roberts, William 299
Robin, Gabriel 298
Rogers, Byron 157
Romanticism 21, 25, 30, 38, 40, 44, 48,
    57, 74, 84, 110, 111, 175, 250, 289,
    295, 304, 306
Roosevelt, F. D. 39
Rothko, Mark 304
'Rouen Cathedral, Full Sunshine'
    (Monet) 233, 276–7
Rousseau, Henri 279–80
Rowlands, Wil 287, 312
Rowntree, Kenneth 41, 47, 48, 53,
    55–6
Royal Academy of Art 42
Royal Hotel (Cardiff) 8
Royal Watercolour Society 41, 42

'S. L. i R. S. (An Imagined Greeting)'
    (Humphreys) 96
St David's Head 54

St John's Gospel 226
St Matthew's Gospel 168
Saint-Gaudens, Augustus 164
*Sands of the Well* (Levertov) 251
Scholastics, the 190
Schopenhauer, Arthur 225
Schweitzer, Albert 246
Scotland 38, 39, 40, 51
Scott, Captain R. F. 8
Scottish Colorists 305
Second World War 13–15, 17, 18–23,
    24, 26–7, 31, 34, 39, 40, 44, 95, 113,
    153, 162, 166, 168, 200, 249, 301
*Sea Wolves, The* 157
Seattle 241, 257
'Self-Portrait in a Convex Mirror'
    (Parmigianino) 263
Shahn, Ben 234, 278–9, 288–9, 316–17
Shakespeare, William 45, 136, 145,
    237–8
Shaw, George Bernard 223
Shelley, P. B. 44
Shrewsbury 58, 162
*Sickness Unto Death, The*
    (Kierkegaard) 197
Siddons, Sarah 55
Sidgwick, J. B. 24–5
Siena 319
*Silex Scintillans* (Vaughan) 257
Simic, Charles 263
Smet, Gustave de 270
Smith, Dave 263
'Snake Charmer, The' (Rousseau)
    279–80
Snowdon 37, 54, 55, 111; *see also*
    Wyddfa, Yr
Snowdonia 37, 54, 307; *see also* Eryri
Soar-y-Mynydd, chapel 47–8
Society for the Protection of Ancient
    Buildings 40
Socrates 188, 189–90, 191, 205–6
Solzhenitsyn, Alexander 2

South Stack lighthouse 73
Spengler, Oswald 213
Stalingrad, siege of 15
Steiner, George 216
Steiner, Wendy 303
Stevens, Wallace 6, 178, 209, 252, 302
'Still Life' (Hofer) 278
Stirling 150
Strand, Mark 263
Stravinsky, Igor 28
'Suburbs of the paranoiac-critical Town' (Dalí) 301
Surrealism 230, 232, 233, 266, 286, 287, 289, 293, 294–303, 304, 308, 314
*Surrealism* (Read) 293, 294–5, 298
Swansea 94, 241, 313
Swedish Academy 241
Swift, Jonathan 175
Symbolism 314

Taliesin 151, 152
Tambimuttu, M. J. 13
Tanguy, Yves 300–1, 302
Taylor, Mark C. 171–2
Tchaikovsky, Peter Ilyich 208
'Terre d'ombre' (Tanguy) 300–1
*Tesserae* (Levertov) 244, 246, 253–4, 255
Thatcher, Margaret 108
'Thinking about Paul Celan' (Levertov) 261
'Thirty Welsh Paintings of Today', exhibition 316
Thomas, Brynmor 10
Thomas, Caitlin 13
Thomas, Dafydd Elis 90, 91, 105, 108
Thomas, Dylan 13, 15, 17, 93, 95, 96, 313
Thomas, Edward 88, 260
Thomas, George 165
Thomas, Gwydion 3, 166
Thomas, Gwyn 3

Thomas, Ned 123, 135, 145
Thomas, R. S.
 and Abercuawg poems 9, 76, 83–4, 85, 88, 147, 148–51, 153–4, 158, 162, 166, 168–9
 and Anglicisation 71–2, 104, 107
 and Anglo-Welsh writing 51–2, 95, 97, 109, 149, 153
 and anthropology 23–5, 54
 and autobiography 9–10, 117, 145, 182, 183, 193–7, 198, 199–216, 220, 236, 296–7
 and bilingualism 5, 45
 birth of 118–22, 123–4, 125, 196,199, 253, 287
 and capitalism 71–2
 character 1, 3–6, 7–9, 10, 62
 childhood 67–8, 88, 129, 202
 death of 1, 10, 11, 212, 238, 293, 311–12
 and England/Englishness, English language 53, 96, 97, 98, 101, 102, 149
 and family 4, 5, 9, 117, 122–45, 194, 195–6, 202, 203, 285, 287
 and God 1, 4, 7, 8, 16, 29, 32–3, 72, 89, 119, 123, 128, 136, 173, 177, 178–9, 186–7, 190, 204, 212, 214, 220–1, 222–4, 225–8, 232–3, 234–5, 241–4, 247, 248, 252, 257–8, 264, 287, 288, 290, 301, 302, 311, 319
 and hill country 23, 25, 26, 27, 76, 81, 158, 200, 304, 305
 and Iago Prytherch 2, 3, 7, 8, 10, 11, 16, 17, 18, 20, 22, 23, 24, 27, 32, 48–9, 60–2, 70, 71–3, 74–5, 76, 78–9, 82, 97–8, 123, 158–9, 168, 212, 264, 290, 317, 319
 and identity 46, 56–7, 58, 61–2, 195, 196, 220, 295–6
 and industrial areas 98, 99, 100–1, 105

and intimacy 3–4, 10, 61, 77, 119, 122, 269
irony 1, 2, 7, 21, 26, 70, 104–5, 110, 112, 124, 135, 173–4, 181–2, 183, 184–5, 186, 186–8, 189, 190, 191
and landscape 10, 11, 37–8, 48–9, 51–2, 60, 74, 87, 103, 107, 184, 304
and language 220, 224, 225–9, 231, 237, 252, 264–5, 283, 302
Liverpool complex 37, 46
and the Machine 21, 120, 173, 174, 180, 250
and marriage 5, 38–9, 42, 44, 45, 47–9, 50, 51, 56, 62–3, 122, 131, 132, 135–6, 137–8, 139–44, 154, 155, 156, 186, 194, 282–3, 311; see also Eldridge, Mildred
and military men 155–7, 162
and nationalism 5, 97, 104, 100, 107, 108–9, 165
and natural world 28–30, 72, 74, 76, 107, 119, 180, 133, 243, 247–8, 249–50
and Nobel Prize for Literature 241
and Nonconformity 47–8
and pacificism 150–1, 153, 154, 156, 159, 163
and painting 8–9, 10, 38–9, 51, 144, 183–4, 230–4, 264–5, 266–90, 293–6, 297–319
and physical courage 8, 19–20, 154–5, 157, 159, 161, 162, 163, 164
as poet 1–3, 4, 6–7, 8, 9, 57–60, 69–70, 90, 98, 125, 137, 150, 166, 207–10, 258, 259–60, 274
as priest 1, 26, 212, 274, 284, 285
relationship with father 6, 121, 126–8, 129, 130–2, 155, 195, 287
relationship with mother 3, 6, 8, 67, 68, 101–2, 109, 117, 121, 123–5,

132, 147, 155, 195, 282, 287, 296, 319
relationship with son 3–4, 132–5, 138–9, 166
religious poetry 2, 9, 10, 29, 89–90, 107, 171–5, 176–7, 178–83, 184–5, 186–9, 190–1, 194–5, 215, 225–7, 241–2, 258, 266; see also Thomas, R. S.: God
and responsibility of English-language writers in Wales
and rural communities 16, 43–4, 68, 69–71, 97–8, 109, 151
second marriage 4
and the self 8, 27, 56, 172, 174, 179, 183, 193, 194–7, 198, 199–202, 206–7, 208, 209–10, 211, 212, 214–15, 234–7, 295, 296, 297–9, 302, 319
and socialism 100
theology 79–10, 119, 174–5, 178, 180–1, 182, 186–7, 224
and time 230–4, 238–9, 264, 265
and Wales 8, 10, 11, 37–8, 44, 45–66, 68, 73, 74, 79, 89, 90, 91, 99, 102, 107, 110, 111–12, 113, 136, 159, 169, 249–50, 304–5, 319
and war 15–23, 24, 26–7, 30–1, 34, 37
and Welsh language and culture 5, 85, 93, 95, 96, 97, 99, 100, 101, 102–3, 107, 147–50, 152–3, 241, 308
and Welshness 37–8, 62, 80, 88–9
wit 7, 143, 178, 280
and women 27, 135, 280–3, 284–6, 299
Thomas, R. S., works
'Abercuawg' 148–9, 150–1, 153–4, 169; see also Thomas, R. S. and Abercuawg poems
'Absinthe' (Degas) 281

'Afforestation' 82, 83, 111
'After Jericho' 228–9, 252
'Airy Tomb, The' 32
'Album' 126–7, 128
'Anniversary' 133, 139
'Annunciation by Veneziano, The'
    230–1, 319
'Anybody's Alphabet' 232, 252
'At the End' 311–12
'Beach at Sainte-Adresse, The' 271
'Belle Angèle, La' 281–2
*Between Here and Now* 226, 230, 231,
    232, 233, 264, 266, 267, 271, 287,
    293
'Birch Tree' 28–9
'Blondes' 82
'Border Blues' 109, 110, 161–2
'Boy's Tale, The' 128–9, 132
*Bread of Truth, The* 76, 83, 86, 126
'Breton Landscape, the Mill' 184,
    276
'Bridge at Maincy, The' 272–3
'Bright Field, The' 247
'Cain' 179
'Captain Cook's Last Voyage' 234,
    290
'Card Players, The' 317
'Careers' 138–9
'Coming, The' 179, 244
'Composition' 276, 277
'Countering' 141–2
*Counterpoint* 2, 180
'Country Church (Manafon)' 28,
    29–30, 51
'Credo' 181–2, 186
'Cynddylan on a Tractor' 158
'Dancing Class, The' 282
'Dau Gapel' 47
'Depopulation of the Welsh Hill
    Country, The' 26, 306
'Drawing by a Child' 286–7
'Earth' 175

'Echoes' 176–7, 178, 223
*Echoes Return Slow, The* 19, 20–1,
    26, 30, 117, 118, 121, 123, 127–8,
    133, 134, 143, 154, 156, 182, 183,
    193–7, 198, 199–216, 220, 236,
    255–6, 287, 296, 297
'Eviction' 83
'Family Reunion' 231, 279, 280
'Father and Child' 234, 278–9,
    288–9
'Fathoms' 236
'Ffynnon Fair' 187–8
*Frequencies* 126, 148, 227, 228
'Fugue for Ann Griffiths' 112
'Gap, The' 119, 319
'Geriatric' 4, 185–6
'Grave Unvisited, A' 80
'Guernica' 233–4, 270, 288, 289
'Emerging' 227–8
*Experimenting with an Amen* 2
'He agrees with Henry Ford' 101,
    165
'He and She' 139–40
'He is sometimes contrary' 101
'Hearth, The' 143–4
'Hill Christmas' 247
'Hireling' 71
'His condescensions are short-
    lived' 164–5
*H'm* 89, 143, 172, 174, 175, 177, 178,
    222–3, 224, 243, 250, 316
'H'm' 243–4
'Homage to Paul Klee' 233, 287
'Homo Sapiens 1941' 21–2
'I look out' 143
*Ingrowing Thoughts* 230, 232, 233,
    264, 266, 286, 287, 288
'Invasion on the Farm' 74–5
'Island, The' 223
'It' 120
'It hurts him to think' 101–2
'Jane Avril Dancing' 282

'Jaromir Hladik' 219–20
'Justine Dieuhl' 282
Laboratories of the Spirit 180, 183, 230
'Labourer, A' 22, 27
'Lady with a Parasol' 280
'Land, The' 309
'Lecturer, A' 110
'Line from St David's, A' 110
Llwybrau Gynt, Y 67
'Looking at Sheep' 111
'Louveciennes Road, The' 272
'Mademoiselle Dihau at the Piano' 271, 283–4
'Making' 178–9, 223
'Marriage' 135, 137–8
Mass for Hard Times 2, 144, 180, 181, 186, 219, 226
'Memories of Yeats Whilst Travelling to Holyhead' 57–9
'Meeting, The' 270–1
'Minister, The' 305
'Moon in Lleyn, The' 188–9
Mountains, The 38, 70
'Movement' 76
'Musicians in the Orchestra, The' 285–6
Neb 18–19, 21, 29, 70, 71, 117, 123, 125, 127, 133, 145, 154, 156, 159, 183, 193, 194, 235, 296–7
'No Time' 5, 186
No Truce With the Furies 2, 4, 144, 186, 215, 222, 227, 232–3, 242, 287
'Nocturne by Ben Shahn' 316
'Nuit Vénitienne, La' 234, 289
'On the Portrait of Joseph Hone by Augustus John' 18
'On the Shore' 82–3
'On the Threshold of Liberty' 234, 289–90
'Once' 172–4

'One, The' 2
'Other' 223
'Other, The' 120
'Out of the Hills' 23, 26, 49–52, 56, 58, 59, 306
'Patriot, The' 112, 113, 159, 161
'Peasant, A' 16, 22–3, 60–2, 158, 162, 168
'Petition' 177, 178
Pièta 88
'Pissarro: Kitchen Garden, Trees in Bloom' 232, 265
'Pissarro: Landscape at Chapnoval' 232
'Play' 232
'Portrait of a Girl in a Yellow Dress' 268–9
'Portrait of a Young Woman' 273–4
'Portrait of Madame Gaudibert' 232, 280–1
'Portrait of Madame Renou' 275–6
'Prayer, The' 315
'Propaganda' 17
'Provincial, The' 112
'Question, The' 33–4
'Reason, The' 226, 227
'Remembering' 186
'Repeat' 223
'Reservoirs' 103
'Rhodri' 71
'River, The' 174–5, 244
'Rouen Cathedral, Full Sunshine' 233, 276–7
'Rough' 186–7
'S.K.' 233, 234–5
'Sailors' Hospital' 132
'Salt' 130–1
'Saunders Lewis' 161
'Sea-watching' 260
'Self-portrait' 183
'Senior' 313–14
'Servant' 72–3

'Seventieth Birthday' 142
'Small Window' 304–5
'Snake Charmer, The' 279–80
'Soliloquy' 223
'Some Contemporary Scottish
    Writing' 31, 49, 51, 57, 61–2
'Son, The' 132
'Song' 27–8
*Song at the Year's Turning* 17, 22
'Song for Gwydion' 132–3
'Sorry' 125–6
'Still' 186
'Still Life' 278
*Stones of the Field, The* 17, 18, 19, 21,
    22, 23, 27, 28, 29, 30, 31–4, 39, 46,
    47, 51, 53, 56, 57, 60
'Suddenly' 187
'Symbols' 227
*Tares* 69, 76, 139
'Thought from Nietzsche, A' 32
'Tidal' 311
'Time's Disc Jockey' 212–13
'To pay for his keep' 105, 106–7,
    165
'Toast' 111
'Two Children Menaced by a
    Nightingale' 234, 289
'Untamed, The' 76–7
'Via Negativa' 190, 224, 243
'Watcher, The' 75, 76
'Way of It, The' 140–1, 248
'Welcome' 86–7, 104–5
'Welsh' 109
Welsh Airs 108–14, 308
'Welsh Hill Country, The' 304, 306
'Welsh History' 150, 161
'Welsh Landscape' 306–8
'Welshman at St James' Park, A'
    79–81, 82, 83, 110
'Welshman to Any Tourist, A' 104
*What is a Welshman?* 99–102, 104–7,
    162–5

'White Tiger, The' 119, 225
'Winter Retreat' 30
'Words' 232
'Words and the Poet' 84
*Young and Old* 172
'Young Woman Sewing' (Cassatt)
    281

Tillich, Paul 186, 190
Tintern 111
'Tlön, Uqbar, Orbis, Tertius' (Borges)
    178, 221, 229
Tomos, Gwyneth 305
'Torso of an Archaic Apollo' (Rilke) 252
Toulouse-Lautrec, Henri 282
Toyen (Marie Čermínová) 302
Toynbee, Arnold 213
Traeth Maelgwn 111
Tregaron 162, 163, 164
Trevelyan, G. M. 40
'Trust' (Mroczkowska) 310–11
Tryweryn 87, 102–3
Tudor, Henry (Henry VII) 82
Turner, Graham 3
Turner, J. M. W. 41, 44
'Two Children Menaced by a
    Nightingale' (Ernst) 234, 289
*Tynged yr Iaith* (Saunders Lewis) 90–1,
    103–4, 105, 160, 161

*Unbearable Lightness of Being in
    Aberystwyth, The* (Pryce) 10–11
United States of America 43, 94, 249,
    263
University College of North Wales,
    Bangor 37, 123
University College of Wales,
    Aberystwyth 23

Vale, Edmund 40, 45
Van Gogh, Vincent 183
Vaughan, Henry 257

Velázquez, Diego 63
Veneziano, Domenico 230–1
Vernon, Elisabeth 4
Victoria and Albert Museum 41
'Vie Vénitienne, La' (Eluard) 234, 289
Vietnam War 249
*Voyages*, V (Crane) 141

Wales 14, 37, 39, 40, 42–4, 47, 49, 51,
    74, 91, 111, 161, 304, 307
*Wales* 23, 24, 25, 26, 31
'Wales: Its Character and its Dangers'
    (Vale) 40
'Wales and America' (Powys) 25
Wallasey 94, 113
Ward, J. P. 143
*Waste Land, The* (Eliot) 21, 173, 177
Watkins, Vernon 13, 14, 313
Webb, Harri 11, 14, 317
'Welsh Aboriginals' (Powys) 25
*Welsh Journal* (Hooker) 256
Welsh language 5, 19, 43, 44, 54, 83,
    84–6, 87–8, 90, 91, 95, 96, 98, 99,
    100, 103–4, 106, 107, 108, 112,
    149, 157, 160, 163
Welsh-language culture 54, 85, 95, 98,
    99, 264
Welsh literary tradition 83, 94, 95,
    96–7, 98, 99, 103, 147–8
Welsh-medium schools 108
'Welsh Station' (Sidgwick) 24–5
Westover, Daniel 168
'What One Receives from Living Close
    to a Lake' (Levertov) 259–60

Whitman, Walt 31, 57, 128
*Wild Wales* (Borrow) 44
Williams, Huw Owen, *see* Menai,
    Huw
Williams, Sir Ifor 151
Williams, Kyffin 306
Williams, Raymond 71
Williams, Rowan 313
Williams, Waldo 313
Williams, William Carlos 245, 263,
    283–4
Williams Parry, R. 160–1
Williams-Ellis, Clough 40
Wimbledon Art School 42
'Winter' (McIntyre) 305
Wirral, the 37
Wordsworth, William 40, 44, 45, 75–6,
    111, 149, 230, 260
Wright, Charles 263
'Writers on Art' series 263
Wyddfa, Yr 31; *see also* Snowdon
Wyschogrod, Michael 199

Yeats, W. B. 6, 17–18, 20, 38, 57–60, 84,
    88, 94–5, 105, 136, 142, 188, 189,
    213, 238, 257
Young, Douglas 31
'Young Woman Sewing' (Cassatt) 281
Ysbaddaden Bencawr 3
*Ysbrydoliaeth/Inspiration*, exhibition
    304–5
Yspytty Cynfyn 55

Zimbabwe 308